RESURRECTION

RESURRECTION

Theological and Scientific Assessments

Edited by

TED PETERS
ROBERT JOHN RUSSELL
MICHAEL WELKER

WILLIAM B. EERDMANS PUBLISHING COMPANY
GRAND RAPIDS, MICHIGAN / CAMBRIDGE, U.K.

Wm. B. Eerdmans Publishing Co.
255 Jefferson Ave. S.E., Grand Rapids, Michigan 49503 /
P.O. Box 163, Cambridge CB3 9PU U.K.

Printed in the United States of America

07 06 05 04 03 02   7 6 5 4 3 2 1

Library of Congress Cataloging-in-Publication Data

Resurrection: theological and scientific assessments /
edited by Ted Peters, Robert John Russell, Michael Welker
p.   cm.
Includes bibliographical references.
ISBN 0-8028-0519-1 (pbk.: alk. paper)
1. Resurrection.   2. Religion and science.
I. Peters, Ted, 1941-   II. Russell, Robert J.
III. Welker, Michael, 1947-

BT873.R47   2002
236′.8 — dc21

2002073887

www.eerdmans.com

Contents

CONTENTS

PART III
RESURRECTION AND THE LAWS OF NATURE

PART IV
RESURRECTION, NEW CREATION, AND CHRISTIAN HOPE

Contents

Introduction:
What Is to Come

TED PETERS

"If Christ has not been raised, then our proclamation has been in vain and your faith has been in vain" (1 Cor. 15:14). In raising this challenge within Scripture, St. Paul is assuming that the faith of a Christian is in principle falsifiable. Faith could be falsified if the claim that Jesus Christ rose from the dead could be falsified. Without Easter, Christian hope, trust, and passion are all in vain.

Such a falsification could come in two forms, one looking backward and one looking forward. Looking backward, we could imagine evidence put forward to claim that Jesus hung on the cross, died, and remained dead. We could imagine a historical argument claiming that the Easter resurrection did not occur in the manner that the Christian faith has presumed. Looking forward, we could imagine a future without a consummation, without the new creation promised by the Easter resurrection. Inextricably built into the Easter resurrection is the proleptic anticipation of the future resurrection of humanity at the arrival of the eschatological kingdom of God. The resurrection of Christ, according to Christian faith, was not merely an extraordinary event in Jesus' biography; it was the advent of the world's transformation. Without the consummation of this transformatory promise, the Christian faith is in vain.

With the rise of empirical methods in science during the eighteenth century, Western European literati began to doubt the Christian claim that Jesus rose from the dead on Easter. During the centuries immediately prior, with the rise of the Age of Reason, life after death was resolutely affirmed. It is rational to believe in a universal afterlife, said philosophers of religion; any reasonable person can see that this is the case. However, as reason yielded to experiment and no experiments could be conceived that would demonstrate life beyond the grave, doubt gained a grip on the Western mind.

The laws of nature became seen as uniform, everywhere and always applicable. The laws of nature never go on a holiday; they never open a date on the calendar for miracles or other transcendent interventions. And, accordingly, one of these laws is that dead people stay dead. Because every dead person observed has stayed dead, it was easy to argue inductively that all people who die remain dead. None rises. By analogy and by assuming uniformity in nature, the observable finality of death became applied to the unobservable event of Jesus' alleged resurrection. Because nobody else can rise, neither could Jesus. So, the argument goes.

What are we to do? As Robert John Russell points out in chapter one, two basic strategies seemed to present themselves to Christian thinkers, the objective strategy and the subjective strategy. The objectivists found themselves embracing empirical science, accepting the task of identifying universal laws of nature derived from empirical observation. When it comes to the Easter resurrection of Jesus, however, objectivist theologians dubbed this an exception. Some said it was a miracle, a divine intervention that temporarily violated the otherwise uniform laws of nature. More recently some objectivists have said that the Easter resurrection was a contingent historical and natural event, the first instantiation of what will become a new law of nature when God raises all the dead.

Like the objectivists, the subjectivists accepted fully the empirical advances of modern science; and they ceded to science the uniformitarian scope of the laws of nature. The assumption they adopted was that nothing happens in nature that scientists cannot describe. This rules out any miraculous intervention at Easter; but it does not rule out nonmiraculous workings of God's Spirit. The Easter resurrection, then, is said to be an event in the minds and hearts of Jesus' disciples, an event in the consciousness of what became the church. Jesus' resurrection becomes a symbol of personal transformation; what allegedly happened historically to the body of Jesus on Easter becomes applied to what happens existentially to the spirit of Jesus' followers. Affirming the resurrection, the subjectivist strategy removes it from the objective realm of scientific fact and places it in the subjective realm of interpretation and meaning. One implication of the subjectivist move is that it renders the resurrection nonfalsifiable because no one can falsify what happens in human subjectivity. According to this strategy, Christian faith is immune from the challenge of modern science.

TED PETERS

Entropy and Eschatology

Like vines on a trellis, these two strategies grew up together when the challenge had to do with looking backward, with the challenge regarding the historicity of the Easter event and related matters. More recently, the challenge is coming from future consciousness, from looking forward. Specifically, the second law of thermodynamics and Big Bang cosmology raise questions for Christian eschatology. The second law of thermodynamics affirms that in a closed system energy flows in only one direction, from hot to cold, not the reverse. If the Big Bang back at the beginning was the hottest moment in the history of the cosmos, and if the universe is open and expanding without limit, then the future we look forward to is one of increased entropy, of dissipation into equilibrium. In short, the universe is destined to freeze itself out of existence. If, on the other hand, the universe is closed and finite, then gravity will cause it to recollapse into another dense fireball; and it will explode again. Either way the present cosmos will come to an end. Whether freeze or fry, the future of life in our universe is not endless. Like individual sentient beings, the cosmos as a whole is destined for death. At least, this is the picture of the future painted by physical cosmologists.

Does this picture look like the one painted by Christian eschatology? No. Entropy and eschatology appear to be locked in conflict. Christian eschatology does not anticipate a far future at equilibrium that has forgotten its past. Rather, it looks now through a mirror dimly at a bright, shining future, the future of the new creation promised by God in the Easter resurrection of Jesus. The present creation is slated for transformation, and Jesus' Easter resurrection is the microcosm of the promised macrocosmic transformation. "But in fact Christ has been raised from the dead," writes St. Paul, "the first fruits of those who have died" (1 Cor. 15:20). As he rose, so will we. And what we rise into is the new creation.

Rather than consonance, it appears that we have dissonance between physical cosmology and Christian eschatology. If scientists rely on the uniformity of nature, the future they picture must be based on an extrapolation of observations and principles governing the past history of the natural universe. Based on nature's past, no vision of a future transformation, such as Christian eschatology proclaims, can be pictured. Based on our experience with the present creation, no warrant can be given to project a radically new creation. Based on our observation that dead people remain dead, no evidence can be mustered to affirm a future general resurrection.

In principle, then, physical cosmology as scientists pursue it has the potential for falsifying Christian belief in the resurrection. Because entailed in the very notion of the Easter resurrection is the divine promise for the renewal of the whole of creation, the failure of the creation to undergo transformation would invalidate the Christian claim. If natural uniformity wins — meaning that Jesus remained dead, and so will we — then the Christian faith is in vain.

Although we may say "in principle" that the Christian claim is falsifiable, this is not empirically achievable. The final disproof of the Christian claim would require observing the actual dissipation of the universe in the far distant future. No laboratory of the present generation is expected to last that long, and no scientist is likely to live long enough to see it.

Be that as it may, physical cosmology challenges Christian theology to think methodologically. Eschatology, so it appears, ought not rely upon the present state of natural science for conceptual support. If a future new creation actually arrives as God has promised, then its arrival will have to be due to divine intervention. The natural world will not evolve into a new creation on its own. If such a transformation is to take place, it will have to come courtesy of a creative act of God. No one can predict a creative act of God; hence it will remain invisible to present scientific eyes.

The challenge as we have outlined it here affects mainly the objectivists. Or so it would seem. It belongs to the objectivists because here science and theology share the same domain of inquiry — that is, they both deal with the world of nature and history. Theologians claim that the God of Israel is the creator and redeemer of the very same world that natural scientists examine under microscopes and telescopes. They expect some consonance, some overlap between empirical observation and theological conception. When apparent dissonance appears, so does a challenge.

Yet the subjectivists cannot fully escape the challenge of science. Their retreat into subjectivity with nonobjectifiable divine activity in the human spirit provides only a temporary oasis. Science is relentless in its hot pursuit. Along with cosmology, evolution and genetics and neuroscience are hot on the trail of human subjectivity, ready to reduce mind to body, spirit to matter. Scientific explanations may simply undercut the relative autonomy we presume for mind or spirit.

All along, the subjectivist strategy has been leaving a trail of critics challenging its credibility, challenging its attempt to sever the tie between fact and meaning, between science and faith. Its defense has relied upon a Cartesian dualism between body and mind or between object and subject, a dualism that is coming under increasing fire as modernity gives way to postmodernity. Postmodern philosophies emphasize relationality, connectedness, and intersubjectivity. To startling degrees, physicists and cosmologists as well as evolutionary biologists are demonstrating that human subjectivity is deeply embedded in nature's history, in the history of all of nature from the Big Bang to the present. Human subjectivity, it is frequently said, is nature becoming conscious of itself. With this as the contemporary context, privatizing religious meaning in an isolated subjectivity is losing credibility.

There is no "science free" zone today where theology can proceed with its business untrammeled by the kaleidoscopic pictures of reality projected by the various sciences. Whether Christian theologians like it or not, contemporary science forces us to ask questions such as: Did Jesus really rise from the dead? And is the Christian faith credible or vain? The question of the present book is this: *How should we assess the resurrection scientifically and theologically?*

Theological Realism

The task of the present volume is not to falsify Christian belief, nor is it to promote objectivist theology; and it certainly is not to defend biblical literalism. Rather, its task is to place Christian theological reflection into dialogue with the relevant natural sciences, to press toward what we at the Center for Theology and the Natural Sciences call a *creative mutual interaction.*

Such a creative mutual interaction was the goal that led to a set of conferences and to this book. Faculty at the University of Heidelberg and at the Center for Theology and the Natural Sciences at the Graduate Theological Union in Berkeley, California, and from other locations internationally have linked together for interdisciplinary scholarship. Meeting at the *Internationale Wissenschaftsforum* in Heidelberg in 2001, we gathered a seminar team that included research and teaching faculty in physics, biology, neuroscience, Scripture, Egyptology, church history, and systematic theology. We reversed the normal direction of the conversation between science and religion. Normally, the dialogue begins with a new discovery in science, and then religious spokespersons react. In this case, however, we began with a specific theological question: How should we understand the resurrection of the body? We posed the question in such a way as to elicit contributions from various sciences and various disciplines within Christian theology.

The theologians sense that the scientists may have something relevant to offer, but it is not clear yet what it is. The scientists also begin gingerly, looking for orientation toward this new subject matter. We are at the stage of scholarship that Alfred North Whitehead once called philosophical "assemblage," where we are assembling what we surmise to be relevant material but not quite ready yet to formulate a hypothesis or establish a system.

The impetus comes from a shared entelechy within science and within theology, namely, the impetus to know what is real, to have confidence that what we know is rooted in what is true. Only knowledge of reality constitutes truth, and only truth can quench the thirst that leads to research. So the faith of theologians here is seeking fuller understanding; and the suspicion is that what scientists know about the future of the cosmos and about the workings of the human body may be relevant for understanding Christian eschatological promises for a new creation and for the resurrection of the body.

The point of departure is difficult. We recognize, as Michael Welker says in his chapter, that we find ourselves in worldwide cultural communication but with multiple rationalities. Neither science nor theology offers a single thought system that encompasses the length and breadth of human experience and meaning; nowhere in the world can we find a metarationality that offers a single inclusive, comprehensive, and coherent *Weltanschauung* or worldview.

Within this pluralism of rationalities, however, science and theology share something in common. Both are driven by ontological thirst, by the thirst to know reality as it is. Both shun delusion. Both are pursued by *truth-seeking communities*. Both are willing to subject ordinary knowledge to scrutiny and to humbly accept correction, revision, and reorientation. Oh yes, we are aware of the exceptions. We are aware of the reductionists and the Marxists who equate science with atheism; and we are aware of the religious dogmatists who in fragility defend outdated authority. But when science is at its best and theology is at its best, both are prosecuted by truth-seeking communities open to reorientation by what they learn about reality in a process I call "hypothetical consonance."

From the Big Bang to the New Creation

What Robert John Russell does in his chapter is create a common domain of discussion for both scientific and theological visions of the cosmic future. Big Bang cosmology as we have come to know it in science has found remarkable consonance with the doctrine of creation arising out of the Bible: the cosmos is contingent, timebound, and historical. But this remarkable consonance deals primarily with the past. When we scientifically project scenarios into the future, we provoke dissonance with theological eschatology. The freeze or fry scenarios for the far future do not fit with the Easter promise of a coming new creation. Without resolving the tension, Russell recommends a number of guidelines for follow-up, one of which is that theology offers a reconceptualization that suggests theory choice for future scientific research.

Russell can advise that theology might have some indirect influence on the scientific conversation because he affirms that the two disciplines share a common domain. For Russell, the Easter resurrection of Jesus is the first instantiation of a new law of nature. Rather than a miracle that violates nature's laws, resurrection is a divinely instituted event that changes nature's laws. In the future all of us will rise, naturally.

At this point in history, however, we can say this theologically but not scientifically. This places theology in the position of risking falsification by science; and in a sense it places current science in the position of risking falsification by theology. If the future brings new creation, then current scientific prognostications will need correction. If the future brings what scientific cosmologists predict, freeze or fry, then theological hope will be dashed.

When we turn to the chapter of the cosmic story that deals with the evolution of life on earth, the situation is a bit more ambiguous. On the one hand, evolution over deep time has brought marvelous changes. On the other hand, we cannot understand biological life without its being fed by death, by predation. Can we extrapolate from present biology to a deathless eschatology? Not likely, says Jeffrey Schloss. If we are to trust in an eschatological hope, it will have to rest on the promise of something radically new, a reality that transcends nature as we have known it thus far.

If the dire predictions of the physicist's eschatology are fulfilled, John Polkinghorne argues, we must conclude that "all is vanity." If after billions of years evolving carbon-based life proves to have been but a transient episode in cosmic history, then this puts a very serious question to theology about the ultimate intentions of the Creator. The answers to these questions must be found beyond the simple extrapolation of scientifically influenced expectation. Polkinghorne contends that a faithful Creator is not bound to maintain nature's laws unchanged. That faithful Creator will provide *ex vetera* an eschatological transformation of cosmic matter. In the process of transforming the material universe, God will draw into the divine memory the pattern of information that constitutes the human soul; and in the eschaton God will reinstate human personhood within the transformed material creation. Note what Polkinghorne is saying here: the human soul consists of an informational pattern that can be extracted from our present earthly bodies and reinstated in a future resurrected body.

Such a discussion reminds us that some materialist or reductionist scientists have proposed cybernetic immortality. These scientists in the field of Artificial Intelligence (AI) would upload into computers the informational patterns of the human brain that are identified with the soul and then transfer them to a new physical platform, perhaps to a robot. Our personal identity would continue carried by the informational pattern that, like software, would be booted up in new and more durable hardware. We could then exist as long as the machine in which we reside exists. We would gain more time than biological organisms normally have. Cybernetic immortality constitutes a scientized eschatology that results from human technological achievement.

The theologians writing in this volume would object to visions of cybernetic immortality because resurrection as Christians conceive it will be the result of an act of God, not the achievement of technological advance. Noreen Herzfeld, in her chapter, objects for two reasons. First, cybernetic immortality sounds like science fiction, not science. It is simply not scientifically feasible. Second, although it is materialistic, it reduces the human self or person to information patterns, to an immaterial form. Herzfeld, in contrast, holds that our finite bodies belong essentially to our identity. Curiously, cybernetic immortality is dualistic even while materialistic.

Detlef Linke is less likely to permit an exuviation of the soul's information from the body. Even though neuronal activity constituting the interaction of brain and body is not isomorphic with human consciousness or behavior, the stability structure of the neuronal substrate retains memory; and it provides the parameters for conscious activity. When speculating about resurrection, a transfiguration of the body would necessarily change one's consciousness significantly. Does this mean that we cannot disembody the soul's informational pattern and reestablish it in a subsequent bodily make-up?

What biblical resources may we rely on for clues here? Returning exegetically to the Pauline corpus in the New Testament, Peter Lampe argues that the Apostle to the Gentiles employed a holistic integration of body and soul. Without a body there is no legitimate usage of "resurrection." The resurrection must be physical. Yet some sort of interim period described as existing "in Christ" describes our passage from the present aeon to the new aeon. Could this be the information pattern or soul remembered by God that Polkinghorne and others describe? Lampe hints that Paul provides no metaphysical elaboration and, thus, no handle for science to gain an explanatory grip.

Hans-Joachim Eckstein draws our attention to the Lukan corpus and the strange concern of Luke to stress physicality in the resurrection. For Luke the grave is empty, and the risen Jesus is portrayed as so physical that he can even eat fish for breakfast. Eckstein is puzzled that the exaltation of Jesus to become the "Lord and Messiah" (Acts 2:36) in glory seems to bypass the need for a return to the physical body. He contends with a pun that the Lukan concern for how *full* Jesus' grave was risks *emptying* faith in resurrection.

Frank Crüsemann also uses Scripture to discuss Jesus' resurrection, but his goal is to emphasize the continuity, rather than the discontinuity, between the treatment of resurrection in the Hebrew Scriptures and the New Testament. Crüsemann thus highlights the importance of interpreting the resurrection of Jesus in a much larger historical and cultural context, which includes the faith of Abraham and the promises of God that define and shape the history of the Israelites. He concludes with two important theses. First, that the resurrection of the dead is a predicate of God the creator and thus cannot be developed exclusively on the basis of a Christology. Second, the appearances of the resurrected Jesus actualize God's promise to the Gentiles and give the impetus for their inclusion in the disciples' commission to preach and baptize in Jesus' name.

Where Polkinghorne, Herzfeld, Lampe, Eckstein, and Crüsemann leave us is with the question of personal identity. When it comes to the paradoxical dialectic between continuity and discontinuity as Jesus or as we pass through death to resurrection, who is it that rises? How is the Easter Christ the same Jesus who was crucified? If we are to rise, what aspect of us rises so that we know it will be we and not something or someone distinct from us? What continues beyond death? Our body? Our mind? Our soul? Our pattern of information? Nothing? Everything?

Enter Nancey Murphy. Murphy is an advocate of nonreductive physicalism — that is, she denies substance dualism with its concept of an independent immortal soul. A human self is always an embodied self. Therefore, identity in the resurrection must retain continuity with our bodies, with our individual biographies while living our earthly lives. If we are renewed in the resurrection, what remains the same? The physical elements of our present body? Our consciousness? Our memories? What decisively maintains continuity is our moral character, she argues. Our identity as persons is as much dependent on our character as it is on memory, consciousness, and body. So, if God were to replicate us out of different "stuff" according to our information pattern, we would not be ourselves unless we continued to possess our virtues (and vices?), our affections, and our moral perceptions.

Who controls our identities? Does the self? Does God? When we die, we lose control over our identity. We may be remembered, but which memories live on are beyond our control. We tend to think that subjective immortality is a way of containing our identity in our self, whereas objective immortality is an identity that resides in the memories of our heirs or in God's memory. Objective immortality belongs to someone else's subjectivity, not to ours. Andreas Schuele weighs these matters and concludes that resurrection requires us to work on understanding the relation between contained and uncontained identities. Already in this life this side of death, our identities can grow in Christ. Identity in Christ now is like earnest money, a down payment, a prolepsis, or first fruits (1 Cor. 15:20) of what is to come in the resurrection. Losing control of our identity in death does not mean we lose our identity, especially when God promises resurrection.

Finally, why has the Christian doctrine of resurrection appeared in the history of human culture? Does it function as a political opiate to legitimate hereditary kingship, as Jan Assmann suggests it did in ancient Egypt? Does it function as an ethical opiate to inoculate us against ecological responsibility, an issue that Ernst Conradie addresses? Does it function as encouragement by promising triumph for the church militant, as we see in Bernd Oberdorfer's exposition of Schleiermacher? Does it function as a beacon of *shalom*, an eschatological rest for us who are anxious over the transience of time, as Dirk Evers avers? Or, finally, is the concept of resurrection a theological explication of the historical event of Easter, a reflection on the apostolic experience with the risen Lord who promised that we would in the future feast with him in paradise? If the latter, then one question to pose is this: Can we trust in the truth of this promise? The dialogue between science and theology is an attempt to provide critical appraisal and to gain intelligibility regarding the content of this eschatological promise.

Our assembled team of scientists and theologians begins with faith and then seeks to expand and deepen our understanding. Here we have taken what might turn out to be the first step down a long road. This is the faith.

Since One, for love, died on a tree
And in the stony
Tomb has lain,
Behold I show a mystery:
All sepulchers
Are sealed in vain!

John Richard Moreland, 1880-1947

The understanding still lies on the horizon.

PART I

RESURRECTION AND
ESCHATOLOGICAL CREDIBILITY

Bodily Resurrection, Eschatology, and Scientific Cosmology: The Mutual Interaction of Christian Theology and Science

ROBERT JOHN RUSSELL

Blessed be the God and Father of our Lord Jesus Christ! By his great mercy he has given us a new birth into a living hope through the resurrection of Jesus Christ from the dead.

1 PETER 1:3

The defining kerygma of Christian faith, the resurrection of Jesus, plays a crucial role in New Testament scholarship and systematic theology, yet the resurrection has seldom been discussed carefully in light of the challenges raised by contemporary natural science. Ironically, this also holds true for the rapidly growing field of theology and science, where such interactions are the field's *raison d'etre!* The purpose of this paper is to undertake this discussion.

After a brief overview of Big Bang cosmology, I give as examples two theological areas where the resurrection is particularly crucial: evil and theodicy, and eschatology. I then summarize competing positions on the resurrection in New Testament research. My intention is not to enter into the ongoing scholarly debates over the meaning of the resurrection of Jesus. Instead it is to adopt the "worst case scenario" for the credibility of Christianity, the bodily resurrection, because this position raises serious, and perhaps un-

---

This essay was supported in part by a research and writing grant from the Philadelphia Center for Science and Research. The author gratefully acknowledges George Ellis, Nancey Murphy, Ted Peters, Bill Stoeger, and Claude Welch for detailed discussions of this and related essays.

3

solvable, conflicts and contradictions with science. I then turn directly to theology and science where, despite numerous significant advances over the past forty years, the resurrection has received little sustained attention. This actually makes the task well worth pursuing since the bodily resurrection represents a test case of the highest order for those of us who urge that theology and science should be in a posture of constructive interaction rather than one of outright conflict.

To move forward, I will suggest an expansion of the current methodology in theology and science that places them in a dynamic relation I call "creative mutual interaction." I close by offering guidelines and specific suggestions for reconstructing eschatology in light of science and for exploring new approaches to physical cosmology in light of eschatology.[1]

The Challenge of Big Bang Cosmology

(I)f it were shown that the universe is indeed headed for an all-enveloping death, then this might . . . falsify Christian faith and abolish Christian hope.[2]

JOHN MACQUARRIE

To consider the universe from a scientific perspective, we must turn to physics and Big Bang cosmology.

Big Bang Cosmology and the Far Future[3]

During the 1920s, telescopic observations by Edwin Hubble showed that galaxies surrounding our Milky Way were receding from us at a velocity propor-

1. For an initial discussion of the latter see Robert John Russell, "Eschatology and Physical Cosmology: A Preliminary Reflection," in *The Far Future Universe: Eschatology from a Cosmic Perspective*, ed. George F. R. Ellis (Philadelphia: Templeton Foundation, 2002).

2. John Macquarrie, *Principles of Christian Theology*, (New York: Scribner's, 2d ed. 1977 [1966]), ch. 15, esp. pp. 351-62.

3. For a nontechnical introduction, see James Trefil and Robert M. Hazen, *The Sciences: An Integrated Approach* (New York: John Wiley, 2d rev. ed. 2000), ch. 15; George F. Ellis and William R. Stoeger, S.J., "Introduction to General Relativity and Cosmology," in *Quantum Cosmology and the Laws of Nature: Scientific Perspectives on Divine Action*, ed. Robert J. Russell, Nancey C. Murphy, and Chris J. Isham, Scientific Perspectives on Divine Action Series (Vatican City State: Vatican Observatory Publications; Berkeley, Calif.: Center for Theology and the Natural Sciences, 1993), 33-48. For a technical introduction, see Charles W. Misner, Kip S. Thorne, and John Archibald Wheeler, *Gravitation* (San Francisco: W. H. Freeman, 1973), pt. 6.

tional to their distance. With this finding the expansion of the universe, as described by Einstein's General Theory of Relativity, had been discovered!

There are three possible types of expansion. The first type is the closed model: the universe has the shape of a three-dimensional sphere of finite size. It expands up to a maximum size, approximately 100 to 500 billion years from now, then re-contracts. The second two types are open models. In both the "flat" and "saddle-shaped" models, the universe is infinite in size and will expand forever. All three came to be called "Big Bang" models because they describe the universe as having a finite past life of 10 to 15 billion years and beginning at time "t = 0" in an event of infinite temperature and density and zero volume.

Inflationary Big Bang and Quantum Cosmologies[4]

Since the 1970s, a variety of problems in the standard Big Bang model have led scientists to pursue inflationary Big Bang and quantum cosmology. According to *inflation,* at extremely early times (roughly Planck time, 10^{-43} seconds after t = 0) the universe expanded exponentially rapidly, then quickly settled down to the slower expansion rates of the standard Big Bang model. During inflation, countless domains may arise, separating the overall universe into many universes, each huge portions of space-time in which the natural constants and even the specific laws of physics can vary. In *quantum cosmology* our universe is part of an eternally expanding, infinitely complex mega-universe. Quantum cosmology, however, is a highly speculative field since the theories involving quantum gravity, which underlie quantum cosmology, are notoriously hard to test empirically.

Big Bang and the Far Future: Freeze or Fry

Even if inflationary or quantum cosmologies prove of lasting importance, the visible universe from Planck time to the present is described by Big Bang cos-

---

4. For a nontechnical introduction see Donald Goldsmith, *Einstein's Greatest Blunder? The Cosmological Constant and Other Fudge Factors in the Physics of the Universe* (Cambridge, Mass.: Harvard University, 1995), chs. 10 on. For a more technical introduction see Chris J. Isham, "Creation of the Universe as a Quantum Process," in *Physics, Philosophy, and Theology: A Common Quest for Understanding,* ed. Robert J. Russell, William R. Stoeger, S.J., and George V. Coyne, S.J. (Vatican City State: Vatican Observatory Publications, 1988), 375-408; Edward W. and Michael S. Turner Kolb, *The Early Universe* (Reading: Addison-Wesley, 1994).

mology, and there are two scenarios for its far future: freeze or fry. Freeze: if the universe is open or flat, it will expand forever and continue to cool from its present temperature (about $2.7°K$), asymptotically approaching absolute zero. Fry: if it is closed, it will expand to a maximum size in another one to 500 billion years, then re-collapse to an arbitrarily small size and unendingly higher temperatures, somewhat like a mirror image of its past expansion. Although the presence of a cosmological constant (Λ) could either accelerate its expansion or, possibly, close the universe, the far future scenarios are still freeze or fry.

What about the future of life in the universe? It turns out that the overall picture is bleak, regardless of whether it is open or closed (i.e., freeze or fry). According to Frank Tipler and John Barrow,[5] in 5 billion years the sun will become a red giant engulfing the orbit of the earth and Mars, and eventually becoming a white dwarf. In 40 to 50 billion years, star formation will have ended in our galaxy. In 10^{12} years, all massive stars will have become neutron stars or black holes.[6] In 10^{19} years, dead stars near the galactic edge will drift off into intergalactic space, and stars near the center will collapse together, forming a massive black hole. In 10^{31} years, protons and neutrons will decay into positrons, electrons, neutrinos, and photons. In 10^{34} years, dead planets, black dwarfs, and neutron stars will disappear, their mass completely converted into energy, leaving only black holes, electron-positron plasma, and radiation, and all carbon-based life forms will be extinct. Beyond this, solar mass, galactic mass, and finally supercluster mass black holes will evaporate by Hawking radiation. The upshot is clear: "Proton decay spells ultimate doom for . . . *Homo sapiens* and all forms of life constructed of atoms. . . ."[7]

Now we can return to our key question: *Can Christian eschatology be seen as consistent with these scientific scenarios?*

5. John D. Barrow and Frank J. Tipler, *The Anthropic Cosmological Principle* (Oxford: Clarendon, 1986), ch. 10; see also William R. Stoeger, S.J., "Scientific Accounts of Ultimate Catastrophes in Our Life-Bearing Universe," in *The End of the World and the Ends of God: Science and Theology on Eschatology*, ed. John Polkinghorne and Michael Welker (Harrisburg, Pa.: Trinity Press International, 2000).

6. If the universe is closed, then in 10^{12} years the universe will have reached its maximum size and re-collapse back to a singularity like the original hot Big Bang.

7. Barrow and Tipler, *The Anthropic Cosmological Principle*, 648.

Four Movements Relating Resurrection, Eschatology, and Cosmology

Four key areas in contemporary theology and New Testament scholarship either move toward, or stem from, a new and vigorous engagement with the central Christian kerygma, the resurrection of Jesus and its eschatological implications. Remarkably, none of them has engaged the challenges raised to them by scientific cosmology. Here I will point to two briefly before engaging two others in depth.

1. The Problem of Evil and Theodicy

The problem of moral evil and theodicy in contemporary theology is immense, particularly in light of the human atrocities of the twentieth century. A pivotal response has been a revised doctrine of God through a "recovery of the Trinity" and a "theology of the crucified God," to use Catherine Mowry LaCugna's and Jürgen Moltmann's terms, respectively. But this, in turn, requires a robust theology of the resurrection and eschatology, and this leads directly to the challenge of contemporary cosmology. Meanwhile, when we consider the problem of natural evil in light of the evolution of life on earth over its 3.8-billion-year history, and thus massive suffering, disease, death, and extinction in nature, the challenge of theodicy is vastly amplified, leading scholars to consider the redemption of nature and an eschatology of "new creation." Again, however, the challenge from physics and cosmology is seldom noted.

2. Christian Eschatology

The nineteenth- and twentieth- century rediscovery of the essentially eschatological dimension of the New Testament kerygma has affected every area of contemporary theology. Among the enormous variety of Christian eschatologies today one finds hope for the transformation of persons, societies, and, in some cases, the world as a whole — a transformation that is both "realized" in the present and yet to come at the end of history. Scientific cosmology need not be seen as challenging those eschatologies that are restricted to spiritual, moral, interpersonal, societal, or historical categories, but when eschatology expands to embrace the environment and the history of life on earth, as suggested above, and when earth is seen as a tiny part of the immense universe, then Christian eschatology runs up directly against the challenge of physical cosmology. According to Peters, "should the final future as forecasted by the combination of big bang cosmology and the second law of thermodynamics come to pass . . . then we would have proof that our faith has been in vain. It would turn out to be that there is no God, at least not the God in whom followers of Jesus have put their faith."[8] Yet little attention has been given this warning.

3. New Testament Debates over the Resurrection and the Eschatology of New Creation

Although New Testament scholars and contemporary theologians hold a diversity of views regarding the resurrection of Jesus, they can be divided roughly into what I call the "objective" and "subjective" interpretations.

According to the subjective interpretation, the resurrection of Jesus is only a way of speaking about the experiences of the first disciples. Although they described the resurrection as having happened to Jesus after his death and burial, it is in fact not about purported events in the new life given to Jesus by God but merely about the experience of renewed faith given the disciples. According to Willie Marxsen, "All the evangelists want to show is that the activity of Jesus goes on. . . . They express this in pictorial terms. But what they mean to say is simply: 'We have come to believe.'"[9] Rudolf Bultmann was one of the most prominent defenders of the subjective interpretation in the twentieth century. Others include John Dominic Crossan, John Hick, Gordon Kaufman, Hans Küng, Sallie McFague, Norman Perrin, and Rosemary Radford Ruether.

According to the objective interpretation, something actually happened to Jesus of Nazareth after his crucifixion, death, and burial: God raised Jesus from the dead, he lives forever with God, and he is present to us in our lives and communities. Hence what happened to Jesus in the resurrection cannot be reduced entirely to the experiences of the disciples as reported in the appearances and the empty tomb traditions. According to Raymond Brown, "Our generation must be obedient . . . to what *God* has chosen to do in Jesus; and we cannot impose on that picture what we think God should have done."[10] Karl Barth was

8. Ted Peters, *God as Trinity: Relationality and Temporality in the Divine Life* (Louisville: Westminster/John Knox, 1993), 175-76.

9. Willi Marxsen, *The Resurrection of Jesus of Nazareth*, trans. Margaret Kohl (Philadelphia: Fortress, 1970), 77, 156.

10. Raymond E. Brown, *The Virginal Conception and Bodily Resurrection of Jesus* (New York: Paulist, 1973), 72.

a prominent defender of the objectivist interpretation. Others include Gerald O'Collins, William Lane Craig, Stephen Davis, Wolfhart Pannenberg, Pheme Perkins, Ted Peters, Janet Martin Soskice, Sandra Schneiders, and Richard Swinburne.

The objective interpretation emphasizes elements of continuity and discontinuity between Jesus of Nazareth and the risen Jesus, holding these in tension by such terms as "transformation," "transfiguration," and "identity-in-transformation."[11] While rejecting anything that reduces resurrection to mere resuscitation, most scholars assert that there is at least a minimal and irreducible element of physical/material continuity as well as personal and spiritual continuity between Jesus of Nazareth and the risen Jesus even while there is radical discontinuity. I will call this view "bodily resurrection" to emphasize its inclusion of physical/material continuity. In contrast to this, a few scholars[12] support what can be called "personal resurrection." Here the resurrection of Jesus includes personal and spiritual continuity but not (or not necessarily) physical and material continuity. Thus, while the appearances are essential components of both views, the empty tomb traditions are also essential to the bodily resurrection approach while supporters of personal resurrection can be agnostic toward the empty tomb traditions or even claim that Jesus' body decayed in the grave like any other body.

Finally, scholars who support the bodily resurrection of Jesus, and with it the empty tomb traditions, normally connect his resurrection with the general resurrection at the end of time and the coming of a new creation. By analogy with the resurrection, the new creation will be a transformation of the world as a whole and all that is in it. Thus the new creation will be both continuous and discontinuous with the present world, and, as with the resurrection of Jesus, the elements of continuity include something of the physical/material character of this world.

In this chapter I will assume the bodily resurrection approach and thus the eschatological transformation of the universe into the new creation precisely because it is this position that runs into the greatest challenge from science. Thus I am not not making a normative or dogmatic argument that the bodily resurrection is the only approach Christians can or should hold. What I am suggesting is methodological, namely, that the bodily resurrection ap-

---

11. Gerald O'Collins, S.J., *The Resurrection of Jesus Christ* (Valley Forge, Pa.: Judson, 1973), 95.

12. See, e.g., Thorwald Lorenzen, *Resurrection and Discipleship: Interpretive Models, Biblical Reflections, Theological Consequences* (Maryknoll: Orbis, 1995), esp. ch. 8.

proach, and entailed by it the eschatological transformation of the universe in the new creation, poses an extraordinarily powerful "test case" for the claim that theology and science can avoid conflict and be in a relationship of creative mutual interaction.

4. Resurrection, Eschatology, and Cosmology within Theology and Science: The Surprising Lack of Engagement

The fourth movement is the growing field of theology and science. Against competing claims that theology and science are necessarily in outright conflict or that they are two separate worlds, there has been enormous progress, now on an international scale, in relating theology and science through dialogue and interaction. Over the past four decades, physics, cosmology, evolution, genetics, and other areas of the natural sciences have been introduced into constructive theological discussions. The beginning of the universe at "t = 0" in Big Bang cosmology and the apparent "fine-tuning" of the universe for the possibility of the evolution of life are seen by many as consonant with a theology of creation *ex nihilo*. Similarly, evolutionary and molecular biology are routinely taken as fully consistent with a theology of continuous creation: God works in and through, even while sustaining in their being and regularity, the very processes of nature that the natural sciences study through methodological naturalism. Particular attention has been given to the goal of articulating objectively special, *noninterventionist* divine action by searching for genuine openness (indeterminism) in nature.[13] Surprisingly, however, little attention has been given to the resurrection of Jesus and its eschatological implications in light of science.[14]

This lack of attention is particularly ironic since the same methodological framework that has played an essential role in making it possible for the field of theology and science to grow so richly over the past four decades should have prevented us from sidestepping the crucial issues raised by cosmology for Christian eschatology. To see this, we need to summarize two of its central claims,[15] epistemic hierarchy and analogous methodologies, which

13. See the series of five volumes on divine action, the CTNS/Vatican Observatory publications, distributed by the University of Notre Dame Press.

14. Stoeger, "Scientific Accounts of Ultimate Catastrophes in Our Life-Bearing Universe," 19-20.

15. Critical realists also claim that language is intrinsically metaphorical, and they defend a referential theory of truth warranted in terms of correspondence, coherence, and utility.

build directly on the pioneering writings of Ian Barbour[16] as well as on those of Arthur Peacocke,[17] Nancey Murphy,[18] Philip Clayton,[19] John Polking-horne,[20] and many others.

The first claim is that the sciences and the humanities, including theology, can be placed in a series of epistemic levels that reflect the increasing complexity of the phenomena they study. In this "epistemic hierarchy," lower levels place *constraints* on upper levels (against "two worlds"), but upper levels cannot be reduced entirely to lower levels (against "epistemic reductionism"). Thus, physics places constraints on biology and neurophysiology on psychology. On the other hand, the processes, properties, and laws of the upper level (e.g., biology) *cannot be reduced* entirely to those of the lower level (e.g., physics).

The second claim is that, within this hierarchy, each level involves similar methods of theory construction and testing. Thus theological methodology is analogous to scientific methodology (though with several important differences).[21] This claim is both a *description* of the way many theologians actually work and a *prescription* for progress in theological research. Theological doctrines are to be seen as working hypotheses held fallibly, constructed through metaphors and models, and tested in light of the data of theology *now including the results of the sciences.*

It is helpful to combine these two ideas — epistemic hierarchy and analogous method — into a single diagram (see p. 12; for now, disregard paths 6, 7, and 8) and limit the conversation to physics and theology.[22] Here five paths

16. Ian G. Barbour, *Religion in an Age of Science,* Gifford Lectures, 1989-90 (San Francisco: Harper & Row, 1990).

17. Arthur Peacocke, *Theology for a Scientific Age: Being and Becoming — Natural, Divine and Human* (Minneapolis: Fortress, enlarged ed. 1993). See particularly Fig. 3, p. 217, and the accompanying text.

18. Nancey Murphy, *Theology in the Age of Scientific Reasoning* (Ithaca, N.Y.: Cornell University, 1990). While Murphy has contributed to the development of a methodology for relating theology and science, she is highly critical of the term "critical realism." See her book *Anglo-American Postmodernity: Philosophical Perspectives on Science, Religion, and Ethics* (Boulder, Colo.: Westview, 1997).

19. Philip Clayton, *Explanation from Physics to Theology: An Essay in Rationality and Religion* (New Haven, Conn.: Yale University, 1989).

20. John C. Polkinghorne, *The Faith of a Physicist: Reflections of a Bottom-up Thinker,* Theology and the Sciences Series (Minneapolis: Fortress, 1994).

21. There are, of course, important differences between the methods of theology and the natural sciences, as Barbour and others stress carefully.

22. One could do a more complicated diagram with physics, biology, and theology, for example, and one would need to include the influences of physics on both biology and theology as well as the influences of biology on theology. Etc.!

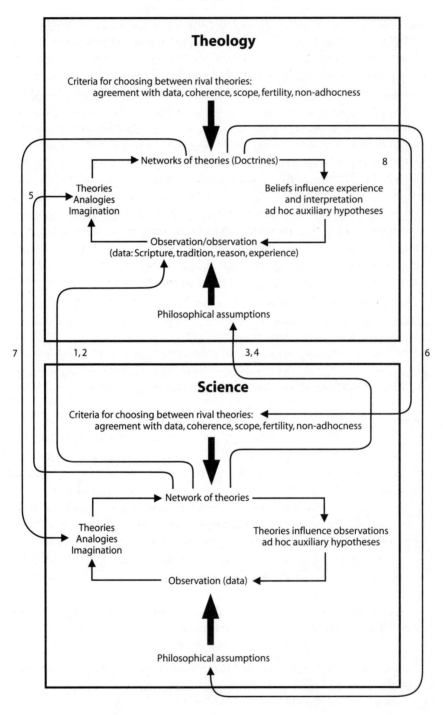

lead from physics to theology. (1) Theories in physics can act *directly* as data that place constraints on theology. For example, a theological theory about divine action should not violate special relativity. (2) Theories can act *directly* as data either to be "explained" by theology or as the basis for a constructive theological argument. For example, t = o in standard Big Bang cosmology can be explained theologically via creation *ex nihilo*. (3) Theories, after philosophical analysis, can act *indirectly* as data for theology. So an indeterministic interpretation of quantum mechanics can function within theological anthropology by providing a physical precondition for the bodily enactment of free will. (4) Theories in physics can also act *indirectly* as the data for theology when they are incorporated into a fully articulated philosophy of nature (e.g., that of Alfred North Whitehead). Finally, (5) theories in physics can function *heuristically* in the theological context of discovery by providing conceptual or aesthetic inspiration. So biological evolution may inspire a fresh interpretation of God's immanence in nature. For convenience, I will use the symbol "SRP → TRP," suggested by George Ellis,[23] to indicate these five ways in which scientific research programs (SRPs) can influence theological research programs (TRPs).

We are now prepared to see clearly why the problem of eschatology and cosmology is forced on us by the same methodological framework that has made possible the fields of theology and science: scientific cosmology (e.g., Big Bang cosmology, inflationary Big Bang, quantum cosmology, etc.) is part of physics (e.g., relativistically correct theories of gravity applied to the universe). Therefore the predictions of "freeze or fry" — or their scientific replacements in the future — must place constraints on and challenge what theology can claim eschatologically. No appeal to contingency, quantum physics, chaos theory, ontological unpredictability, novelty, emergence, the future, or metaphysics alone will be sufficient to solve this problem.

Arthur Peacocke and John Polkinghorne have given somewhat detailed treatments of eschatology and cosmology. They both defend the objective interpretation of the resurrection of Jesus, but they differ in their support of what I am calling personal versus bodily approaches, and this, in turn, determines the degree to which scientific cosmology challenges their position.

According to Peacocke,[24] there are two options for understanding the resurrection: (1) to affirm continuity, in which Jesus' body undergoes a "fundamental transformation" into his risen state — what I am calling "bodily

---

23. This is a slight modification of George's actual suggestion (private communication).

24. Peacocke, *Theology for a Scientific Age*, 279-88.

resurrection," and (2) "to remain agnostic, recognizing that the historical question remains open — that is, to be open to either bodily or personal resurrection." Both views, in Peacocke's opinion, retain the "essential core" of Christian belief: that the whole person of Jesus was glorified, his identity was preserved, he now exists united with God, and he appeared to the disciples. As Peacocke develops his argument, however, it becomes clear that he actually favors "personal resurrection" and not just what he calls option (2). For example, he rejects option (1), bodily resurrection, because it makes the relation of Jesus' death to ours, and the relation between the continuity of our personal identity and the transformation of our bodies, problematic since, unlike those of Jesus' body, our constituents will decay and disperse about the globe where they will contribute to other organisms.[25] That Peacocke leans toward personal resurrection is further indicated by his discussion of eschatology and its focus on "the axis between man *[sic]* and God in the *present* experience." Our hope is that the purposes of God will "finally achieve their fulfillment beyond space and time within the very being of God himself. . . . [M]an's true citizenship is in heaven and . . . his true destiny lies beyond space and time. . . ."[26] The ultimate destiny of humanity is the "beatific vision" as expressed in Dante's *Paradiso.*[27]

Polkinghorne[28] has argued extensively for the bodily interpretation and the historicity of the empty tomb. He disagrees with the claim that Jesus must share our lot in regard to bodily corruption in the grave. Instead the empty tomb means that "matter has a destiny," though a transformed one. Polkinghorne rejects eschatological views based strictly on the processes of nature, including the "fantastic, and curiously chilling, programme" labeled "physical eschatology" of Frank Tipler. Instead, our hope must rest in God and not in God's creation. He also rejects a dualist view of human nature as an embodied soul; instead we are a psychosomatic unity. Death is the dissolu-

---

25. See also Peacocke, *Theology for a Scientific Age,* 332. Note Peacocke's use of Hans Küng, *On Being a Christian* (Garden City, N.Y.: Image Books/Doubleday, 1976/1984), 364-66, as a further indication of his distance from the "bodily" view. This is the reference O'Collins uses in his argument against Küng. See Gerald O'Collins, S.J., "The Resurrection: The State of the Questions," in *The Resurrection: An Interdisciplinary Symposium on the Resurrection of Jesus* (Oxford: Oxford University, 1997), 13.

26. A. R. Peacocke, *Creation and the World of Science: The Bampton Lectures, 1979* (Oxford: Clarendon, 1979), ch. 8.

27. Peacocke, *Theology for a Scientific Age,* 344-45.

28. John Polkinghorne, *The Way the World Is* (Grand Rapids: Eerdmans, 1983), ch. 8; Polkinghorne, *The Faith of a Physicist,* chs. 6, 9, esp. 163-70; John C. Polkinghorne, *Serious Talk: Science and Religion in Dialogue* (Valley Forge, Pa.: Trinity Press International, 1995), ch. 7.

tion of this unity, but at the resurrection we will be re-created by God in the "new environment."

How will God create this new environment? Here we see the crucial importance of the empty tomb: just as Jesus' body was transformed into the risen and glorified body, so the "matter" of this new environment must come from "the transformed matter of this world": "[T]he new creation is not a second attempt by God at what he *[sic]* had first tried to do in the old creation. . . . [T]he first creation was *ex nihilo* while the new creation will be *ex vetere* . . . the new creation is the divine redemption of the old. . . . [This idea] does not imply the abolition of the old but rather its transformation."[29] Creation *ex vetere* means that "the present created order [has] . . . a profound significance, for it is the raw material from which the new will come." It underscores our concern for our planetary environment, and it offers the only viable response to the problem of suffering and thus theodicy. Clues to what the new heaven and earth will be like might come from the themes of continuity and discontinuity found in the Gospel accounts of the resurrection and in the Eucharist. Moreover, we might get help in understanding the continuities from science or, more precisely, what Polkinghorne calls "metascience . . . the distillation of certain general ideas from the scientific exploration of many particulars."[30]

In sum, by favoring the personal interpretation of the resurrection of Jesus and, with it, an eschatology restricted to the vision of God, Peacocke avoids the challenge of cosmology with its bleak predictions of freeze or fry. Polkinghorne, on the other hand, is clearly committed to the bodily resurrection of Jesus, including the empty tomb. He then must acknowledge the challenge raised by scientific cosmology. Although he never explicitly rejects the predictions of freeze or fry, I take this as implicit in his support of *ex vetere*. If we are to move beyond this point in pursuing the "worst case scenario," we will need an expanded methodology.

---

29. Polkinghorne, *The Faith of a Physicist*, 167.

30. John Polkinghorne, "Eschatology: Some Questions and Some Insights from Science," in *The End of the World and the Ends of God: Science and Theology on Eschatology*, ed. John Polkinghorne and Michael Welker (Harrisburg, Pa.: Trinity Press International, 2000), 29-30.

ROBERT JOHN RUSSELL

Methodology and Guidelines for New Research in Scientific Cosmology and in Eschatology

I see that you believe these things are true because I say them.
  Yet, you do not see how.
Thus, though believed, their truth is hidden from you.

DANTE ALIGHIERI[31]

If it is impossible, it cannot be true. But if it is true, it cannot be impossible.

Clearly, if one assumes the current methodology in theology and science, and if one starts with the bodily resurrection of Jesus and an eschatology of cosmological transformation, then one seems forced into a direct contradiction with the predictions of contemporary scientific cosmology. To move forward, I propose that we expand our methodology to allow for genuine interaction between theology and science.

A New Methodology to Meet the Challenge: The Mutual Creative Interaction of Christian Theology and Natural Science

Earlier we delineated five paths of influence by science on theology. Now, let me reverse the direction of influence by adding three new paths (see the diagram on p. 12, paths 6, 7, and 8). These paths represent the possible influences of theology on the philosophical assumptions that underlie science, and a heuristic source of inspiration functioning within the initial phase of current research often called the "context of discovery." I will again use Ellis's suggestion to represent these paths as TRPs → SRPs.

The first new path deals with underlying philosophical assumptions in science. It is now abundantly clear that, historically, theological ideas provided some of the philosophical assumptions that underlie scientific methodology. Historians and philosophers of science have shown in detail how the doctrine of creation *ex nihilo* played an important role in the rise of modern science by combining the Greek assumption of the rationality of the world with the theological assumption that the world is contingent. Together these helped give birth to the empirical method and the use of mathematics to represent natural processes.[32]

---

31. Dante Alighieri, *The Divine Comedy,* trans. John Ciardi (New York: W. W. Norton, 1970), The Paradiso, canto XX, vv. 88-90.

32. To view nature as created *ex nihilo* implies that the universe is contingent and ra-

The second and third new paths deal with the context of discovery in science. My view is that theological theories can act as sources of inspiration in the construction of new scientific theories. An interesting example is the subtle influence of atheism on Hoyle's search for a "steady state" cosmology.[33] Theological theories can also lead to or be suggestive of selection rules within the criteria of theory choice in science. For example, if one considers a theological theory to be true, then one can delineate what conditions must obtain within physics for the possibility of its being true. These conditions in turn can serve as motivations for an individual research scientist or group of colleagues to pursue a particular scientific theory.

The asymmetry between theology and science should now be quite apparent: theological theories do *not* act as data for science, placing constraints on which theories can be constructed in the way that scientific theories do for theology. Still, unlike the more limited methodology that still dominates the field of theology and science, theology can now have an influence on science: it can play a constructive and heuristic role within the implicit philosophy of nature that undergirds science and within the explicit context of scientific discovery. Together the eight paths portray science and theology in a much more interactive mode. I suggest calling this *the method of creative mutual interaction*. It involves two interconnected steps: following paths 1-5, we construct a more nuanced understanding of eschatology in light of physics and cosmology (SRPs → TRPs), and following paths 6-8, we search for a fresh interpretation of, or possibly revisions of, current scientific cosmology in light of this eschatology (TRPs → SRPs).

A sign of real progress in theology and science therefore will be that both sides find the interaction fruitful within their own disciplinary standards of progress. If such a project is at all successful, it might eventually be possible to bring these two trajectories together, at least in a very preliminary

---

tional. These are two of the fundamental philosophical assumptions on which modern science is based. See, e.g., Michael Foster, "The Christian Doctrine of Creation and the Rise of Modern Science," in *Creation: The Impact of an Idea*, ed. Daniel O'Connor and Francis Oakley (New York: Scribner's, 1969); David C. Lindberg and Ronald L. Numbers, eds., *God and Nature: Historical Essays on the Encounter between Christianity and Science* (Berkeley: University of California, 1986); Gary B. Deason, "Protestant Theology and the Rise of Modern Science: Criticism and Review of the Strong Thesis," *Center for Theology and the Natural Sciences Bulletin* 6.4 (Autumn 1986); Christopher B. Kaiser, *Creation and the History of Science*, The History of Christian Theology Series, no. 3 (Grand Rapids: William B. Eerdmans, 1991).

33. Helge Kragh, *Cosmology and Controversy: The Historical Development of Two Theories of the Universe* (Princeton: Princeton University, 1996).

way, to give a more coherent overall view of the history and destiny of the universe than is now possible, in light of the resurrection of Jesus and its eschatological completion in the *parousia*.

This project, however, is clearly a long-term undertaking, requiring the participation of scholars from a variety of fields in the sciences, philosophy, and theology. How might we begin it? I believe we first need guidelines that point us in a fruitful direction. Using them, we can begin to explore specific ways to enter into the research.

General Philosophical Guidelines for Constructive Theology (G1-G4)

We begin with guidelines for constructing theology in light of contemporary science. Our first four guidelines deal with overall philosophical and methodological issues in constructive theology. *Note:* These guidelines hold for *theological* research in light of science. They do *not* hold for scientific research (for which see Guidelines 8-10 below). This is particularly true for Guideline 1 since scientists must assume the principle of analogy and, more specifically, the universal applicability of the laws of nature if they are to test their theories by empirical evidence.

Guideline 1: Rejection of Two Philosophical Assumptions about Science: The Argument from Analogy and Its Representation as Nomological Universality

The first guideline deals with the fundamental challenge physical cosmology poses to the kind of eschatology we are considering here, namely, one based on the bodily resurrection of Jesus. In bare form, the challenge is this: if the predictions of contemporary scientific cosmology come to pass, then the *parousia* will not be just delayed; it will never happen. And if this is so, then the logic of Paul in 1 Corinthians 15 is inexorable: if there will never be a general resurrection, then Christ has not been raised from the dead and our hope is in vain. The challenge can also be seen as coming from theology to science: if it is in fact true that Jesus rose bodily from the dead, then the general resurrection cannot be impossible. This must in turn mean that the future of the universe will not be what scientific cosmology predicts.

We seem to be at loggerheads. How are we to resolve this fundamental challenge? My response is to recognize that the challenge is *not* from science but from the philosophical assumptions that we routinely bring to science, namely, that scientific predictions hold without qualification. This assumption involves two arguments: (1) at its most *fundamental* level, the future will be just like the past (or what one can call "the argument from analogy"). (2) The same laws of nature that govern the past and present will govern the future as well (or what one can call "nomological universality").

It is quite possible, however, to accept a very different assumption about the future predictions of science while accepting all that science describes and explains about the past history of the universe. The first step is deciding whether the laws of nature are descriptive or prescriptive. At this point, as William Stoeger argues, science alone cannot settle the matter.[34] A strong case can then be made on *philosophical* grounds that the laws of nature are descriptive. One can, in turn, claim on *theological* grounds that the processes of nature that science describes are the result of God's ongoing action as Creator; their regularity is the result of God's faithfulness. But God is free to act in radically new ways, not only in human history but also in the ongoing history of the universe, God's creation.

Another way of making this case is to recognize that all scientific laws carry a *ceteris paribus* clause, that is, their predictions hold "all else being equal." But if God's regular action accounts for what we describe through the laws of nature, and if God will act in radically new ways to transform the world, then of course all else is *not* equal.[35] We could say that the "freeze or fry" predictions for the cosmological future might have been applicable had God not acted at Easter and if God were not to continue to act to bring forth the ongoing eschatological transformation of the universe.

Guideline 1 also places a crucial limitation on nomological universality. The limitation is that, though they are clearly applicable to the universe as a whole in its past and present, the laws of nature as we now know them cannot be arbitrarily extended to the future. In short, we could say that the "freeze or fry" predictions for the cosmological future might have applied had God not acted at Easter and were God not to continue to act to bring forth the ongoing eschatological transformation of the universe.

34. William R. Stoeger, S.J., "Contemporary Physics and the Ontological Status of the Laws of Nature," in *Quantum Cosmology and the Laws of Nature,* ed. Russell, Murphy, and Isham, 209-34.

35. I am grateful to Nancey Murphy for stressing this point to me (private communication).

Guideline 2: Eschatology Should Embrace Methodological Naturalism regarding the Cosmic Past and Present: The Formal Argument

Any eschatology that we might construct must be scientific in its description of the *past* history of the universe. More precisely, it must be constrained by methodological naturalism in its description of the past: it should not invoke God in its explanation of the (secondary) causes, processes, and properties of nature.[36]

This guideline is a formal argument. It separates this proposal as sharply as possible from such approaches as "intelligent design" insofar as they are critical of the physical and/or biological sciences for not including divine agency in its mode of explanation.

Guideline 3: Big Bang and Inflationary Cosmology as a "Limit Condition" on Any Revised Eschatology (Paths 1 and 3): The Material Argument

Guideline 3 is a material argument. It follows paths 1 and 3 by stating that standard and inflationary Big Bang cosmologies, or other scientific cosmologies (such as quantum cosmology), place a limiting condition on any possible eschatology. All we know of the history and development of the universe and life in it will be data for theology, particularly as interpreted philosophically.

Guideline 4: Metaphysical Options: Limited but Not Forced

In revising contemporary eschatology there are a variety of metaphysical options from which we may choose; they are not forced on us, or determined by science. On the one hand, since eschatology starts with the presupposition of God, it rules out reductive materialism and metaphysical naturalism. By taking on board natural science, other metaphysical options become unlikely candidates, including Platonic or Cartesian ontological dualism. On the other hand, several metaphysical options are compatible with science and Christian theology, including physicalism, emergent monism, dual-aspect monism, ontological emergence, and panexperientialism (Whiteheadian metaphysics).

---

36. It is crucial to note that the commitment to methodological naturalism does not carry any ontological implications about the existence/nonexistence of God (i.e., it is not inherently atheistic).

Guidelines for Specific Theological Construction in Light of Science (G5-G7)

We must now begin the enormous job of revisiting our understanding of eschatology in a way that takes up and incorporates all the findings of science, and particularly scientific cosmology, without falling back into the philosophical problem Guideline 1 is meant to address.

Guideline 5: "Transformability" and the Formal Conditions for Its Possibility (the "Such That"[37] or "Transcendental" Argument)

Our starting point is that the new creation is not a replacement of the old creation, or a second and separate creation *ex nihilo*. Instead, God will transform God's creation, the universe, into the new creation *ex vetere*, to use Polkinghorne's phrase. It follows that God must have created the universe *such that it is transformable*, that is, that it can be transformed by God's action. Specifically, God must have created it with precisely those conditions and characteristics that it needs as preconditions in order to be transformable by God's new act. Moreover, if it is to be transformed and not replaced, *God must have created it with precisely those conditions and characteristics that will be part of the new creation.* Since science offers a profound understanding of the past and present history of the universe (Guidelines 2, 3), science can be of immense help to the theological task of understanding something about that transformation if we can find a way to identify, with at least some probability, these needed conditions, characteristics, and preconditions. Using our previous discussion of the bodily resurrection and the new creation, I will refer to these conditions and characteristics as "elements of continuity."

Guideline 5 can be thought of as a *transcendental* or "such that" argument.[38] A simple analogy would be that an open ontology could be thought of as providing a precondition for the enactment of voluntarist free will, but certainly not the sufficient grounds for it. Science might also shed light on which conditions and characteristics of the present creation we do *not* expect to be continued into the new creation; these can be called "elements of discontinuity" between creation and new creation. Thus physics and cosmology

---

37. See in particular the articles by Noreen Herzfeld, Nancey Murphy, Ted Peters, Jeffrey Schloss, and Michael Welker in this collection.

38. I am grateful to Kirk Wegter-McNelly for suggesting the term "transcendental" here (private communications).

might play a profound role in our attempt to sort out what is truly essential to creation and what is to be left behind in the healing transformation to come.

Guideline 5 gives to the terms "continuity" and "discontinuity," found in the theological literature on the resurrection of Jesus, a more precise meaning and a potential connection with science. With it in place we can move eventually to a material argument and ask just what those elements of continuity and discontinuity might be.

Guideline 6: Continuity within Discontinuity: Inverting the Relationship

Closely related to the previous guideline is a second formal argument about the relative importance of the elements of continuity and discontinuity. So far in theology and science, discontinuity has played a secondary role within the underlying theme of continuity in nature as suggested by the term "emergence." Accordingly, irreducibly new processes and properties (i.e., discontinuity) arise within the overall, pervasive, and sustained background of nature (i.e., continuity). Thus biological phenomena evolve out of the nexus of the physical world, the organism is built from its underlying structure of cells and organs, mind arises in the context of neurophysiology, and so on. Now, however, when we come to the resurrection and eschatology, I propose we *invert* the relation: the elements of continuity will be present, but within a more radical and underlying discontinuity as is denoted by the *transformation* of the universe by a new act of God *ex vetera*. With this inversion, discontinuity as fundamental signals the break with naturalistic and reductionistic views such as "physical eschatology," while continuity, even if secondary, eliminates a "two-worlds" eschatology.

This has important implications for our search for candidate theories. It *eliminates* "noninterventionist objective special divine action" as a candidate since it does not involve a transformation of the whole of nature. Indeed, these approaches presuppose that it is the continual operation of the usual laws of nature that makes objective special divine action possible without the need for the violation or suspension of those laws. But the bodily resurrection of Jesus directs us toward a much more fundamental view: the radical transformation of the background conditions of space, time, matter, and causality, and, with this, a permanent change in at least most of the present laws of nature.[39]

---

39. I agree with O'Collins's criticism that previous work on noninterventionist divine

Guideline 7: "Relativistically Correct Eschatology": Constructing Eschatology in Light of Contemporary Physics (Paths 1, 2, and 3)

Although we will set aside the predictions Big Bang offers for the cosmic future, we must be prepared to reconstruct current work in eschatology in light of contemporary physics — specifically relativity and quantum physics — as well as what cosmology tells us about the history of the universe, following paths 1 and 2. I will refer to this project as the attempt to construct a "relativistically correct Christian eschatology."

Guidelines for Constructive Work in Science (G8-G10)

Our project also involves the question of whether such revisions in theology might be of any interest to contemporary science — at least for individual scientists who share eschatological concerns such as are developed here, and are interested in whether they might stimulate a creative insight into research science. Very different guidelines hold for scientific research. Scientists should set aside the preceding guidelines, which apply only to theological research, and consider instead Guidelines 8-10.

Guideline 8: Theological Reconceptualization of Nature Leading to Philosophical and Scientific Revisions (Path 6)

Here we move along path 6 in discovering whether a richer theological conception of nature both as creation *and* as new creation can generate important revisions in the philosophy of nature that currently underlies the natural sciences, the philosophy of space, time, matter, and causality in contemporary physics and cosmology.

Guideline 9: Theology as Suggesting Criteria of Theory Choice between Existing Theories (Path 7)

We can also move along path 7 to explore philosophical differences in current options in theoretical physics and cosmology. The theological views of re-

---

action did not deal with the problem of the resurrection. See O'Collins, "The Resurrection," p. 21 n. 52.

search scientists might play a role in selecting which theoretical programs to pursue among those already on the table (e.g., the variety of approaches to quantum gravity).

Guideline 10: Theology as Suggesting
New Scientific Research Programs (Path 8)

Finally, we can move along path 10 and suggest the construction of new scientific research programs whose motivation stems, at least in part, from theological interests.

In closing this section I want to stress once again that all such programs in science would have to be tested by the scientific communities (what is often called "the context of justification") without regard for the way theology or philosophy might have played a role in their initiation ("the context of discovery").

SRPs → TRPs: Reconstructing Christian Eschatology as Transformation in Light of Science

Our fundamental problematic is clear: we must reconstruct Christian eschatology to be consistent with both our commitments to the bodily resurrection of Jesus and thus an eschatology of transformation, *and* with scientific cosmology regarding the past history and present state of the universe and its basis in such foundational theories as special and general relativity and quantum mechanics.[40] Is such a project possible? I believe this is a genuinely open research question; it cannot be answered in advance of actually attempting to carry it out.

As a first step, we could follow Guidelines 5 and 6, focusing on continuities, discontinuities, and their preconditions that are part of that transformation. These may be found in certain suggestive eschatological hints gleaned from the resurrection of Jesus and the reign of God depicted in the New Testament and its glimpses in the living body of Christ, the church, and keeping clearly in mind the apophatic character of this material.

---

40. The project would eventually include attempts to bring these together in quantum theories of gravity and the like.

Continuities and Discontinuities

(a) Hints of continuity from the *resurrection of Jesus:* he could be touched, he could eat, break bread, be seen,[41] heard, and recognized. These instances of "realized eschatology" are suggestive of an extended domain of the new creation proleptically within the old, a domain that ceases with the ascension, but that, when present, includes Jesus, the disciples, and their surroundings.[42] Hints of discontinuity: these encounters with the risen Lord break with a mere resuscitation and with normal limitations on physicality. (b) Hints of continuity from the *reign of God* in the New Testament and in the church: the new creation will include persons-in-community and their ethical relations.[43] Hints of discontinuity: in the reign of God, it will "not be possible to sin," compared with the present creation in which it is "not possible not to sin," to use Augustine's apt formulation. (c) Hints of continuity from the problem of *personal identity* between death and the general resurrection in historical and contemporary theology: (1) Paul's analogy of the seed;[44] (2) numerical, material, and/or formal continuity between death and general resurrection in historical Christian thought.[45] Hints of discontinuities: though death awaits all people now, the general resurrection, like that of Jesus at Easter, will not be a resuscitation; Paul's fourfold contrast.[46]

Preconditions for These Continuities and Discontinuities

Next we look for the preconditions that make possible these continuities and discontinuities. One way is to move epistemically down the disciplinary hierarchy, focusing on those characteristics that make possible the elements of

41. Does "seeing" require "grace"? See the debate between O'Collins and Davis in O'Collins, *The Resurrection.*

42. Michael Welker offers a very imaginative formulation of the relation between the reign of God as already present and as apocalyptic in terms "eschatological complementarity." See his chapter in this volume.

43. For a very creative development of this theme, see the chapter by Nancey Murphy in this volume.

44. 1 Corinthians 15:35ff.

45. Caroline Walker Bynum, *The Resurrection of the Body in Western Christianity, 200-1336* (New York: Columbia University, 1995); Sandra Schneiders, "The Resurrection of Jesus and Christian Spirituality," in *Christian Resources of Hope* (Dublin: Columba, 1995), 81-114. See also the article by Brian Daley in this volume.

46. 1 Corinthians 15:42ff.

continuity or lead to those of discontinuity. For now, I will set aside the many levels to be found in the social, psychological, and neurosciences, and move directly to physics. Here we find a variety of themes that underlie our discussion of continuity and discontinuity. A central one is temporality, or the theological loci, the relation of time and eternity. Another is ontological openness as a precondition for persons-in-community to act freely in love (i.e., assuming incompatibilist freedom). Still others include ontological relationality since creation and new creation are the acts of the triune God.[47] It is arguable that mathematics as we now know it will be present in the new creation if it is in some sense grounded in the mind of God.[48]

The Theological Research Program (TRP): Reconstructing Eschatology

The next step is to undertake a reconstruction of Christian eschatology in light of these arguments and, following Guidelines 3 and 7, in light of contemporary science and cosmology,. This will clearly require extensive research far beyond the limits of this chapter. Nevertheless, some hints of the way forward can be found in focusing, briefly, on one aspect of that project: the relation of time and eternity.

A crucial argument shared widely among contemporary trinitarian theologians[49] is that eternity is a richer concept of temporality than timelessness or unending time. In essence, eternity is the source of time as we know it, and of time as we will know it in the new creation. Eternity is the fully temporal source and goal of time. Barth calls it "supratemporal." Moltmann calls it "the future of the future," and Peters refers to the future as coming to us

---

47. Polkinghorne has made very similar suggestions in "Eschatology," esp. 29-30.

48. Robert John Russell, "The God Who Infinitely Transcends Infinity: Insights from Cosmology and Mathematics into the Greatness of God," in *How Large Is God,* ed. John Marks Templeton and Robert L. Herrmann (Philadelphia: Templeton Foundation Press, 1997).

49. For a helpful overview of trinitarian theologians on the problem of "time and eternity," see Peters, *God as Trinity,* and Robert John Russell, "Time in Eternity," *Dialog* 39.1 (March 2000). There are, of course, fundamental problems in contemporary discussions of the doctrine of the Trinity. These include the source of the doctrine (is it analytic or synthetic?), the meaning of the divine persons, their principle of unity, the relation of the economic and the immanent Trinity, and so on. Here I am not attempting to adjudicate between these issues. I am simply lifting up some themes that, arguably, most trinitarian formulations have in common in order to suggest ways to start the conversation with science.

(adventus) and not merely that which tomorrow brings *(futurum)*. Pannenberg claims that God acts proleptically from eternity: God reaches back into time to redeem the world, particularly in the life, ministry, death, and resurrection of Jesus. In this approach the relation between time and eternity is modeled on the relation of the finite to the infinite. Here the infinite is not the negation of the finite (as in the Platonic/Augustinian view of eternity as timelessness); instead the infinite includes while ceaselessly transcending the finite.

In my opinion, this view of eternity includes at least five distinct themes: (1) co-presence of all events, where distinct events in time are nevertheless present to one another without destroying or subsuming their distinctiveness; (2) "flowing time," where each event has a "past/present/future" (ppf) structure or an "inhomogeneous temporal ontology"; (3) duration, where each event has temporal thickness in nature as well as in experience, and events are not pointlike present moments lacking an intrinsic temporal structure; (4) prolepsis, where the future is already present and active in the present while remaining future, as exemplified by God's act in raising Jesus from the dead; and (5) the global future, where there is a single global future for all of creation so that all creatures can be in community.

Note: the combination of flowing time and co-presence in eternity means that all events can be "simultaneously present" and available to each other (à la Boethius) and yet each event retains its own unique identity. Thus in the new creation "flow" keeps "co-presence" from reducing to *"nunc"* while "co-presence" keeps "flow" from reducing to a stream of isolated moments.

Our guidelines now lead to three questions: (1) Which of these themes are already present in creation and thus are elements of continuity in its transformation into the new creation? (2) Which themes are not yet present in creation but instead represent elements of discontinuity, emerging only in the new creation? (3) And regarding the latter, does the universe at present include the preconditions for the possibility of their coming to be in the new creation? The answer to these questions will require a careful discussion of time in physics and cosmology. It will also require us to reformulate these theological themes in terms of our current understanding of time as drawn from twentieth-century physics and cosmology.

Though the reformulation has only begun, I can nevertheless anticipate possible responses to the three questions. To the first, I would argue that flowing time and duration are objective features in nature, though this is debatable. Time in special relativity is subject to conflicting interpretations (e.g., "block universe" as well as "flowing time"). Moreover, lacking co-presence, "flowing time" for us means an isolated present with a vanishing past and a not-yet-realized future. Following path 3, I would introduce a "co-present flowing time" interpretation of special relativity into the theological discussion of time and eternity. Duration is a harder problem, since contemporary physics assumes a pointlike or durationless view of time. I believe a case can be made for duration in nature by drawing on Pannenberg's arguments.[50]

To the second and third questions, I would identify co-presence, prolepsis, and the global future as elements of discontinuity, and thus search physics for their preconditions in nature. For example, the transformation of flowing time into co-present flowing time would seem plausible if one could argue that the inhomogeneous ontology of flowing time does not logically exclude the possibility of distinct temporal events being co-present. Preconditions for prolepsis could include backward causality, violations of local causality, and violations of global causality. Finally, a global future, while excluded by special relativity, is theoretically possible in general relativity where the topology of the universe is contingent on the distribution of matter.

The theological task now will be to reconstruct eschatology with these insights in mind and with our theological concepts reformulated in light of contemporary physics. For example, time and space are treated as independent quantities in classical physics. Similarly, theological treatments of eternity and omnipresence typically take for granted independent treatments of time and space. But time and space are placed in a complex interrelationship in special relativity and further linked with matter in general relativity. Our task then will be to reformulate such theological categories as eternity and omnipresence in light of special and general relativity with an eye to "co-present flowing time" and time as duration. Similar theological reconstructions will hold for the treatment of time and space in quantum mechanics, and so on.

50. In brief, Wolfhart Pannenberg claims that duration was part of the biblical and early Western understanding of time, that it was lost in Augustine's separation of subjective and objective time, and that modern physics inherited the latter, durationless view. He then points to recent philosophy where attempts have been made to view physical time in terms of duration, as in the writings of Bergson, Heidegger, and Whitehead, whose roots lie, in part, in Christian theology. See Wolfhart Pannenberg, "Theological Questions to Scientists," in *The Sciences and Theology in the Twentieth Century*, ed. A. R. Peacocke (Notre Dame: University of Notre Dame, 1981); Wolfhart Pannenberg, *Metaphysics and the Idea of God* (Grand Rapids: Eerdmans, 1990); Wolfhart Pannenberg, *Systematic Theology*, trans. G. W. Bromiley (Grand Rapids, Mich.: Eerdmans, 1991), vol. 1; Wolfhart Pannenberg, *Toward a Theology of Nature: Essays on Science and Faith*, ed. Ted Peters (Louisville: Westminster/John Knox, 1993).

TRPs → SRPs: New Research in Physics and Cosmology

Our methodology of mutual interaction includes a second agenda: explore ways in which a revised eschatology as suggested above leads to a revised philosophy of nature as it underlies science, to criteria of theory choice among current theories in science, and to the construction of new scientific research programs.

The first project, revising eschatology in light of science, is still in its very early stages. Until more has been accomplished, we might pursue the second agenda by a more limited approach: begin with our existing eschatology and the *same* elements of continuities, discontinuities, and their preconditions as listed above, and ask now what SRPs they might suggest. Once again, since temporality is such a predominant theme here, we could start with the theme of "time and eternity,"[51] but now we will explore its implications for current physics and cosmology in two ways. (1) We begin with those aspects of temporality in nature that constitute elements of continuity and of discontinuity in respect to the eschatological transformation of the world. This time, however, the analysis should lead to interesting questions about time in current physics. (2) We also will consider aspects of temporality that physics may have overlooked but which, from the perspective of eschatology, might be expected to exist at present. If physics were reconsidered with them in mind, could it generate concrete suggestions for research programs in physics? For example, let us return to the debate over "flowing time" versus the "block universe" in special relativity. Here the absence of absolute simultaneity undercuts most approaches to "flowing time." Can we construct a new interpretation of special relativity that is consistent with "flowing time" but avoids these problems? I will label this SRP 1. Alternatively, one might attempt to revise special relativity to support a "flowing time" interpretation over a "block universe" interpretation, which I will designate as SRP 2. Interestingly, most interpretations of quantum mechanics presuppose "flowing time." See, for example, the importance of the absolute present to the "measurement problem" in the Copenhagen interpretation. But technical problems in this interpretation have led some scholars to consider either constructing an alternative interpretation of quantum mechanics that supports "flowing time" and avoids these problems (SRP 3), or a modification of quantum mechanics

---

51. The focus on "time and eternity" is particularly appropriate for our task here since most contemporary theologians root their eschatology within the framework of *creatio ex nihilo*. Thus much of what they claim about time and eternity applies to the universe as present and new creation, and not only as it will be as the new creation.

that supports "flowing time," such as nonlinear or stochastic versions of the Schrödinger equation (SRP 4). Finally, one might pursue Pannenberg's arguments that duration should be found in nature by searching for a mathematical way to represent time as duration and then exploring its implications for research physics (SRP 5). In sum, we are asking what an expanded scientific conception of nature would be like if it were inherited from eschatology instead of creation theology, and what ramifications this might have for current science. This program is currently in process.

Theological Realism and Eschatological Symbol Systems

MICHAEL WELKER

There are many definitions of "theological realism." A minimalist definition states that theological claims should be compatible with possible experience. The measures for possible experience need continuous testing, and negotiation in and among truth-seeking communities.[1] Truth-seeking communities seek to interrogate and to heighten certainty and consensus without reducing truth to certainty and consensus. Truth-seeking communities can do this because they also want complex states of affairs to be made accessible in repeatable and predictable ways. Since they aim at the co-enhancement of certainty and consensus and content-loaded, shared insight, they also guard against reducing truth to the — possibly trivial — repeatable, predictable, and correct investigation of the subject under consideration.

Since truth-seeking communities concentrate on different topical areas, use different rationalities, and pursue different goals, these negotiations on what could count as possible experience are not easy; they are even loaded with conflict.[2] Those, however, who shy away from this burden and conflict enter the risk of working with reductionistic or even ideological notions of reality and rationality. They run the risk of reducing truth-seeking communities to communities that aim at preserving certainties and routines. The sci-

---

1. Cf. John Polkinghorne, *The Faith of a Physicist* (Princeton: Princeton University, 1994), 149; *Faith, Science, and Understanding* (New Haven: Yale University, 2000), 29-30; John Polkinghorne and Michael Welker, *Faith in the Living God: A Dialogue* (London: SPCK; Minneapolis: Fortress, 2001), esp. ch. 9.

2. A careful description of a potentially fruitful scenario in the case of a discourse between theology and the sciences on eschatological topics is given by Robert John Russell in this volume.

ence-and-theology discourse is one example of the attempt to work boldly against the segmentation of knowledge and the reduction of experience to areas of well-established routines to preserve mere certainty and security of expectations.[3]

Theological Realism as Ambitious Enterprise

In his famous disputation on the human person, his *Disputatio de homine* of 1536,[4] Martin Luther states that philosophy — namely, Aristotelian philosophy — can only define the mortal and worldly human being. When philosophy speaks of the rational being, the *animal rationale,* it tries to grasp something divine in the human being by reference to the power and majesty of reason. But if one looks more closely at what this philosophy really knows about the human person and his or her destiny, one is rather disappointed. Aristotelian philosophers are quite insecure about what shapes the human being and his or her existence; they offer only vague talk about the "shaping cause" that they call "the soul."

Luther says that, over against philosophy, theology gives us a much fuller account of the human person when it speaks of the person as God's creature, made of flesh and a living soul, and from the beginning formed as an image of God, called to be fruitful, to multiply, and to rule the earth, destined for eternal life. Theology then talks about the fall, the subjugation of the human being to sin and death, and his or her inability to overcome the evil forces by his or her own power. Finally, theology speaks of the saving work of Christ, who freed human beings and gave them the gift of eternal life.[5]

In the light of these theological insights, Luther challenges such illusionary philosophical statements as the idea that human reason always aims at "the good" or even at "the best," and that human beings have the power to choose between good and evil. He concludes that in this life human beings — like all the other creatures — live under the powers of sin and futility. But they are at the same time God's material for a future life in which they will be restored and completed as the *imago Dei,* the image of God.[6]

It is clear that Luther extends the focus on human life greatly by bring-

---

3. This does not mean that security of expectations is not a most important good for religious communication. Cf. Michael Welker, "Security of Expectations: Reformulating the Theology of Law and Gospel," in *Journal of Religion* 66 (1986): 237-60.

4. *Weimarer Ausgabe,* 39.1.175-77.

5. *Disputatio de homine,* theses 21-23.

6. Ibid., theses 35-38.

ing in real and possible experiences of sin, death, self-endangerment, and futility. The open question is whether and how the theological symbols he evokes can honestly and convincingly disclose and illuminate these areas of experience. Does theology, indeed, give a fuller account of human reality, or does it reach out into areas of fiction and fantasy?

In a way strikingly similar to that of Luther, the twentieth-century theologian Karl Barth, in the doctrine of creation in his *Church Dogmatics*,[7] investigates various philosophical and scientific anthropologies. He arrives at the conclusion that naturalistic, idealistic, and existentialistic anthropologies have offered us only "phenomena of the human being." They have not shown us "the real human being." Based on his own, early thorough and penetrating interpretation of the atheistic philosophy of Ludwig Feuerbach,[8] Barth first praises Feuerbach's anti-idealistic anthropology. He suggests that Feuerbach, with his emphasis on the sensuality and the intrinsic sociality of the human being, had at least some glimpses from afar into what Barth calls "the real human being." However, Feuerbach's great problem and error, according to Barth, is that he dismisses creaturely mortality and the dominance of the power of sin over human existence.[9] Barth is convinced that only a christologically oriented view can focus on the profound lostness of human existence and on God's care and intention for this existence, namely, its participation in the divine glory.

When modern scientists are confronted with such statements of genius theologians like Luther and Barth, it seems quite likely that many of them react with a mixture of irony and bewilderment. What is the basis on which these theologians speak? Religious narratives of the past and lofty ideas of a future life, the image of God, and divine glory seem to be the ground of what appear to be pretentious claims to focus on "the real human being." What is

---

7. *Church Dogmatics* III/1-4, esp. III/2, 71ff.

8. Karl Barth, "Ludwig Feuerbach," in *Die Theologie und die Kirche: Gesammelte Vorträge* (München: Kaiser: 1928), 2:212ff.; this is a chapter in a course on theology and philosophy that Barth gave in Münster in the summer of 1926. The later, much weaker publication of this course replaced the stronger version of the original lecture on Feuerbach. Cf. K. Barth, *Die protestantische Theologie im 19. Jahrhundert: Ihre Vorgeschichte und ihre Geschichte* (Zürich: Evangelischer Verlag, 1946), 484ff. See also "Feuerbach, 1922," in K. Barth, *Vorträge und kleinere Arbeiten, 1922-1925*, ed. Holger Finze, Gesamtausgabe 19 (Zürich: Theologischer Verlag Zürich, 1990), 6ff.

9. Barth, "Ludwig Feuerbach," 237, follows Hans Ehrenberg, introduction to Ludwig Feuerbach, *Philosophie der Zukunft* (Stuttgart: Frommann, 1922), 94, who states, Feuerbach sei "als 'getreues Kind seines Jahrhunderts' ein 'Nichtkenner des Todes' und ein 'Verkenner des Bösen' gewesen."

the reality status of such claims? Do they have any connection to real phenomena and real experience? Can they meet any challenges to sustain truth claims? In the following reflections I intend to affirm the theological claims. I will undertake this very difficult task by investigating several biblical eschatological symbol systems.[10] According to a widespread prejudice, eschatological symbols seem to point to a realm "totally other" than the reality we can experience. As we have elaborated in a multi-year discourse between scientists and theologians, the biblical eschatological symbols and texts express an interesting relation between this creation and the "new creation": "most eschatological symbols and texts in the classical and canonical religious traditions . . . speak of the *continuity and discontinuity* between this world and the world to come."[11] Like Luther and Barth in their focus on the "real" human being, eschatological symbols and symbol systems indeed focus on possible experiences and a reality that should not be ignored or even given up by the sciences. I should like to name this reality the *reality of the fullness of life,* understood as both individual and communal life "in God."

The Resurrection of Christ as the Presence of the Fullness of His Life and His Personhood

For a long time the general understanding of "resurrection" was dominated by a confusion of resurrection and physical reanimation and resuscitation — and great skepticism over against this. Time and again, famous and would-be-famous New Testament scholars made a splash in the media by assuring the interested public that the resurrection texts of the New Testament speak of a reanimation of the dead Jesus but that today human beings are not going to be persuaded that dead persons can be reanimated. Therefore the experience and reality of the bodily resurrection must be called into question.[12]

---

10. By "symbol systems" I understand connections of symbols with rationalities that can be explored and disclosingly reinvested in other realms of experience or at least fruitfully contrasted with other connections of symbols operating in different realms of experience.

11. Cf. Polkinghorne, "Introduction: Science and Theology on the End of the World and the Ends of God," in *The End of the World and the Ends of God: Science and Theology on Eschatology,* ed. John Polkinghorne and Michael Welker (Harrisburg, Pa.: Trinity Press International, 2000), 1-13; M. Welker, "Resurrection and Eternal Life: The Canonic Memory of the Resurrected Christ, His Reality, and His Glory," in Polkinghorne and Welker, *The End of the World and the Ends of God,* ed. Polkinghorne and Welker, 279-90; *Faith in the Living God,* 40ff., 60ff.

12. Cf. Rudolf Bultmann, "Neues Testament und Mythologie: Das Problem der Ent-

A theology concerned about its academic reputation avoided this topic or at best gave it a niche under the cloak of existentialist and supernaturalist figures of thought. In this situation, Wolfhart Pannenberg and others proposed that we take account only of the appearances of light attested in the New Testament's resurrection witnesses, not the reports of personal encounters with the resurrected Christ and the empty-tomb traditions.[13] On this view appearances of light and visions, to which historicity can be attributed, are the foundation of the testimonies to the resurrection. This proposal, though, remained unsatisfying. It had to leave out most of the Synoptic resurrection accounts. It also left open the question of how precisely the pre-Easter Jesus could be perceived in a new form in the appearances of light.

Ironically, the calm awareness of several disturbing complexities in the New Testament resurrection accounts led us out of the two dead-end streets: the disputes about the pros and cons of resurrection understood as resuscitation, and the dispute about the either-or of resurrection as historical or subjective or even psychopathic visions.

1. The New Testament accounts present us with a *strange tension between palpability and appearance.*[14] The resurrection of Christ is clearly not a physical reanimation and resuscitation. Only if we isolate a few biblical verses from their contexts in a biblicistic manner can we be led to think that the resurrection of Christ was a mere reanimation of the pre-Easter Jesus. The most graphic of all affirmations that the presence of the resurrected

---

mythologisierung der neutestamentlichen Verkündigung," in *Kerygma und Mythos*, Bd. 1 (Gütersloh: Gütersloher, 3. Aufl. 1988); Gerd Lüdemann, *Die Auferstehung Jesu: Historie, Erfahrung, Theologie* (Göttingen: Vandenhoeck & Ruprecht, 1994); "Zwischen Karfreitag und Ostern," in *Osterglaube ohne Auferstehung? Diskussion mit Gerd Lüdemann,* ed. Hansjürgen Verweyen (Freiburg/Basel/Wien: Herder, 1995), 13ff.

13. Wolfhart Pannenberg, *Grundzüge der Christologie* (Gütersloh: Gütersloher, 6. Aufl. 1982), 85ff.

14. I have elaborated this in "Resurrection and the Reign of God," in *The 1993 Frederick Neumann Symposium on the Theological Interpretation of Scripture: Hope for the Kingdom and Responsibility for the World, The Princeton Seminary Bulletin,* supplementary issue, no. 3, ed. Daniel Migliore (Princeton: Princeton Seminary, 1994), 3-16; and in "Auferstehung: Dietrich Ritschl zum 65. Geburtstag," *Glauben und Lernen* 9 (1994): 39-49; similar results are offered by Joachim Ringleben, *Wahrhaft auferstanden: Zur Begründung der Theologie des lebendigen Gottes* (Tübingen: Mohr-Siebeck, 1998); more recently, Bernd Oberdorfer, "'Was sucht ihr den Lebendigen bei den Toten?' Überlegungen zur Realität der Auferstehung in Auseinandersetzung mit Gerd Lüdemann," and Günter Thomas, "'Er ist nicht hier': Die Rede vom leeren Grab als Zeichen der neuen Schöpfung," both in Hans-Joachim Eckstein and Michael Welker, *Die Wirklichkeit der Auferstehung* (Neukirchen: Neukirchener, 2002).

had all the signs of palpability and physicality is found in Luke 24: When the disciples and their companions think "they [are] seeing a ghost," the resurrected points at his flesh and bones and even eats a piece of fish before them. He then "opens their minds to understand the scriptures" and tells them to wait for the outpouring of the Spirit in order to begin the proclamation of the gospel throughout the world. Finally it says: "While he was blessing them, he withdrew from them and was carried up into heaven" (Luke 24:51).

A similar connection of palpable presence and withdrawal, of palpability and appearance, is expressed in the Emmaus story, also in Luke 24. It states that the eyes of the disciples who encountered the resurrected Christ were kept from recognizing him (24:16). This speaks even more clearly against resuscitation than against the impression that they see a ghost. The disciples' eyes are opened, and they recognize the resurrected when the resurrected Christ takes bread, blesses it, breaks it, and gives it to them. But already in the next sentence the text explicitly states: "And he vanished from their sight" (24:31). After the opening of their eyes to the presence of the resurrected Christ, he vanishes from sight. Instead of bemoaning this and complaining about a spooky event, the disciples now retrospectively recognize that they had a feeling of the presence of the resurrected even before their eyes were opened in the ritual act in table fellowship. "They said to each other, 'Were not our hearts burning within us while he was talking to us on the road, while he was opening the scriptures to us?'" (24:32). Then they bear witness to the resurrection before others.

This tension between palpability and appearance is characteristic of most of the resurrection accounts of the canonic traditions. The so-called longer ending of Mark speaks of an appearance of the resurrected "in another form" (Mark 16:12). Paul encounters the resurrected Christ in light appearances, which in themselves clearly speak against a mere physical reanimation. John speaks of a sudden appearance of the resurrected "when the doors of the house were locked" (John 20:19). In no case do the biblical witnesses give the impression that the post-Easter Christ lived together with his disciples or with other persons in the same way as the pre-Easter Jesus. Although they claim that there is both identity and continuity between the pre-Easter and the post-Easter Jesus Christ, they point to a complex identity and continuity that needs to be unfolded.

2. Connected with this tension between palpability and appearance is the double reaction of worship and doubt to the presence of the resurrected (Matt. 28:17). The touch of the resurrected is experienced as a revelation of God, as a theophany. The disciples and the women fall down before the resur-

rected. "My Lord and my God!" exclaims the disbelieving Thomas. Not: "How good to see you among us again, Jesus!"

3. It is consistent with this complicated picture that the discovery of the empty tomb and the more or less spectacular appearances of heavenly messengers do not yet generate resurrection belief. The first reactions to the empty tomb are fear and silence (Mark 16), the worry or the public rumor that a theft of the corpse has taken place (Matthew 28; John 20), or the belief that the claim of the resurrection was mere talk of women (Luke 24).

4. It is important to see that the encounters with the resurrected Christ as witnessed by the Scriptures take very different forms, from visions of light to the appearance of a person with all the impressions of palpability. It is not the case that just one spectacular experience leads to the belief in the resurrection. Not from a single appearance, but rather from *a variety of appearances* arises the firm conviction: the resurrected Christ was and is with us.[15] These appearances are connected with symbolic, liturgical, or missionary acts that will all be constitutive for the life and the worship of the early church: for instance, the greeting, "Peace be with you!" the breaking of the bread, the opening of the Scriptures, the disclosure of the secret of the Messiah, the blessing and sending of the disciples, and other ritualized actions and signs. The biblical texts do not try to smooth over the problems connected with this presence. They describe the fear, the doubt, the derision, and the disbelief connected with this reality. On the whole, the resurrection witnesses very calmly acknowledge that this presence is not a simple empirical reality, although it bears several characteristics of such a reality.

The connection with the risen Christ grows out of different experiences that can accurately be termed "testimonies." This term points, on the one hand, to the personal authenticity and certainty of the experience and, on the other hand, to its fragmentary and perspectival character. Francis Fiorenza has emphasized that this character of testimony is indispensable. He has

---

15. I made this point in "Die Gegenwart des auferstandenen Christus als das Wesentliche des Christentums," in *Das ist christlich: Nachdenken über das Wesen des Christentums*, ed. W. Härle, H. Schmidt, and M. Welker (Gütersloh: Gütersloher, 2000), 91-103. Sarah Coakley, "The Resurrection and the 'Spiritual Senses': On Wittgenstein, Epistemology and the Risen Christ," in *Powers and Submission: Spirituality, Philosophy and Gender* (Oxford: Blackwell, 2002), has recently called attention to the fact that an epistemology of the resurrection testimonies must take note of the polyphony of senses addressed by the resurrection: "Our continuing difficulties in expressing the reality of a risen Christ who cannot finally be grasped, but rather 'seen' — 'not with the eyes only'" are to be traced back to the richness of knowledge that comes with the presence of the resurrected. See also the contribution of Nancey Murphy in this volume.

shown that these necessarily multiple testimonies push toward metaphorical speech when they point to each other and also seek to thematize the complex reality to which they point perspectivally.[16]

To indicate the continuity between the pre-Easter and the post-Easter Christ, the biblical traditions use the term "body." The biblical texts clearly state that the stories of the empty tomb allow for different interpretations. Very realistic and extreme supernaturalistic versions are possible. However, they all have in common that Jesus Christ's pre-Easter body is not available for an autopsy or for physical inspection.[17] A transformed body, a transfigured body, a body that is also called "spiritual" or "glorified" (cf. Rom. 15:46; Phil. 3:21) is the body of the resurrected. This body represents the essential marks of personal identity in such complexity and fullness that, on one hand, its recognition can become much more complicated than the recognition of a merely biological body. On the other hand, this transfigured body can open many more routes of recognition, community, and identification than a merely natural body.

By insisting on the aspect of palpability in the midst of appearances the biblical texts indicate and even emphasize that the resurrected body is not the product of mere imagination or fantasy. Grounded in the life and person of the pre-Easter Jesus, the resurrected body generates memories and imaginations. It produces a living cultural and canonic memory[18] shaped by the life of the pre-Easter Jesus and the revelation of the resurrected Lord. This fact — that the cultural and canonic memory is shaped by Jesus' pre-Easter life — allows us *to affirm the objectivity of the transfigured body.* It is indeed not the product of fantasy. It is also not just a poly-individual and communal recollection. A living cultural and canonic memory not only shapes individual and communal modes of experience and expectation. The very lives and bodies of

16. Francis Schüssler Fiorenza, "The Resurrection of Jesus and Roman Catholic Fundamental Theology," in *The Resurrection: An Interdisciplinary Symposium on the Resurrection of Jesus,* ed. S. T. Davis, D. Kendall, and G. O'Collins (Oxford: Oxford University, 1997), 213-48, 238ff.

17. Cf. Hans-Joachim Eckstein's contribution to this volume. Gerd Lüdemann's remark, "The factual statement of Jesus' decomposition is to me the starting point of all further work on questions in the context of his 'resurrection,'" thus shows poor exegetical and theological perception. "Zwischen Karfreitag und Ostern," in *Osterglaube ohne Auferstehung? Diskussion mit Gerd Lüdemann,* ed. Hansjürgen Verweyen (Freiburg/Basel/Wien: Herder, 1995), 13ff., 27 (translation M. W.).

18. Cf. *The End of the World and the Ends of God,* ed. Polkinghorne and Welker, 284ff., with references to Jan Assmann's concept of "cultural memory" (Jan Assmann, *Das kulturelle Gedächtnis* [Munich: Beck, 1992]) and the difference between communal, cultural, and canonic memory.

the bearers of this memory are *shaped by the very person and life who constitutes and sustains this memory.*[19] On the basis of the cultural and historical objectivity of the transfigured body, we can acknowledge that the appearances characteristic of this body become present together with Christ's witnesses. As Luther and Barth rightly state: "Der auferstandene Christus ist nicht ohne die Seinen,"[20] the resurrected Christ is not without his witnesses. The participation of the witnesses in this presence is of the utmost soteriological importance.

The transfigured body of the resurrected calls for the participation of the witnesses in the glorified life, a participation that in turn transforms the lives of the witnesses. They become "one with Christ," they take part in the divine life, they become transformed by God's own creativity[21] "from glory to glory." The explanation of this process within the realms of the symbol system of the resurrection is difficult. We see tensions in the canonical traditions that deal with participation in the life of the resurrected Christ. 2 Timothy, for instance, warns against those "who have swerved from the truth by claiming that the resurrection has already taken place" (2 Tim. 2:18). Other texts, such as Colossians 3:1, exhort believers, "So if you have been raised with Christ, seek the things that are above, where Christ is. . . ." Do we participate already in the resurrection — or is it a future event? Or is it both? What experiences are connected with the presence of the fullness of life of the resurrected Christ in canonic memory? It is helpful to turn to other eschatological symbols to find a way out of this difficulty.

Resurrection Explained with the Assistance of Other Eschatological Symbol Systems

Eschatological symbols such as "the reign of God" offer us considerable assistance in the difficult disclosure of both the continuity and the discontinuity of this life and life in the "world to come." The claim that all the eschatological symbols just mean "the same" cannot be maintained. They do not point at a vague or even miraculous "transformation" that should be left to pious

19. With Jeffrey Schloss, "Evolutionary Eschatology," one could speak of an eschatological "intensification" of our life, not just a continuation.

20. Cf. *Kirchliche Dogmatik* IV/2, 63.

21. Cf. John Polkinghorne, *The Faith of a Physicist,* 162ff. and the conclusion of Ted Peter's contribution in this volume. See also Andreas Schuele, "Gottes Handeln als Gedächtnis. Auferstehung in kulturtheoretischer und biblisch-theologischer Perspektive," in H.-J. Eckstein and M. Welker, *Die Wirklichkeit der Auferstehung.*

guesswork. However, *if we want to profit from this offer we have to respect the inner consistencies and rationalities of the different symbol systems.* This does not mean that the different symbol systems cannot illuminate each other. I would like to show that the symbol system connected with the "reign of God," which seems to focus more on communal transformation than on individual bodily existence, can help us to understand the connection between the resurrection of Christ (as a past event), the participation of humans in this resurrection in faith and through the working of the Holy Spirit (a present event), and the resurrection on the "last day" (a future event) of which, for instance, the Apostles' Creed speaks.

It is Luke who occasionally connects the two different symbol systems explicitly, the symbol system of the reign of God and that of the resurrection: when Jesus says that those who have shown mercy to the poor, the crippled, and the blind will be "repaid at the resurrection of the righteous," one of the "dinner guests" responds with the formula, "Blessed is the one who will eat bread in the kingdom of God!" (Luke 14:14, 15; cf. Luke 20:35).

The symbol system of the reign of God in itself exhibits a very important *eschatological complementarity,*[22] and it does so in a much clearer way than the symbol system of the resurrection. What does this *eschatological complementarity* mean? On the one hand, the reign of God is pictured as an emergent reality in which — in multifarious experiences and acts of love, care and forgiveness — a new reality latently breaks through, endangered and clouded from all sides, visible only to eyes of faith. On the other hand, the reign of God comes fully only at the complete theophany at the end of time.[23] This theophany at the end of time must not be located in just one specific temporal slot in world history. It is the "last day" of *all times,* equally close to and distant from all parts of history. In this respect the full theophany of the end of time is a (co-)present reality with all times, which necessarily cannot be adequately expressed by any specific development in world history.

22. I am aware of the risks that come with the transport of a technical term from one area of knowledge into another. The strong analogies of the necessary disclosure of one reality in two different forms with different epistemological complexities and gains encouraged me to take this risk. I am grateful to Robert John Russell for supporting me with insights and literature on this topic. The technical and methodological discussion of my transfer requires a chapter of its own.

23. Cf. John Polkinghorne, "Eschatological Credibility: Emergent and Teleological Process," in this volume. See also Michael Welker, "The 'Reign' of God," *Theology Today* 49 (1992): 500-515; Michael Welker and Michael Wolter, "Die Unscheinbarkeit des Reiches Gottes," in *Marburger Jahrbuch Theologie,* 11, ed. W. Härle and R. Preul (Marburg: Elwert, 1999), 103-16.

The texture of emergence, necessarily accompanied by doubt and the unavoidable inability to clearly locate the reality of the general resurrection, corresponds on the level of historical time to the eschatological reality of the theophany of the end of time (cf. Matt. 24:23; Mark 13:21; Luke 17:21, 23). In the New Testament traditions the eschatological complementarity of the emergent reality of the reign of God and of its full eschatological disclosure are expressed in the notion of the "coming reign" and its "nearness." These expressions reflect the necessary inability of specific historical settings to encompass the fullness of life, the fullness of reality.

The symbol of the resurrection, as a symbol of the defeat of death and sin, is not easily compatible with the rationality of emergence. The gradual and partial transformation of bodily existence can hardly be expressed in the language of the symbolism of the resurrection. It is difficult to think of resurrection "in the making." Resurrection and the theophany of the end of time seem to coincide. But if this was all that could be said, we would be left with an abstract eschatological transcendence, which the poet Friedrich Schiller grasped in his poem *The Pilgrim* with the words: "Ach, der Himmel über mir/ Will die Erde nie berühren,/Und das Dort ist niemals Hier." (Alas, heaven above me/Will never touch the earth,/And what's there is never here.)[24]

It is the resurrection of the pre-Easter Jesus Christ that opens a salvific perspective in this painful situation. His resurrection *did take place in a certain spatio-temporal slot in history.* And the reality of his resurrection is shaped by a specific bodily existence in space and time. The resurrection brings forth this bodily existence in its fullness.[25] It becomes a reality in the

---

24. Friedrich Schiller, *Sämtliche Gedichte: Zweiter Teil,* Deutscher Taschenbuch Verlag, Gesamtausgabe 2:171-72.

25. In "Who Is Jesus Christ for Us Today?" *Harvard Theological Review* (2002), I have argued that this has an impact on a deeper understanding of "history." The new interest in the resurrection seems to be connected with the replacement of an "archeologistic" understanding of history (with an enthusiasm about "excavating Jesus") with a new paradigm. "In this new paradigm of that which is historical we start with the assumption that at any and every point in time and space we can in principle open a continuum of memory and expectation. At every point both past and present we can in principle draw out a horizon constituted by past, present, and future. Historians must give account for their choice of both primary contexts of memory and expectation and bearers of those contexts, who in turn must be historically accessible. Historians must also reckon with the possibility of other contexts of memory and expectation which stand in temporal and spatial proximity to their chosen contexts, but which entail divergent presentations of historical persons and events. Concretely, we must consider the likelihood that Jesus had a different impact on the rural population of Galilee than on the urban population of Jerusalem. We must consider the likelihood that those who wished to hold high the Mosaic law or the Temple cult in the face of the Roman

mode of an engaging and transforming *incorporated word or message: the gospel.* It allows for participation in this reality — that is, a reality of what the sciences would call "transforming information." And this participation involves those who participate in it in "the life and world to come." Learning from the symbolism of the reign of God, we can see clearly that here again we focus on an emergent reality. For good reasons we have to acknowledge the necessary inability to locate clearly the reality, which historically corresponds to the eschatological reality. Nobody can say: this part of my life and body already lives the life of the resurrection.

With a third set of symbol systems the New Testament traditions find ways to help us and give us orientation in this vexing situation. In the community of Christ, mediated by faith, by participation in the sacraments, and by the *imitatio Christi,* believers at least move toward the resurrection and the life to come or even already participate in it (cf. John 11:25; Rom. 6:5; Phil. 3:10-11; Col. 2:12). Paul speaks of the rescuing Spirit by which God, "who raised Christ from the dead, will give life to your mortal bodies also through his Spirit that dwells in you" (Rom. 8:11). The Spirit is the divine power by which the fullness of the divine and eternal life — revealed in the life of Christ — permeates human souls and bodies. The powers of love, justice, mercy, and truth permeate the creation mediated through the body of Christ and through the members of this body that are physically embodied human persons. In this process human beings become part of "the Word," bearers and mediators of "the gospel."[26] They incorporate God's message for God's creation, and they participate in the divine power and life that sustains, rescues, and ennobles the creation and will never perish.

---

occupation perceived Jesus differently than those who wanted to embrace Roman culture. We must consider the likelihood that those whom Jesus met with healing and acceptance must give a different testimony about him than those whose main impression of Jesus came in the conflicts with Rome and Jerusalem." The life of the resurrected integrates and unfolds this polycontextual existence in an indefinite richness and intensity. It is the life of the historical Jesus itself that gives rise to and nourishes a specific multiplicity of expectations and experiences. It is this life that opens a specific space for images of Jesus that stand in tension, even in conflict with one another. The refined view of that which is historical challenges us to reconstruct a reality that requires forms of symbolic representation that can no longer be dismissed as products of fantasy by an archeologistic mind-set.

26. Cf. the contribution of Peter Lampe in this volume.

Eschatological Credibility:
Emergent and Teleological Processes

JOHN POLKINGHORNE

Although, as far as we know, life appeared in the universe only when it was eleven billion years old, and self-conscious life only after fifteen billion years of cosmic history, there is a real sense in which the universe was pregnant with life from the very beginning. The insights of the Anthropic Principle[1] indicate that the physical fabric of the world after the Big Bang had to take a very precise and specific form for the possibility of carbon-based life to be realizable at all. Such considerations in themselves already raise the teleological question of whether there has been something going on in the happenings of the universe's history. Such "fine tuning" does not look like just a happy accident.[2] Is there, then, a purpose behind cosmic process? The question is relevant to eschatological thinking since if past history were to lack meaning, there would be no reason to anticipate future fulfillment.

Note that this teleological questioning, although it arises from scientific insight, points us beyond what can be the subject matter of science. The latter has to be honest enough to recognize that its success has been purchased by its self-limited modesty in addressing only limited kinds of questions. Anthropic discussion considers the actual form of the laws of nature, a matter that science itself can only treat as the unexplained basis of its account of natural process. Therefore, if a new natural theology contributes to this meta-scientific discussion, it does so as a complement to science and not in conflict

1. John Barrow and Frank Tipler, *The Anthropic Cosmological Principle* (Oxford: Oxford University, 1986); see also Christian de Duve, *Vital Dust* (New York: Basic Books, 1995).

2. John Leslie, *Universes* (London: Routledge, 1989); see also John Polkinghorne, *Reason and Reality* (London: SPCK; Harrisburg, Pa.: Trinity Press International, 1991), ch. 6.

with it. This contrasts with the old style natural theology (such as William Paley's appeal to God as the divine watchmaker who designed and constructed the ingenious mechanisms of nature), which presented itself as a rival to scientific explanation for such events as the development of the optical system of the eye.

Questioning of the significance to be attached to the fruitfulness of the world intensifies when we go on to consider some recent developments in scientific understanding. For the first time, scientists are beginning to gain detailed insight into the behavior of complex systems. The resource that has enabled this advance to be made has been provided by computer modeling. Although the systems currently treatable in this manner fall very far short of the complexity of even the simplest living bacterium, the work already displays extremely interesting and unexpected hints of a new kind of natural behavior. These insights center on the ability of complex systems spontaneously to generate astonishing degrees of large-scale order.

The Emergent Properties of Complexity

A simple but instructive example can be drawn from the work of Stuart Kauffman.[3] He considers a digital model whose logical analogue in terms of a physical system would be as follows. An array of light bulbs is set up in which the behavior of each bulb (on or off) is influenced by the on/off behavior of two other bulbs somewhere else in the system. They do not have to be neighbors of the first bulb, but they can be anywhere else in the array. The correlation imposed is such that, in the next state of the system, a bulb will be more likely to be on if its two correlates are on now. All the bulbs in the array are subject to correlations of this kind. (Technically, the system corresponds to a logical entity called a Boolean net of connectivity two.) The system is started off in a randomly selected configuration, with some bulbs on and some bulbs off, and it is then allowed to develop according to the prescribed rules.

One might have expected that the network would continue to flicker away haphazardly forever. That is not the case, however. If the strengths of the correlations are suitably chosen within a certain range, the system soon settles down to cycling through a limited set of patterns of illumination, whose number is roughly the square root of the number of elements in the array. If there are 10,000 light bulbs, they will soon become illuminated in a cycle of about a hundred different patterns. Since there are approximately 10^{3000} dif-

3. Stuart Kauffman, *At Home in the Universe* (Oxford: Oxford University, 1995), ch. 4.

ferent possible states of illumination in which the whole array might be found, the observed effect implies the spontaneous generation of an altogether astonishing degree of order.

The investigation of the emergent properties of complexity is still at the "natural history" stage of depending on the study of specific computer models. The work has revealed the existence of these unanticipated and significant order-generating properties, but the general theory that must surely underlie these remarkable instances of particular behavior is currently unknown. I believe that gaining understanding in this area is likely to be among the most important scientific advances that we can hope for in the twenty-first century.

This strong propensity for the emergence of pattern powerfully suggests that the conventional scientific picture of basic natural process requires enlargement. Until now, science's main technique has been that of "divide and rule," the methodological tactic of splitting systems up into their component parts. It has been a successful strategy to follow because of the simplicity that often results from such a "bits and pieces" approach. Important insights were achieved, expressed in terms of the exchange of energy between constituents. It is becoming clear, however, that there are important properties pertaining to the system as a whole that can never be discovered in this reductionist fashion. The study of complexity has already suggested that we shall also need a complementary account, framed in terms of wholes rather than parts and concerned with information (the specification of dynamic pattern) rather than with energetic exchanges.

Kauffman has been particularly interested in the relevance that these new ideas may prove to have for biological thinking. He suggests that some of the homologous structures that comparative anatomists discern in their studies of different species may have their origin in certain universal pattern-forming tendencies possessed by matter. Conventional neo-Darwinian thinking supposes these similarities to have arisen from the contingent particularity of a common historical ancestor. Kauffman suggests that, in fact, they may be ahistorical features due to the inbuilt tendency for complex systems to generate specific kinds of order. (Remember those hundred particular patterns that emerged from the 10^{3000} possibilities of the light bulb array.)

These ideas are still at an early stage. Much remains to be done, and many contentious points remain to be resolved. Nevertheless, autopoiesis (the self-generation of order) has been placed firmly on the scientific agenda. It seems entirely possible that certain holistic laws of nature, presently unknown to us, control many emergent phenomena and are needed to complement the constituent laws of nature that have so long been familiar to us. It seems likely that information may very well prove to be as significant a category for understanding the processes of the world as energy undoubtedly is.

Holism, Atheism, and Theism

Metascientific evaluation of these developments displays the ambiguity that is characteristic of the search for wider worldviews. If there are holistic laws of fruitful generation of the kind I am suggesting, the atheist can point to them as supporting a purely naturalistic account of the process of the world. On the other hand, the theist can point to the astonishing degree of fertile potential built into natural law and inquire whether it is sufficient simply to treat this as brute fact ("a happy accident"), or whether it does not raise yet more intensely the question whether such remarkable properties become fully intelligible only if we believe them to be expressions of the mind and purpose of a divine Agent, whose will lies behind the intrinsic fruitfulness of the universe.

Certainly, no one who holds a doctrine of creation will suppose that God and the laws of nature exclude each other, for the regularities of those laws will be understood by the theist to be reflections of the faithfulness of the Creator who ordains them. The theist will also understand these laws not as being immutable necessities, but as holding simply for as long as the Creator determines that they should do so. God will not act in a capricious or trivially magical way to subvert the reliability of creation, but neither can God be denied the possibility of doing something totally new when it is appropriate to the divine will and faithful purpose to do so. Such a circumstance could arise if creation were to run down to the point where its current process no longer held out any prospect of further future fertility.

The argument relating to autopoietic laws of nature seems to be somewhat different from that involved in our earlier brief consideration of the Anthropic Principle. There the issues were comparatively clear-cut. It is an undeniable fact that if the laws of nuclear physics were not exactly what, in fact, they are, the stars would be unable to produce carbon in their interior nuclear furnaces. There would then be no possibility of carbon-based life, simply because there would be no carbon. In the anthropic case, there is no available naturalistic explanation of the strength of the nuclear forces — hence the atheist who wants to deflect the threat of theism is driven to the rather desperate metaphysical expedient of supposing that there is an infinite number of other universes, unknown and unknowable by us, from which vast portfolio our world has fortuitously proved to be the one where life could actually develop. We have seen, by contrast, that autopoiesis is rather more metaphysically ambiguous and the outcome of the argument more disputable.

Cosmic Death as Theological Threat

Nevertheless the theist, contemplating past cosmic history and the evolving fruitfulness of the universe to date, can, with integrity, claim that the belief that the world is a creation offers an intellectually satisfying understanding of the intrinsic, *inbuilt* fruitfulness that has made all this possible. Yet, when our eyes turn to the cosmic future, the picture darkens. Not only are there many hazards that could threaten the continuance of life on earth (a large meteor impact; a nearby supernova explosion drenching the planet with lethal radiation, the certainty that in five billion years the sun will turn into a red giant), but the whole universe itself is condemned to eventual futility. It is as scientifically sure as it can be that the cosmos will end either in the dying whimper of decay or in the bang of collapse into the melting pot of the big crunch.[4] In the end, the extrapolation of current process, as science understands it, leads to the inescapable conclusion that "all is vanity." Of course, these dire predictions lie very many billions of years into the future. Yet, though the timescale is extremely long, the knowledge that carbon-based life will eventually prove to have been but a transient episode in cosmic history puts a serious question to theology about the ultimate intentions of the Creator. If there is an answer to be found it will necessarily go beyond the simple extrapolation of scientifically influenced expectation. Theological dilemmas ultimately demand theological resolutions. We have already argued that a faithful Creator is not bound to maintain creation unchanged beyond the period of its natural fruitfulness.

Although ultimate issues of destiny are fundamentally theological in character, scientific considerations of the kinds discussed nevertheless provide a necessary context for contemporary eschatological thinking. We have discovered that the universe is both fertile and ultimately futile. Our conception of the nature of the physical world begins to embrace information as well as energy, relational structure as well as constituent atomism. The expression of Christian hope for an ultimate redeemed reality has always been conditioned by its contemporary understanding of the nature of present reality.[5]

4. See John Polkinghorne and Michael Welker, eds., *The End of the World and the Ends of God* (Philadelphia: Trinity Press International, 2000), chs. 1 and 2.

5. See Brian Daley, "A Hope for Worms: Early Christian Hope," in this volume.

That is because resurrection hope is necessarily engaged with a tension between continuity and discontinuity.[6] This follows from the fact that its picture of the new life to come is framed in terms of its being the eschatological transformation of the old life, and not simply the latter's abolition and replacement. Eschatology, therefore, must make the best use that it can of current insight into the character of creation. Consideration of past attempts to use this strategy reminds us of its limitations (think of Gregory of Nyssa's notion of the reassembly of the atoms that "belong" to the body of an individual human soul — an idea that makes no sense to us with our knowledge of the material flux that sustains biological life), but the endeavor remains an indispensable element in our thinking. An exploration of eschatological credibility today must, among other factors, make full use of the resources for understanding and conjecture that science can offer it.

Cosmic death, as well as the even more certain fact of individual human death, forces the issue of whether the universe is truly a cosmos or simply a chaos, whether history makes total and lasting sense or whether, ultimately, it is pointless, being, as Macbeth said, "a tale told by an idiot, full of sound and fury, signifying nothing." One could scarcely imagine a more challenging issue for theology.

Divine Faithfulness versus Evolutionary Optimism

An adequate theological response must rest on two foundational beliefs. The first is that all eschatological hope is predicated on the everlasting faithfulness of God. It cannot be based on a kind of evolutionary optimism that depends solely on the extrapolation of present process.[7] That would be reliance on a delusory hope, for there is no natural expectation that stretches beyond death, whether the death is that of the human individual or that of the universe. The fact of mortality is real, but it is not ultimate reality, for only God is that. Jesus made this point clearly and decisively in his well-known confrontation with the Sadducees. He pointed out to them that the God of Abraham, Isaac, and Jacob is the utterly faithful and reliable God, the God "not of the dead, but of the living" (Mark 12:27). Here alone is to be found the ground for an everlasting hope.

The second is that all creation must matter to the Creator in ways that are appropriate to its nature. Therefore, all creatures must ultimately find

---

6. Polkinghorne and Welker, *The End of the World and the Ends of God,* passim.

7. See Jeffrey Schloss, "From Evolution to Eschatology," in this volume.

their true fulfillment. The form that fulfillment will take will surely vary with the kind of creature involved. I do not believe that every bacterium that has ever lived will be resurrected to enjoy an everlasting destiny. But neither do I believe that it is only human beings that really matter to God forever. Theology has often been excessively anthropocentric in its concerns, as if history were simply the few tens of thousands of years of cultural record, and as if the rest of creation just provided the stage scenery before which the human play is being acted out. We need to heed the rebuke delivered to Job out of the whirlwind and lift our eyes to see the many concerns that the Lord has in what is going on around us (Job 38–42). The New Testament is strikingly free from this narrowness of vision. The Word is the one by whom all *things* were made (John 1:3); the cosmic Christ is the one through whom all *things* are redeemed by the blood of his cross (Col. 1:20). Perhaps most remarkable of all is the insight that Paul conveys in Romans with his picture of the whole creation waiting with eager longing to be set free from the bondage of decay and to obtain the freedom of the glory of the children of God (Rom. 8:19-21). Unless one has an eschatological conception whose scope is cosmic in range, the nonhuman dimension of the present creation would seem to possess no lasting value and ecological concern would then be seen simply as a matter of prudent human provision for its own needs.[8]

The emphasis on the prospect of a redemption of cosmic scope is surely reinforced by the message of the empty tomb. Its implication is that the Lord's risen and glorified body is the transmuted form of his dead body. What is involved, of course, is the eschatological transformation of resurrection and not the banality of resuscitation. The risen Christ has a body, still carrying the scars of the passion, but it possesses wholly new properties, so that he appears and disappears within locked rooms. Even less is the tomb empty because of the disposal of what was just a material irrelevance that had proved to be no longer necessary for Christ's future because his ultimate destiny was to be purely spiritual in character. The emphasis on the corporeal aspects of the risen Christ that we find in the later writings of the New Testament[9] makes a similar point.

The message seems clear. In Christ there is a destiny for *matter* as well as for men and women. I believe that a downplaying of the empty tomb and of the bodily resurrection, evident in a good deal of contemporary theological discussion, is a severe impoverishment of our eschatological understanding.

---

8. For a different approach to this last point, see Ernst Conradie, "Resurrection, Finitude, and Ecology," in this volume.

9. See Hans-Joachim Eckstein, "Bodily Resurrection in Luke," in this volume.

Continuity and Discontinuity

How do these theological considerations relate to the scientific points made earlier? We have already noted that much eschatological thinking centers on seeking a resolution of the tension between continuity and discontinuity. There must be sufficient continuity for it to be possible truly to say that Abraham, Isaac, and Jacob live again in the kingdom of God, and are not just new characters who have been given the old names. Another way of expressing continuity, as I have emphasized elsewhere,[10] is to understand that the new creation arises *ex vetere*, as the redeemed transformation of the old creation, and not as a second, totally new, creation *ex nihilo*. Yet there must also be sufficient discontinuity to insure that the new creation is not just a redundant repetition of the old. Any notion of a kind of eternal return is the very negation of hope. Paul wrestles with these problems in 1 Corinthians 15, as he struggles to articulate his ideas in terms of a "physical" body and a "spiritual" body.[11] The repetition of *sōma* in these formulas is an expression of continuity, while the disjunction of those untranslatable adjectives *psychikon* and *pneumatikon* is an expression of discontinuity.

A traditional way of understanding how the continuity of human individuals may be preserved in the course of eschatological transformation has been in terms of the resurrected reembodiment of the soul. I think that something like this language is still indispensable for the credible articulation of Christian hope, but its content requires reexamination in the light of contemporary understanding of human nature.

The point at issue is what could be the meaning of the soul. I do not think that a dualist conception of the human being, either of a Platonic or of a Cartesian kind, is any longer possible for us. Our evolutionary line of connection with earlier forms of animal life, together with our awareness of the effect of drugs and brain damage on human mental experience, encourages very strongly the view that we are psychosomatic unities — "animated bodies rather than incarnated souls," to use a famous phrase. Of course, this conclusion would scarcely come as a shock to the writers of the Hebrew Bible. But how, then, are we to understand the human soul, particularly in relation to eschatological thinking, if it is not a separable spiritual component that survives the death and decay of the body that once housed it?

The nature of the human person, and the related question of what

10. John Polkinghorne, *Science and Christian Belief/The Faith of a Physicist* (London: SPCK; Princeton: Princeton University, 1994), ch. 9.

11. See Peter Lampe, "Paul's Concept of a Spiritual Body," in this volume.

could constitute the preservation of human identity in circumstances that go beyond those able to be discussed in terms of observed bodily continuity, is the concern of many contributors to this volume.[12] Valuable though such discussions undoubtedly are, and crucial as the issue is to the consideration of the rationality of resurrection, it is clear that theological anthropology is still insufficiently developed to be able to provide unequivocal answers that settle all our perplexities for us. As a contribution to the ongoing debate, I wish to sketch an approach that makes use of the concept of information, based on a generalization from those incipient scientific studies of complex systems that I have suggested encourage us to think that this is a direction in which we may seek future developments leading to further enlightenment. Because of a desire to retain some contact with the theological thinking of earlier generations, I shall continue to use the language of "soul," though I realize that some might prefer another term, such as the core of the "person" or the "self."

If we are to use the term "soul," it surely must be capable of being understood as referring to "the real me." What that might mean is problematic within life as well as beyond death. What could be the carrier of continuity that links me today with the young schoolboy in the photograph of sixty years ago? It is certainly not the matter of my body that plays that role. That is changing all the time, through wear and tear, eating and drinking. None of us has many atoms in our bodies today that were there even two years ago. Materially, we are in a state of flux.

The Soul as Information-Bearing Pattern

I think that we must understand the soul as being the almost infinitely complex, dynamic, information-bearing pattern in which the matter of our bodies at any one time is organized. This is what develops continuously in life and what constitutes the connection between ourselves as we were in youth and as we are today. You will recognize that this is an old idea presented in modern dress, for I am saying that the soul is the form of the body, a thought that would not have seemed strange either to Aristotle or to Thomas Aquinas, though perhaps I wish to think more dynamically about it than they would have been inclined to do.

Of course, this concept is only cloudily formulated in what I have said. I do not think that today we have the ability to make the idea more precise. At

12. See the contributions of Nancey Murphy, Ted Peters, and Andreas Schuele in this volume.

least one can say that it is consonant with what I earlier have been claiming about the developing recognition of the importance of information (pattern) in the scientific account of the process of the world, though the concept of the human soul goes very far beyond anything that we can derive directly from studies of moderately complex systems. In a *very* crude image, one might say that the soul is the software running on the hardware of the body. However, this is an extremely inadequate way of speaking, for I believe that we have good reasons to believe that human beings are something much more subtle than simply "computers made of meat."[13] Moreover, as part of the effort to frame a just account of the richness of human life, I think there will be a need to extend the rather atomistic picture of an individual human being that I have used until now. "What I am" is not simply carried by my body, but also by the nexus of relationships within which my life develops. We have good reason to believe that the embodiment of that pattern that is the soul is not something that terminates at the surface of the skin. It is significant that one of the ways in which Christian hope of fulfillment is formulated is in the collective terms of our incorporation into the body of Christ.

In natural terms, the pattern that is me, whatever form it actually takes, will be dissolved at my death, as my body decays and my relationships are reduced simply to the fading retention of memories by others. Yet it seems an entirely coherent belief that the everlastingly faithful God will hold that pattern perfectly preserved in the divine memory,[14] and then reembody it in the ultimate divine eschatological act of resurrection at the last day, as the new creation enters into the unfolding fullness of time.

In these terms, the soul is indeed still to be understood as the carrier of continuing human identity, linking this world to the world of the life to come. Its intermediate state between death and resurrection, held in the divine memory, could amount to more than a static retention, for it could involve also the possibility of a process of redemptive transformation through closer contact and interaction with the reality of God. Yet, this intermediate state would be less than fully human since the restoration of full humanity would require the further resurrection act of reembodiment.[15] It would be something like the life of shades in Sheol, though the emphasis on the role of the

13. See Roger Penrose, *The Emperor's New Mind* (Oxford: Oxford University, 1989); John Searle, *Minds, Brains, and Science* (London: BBC Publications, 1984); and Noreen Herzfeld, "Cybernetic Immortality versus Christian Resurrection," in this volume.

14. See Dirk Evers, "Memory in the Flow of Time and the Concept of the Resurrection," in this volume.

15. See the discussions of the intermediate state by Peter Lampe and Hans-Joachim Eckstein in this volume.

divine memory would enable it to be understood in a much more positive sense than one finds in most of the Hebrew Bible. The picture being suggested for postmortem, preresurrection life could correspond to what Paul had in mind when he spoke of the possibility of being "unclothed" (2 Cor. 5:4). There is also, of course, the possibility that, though humans die at different times, all arrive together at the day of resurrection, without the need for an intermediate state at all.[16] This is conceivable because, though the new creation is the redemption of the old creation, the two worlds need not share a single time, requiring that the one simply follow consecutively upon the other. Their mutual relationship can be more subtle in its character than that.[17] Indeed, the appearances of the risen Christ, and the present participation in eternal life that is the realized dimension of eschatological hope, particularly experienced in the Eucharist, imply some degree of "alongsidedness" and even interaction between the two worlds.

We must then go on to ask, "What will be the medium for this resurrection reembodiment?" Obviously it will not be the matter of this present world. "Flesh and blood cannot inherit the kingdom of God, nor does the perishable inherit the imperishable" (1 Cor. 15:50). To suppose otherwise would be to embrace the despair of living again in order to die again. The matter of this universe has a physical character that is appropriate to its evolutionary role as the medium within which creatures, existing at some epistemic distance from their Creator, are allowed to be themselves and to make themselves. In this world of the old creation, death is necessary because it is the inescapable cost of the possibility of the coming-to-be of new life. In this world, cellular mutation both drives the evolutionary development of new life and is the cause of the presence of cancer in creation.

Redeeming Matter

There is no reason to believe, however, that this is the only kind of world that God can creatively hold in being. The theological principle of a degree of discontinuity between the old creation and the new creation permits us to conceive in a general way what it is beyond our powers to articulate in particular detail, namely, a world whose "matter" and "physics" is such that "Death will be no more; mourning and crying and pain will be no more, for the first things have passed away" (Rev. 21:4). This is a coherent theological possibility

16. Polkinghorne, *Science and Christian Belief/The Faith of a Physicist,* 173.
17. Ibid.

because that new world will no longer exist at a distance from its Creator but, through the cosmic Christ, will be integrated with the life and energies of God in a new and most intimate fashion. This redeemed relationship is why eschatological process will be so different from present process. The new creation will have been given its release from bondage to decay because it has "obtain[ed] the freedom of the glory of the children of God" (Rom. 8:21). Presently we live in a world that contains sacraments; the world to come will be wholly sacramental. In the "matter" of that world we shall see God's eschatological purpose fulfilled in the whole created order. I have expressed this hope by asserting that "One might say that panentheism is true as an eschatological fulfillment, not a present reality."[18] Our Orthodox friends are surely right when they say that the final end of creatures is *theosis,* a sharing in the life of God.

These thoughts are both exciting and mysterious. Our only real clue to making sense of them lies in our knowledge of the risen and glorified Christ, whose resurrection is both the foretaste and the guarantee of what I have been trying to speak about.[19] There are, however, some additional things one might try to say. Because the new creation arises *ex vetere,* we may anticipate that there will be a degree of continuity as well as discontinuity when its properties are compared with those of the old creation. In our present universe science understands space, time, and matter to be integrated in the single scheme of general relativity. This kind of "package deal" seems to me likely to continue in the new creation in a redeemed form. It is intrinsic to human beings to be embodied; I believe that it is also intrinsic to human beings to be temporal. The life of the world to come will not be a timeless moment of illumination, but it will be the everlasting exploration of the inexhaustible riches of the divine nature, now made accessible to us in a clear and intimate way, beyond what is possible in this life, even for the greatest of the saints. Certainly our ultimate destiny will not be boring, for it will involve the most exhilarating kind of life imaginable.[20]

The concept of the life of the world to come as being one of endlessly continuing spiritual progress and exploration is to be found in some of the Fathers, most notably in Gregory of Nyssa.[21] For us today it is an expectation reinforced by our understanding of the evolutionary character of creation

18. Ibid., 168.

19. See Nancey Murphy on the resources of eschatological epistemology, in this volume.

20. See Günter Thomas, "Resurrection and Divine Judgment," in this volume.

21. See Brian Daley in this volume.

and the associated doctrine of divine *creatio continua*.[22] The patient and subtle God who works through unfolding process in this world of the old creation may be expected to bring about eschatological fulfillment in a correspondingly gentle and developmental manner. In fact, there surely can be no other way in which finite creatures can adequately encounter the infinite reality of their Creator in a nondestructive fashion. Hence the significance of the necessary eschatological tension recognized by Michael Welker[23] between the once-for-all act of resurrection and the continuing reign of the kingdom of God.

A Credible Hope

Eschatological thinking inevitably involves an element of speculation as to its details. Its scope is necessarily limited in terms of what can be comprehended within this life. Yet it is by no means an exercise in fantasy. Rather, it is an exploration of possibility that can be carried far enough to "defeat the defeaters" by showing that its discourse is reasonable and its hopes well motivated. I believe that scientific insight and theological understanding can be combined to enable us to embrace a credible hope, framed not in terms of a spiritualist notion of survival but in terms of the Christian concept of death and resurrection, a hope whose substance has already been manifested in the resurrection of our Lord Jesus Christ and whose reliability is founded on the faithfulness of the God of Abraham, Isaac, and Jacob.

22. Arthur Peacocke, *Creation and the World of Science* (Oxford: Oxford University, 1979), ch. 6.

23. See Michael Welker, "Theological Realism and Eschatological Symbol Systems," in this volume.

From Evolution to Eschatology

JEFFREY P. SCHLOSS

The huge price of dread which life had to pay from the first, and which steadily mounted with its ascent to more ambitious forms, stirs up the question about the meaning of this venture, and, once asked, never lets it come to rest again. In this question, asked at last by man, as presumptuous as it is inevitable — as presumptuous indeed as the attempt of form undertaken by substance at the dawn of life — the initially problematical nature of life has, after eons of mute insistence, found voice and speech.[1]

If naiveté is the failure of an untutored imagination to appreciate the density of a problem, and presumption is the confidence of an overly enthusiastic imagination to penetrate it, I fear that even attempting to address the issue of scientific perspectives on eschatology entails the risk of simultaneously committing both errors. But perhaps that is just as it should be. The dialectical tension between the two poles is both necessary and desirable in meaningfully construing a "reason for the hope that is in us," and dialogue between science and religion may help us navigate the construal. Scientific perspectives may help us avoid the naive indulgences of disengaged theological idealism; theology may call us from the presumption of reducing the world to fit our currently limited, and often distorted, scientific understanding.[2]

1. Hans Jonas, *The Phenomenon of Life: Toward a Philosophical Biology* (New York: Harper and Row, 1966), 6.

2. Fraser Watts, "Subjective and Objective Hope: Propositional and Attitudinal As-

Organismal Life in This World and the Next

The biologist reflecting on the issue of resurrection cannot escape doing so at two different levels of biological ontology — organismal and ecological. With respect to the organismal, the most immediate and vexing question that arises (but by no means the most helpful one to pursue) is how on earth (or in heaven) could such a thing happen? While this seems unsophisticated, it may be precisely its unsophistication that makes it salient. When my young toddler asked awhile back, "Mommy, how does God get us to heaven, in his airplane?" his older brothers laughed him to scorn, for they were savvy enough to understand that the eternal, disembodied soul does not need material contrivances to make its heavenly ascent. But of course their less mature sibling was right, perhaps by very virtue of his juvenile literalism. Since the biblical notion of eternal life is coupled to physical resurrection and continued embodiment, pondering this in all its material concreteness may (or may not) turn out to be a cul-de-sac, but it will not take us in the wrong direction. It is only in exploring the premise of continuity that we will uncover the contours of discontinuity. If we start with complete discontinuity, we not only slothfully avoid the hard work of contemplation but also languish in idealism. How can a man enter the womb and be born a second time? Who can be saved if a camel must get through a needle's eye? How can we eat Christ's flesh and blood? These ostensibly naive questions in the Gospels reveal not just brute misunderstanding but also the appropriately earnest conviction that Christ's statements describe some sort of tangible reality.

A second, more profound but also potentially more tractable question at the organismal level is, What does it *mean* to be resurrected, to have a new body, to have eternal life? If we understand the biblical promise of eternal life as involving not just additional time tacked on to life as usual, but life transformed, healed, and deepened — increased qualitatively, not just quantitatively — then it would help to consider what life itself *is*. And if we believe the living God has, in the language of Scripture, genuinely "given life to these mortal bodies," not just imprisoned immaterial life within the dead confines of cytoplasmic machinery, then the study of living beings is a fitting conversation partner for theological reflection on what it might mean to have more of this "livingness."

The above questions become magnified at a higher scale of biological

---

pects of Eschatology," in *The End of the World and the Ends of God: Science and Theology on Eschatology*, ed. John Polkinghorne and Michael Welker (Harrisburg, Pa.: Trinity Press International 2000).

ontology if we consider both the biological and biblical notions that organismal life is embedded in a larger creation, entailing communities of ecological interdependence, human engagement, and divine indwelling. Thus emerges the ecological–evolutionary level of integration. Such communal realities entail, as Evelyn Hutchinson has famously said, "the evolutionary play on the ecological stage." The lines, players, and even the plot may change over evolutionary time, though they are ever constrained by the props and setting and choreographic syntax of the ecological moment. With respect to resurrection, then, it involves not just a beanbag of individual bodies that are wafted up to eternal ascent, but being planted anew and flourishing in a suitable environmental substrate, a "new heaven and earth." This environment is not only hospitable to sustaining the eternal life of resurrected humanity, but if we take scriptural descriptions seriously, in some sense it contains other living beings as well but no death, no predation, no tears or sadness, no lack, no sexual bonding, and not even any night.

As if organismal resurrection were not difficult enough to ponder, this new world is almost unrecognizable to us in terms of our own; and yet, the very recognition of differences hinges on continuities. It is not the alien absence of familiar predators and the presence of entirely novel, unearthly creatures, but transformed earthly creatures: the lion lying down with the lamb. It is not that we will not need food, but there will be new food. It is not that we will not need energy, or that there will be untransmitted, mystical animation with neither day nor night, but that there will be eternal day, with God himself providing light. To be sure, these images are intended to be taken metaphorically and not literally. (Indeed, what else could be the case? And yet, perhaps the very distinction between metaphor and referent evaporates in the heat of pure heavenly reality.) But even in their figurativeness, metaphors are metaphors of something, not nothing. To reflect on the something means pushing continuities as far as we can, to engage and clarify the margins of discontinuity. How could such a world come about? What would it mean to inhabit such a realm, again in terms of what we know about *life?*

I propose to reflect on these questions in what others have described as three different modes of engagement between science and theology, entailing three different levels of risk. I do this as an organizational template, not because it represents a taxonomic scheme for science-religion dialogue. First and most modestly, steering clear of both natural theology and theology of nature, and avoiding the attempt to have science inform theology by way of content, science may nevertheless provide concrete experiences to the conceptual images encountered in divine revelation or theological reflection.

C. S. Lewis maintains that the natural world will not teach us that God is glorious, but having learned it elsewhere, nature will furnish substance to the experience of glory. Or it provides a reservoir of metaphors for truths outside our immediate experience. We must die like a seed in order to bear fruit for the kingdom, but it is Jesus and not seeds who teaches us this truth. Although I shall argue that this dichotomy is too simplistic, it is a starting point for discussion.

Second, more ambitiously, we may attempt to contribute to our theological understanding by assessment and extrapolation of scientific understanding. Traditionally, natural theology has entailed this enterprise, especially with the backward extrapolation to ultimate origins or design. But we also employ more proximal historic extrapolation, in hermeneutic and textual analytic engagement with Scripture, and biblical, archeological attempts to inform understandings important to a faith embedded in a sacred history of divine providence. Indeed, so important is the look backward that people of faith often make provision for enabling it: stones at Bethel and psalms of remembrance constitute the effort to facilitate this backward extrapolation so important to anchoring faith in the real world. And where we do not have such stones, we seek their logical equivalents: arguments for Christ's resurrection[3] entail an attempt to provide reasonable grounds for extrapolating back to an event that, in itself, is beyond empirical verification or rational explanation. Similarly, then, we may attempt to extrapolate forward — either to confirm the credibility of or at least to help explore the dimensions of — scriptural eschatological promises.

Third, and most riskily, we may engage margins of discontinuity between theology and science with an eye toward genuinely two-way exchange, where theology does not unilaterally accommodate itself to scientific assertions but "pushes back" with the intention of either modifying or at least informing scientific thinking. The strong and of course riskiest version of this program involves faith-coupled (though not theologically argued) revisionist science, such as current theories of "intelligent design," Gaia, or the various ideologically motivated revisionist theories of ethnic variation that opposed widely accepted eugenic and racial science in the middle quarter of the twentieth century. (It turns out that the empirical support for the most egalitarian of these views did not become compelling until fifty years later.) A weaker version of this program, and one that I will explore here, entails the

---

3. Michael Welker, "Resurrection and Eternal Life: The Canonic Memory of the Resurrected Christ, His Reality, and His Glory," in *The End of the World and the Ends of God*, ed. Polkinghorne and Welker, 279-90.

notion that theology can serve as a reservoir of, or "treasure map" to, hypotheses to be investigated by traditional scientific means, but which may not be suggested by extrapolations of prevailing theory itself.[4] Contemporary investigations of the relationship between prayer or religious involvement and morbidity or of the capacity of human nature for genuine altruism are examples of hypotheses that are suggested by religious belief, are not entailed by current scientific theory, but are fully investigable by scientific methodology. In a similar fashion, then, certain eschatological notions may suggest research agendas for evolutionary analyses at both organismal and ecological scales, or at least help us to stay clear about what we are not yet really clear about. "Christian hope paradoxically enriches our knowledge by protecting our nascence from illusion."[5]

"Intelligibility is the key to reality, but reality is what funds intelligibility,"[6] say John Polkinghorne and Michael Welker. To gain eschatological intelligibility, we will look at biological intelligibility.

Ecological Scale: Ideal versus Actual Niche

One of the most fundamental relationships in environmental physiology involves the observation that most aspects of organismal performance at manifold organizational levels (from enzyme activity to whole-organism functioning) correlate with environmental variability (e.g., temperature, pH) in a quasi-normal curve that has an optimal peak and two tails of diminishment, much like the frequency of simple morphological traits.[7] If one integrates such curves of organism-environmental interactions along multiple axes, the conceptual result is an "n-dimensional hyperspace" — not a habitat but a conceptual integration of ecological requirements or an ecological niche. In cases where these variables scale along an environmental gradient (such as mean temperature up an altitudinal or latitudinal cline, or soil salinity in a salt marsh), we can map organismal distribution along the same axis of abiotic variability. It displays a similar curve, with a central optimal peak and

4. See Robert John Russell's article, "The Relevance of Tillich for the Theology and Science Dialogue," in *Zygon* 36.2 (2001): 269-308. See also Russell's chapter in this volume.

5. Nicholas Lash, "Production and Prospect: Reflections on Christian Hope and Original Sin," in *Evolution and Creation*, ed. E. McMullin (Notre Dame, Ind.: University of Notre Dame, 1995), 281.

6. *The End of the World and the Ends of God*, 4.

7. P. Calow and C. R. Townsend, *Physiological Ecology: An Evolutionary Approach to Resource Use* (Sunderland, Mass.: Sinauer, 1981).

diminishing tails of abundance. However, the interesting thing is that, while distribution is not uncorrelated with performance, the peak of maximal abundance rarely conforms to the peak of optimal performance.

This gap between the ideal and actual conditions of an organism's life history has resulted in the distinction between what is termed, appropriately if not imaginatively, the ideal versus actualized niche. While there are many causes for this disjunction, the primary one is held to be the shifting or compression of the organismal niche in response to competitive displacement by other species. It turns out that recent studies also have shown that a similar phenomenon of suboptimality occurs in the social environment as a result of competition *within* species: individuals occupying low-ranking positions in the dominance gradient suffer displacement from their own internal physiological optimum.[8] It is literally sickening to be marginalized. Conversely, in both the environmental and social environments, relaxation of competition results in rebounding or competitive release, associated with niche expansion in the former and increased physiological robustness in the latter. In an empirically detectable sense, many organisms appear to groan physiologically under the ecological burden of competitive displacement.

I cite this phenomenon not in an attempt to provoke an extrapolation to heaven or an eschatological future, but to suggest how science can provide images for eschatological reflection on both heaven and earth. I will confess that I often think of heaven, whose builder and maker is God, as a place or a time of ultimate competitive release, where not only the creatures are free to occupy their ideal niche but the niche hyperspace itself may undergo transformative niche expansion. And the earth, after centuries of saccharine depiction by romanticism and natural theology, is seen by contemporary ecology as filled with ambiguous partial correlations between creaturely needs and temporal provision. Indeed, this ambiguity has fueled virulent debates between evolutionary biologists over the depiction of the natural world.[9] The sense of ambiguity comports with an ancient ambivalence toward the creation in the Chris-

---

8. R. Sapolsky and J. Ray, "Styles of Dominance and Their Physiological Correlates among Wild Baboons," *American Journal of Primatology* 18.1 (1989): 1-15; C. E. Virgin and R. Sapolsky, "Styles of Male Social Behavior and Their Endocrine Correlates among Low-ranking Baboons," *American Journal of Primatology* 42.25 (1997): 25-39.

9. George Williams, "Huxley's Evolution and Ethics in Sociobiological Perspective," *Zygon* 23.4 (1988): 383-407; George Williams, "Mother Nature Is a Wicked, Old Witch," in *Evolutionary Ethics*, ed. Matthew H. Nitecki and V. Doris (Albany: State University of New York, 1993); Sarah Blaffer Hardy, "Response to George Williams," *Zygon* 23.4 (1988): 409-11; Lynn Margulis and Dorion Sagan, *Slanted Truths: Essays on Gaia, Symbiosis, and Evolution* (New York: Springer, 1997).

tian revelation.[10] The psalmist affirms that the "lion roars to God for its prey," yet "even the young lions suffer lack." The creation is good and "the earth is the LORD's," yet it is "subjected to futility" and "groans in travail." Unlike the physical sciences, biology cannot escape describing the stress on teleonomic systems.[11] This is not a mere matter of noting that all organisms struggle against entropy,[12] or even that living things ultimately lose that battle in death. We surely do not need science to point this out. But the competition-induced disjunction between actually lived and ideally attainable conditions for optimal functioning is something that is ecologically evident.[13]

Having said this, I must be quick to point out three qualifications of both the content and the use of these notions of ecological constraint. First, some have understandably criticized the concepts of ideal and actualized niches on scientific and philosophical grounds, as entailing an essentialism characteristic of Aristotelian biology but being inappropriate for a biological science that eschews final causes. Most biologists no longer believe that animals have souls that order their embodied existence, and that they can be displaced by violence from their development toward perfection of form. For two reasons they claim that it is inappropriate to read into nature an ideal niche, or to take the image from nature to inform theological reflection. The first is that there is no such thing as an ideal niche that organisms "want" to occupy, but what we inevitably do is occupy an optimal niche, comprised of optimized design trade-offs between conflicting variables. However a response to this is that optimality itself is still a matter of vigorous debate in ecology, and even if it exists, it is only a statistical construction that most individual organisms do not occupy. The second is that the distinction between ideal and actual niches has teleological implications, entailing the assumption that there is a niche that, theoretically or ideally, an organism "should" occupy. A response to this is that biology, unlike the physical sciences, is unavoidably ridden with teleology:[14] the very distinction

---

10. Holmes Rolston III, "Does Nature Need to Be Redeemed?" *Zygon* 29.2 (1994): 205-29; and Paul Santmire, *The Travail of Nature: The Ambiguous Ecological Promise of Christian Theology* (Minneapolis: Fortress, 1985).

11. Jonas, *The Phenomenon of Life*; Robert Rosen, *Essays on Life Itself*, Complexity in Ecological Systems Series (New York: Columbia University, 2000).

12. E. Schrodinger, *What Is Life?* (Cambridge: Cambridge University, 1944); Jonas, *The Phenomenon of Life*; Rosen, *Essays on Life Itself*; Eric J. Chaisson, *Cosmic Evolution: The Rise of Complexity in Nature* (Cambridge, Mass.: Harvard University, 2001).

13. Calow and Townsend, *Physiological Ecology*.

14. Robert Brandon, *Concepts and Methods in Evolutionary Biology* (New York: Cambridge University, 1996). See esp. ch. 2, "Biological Teleology: Questions and Explanations."

between homeostatic integration and functional senescence or physiological vigor and pathology is both appropriate and necessary for describing living systems, but not abiotic ones. This is true at both organismal and ecological levels; hence we may speak of the "restoration of damaged ecosystems,"[15] though the issue of what they should be restored *to* is immensely problematic both scientifically[16] and theologically.[17] Even these controversies themselves betray a deep-seated ambiguity in our ability to describe the living world.

Second, we need to be cautious about anthropomorphizing nature by reading our own experience of vexation into ecology and then claiming that science provides an image conciliant with theological notions derived from that same human experience. However, while this warning is surely appropriate, it begs both epistemological and metaphysical questions. Epistemologically, we require our own biotic experience to provide the very concepts we use to engage the external world: even cause and effect are neither innate intuitions nor rational demonstrations but entail derived extensions from the experience of bodily movement through agent causation.[18] Metaphysically, "anthropomorphism" assumes a negative answer to the question of whether the nature of human beings is coextensive with the being of other life forms. Hans Jonas points out that most of our depictions of living things entail not inappropriate anthropomorphism but unavoidable zoomorphism, and that *life* is not describable in terms that do not invoke the tensions between telos and chaos, desire and denial, flourishing and attrition, being and non-being.[19] Scientific investigation of the way living organisms embody and navigate these tensions may provide images for the way we reflect on their eschatological resolution.

> So poised, the organism has its being on condition and revocable. With this twin aspect of metabolism — its power and its need — not-being made its appearance in the world as an alternative embodied in the being itself; and thereby being itself first assumes an emphatic sense: intrinsically qualified by the threat of its negative it must affirm itself, and existence affirmed its existence as a concern. So constitutive for life is the possibility of not-being that its very being is essentially a hovering over this abyss, a skirting of its brink: this state, ever anew to be laid hold of in op-

15. John Cairns, Jr., *Rehabilitating Damaged Ecosystems* (Boca Raton, Fla., Lewis, 1995).
16. Ibid.
17. Rolston III, "Does Nature Need to Be Redeemed?" 205-29.
18. Jonas, *The Phenomenon of Life.*
19. Jonas, *The Phenomenon of Life;* Rosen, *Essays on Life Itself.*

position to its ever-present contrary, not-being, which will inevitably engulf it in the end.[20]

Third, the above two points suggest that the very capacity of the biological world to furnish images that invigorate reflection on eschatology (or any aspect of theology) may ensue from the fact that more is at work than just an experiential palette to color in the paint by number contours provided by revelation. Lewis's distinction between nature providing experiential images and conceptual content for theology may be too simplistic and overly dichotomized: if life entails the imparted being of a living God, then life itself is not a mere metaphor for spiritual realities but a repository of those realities. This must be true if we affirm a middle ground between nihilistic materialism and incorporeal idealism. Thus it could just be that the tension of ideal versus actual niches may not merely represent an illustration of, but a remonstration for, the need for eschatological hope.

Organismal Scale I: Skinless Organisms

"The organic body signifies the latent crisis of every known ontology and the criterion of any future one which will be able to come forward as a science,"[21] writes Hans Jonas. Our organismal experience is foundational for our eschatological speculations.

One of the most fascinating, novel, and challenging concepts to emerge from recent evolutionary theory is the revisionist interpretation of organismal identity entailed by Richard Dawkins's notions of the "skinless organism" or extended phenotype.[22] These notions derive from an unsolved quandary in evolutionary theory involving the observation that some organisms work to pass on others' genes rather than their own. William Hamilton's (1964) famous notion of inclusive fitness partially solved this by reconceptualizing or "enlarging" genetic fitness to include not only offspring but also kin. To solve outstanding cases, Dawkins has made a comparable suggestion for enlargement at the level of the organism. In short, he proposes an extension of the phenotype, or observable expression of genes, to include all the ways in which a given genome orders the environment. Just as a beaver's teeth

20. Jonas, *The Phenomenon of Life*, 4.
21. Ibid., 19.
22. Richard Dawkins, *The Extended Phenotype: The Gene as the Unit of Selection* (Oxford: Oxford University, 1986); Richard Dawkins and Daniel Dennett, *The Extended Phenotype: The Long Reach of the Gene* (Oxford: Oxford University, 1999).

entail the incorporation of environmental resources into a gene-orchestrated reordering we observe as its characteristic phenotypic traits, so does its dam. Hence its *body,* organismal identity, or "phenotype" may be considered to extend beyond the skin, to include all its fitness-enhancing influences on the environment.

This constitutes a brilliant, if not rhetorically sly, response to the counter-reproductive quandary, because any organism that works for the genes of another organism can be deconstructively viewed as the *other* genes' body. The phenotypic characteristics of an organism have always been understood as interactions between genetic information and environmental resources and constraints, but what notions of the skinless organism suggest is that the genetic information effecting the ordering does not have to be inside the skin. Organismal identity becomes fluid, and there is thus ambiguity over "whose" body a body is. The earlier notion that an organism is just a gene's way of reproducing itself was the first move toward reconceptualization of the body;[23] once granted, the more radical but concomitant observation is that the spatial location of the genes does not matter. Margulis has explored contrasting though complementary notions, emphasizing collective identity or symbiotic cooperation rather than individual competition.[24]

The implications of these ideas are far from unhesitatingly accepted, but are vigorously debated in a way that is reminiscent of arguments several decades ago over the nature of species identity and their reality as bounded and irreducible biological units. What the current controversy points to is a relativity, or at the very least an unavoidable ambiguity, in the fundamental biological ontology of the living body or organismal individuality.[25] I want to suggest that this ambiguity in scientific understandings of the body, and the discontinuity between emerging biological accounts and traditional commonsense notions of earthly bodies, reflects an analogous ambiguity within, and discontinuity between, scriptural and commonsense notions of resurrected embodiment.[26] On the one hand, the just and unjust are resurrected to judgment and apparently individual (Matthew 25, but not always) destinies. On the other hand, we are described collectively as the bride of Christ. On the other hand still, we are described as collectively comprising the very body of Christ.

23. George Williams, *Adaptation and Natural Selection* (Princeton: Princeton University, 1966); E. O. Wilson, *Sociobiology: The New Synthesis* (Cambridge, Mass.: Harvard University, 1975); Richard Dawkins, *The Selfish Gene* (Oxford: Oxford University, 1976).

24. Margulis and Sagan, *Slanted Truths.*

25. In *Annual Review of Ecology and Systematics* 11 (1980): 311-32.

26. John Polkinghorne, "Eschatology: Some Questions and Some Insights from Science," in *The End of the World and the Ends of God,* 1-13.

Whether the above images deriving from our earthly experience of the body are analogues or homologues of heavenly reality is another discussion; but whatever the case, we have tended to invoke spirit-flesh or biology-culture dualisms based on commonsense notions of bodily discreteness, in order to make intelligible, or perhaps even dodge, the above ambiguities. For example, we are often represented as individually Christ's body by virtue of radical dualism: his Spirit indwells us, much as our own immaterial soul is taken to inhabit our organic bodies. Or we are viewed as collectively the body of Christ in communal assemblage, involving social cohesion but not organic integration. Thus the parts of the body become a mere metaphor for cultural specialization and cooperation but suggest no new quality of organismal life. However, the fuzzy boundaries of bodily identity associated with new accounts of both symbiotic integration and genetic "action at a distance" provide images (though not mechanisms) for construing how our very *bodies* might be transformed and integrated by God's Word. Polkinghorne maintains, "I do not accept panentheism as a present reality, but I believe it will become an eschatological reality."[27] Indeed, evolutionary biologist David Sloan Wilson argues on strictly scientific, not theological, grounds that some present Christian communities constitute *literal* biological superorganisms.[28]

Organismal Scale II: Soulish Organisms

In contrast to the above claims and controversies about bodily identity, there is a much more fundamental dispute that contends that gene-centric reductions do not merely misconstrue the units of selection or boundaries of the organism, but dismiss or distort the very nature of life. According to many,[29] some Darwinian accounts entail a new dualism not of body/soul or organism/environment, but of genotype/phenotype or germline/*sōma*. The somatic or living comes to be understood both in terms *of* and *for* the genomic or non-living:

27. Ibid., 40.

28. David Sloan Wilson, *The Religious Organism* (Chicago: University of Chicago, forthcoming).

29. Jonas, *The Phenomenon of Life*; Dawkins, *The Selfish Gene*; Hull, "Individuality and Selection"; Leon R. Kass, M.D., *Toward a More Natural Science: Biology and Human Affairs* (New York: Free Press, 1985); Susan Oyama, *Evolution's Eye: A Systems View of the Biology-Culture Divide* (Durham, N.C.: Duke University, 2000).

Thus there arises within the materialist realm itself a strange parody of the Cartesian model of two non-communicating substances. . . . There is on the one hand the blind automatism of a germ history enacted in the subterranean darkness which no light from the upper world penetrates; and on the other hand the upper world of the soma meeting the world in terms of life, pursuing its destiny, fighting its battles, taking the impress of its victories and defeats — and all this being of no other consequence for the hidden charge than that of its being either continued or eliminated. In a reversal of the classical formula, one would have to say that the developed is for the sake of the undeveloped, the tree for the sake of the seed.[30]

The criticism of this view is not so much that it is incorrect, but that it is one-sided or nonrelational. Living organisms are systems that are open at *two* ends, informational and energetic,[31] open to forcings involving interactions with both genes and metabolites, which allow them to function as nonequilibrium dissipative structures that "capture low-entropy states that sustain the state of the system against thermodynamic decay."[32] In emphatic if not altogether precise language, "inanimate objects are moved by forces around them, but living organisms have an internal vitality and vigor allowing them to defy these forces of nature and perform autonomous or *directed actions*."[33] It is this aspect of homeostatic function or teleonomic agency that is so important to living things, as so eloquently described by Konrad Lorenz:

> Life is an eminently active enterprise aimed at acquiring both a fund of energy and a stock of knowledge, the possession of one being instrumental to the acquisition of the other. The immense effectiveness of these two feedback cycles, coupled in multiplying iteration, is the pre-condition, indeed the explanation, for the fact that life had the power to assert itself against the superior strength of the pitiless inorganic world.[34]

Now it is in so asserting themselves that living organisms maintain their structural integrity against entropic deterioration. And it is both this process, and this structural organization itself, which may be viewed as the essence of life.

30. Jonas, *The Phenomenon of Life*, 52.

31. Schrodinger, *What Is Life?*; Rosen, *Essays on Life Itself*.

32. Stuart Kauffman, *The Origins of Order* (Oxford: Oxford University, 1993).

33. John McFadden, *Quantum Evolution* (New York: W. W. Norton, 2000), 256.

34. Konrad Lorenz, *Behind the Mirror: A Search for a Natural History of Human Knowledge* (New York: Harcourt Brace Jovanovich, 1978).

Relational biology can be thought of as the exact inverse of reductionistic ideas. The essence of reductionism is, in a sense, to keep the matter of which an organism is made and throw away the organization, believing that the latter can be effectively recaptured from the former . . . relational biology sought rather to keep the organization and throw away the matter; to treat the organization itself as a *thing,* and recapture specific material aspects through a process of realization.[35]

There are two upshots of this point of view. First of all, there is, in a way, a rehabilitation of the concept of living soul, not in a dualistic or vitalistic sense, but in the Aristotelian sense of functional *telos,* or form for substance. The means by which the genetic material is kept intact become, for the organism, ends in themselves. Organisms open themselves to the environment, respond physiologically, and internalize teleonomic set points; for example, what the organism monitors or "seeks" is temperature, pH, resolution of desire, not fitness.[36]

> . . . such "means" of survival as perception and emotion are never to be judged as means merely, but also as qualities of the life to be preserved and therefore as aspects of the end. It is one of the paradoxes of life that it employs means which modify the end and themselves become part of it. . . . Without these faculties there would be much less to preserve, and this less of what is to be preserved is the same as the less wherewith it is preserved.[37]

Moreover, organisms may achieve these ends to greater or lesser degrees of success. "The end is a standard as well as a goal. Teleological analysis will be concerned both to identify the end and to evaluate how well or badly it is achieved."[38] Thus livingness may be understood to admit itself in degrees, which entail expansion of not only the product but also the process of organismal life. There is a progression of ability to engage and freely respond to the environment along increasing levels of the spatial, temporal, and organizational scale through expanding powers of sensation, locomotion, and cognition. "The ascent of soul has meant the possibility both of an ever-greater awareness of and openness *to* the world, and an ever-greater freedom

35. Rosen, *Essays on Life Itself,* 261.

36. Jeffrey P. Schloss, "Wisdom Mechanisms as Homeostatic 'Laws of Life,'" in *Understanding Wisdom: Sources, Science and Society,* ed. Warren Brown (Philadelphia: Templeton Foundation, 2000), 153-91.

37. Jonas, *The Phenomenon of Life,* 109.

38. Kass, *Toward a More Natural Science,* 257.

in the world."[39] This is not a mystical assertion but an empirical observation of phylogenetic extensions of bodily form and function.

The second and concomitant implication is that the body is not only necessary *for* this awareness and freedom; it is the singular manifestation of it. Disembodied or immaterial life is just as dead — to itself and the world — as non-living matter, both being insensitive to the marvels and challenges of the outside world, the fulfillments and denials of internal desires, and the animating but tension-laden engagement between the two.[40]

Now I want to employ these biological observations for eschatological reflection in two ways. First of all, we may reflect on what it might *mean* to have *more* of life, not just in elongation of temporal quantity but also in intensification of existential quality. In claiming that he came that we "might have life, and have it more abundantly," Jesus indicates that life is to be understood not only as the qualitative antithesis to death but also as a matter of degree; moreover, he challenges the attitude "that seeks to cure the emptiness of life by extending it."[41] Indeed, accounts of the resurrection itself suggest that it did more than "only restore the old pre-Easter liveliness and embodiment of Jesus of Nazareth."[42]

Eschatological Extrapolations from Biology

But what is the more? If we look to organismal biology for suggestions of how life may be had in increasing measure, we see the twofold intensification of ability to withstand equilibrium with entropic forces according to an internal agenda and, at the same time, greater ability to sense and extend oneself into the external world. The first ability is precisely what is entailed by the Pauline exhortation, "Do not be conformed to this world, but be transformed by the renewing of your minds" (Rom. 12:1). The second is what both Jonas and Kass affirm in describing extended engagement with the world through progressively enhanced sensation, locomotion, affect, and cognition, culminating in human beings.[43] Moltmann observes, ". . . human livingness means being interested in life, participating and communicating, and affirming one's own life and the life of others. . . . Our 'soul' is present when we give ourselves up

39. Ibid., 271.
40. Ibid.
41. Ibid., 316.
42. Welker, "Resurrection and Eternal Life," 283.
43. Jonas, *The Phenomenon of Life;* and Kass, *Toward a More Natural Science.*

to something completely, are passionately interested, and, because love makes us strong, do not hold life back but go out of ourselves."[44] It would be wrong, then, to think of life transformed or fulfilled only through the heavenly attenuation of external risk, the transition from the actual to the ideal niche. For more life, there must be a concomitant increase of volitional engagement. Perhaps both are responses to the summoning power of the Word.

The second implication entails our understanding not just of abundant life in general but also of the resurrected body in particular. While "it does not yet appear what we shall be," what we shall be must in some sense be something that does *appear,* that is, to use Rosen's provocative image, we may exchange the matter, but the organization is what is biotically defining and hence retained. This is nicely extended by Polkinghorne's musings,

> In other words, we can hope to revive the Thomistic Aristotelian notion of the soul as the form, or pattern of the body, so that its restoration to psychosomatic existence in a divine act of resurrection constitutes the element that links the one who dies in this world to the one who lives reembodied in the "matter" of the world to come.[45]

I am going to go out on a limb here and suggest that for reasons related to the material ontology of human identity, it makes sense to think of continuity in our bodily form as contributing to the relational quality of eternal life. A less desirable alternative to this approach would entail the extrapolation of pure mystical experience to speculate on human spiritual capacities that would vault over the constraints of embodiment to enable things like nonphysical tactile impressions and hearing, direct awareness of luminous beings, and telepathic exchange of emotions, thoughts, intentions, and spiritual illumination.[46] I do not wish to dismiss either the significance of religious experience or the hope for enhanced capacities to sense the unimaginably wondrous, but I suspect it is more helpful to think of heavenly extensions of experience as related to enhancements of bodily form, in a way analogous to what has occurred in evolutionary phylogenetic development. For example, Portmann provides a compelling description of the relationship between morphology and the sensory and affective state of animals, including the increased capacity for desire enabled by lo-

---

44. Moltmann, "Is There Life after Death?" in *The End of the World and the Ends of God,* 244.

45. Polkinghorne, "Eschatology," 39.

46. Michael Murphy, *The Future of the Body: Explorations into the Further Evolution of Human Nature* (Los Angeles: Tarcher, 1993).

comotion and visual communication facilitated by bilateral symmetry and cephalization.[47] Straus extends this to describe the effects of upright gait in humans, which, along with loss of hair and increase in facial musculature, made our interior life visible to one another.[48] Kass observes that we are the only terrestrial tetrapod that does not move in the direction of our gut, and that is capable of pointing in a direction different than our mouth. Pointing becomes a social gesture, designed to identify something not to ourselves but to others; at the same time it not only specifies something "out there" in a shared world but something "in here" that I am considering. It is, in fact, the body-facilitated analogue of the very telepathy that Murphy wishes to affirm. "Pointing points ultimately to both friendship and philosophy."[49] And, I would add, to heavenly possibilities.

Can we speculate from evolution on what those possibilities might entail?

Evolutionary Eschatology

While there have always been oscillations in the extent to which the evolutionary process is viewed as progressive,[50] with Teilhard de Chardin we have the attempt to extrapolate a scientifically substantive if not indisputably accurate version of evolutionary theory into a comprehensive eschatological scheme. Although his efforts were ambivalently received by both scientists and theologians, more recently there has been a tremendous explosion of both naturalistic and religious evolutionary eschatologies, from the perspectives of cosmology, artificial intelligence, quantum biophysics, chaos theory, complexity theory, process thought, coevolution, symbiosis, new age mysticism, Gaia theory, and nonlocal interactionism.[51] While even a cursory sur-

47. Adolf Portmann, *Animal Forms and Patterns,* trans. Hella Czech (New York: Schocken, 1967).

48. Erwin Straus, "The Upright Posture," in *Phenomenological Psychology* (New York: Basic Books, 1966), 137-65.

49. Kass, *Toward a More Natural Science,* 287.

50. Michael Ruse, *Monad to Man: The Concept of Progress in Evolutionary Biology* (Cambridge, Mass.: Harvard University, 1996).

51. See Chaisson, *Cosmic Evolution* (cosmology); Joel DeRosnay, *The Symbiotic Man: A New Understanding of the Organization of Life and a Vision of the Future* (New York: McGraw Hill, 2000) (artificial intelligence); McFadden, *Quantum Evolution* (quantum biophysics); Jeffrey K. McKee, *The Riddled Chain: Chance, Coincidence, and Chaos in Human Evolution* (New Brunswick, N.J.: Rutgers University, 2000) (chaos theory); Richard Sole and Brian

vey is beyond the scope of this essay, I want to suggest some ways of assessing the issues that may assist distinguishing silliness from salience.

For us to meaningfully extrapolate the evolutionary process to eschatological ends — or even to say it is progressive in any sense at all — requires three things. First of all, we must establish that it is directional. Second, we must argue that the direction of change is something that is humanly valued and/or theologically affirmed, that is, that what we see pro*gress* indeed entails *progress*. And third, we must meaningfully posit that the directional change is actually a progression due to regularities of mechanism rather than contingent coincidences of circumstance, that is, that it is in fact extrapolatable.

Although evolution is held to be nonteleological, this does not mean that it is a-directional. Moreover, while mutation is random, and the only necessary "direction" of selection is reproductive success, for the last fifty years a number of evolutionary directional trends have been accepted as virtually self-evident. Evolution has been widely regarded to entail increases in organismal complexity, ecological diversity, coevolutionary equilibrium, and functional adaptedness. A variety of evolutionary eschatologies, including explicitly theological ones, have been predicated on these trends.

The problem is that each of the above trends is either very difficult to verify or is actually false. Complexity, the most widely cited trend, is quite difficult to quantify. Even in an inanimate molecular system, it is not the mere inverse of entropy, but entails a trade-off between entropic disorder and the highly ordered but rigid state of, for example, a crystalline lattice. It is all the more difficult to assess morphologically and developmentally, but in those studies that have attempted to rigorously characterize biological complexity, it did not appear to increase over evolutionary time.[52] There may be a local increase in abiotic complexity over cosmological time, but that is another issue, and it is often conflated with assertions of increases in biological com-

---

Goodwin, *Signs of Life: How Complexity Pervades Biology* (New York: Basic Books, 2000) (complexity theory); John Haught, *God after Darwin* (Boulder, Colo.: Westview, 2000) (process thought); Philip Hefner, *The Human Factor: Evolution, Culture, and Religion* (Minneapolis: Fortress, 1993) (coevolution); Elisabet Sahtouris, *Earth Dance: Living Systems in Evolution* (San Jose: San Jose University, 2000) (symbiosis); Duane Elgin, *Awakening Earth: Exploring the Evolution of Human Culture and Consciousness* (New York: William Morrow, 1993), and Murphy, *The Future of the Body* (new age mysticism); Margulis and Sagan, *Slanted Truths* (Gaia theory); and Koichiro Matsuno and Stanley Salthe, "Global Idealism/Local Materialism," *Biology and Philosophy* 10.3 (1995): 309-37 (nonlocal interactionism).

52. Daniel McShea, "Complexity and Evolution: What Everybody Knows," *Biology and Philosophy* 6 (1991): 303-24; and Daniel McShea, "Matazoan Complexity and Evolution: Is There a Trend?" *Evolution* 50.2 (1996): 477-92.

plexity by evolution.[53] (The issue of hierarchical organization is considered by some to be a special subset of complexity and will be mentioned below.)

The situation is even less affirming of diversity. It is undisputed that taxonomic diversity manifests no net increase over evolutionary time, but reflects oscillatory crashes and subsequent increases. Morphological (body plan) diversity has held constant since the Cambrian period. Diversity of ecological niches or species interactions does show a rise with the photosynthetic increase of free oxygen and attendant elaboration of the food chain. But there is no evidence of an ongoing directional trend.

Coevolutionary equilibrium fares still worse. For many decades an unquestioned mainstay of parasitology and virology was that infectious agents coevolved with their hosts to minimize pathogenicity over time. This has been firmly demonstrated to be false on both theoretical and empirical grounds: virulence and transmissibility represent trade-offs in life history strategy. Pathogenicity often increases over evolutionary time, depending on infectiousness and host density. This significant reformulation of coevolutionary dynamics represents a big blow to the view that evolution makes for a "kinder, gentler" nature. Nevertheless, many eschatologies still employ this mutualistic scenario in almost saccharine if misanthropic terms. "Just as animals know innately how to share land without killing one another over it, they know innately when they have enough land and food for their needs. An animal may hoard just enough food to get itself through a hard winter, *but no animal except the human one piles up food or takes land beyond its need.*"[54] Would that things were that simple! Porcupines girdle rather than puncture and hence "needlessly" kill trees to tap sweet sap from their phloem; lions consume just the testicles of their kill; oaks manufacture such an abundance of noxious tannins that not only their herbivores but entire watersheds are toxified. So significant is the strategy of subverting the needs of others that Robert MacArthur has added a third form of basic life history strategy to those that evade competition (r) and win competition by efficiency or defense (K): strategists win by sabotage, that is, by taking more than they "need" physiologically and hence maximizing their competitive impact. Indeed, one new suggestion for evolutionary trends is that there is an escalation rather than attenuation of combative "arms races" over evolutionary time.[55]

Finally, with respect to evolutionary progression in functionality, while

---

53. Chaisson, *Cosmic Evolution;* McFadden, *Quantum Evolution.*

54. Sahtouris, *Earth Dance,* 179 (italics in original).

55. G. J. Vermeij, *Evolution and Escalation: An Ecological History of Life* (Princeton: Princeton University, 1987).

evolutionary theorists from Dobzhansky on regard function as the most important concept in biology,[56] its empirical assessment is "a very perilous enterprise that we aren't even close to knowing how to quantify."[57] Indeed, we are not even sure how to define it, much less measure it. And in addition to the consequent empirical uncertainty over whether functionality "improves" over evolutionary time, there is recent theoretical ambiguity about whether it would be expected to do so. If the environment were heterogeneous due to random temporal fluctuation, then there would be no net gain in adaptive fit.[58] And even if the environment itself evidences stasis or predictable change, competitive interactions might subvert the optimization of organismal functionality over evolutionary time (the gap between the ideal and the actual niche). As mentioned above, one hypothesis on the table is that functionality does not *improve*, but functional allocation of resources shifts from reproduction intensiveness of r-strategists to the defense intensiveness of K-strategists,[59] and perhaps to offense intensiveness of alpha strategists.

Are there any candidates for directional evolution about which there is relatively broad agreement? There does appear to be a trend toward higher body temperatures, referred to as maxithermy, and manifest through the sequence of invertebrates, amphibians, reptiles, monotreme, eutherian, placental mammals, non-passerine, and passerine birds. There also appears to be a trend toward increased body size, within these major taxa.[60] Finally, there is directional evolution toward greater energy intensiveness, though this appears to involve episodic jumps rather than a continuous trend[61] and may reflect contingent rather than intrinsic factors.

There are also suggestions for other trends at higher levels of both conceptual integration and speculativeness. One possibility involves increase in

56. Henry Plotkin, *Darwin Machines and the Nature of Knowledge* (Cambridge, Mass.: Harvard University, 1993); and Chaisson, *Cosmic Evolution*.

57. Jeffrey Wicken, *Evolution, Thermodynamics, and Information* (Oxford: Oxford University, 1987); Bruce Weber, David Depew, C. Dyke, Stanley Salthe, Eric Schneider, Robert Ulanowicz, and Jeffrey Wicken, "Evolution in Thermodynamic Perspective: An Ecological Approach," *Biology and Philosophy* 4.4 (1989): 373-405.

58. Daniel McShea, "Possible Largest-Scale Trends in Organismal Evolution: Eight 'Live Hypotheses,'" *Annual Review of Ecology and Systematics* 29 (1998): 293-318.

59. E. O. Wilson, *Sociobiology: The New Synthesis* (Cambridge, Mass.: Harvard University, 1975).

60. N. Newell, "Phyletic Size Increase, An Important Trend Illustrated by Fossil Invertebrates," *Evolution* 3 (1949): 103-24; John Tyler Bonner, *The Evolution of Complexity* (Princeton: Princeton University, 1988).

61. G. J. Vermeij, "Economics, Volcanoes, and Phanerozoic Revolutions," *Paleobiology* 21 (1995): 125-52.

the length and entrenchment of developmental cascades and concomitant decrease in developmental plasticity.[62] Another observes a directionality in the evolution of free-energy dissipative structures that reflects either an increased capacity to dissipate free energy gradients[63] or the more complicated phenomenological sequence typical of both organismal development and ecological succession.[64] Many authors posit an increase in nested, structural depth or the emergence of hierarchical integration.[65] Various schemes describe a series of "major transitions" or steps toward new "levels of organization," including compartmentalization of replicators, standardization of the genetic code and its replication, prokaryote to eukaryote organization, asexual to sexual reproduction, multicellularity, colonial or social integration, and human cultural organization entailing language.[66] Finally, as noted above, there may be a trend that favors K over r strategy and therefore entails increased investment in homeostatic control, longer life spans, greater cognitive fluidity, and higher levels of parental care.[67] Lest this last idea sound like a valuational progression, it should be pointed out that this progression toward K also involves a diminishment of social altruism in the vertebrates.[68]

Now there are a variety of proposals for further integrating the above disparate but not incommensurate observations. But let me cut to the chase by suggesting that, while we have struggled with the conceptualization of just what (if anything) is being "increased" across the phylogenetic development of life, perhaps it is just that: *life*. Of course we must be cautious about sentimental, much less sloppy thinking. Yet it is also true that unlike the physical sciences, biological study begins with the recognition of that which evades operational definition: life from nonlife, male from female, function from pathological dysfunction. And long before evolutionary theory, natural philosophers recognized a "chain of being" that entailed escalating qualities of

62. Kauffman, *The Origins of Order;* Stanley Salthe, *Development and Evolution* (Cambridge, Mass,: MIT Press, 1993).

63. McFadden, *Quantum Evolution.*

64. McShea, "Possible Largest-Scale Trends in Organismal Evolution."

65. George Stebbins, *The Basis of Progressive Evolution* (Chapel Hill: University of North Carolina, 1969); John Maynard Smith, "Evolutionary Progress and Levels of Selection," in *Evolutionary Progress,* ed. M. Nitecki (Chicago: University of Chicago, 1988), 219-30; M. Pettersson, *Complexity and Evolution* (Cambridge: Cambridge University, 1996); Chaisson, *Cosmic Evolution.*

66. Maynard Smith and E. Szathmary, *The Major Transitions in Evolution* (New York: Freeman, 1995).

67. Wilson, *Sociobiology.*

68. Ibid.

life. Although that notion was discarded along with vitalism and natural theology, it turns out that the major phylogenetic links in the chain do correspond to evolutionary history. There has therefore been a rehabilitation of the notion of the "ascent of soul"[69] with the attendant increase in capacities for sensing and cognitively processing the external world, maintaining interior constancy in asserting oneself against the world, and at the same time extending oneself out into the world and "bonding" with other souls in — literally — relational engagement.[70] "It is not enough to call these new and distinct powers merely more complex or more organized forms of life: They represent and make possible new and essentially different ways of life."[71]

Moreover, unfashionable as it has previously been, there is also reaffirmation that humanity is an evolutionary capstone, and that "humankind and its complexities comprise the greatest complexities known in Nature seems indisputable. . . ."[72] E. O. Wilson makes a provocative assertion, invoking a culminating of the K-sequence but a reversing of its associated decreases in social altruism: "Man has intensified the vertebrate traits while adding unique qualities of his own. . . . Exactly how he alone has been able to cross to this fourth pinnacle, reversing the downward trend of social evolution in general, is the culminating mystery of all biology."[73]

Evolutionary Ambivalence

Positing a direction for evolution, and then extrapolating it, provides no intrinsic basis for optimism — eschatological or otherwise — because all depends on whether we *value* the direction of change. Even if we grant the above ambiguous trends as involving real directionalities, they entail an ambivalent valuational legacy.

Increases in energetic intensiveness are associated with coevolutionary arms races and increased competition inhospitable to eschatological hope. And the more nuanced thermodynamic articulations of development in dissipative structures culminate in diminished resilience to external stresses,

69. Kass, *Toward a More Natural Science.*

70. Jonas, *The Phenomenon of Life;* Kass, *Toward a More Natural Science;* Frans De Waal, *Good Natured: The Origins of Right and Wrong in Humans and Other Animals* (Cambridge, Mass.: Harvard University, 1997); Thomas Lewis et al., *A General Theory of Love* (New York: Vintage, 2001).

71. Kass, *Toward a More Natural Science,* 270.

72. McFadden, *Quantum Evolution,* 142.

73. Wilson, *Sociobiology,* 382.

for example, senescence and ultimate deterioration of life — hardly an eschatological goal! Increases in "complexity" are associated with propositions for increased organization of many different kinds, but it is not clear that any of it involves something intrinsically valued or eschatologically affirmed. Indeed, many aspects of both human scientific and religious activity reflect ambivalence about complexity and a premium on simplicity. Einstein says that "things should be made as simple as possible, and no more." Oliver Wendell Holmes would give all "for the simplicity on the other side of complexity."

In contrast to the above, diversity has been valued on aesthetic grounds since Whitehead, and Haught[74] constructed both a theodicy and an eschatological vision based on the diversity-related "maximization of beauty." However, leaving aside the thorny aesthetic question of the relationship between beauty and the dialectic of variability and continuity, we still have the Victorian dilemma of a God who trades beauty for goodness: "some wild poet, working without a conscience or an aim."[75] Thomas Wolfe's critique of Western modernity is that, having lost confidence in the ontological basis of the moral, we have made the aesthetic the *telos* of life: quite literally, we have swapped good taste for good*ness*. A critique of eschatologies based on evolutionary aesthetics is that we have fashioned God after own fallen image, at precisely the cultural moment when theology needs to recall us in eschatological hope to the renewal of his moral image within us.

At this point it might be optimistically pointed out that all of the above miss the really fundamental point, which is the evolutionary amplification of life and both its peak and promise in humanity. Yet humanity, with its ambivalent legacy of capacity for self-transcendent good and self-destructive (and other-annihilating) evil, is precisely part of, if not central to, the problem we are trying to resolve eschatologically. To simply make us more of what we are, even unimaginably more, suggests no cure.

Perhaps, then, if evolution entails an intensification of life, we can think of its eschatological extrapolation as emphasizing the life-promoting, and attenuating the life-denying, aspects of ourselves, and doing the same for all of nature. In a very hopeful sense, it would seem to make us, and the rest of creation, more of what we are already becoming and ultimately should be. The problem with this wonderful image is that evolution reads like a historical drama and not a spiritual allegory. In contrast to optimistic eschatological extrapolations of evolution, "this is not a success story. The privilege of freedom

74. Haught, *God after Darwin*.
75. Alfred Lord Tennyson, *In Memoriam*, ed. Robert H. Ross (New York: Norton, 1973), 23.

carries the burden of need and means precarious being."[76] It is not just that evolutionary history has (and hence evolutionary futures would contain) manifold tragedy. It is that intensifying the very substance of life intrinsically escalates the very experience of suffering, on two counts. First off, death itself is amplified. In a reversal of the classic formula, the coward (or unextended) dies but one death; the brave (hierarchically extended) many. Human beings die at the cellular, organismal, and cognitive levels. So real are these distinctions that one can in fact be alive cellularly but not organismally (as with cardiovascular shock), or organismally but not cerebrally (as in the "brain dead"); and each of these levels of life entails a concomitant death of greater magnitude.

Second, even this side of death, the very intensification of life by definition entails heightened precariousness, anxiety that, in Kierkegaard's phrase, is "dizziness for freedom." Yet this dizziness portends not only fans of exhilaration but also blows of agony. Over the course of the "ascent of soul," with its attendant increase in the scope and resolution of sensory encounter, the persistence and profundity of desire, and ultimately the transformation of desire itself from craving need to appreciative care,[77] we see a simultaneous deepening of capacities not only for fulfillment but also for suffering. The elephant who keeps vigil over its mother's corpse for three weeks, and returns to the site regularly for ten years.[78] The chimp who, after witnessing its mother's torture and killing by poachers, was the only organism besides humans ever observed to have shed tears.[79] The group of twenty-three whales photographically documented to have stayed with an infected conspecific for three days in six feet of water, until it died.[80] In writing this, I am feeling self-conscious about the ostensibly saccharine and sermonic tone. But these observations derive from evolutionary ethology, not theology, and the placement of the "e" makes all the difference. They, do, however have theological implications, for the underlying problem with all evolutionary eschatologies is evolutionary theodicy. Most profoundly, it entails not just the scale of suffering over evolutionary time nor the role of suffering in evolutionary process, but the intensification of suffering as an inescapable consequence of the evolutionary escalation of life.[81]

---

76. Kass, *Toward a More Natural Science*, 4.

77. C. S. Lewis, *The Four Loves* (New York: Harcourt Brace, 1960); De Waal, *Good Natured*; Schloss, "Wisdom Mechanisms as Homeostatic 'Laws of Life.'"

78. De Waal, *Good Natured*.

79. Jane Goodall, *The Chimpanzees of Gombe: Patterns of Behavior* (Cambridge, Mass.: Harvard University, 1986).

80. Robert Trivers, *Social Evolution* (Menlo Park: Benjamin/Cummings, 1985).

81. J. V. Langmead Casserley, *Evil and Evolutionary Eschatology* (Lewiston: Edwin Mellen, 1990).

Thus the impact of thoughtful evolutionary extrapolation is not monolithic optimism but ambivalent longing for something that evolutionary history illuminates the necessity of, but does not assure the attainment of. We long for continuity with life processes that increase the measure of life. Yet we also long for radical discontinuity with the organismal enmeshment of life with suffering, for redemption by a God "whose blessings make rich, and add no sorrow with it." In contrast to buoyant optimism, it is precisely this longing for something the "data" do not demonstrate is coming that may give rise to profound hope.[82]

Eschatological Discontinuities with Biology

Hope involves the longing for and expectation of something that our experience causes us to desire but circumstances do not assure us is coming. But for it to be a hope that confers meaning, indeed for it to be genuine hope at all, and not silly, even psychotic fantasy, it must entail a referent that is in some way coherent with our present sense of the real.

We have been considering the eschatological deepening or intensification of life, generating more "abundance" of life in a way that comports with what we know of life but also transforming it in ways we cannot fully imagine. It turns out that whether this language entails meaningful hope (though not necessarily optimistic expectation) or mere saccharine silliness depends in some measure on how we construe life scientifically. I have already mentioned ambiguities in the conceptualization of the body and attendant debates about the character of the organism. But underlying all this is a still more fundamental, polar disagreement over the nature of life itself. This is widely described as the debate between reductionism and various notions of antireductionism (holism, emergentism, complexity, relational biology) in the description of life and, indeed, other aspects of reality. But for our purposes here I think it may be more helpful to think of it as a controversy between attempts to provide a particularist versus a generalist physical account of life.[83]

The particularist approach views life as an interesting but very rare and specific phenomenon to be explained in the context of laws describing the larger, more general set of abiotic phenomena. In this case, we should not expect to advance the laws of physics by studying life, but, on the contrary, we

---

82. Watts, "Subjective and Objective Hope."
83. Rosen, *Essays on Life Itself.*

must "reduce" or particularize life in a way that comports with physical laws derived from the abiotic. Jaques Monod advances this view in *Chance and Necessity* when he maintains that the living world is a very "special part of the universe — it does not seem likely that the study of living things will ever uncover general laws applicable outside the biosphere." A contrasting approach views life as the more fundamental or conceptually generic phenomenon, of which inanimate matter is only a very particular and constrained subset: ". . . contemporary physics is to biology as Number Theory is to a formalization of it . . . [an organism] is more generic than an inorganic system rather than less."[84] In principle, then, we could advance physics itself by studying this more general assemblage of matter. Einstein commented, "One can best feel in dealing with living things how primitive physics still is."[85] Schrodinger considered organisms repositories of "new physics," and their apparent rarity as a sampling artifact, a view that Monod branded "vitalist." The counterclaim to Monod is that the alternative to reductionism "is not vitalism, but rather a more generic view of the scientific world itself, in which it is the mechanistic laws that are the special cases."[86]

Of course there are other alternatives to reductionism as well, and although I believe there is both empirical and theological warrant for favoring nonreductionist approaches, I do not want to argue the case here either against reductionism, or for a particular version of emergentism, complexity theory, or generic extensionism. What I do want to assert is that the issues are still unresolved: "The question is still open whether life is a quantitative complexification in the arrangement of matter . . . or whether, contrariwise, 'dead' matter, as one extreme of a spectrum, represents a limiting mode of the properties revealed by feeling life, their private reduction to the near-dwindling point of inchoateness: in which case its bare, inertial determination would be dormant, as yet unawakened freedom."[87] I wish to make two comments on the eschatological implications of this open question.

First, if life and other aspects of reality are irreducible to physical laws, then their future is nonextrapolatable from those laws. This is a common though important point that ensues from any perspective that is sensitive to the contingency of historical processes, the chaotic nature of nonlinear processes, or the emergent nature of hierarchical processes. In a sense, not only our knowledge of the future but the future itself is underdetermined by the

84. Ibid., 4.
85. R. W. Clark, *Einstein: The Life and Times* (New York: Avon, 1972), 72.
86. Rosen, *Essays on Life Itself*, 34.
87. Jonas, *The Phenomenon of Life*, 24.

past, though it is also true that this unpredictability is constrained by the boundary conditions of underlying processes: neither contingency, chaos, nor holism can violate natural law and evoke the "impossible." However, the heuristic value of the particularist–generalist framework is that if living systems are not subsets of the abiotic but we need to extend and make more general our scientific laws in virtue of them, then until (if ever) we do this, we do not really know what *is possible*. Moreover, it is not clear that it is possible to know what is possible. If life requires the enlargement of natural law in a way that, because it is more generic rather than more specific, would not be envisionable without the appearance of life itself, then our theory will always lag behind the appearance of the higher-level phenomena "matter is capable of attaining."[88] "In effect, there seems to be no end to the emergence of emergents. Therefore, the unpredictability of emergents will always stay one step ahead of the ground won by prediction."[89] Thus, we do not know what is eschatologically possible — even within the domain of current natural reality — until it happens. Moreover, if we view life as a generic rather than emergent nonreductive phenomenon, then although the future may be discontinuous with the trajectory we plot from the past and present, when we are there, it will be coherent if not continuous with a reality larger than we now understand but that encompasses the now.

Second, I want to suggest that the rhetoric of reduction reflects a grave hermeneutic situation to which both science and eschatology can make an alert contribution. One rather uncontroversial view of the "materialist monism" into which some are attempting to fit contemporary biology is that it represents a residue of the dualistic correction to vitalistic monism or animism that dominated earlier thinking. The benefit of dualism was that it constrained animistic projection and recognized that there could be matter without life; the cost was the complementary conviction that there could be life without matter, and that in fact the essence of life was nonmaterial. It was then perhaps a contiguous methodological step to get rid of "spirit," which was not doing any explanatory work anyway. But it was a huge ontological step, for then life became a mechanistic subset of nonlife. David Oates has observed that the "problem of evil," after Darwin, was turned on its head and became "the problem of goodness" — evil could be assumed; it was goodness that required an explanation. There is an analogous but far more fundamental shift involved in the mechanistic depiction of life: "the lifeless is the true and only foundation of reality. It is the 'natural' as well as the original state of

88. Ibid.
89. Goldstein, as quoted in Solé and Goodwin, *Signs of Life*, 1.

things. Not only in terms of relative quantity but also in terms of ontological genuineness, nonlife is the rule, life the puzzling exception in physical existence. . . . Our thinking today is under the ontological dominance of death."[90] Jürgen Moltmann has observed, "The experience of death is always secondary. Our primary experience is life."[91] In contemporary scientific accounts of reality, the reverse is true.

I do not want to be glib about this critique, for if evolutionary history were not enough to convince us, the cross also testifies to the fact that we must give death its due. But whether the universe reflects a cosmic indifference to life, from which organisms must tentatively and fleetingly wrest their labile existence, or whether the cosmos — by very virtue of the fact that it did "bring forth" life — entails a different, life-promoting ontology, is not a matter that can be decided scientifically. It can, however, inform scientific interpretive frameworks. While it will be evident to anyone who is still reading this essay at this point that I am not a theologian, one of my understandings of the task of theological eschatology is that it is not just to posit a happy future, but to exegete the present in light of promises rooted in the ultimate purpose of existence. A scandalous premise of Christian hope is that death is neither the last word, nor the first. And that is not just because of the promise of resurrection. Rather, it is the opposite: resurrection is a promise because life is the ultimate unit of cosmic ontology — the cosmos was created by, presently consists in, and will be eschatologically consummated in union with the living God. Thus, in both our science and our eschatological reasoning, we would do well to heed the angelic exhortation at the tomb, "Why do you look for the living among the dead?" A great theoretical challenge is to explore depictions of matter that account for its ability to "teem with life," rather than viewing the phenomenon as the divine imposition upon a recalcitrant substrate or an absurdly unlikely and fleeting eruption against all odds.

The Issue of Death

Finally, I must "end" with a discussion of the issue of what becomes of the last enemy, death. I have no desire to speculate on mechanisms or even to contemplate images, but only to reflect briefly on the question of whether it is at all reasonable to imagine life without death; or is it something ridiculous, like a round square or a happy guillotine?

90. Jonas, *The Phenomenon of Life*, 12.
91. Moltmann, "Is There Life after Death?" 239.

The famous evolutionary biologist Theodosius Dobzhansky was once asked, "Is sex necessary?" His answer was, "It may not be necessary, but it is certainly desirable." Interestingly, the same could be said of death at both the organismal and ecological levels. At the organismal level, there are no physiological or thermodynamic reasons why death must occur. In fact, there are several unicellular species that are immortal and one advanced multicellular organism that has not demonstrated any signs of senescence (Bristlecone Pine). The evolutionary interpretation of senescence is not that it represents either biological failure or necessity, but it is an adaptation *built in* to organisms, enhancing fitness by "making room" for progeny. (I am not here speaking of death by external agents like fires or pathogens.) In fact, there are various strategies for coordinating death and reproduction, from short lives with death immediately after reproduction, to long lives with continual reproduction, to long lives with early reproduction and ongoing investment in offspring, to long lives with death after one massive reproductive effort — and they are all interpretable in differing ecological contexts. The bottom line, however, is that death is not physiologically necessary but that it has proven evolutionarily valuable.

The next question, then, is whether death is evolutionarily necessary. At face value the answer would seem to be yes, since evolution is often understood as entailing differential mortality. Strictly speaking, however, evolution by natural selection entails differential reproductive success. Tennyson's "nature red in tooth in claw," in strictly Darwinian terms, should be "nature green in shoot and bloom": the driving force of evolutionary change is excessive fecundity, and therefore random mutation is followed by differential transmission of those variants. It does not require — and often does not even entail — selective mortality. Moreover, as stated above, even where there is selective mortality, it can work in the counterintuitive fashion of facilitating evolutionary advantage, that is, mortality may enhance rather than subvert reproduction. So death is not necessary for evolution, and evolution would still occur if organisms were immortal in an unbounded environment.

However, ecological settings are not unbounded. Therefore, although death is neither physiologically nor evolutionarily necessary, it is necessary if a habitat has finite resources and populations are reproductively increasing without emigration. And, of course, it is also necessary for predators and parasitoids to obtain food at all, since by definition they kill their food. Can we imagine a functioning ecosystem without predators? Several decades ago, classic studies by Paine suggested that predators were necessary for community organization. More recent work suggests that this is not always true, though we certainly cannot imagine earth's present major ecosystems functioning without a hierarchy of predation. One feels silly even considering this, but in reply to the question whether an ecology without predation is conceivable without "magic," the answer would seem to be yes.

The same is true about death more generally. To have a functioning ecology without death would require two things. First, there would be an infinite energy source, or organisms would not be reproducing. I suppose the first does sound like magic (though one wonders what allusions to Christ being the sun entail), but the second is by no means magic and is concordant with teaching on at least sexual reproduction of angels and humans in heaven. Second, energy flow through the ecosystem would have to reflect a balance between rates of energy utilization and productivity; and, assuming that energy is materially incorporated, biomass turnover (to which death substantially contributes in natural ecosystems) would have to entail balanced cycles of consumption and elimination. The farther we go with this the more naive the line of reasoning seems ("Can a man enter his mother's womb a second time?"). But there appear to be, in principle, no biological reasons why death is ecologically necessary. There are, however, thermodynamic reasons why waste is necessary.

Finally, while death is not necessary for life, the *possibility* of death is necessary, that is, life entails the continual overcoming of entropic forces that, if unresisted, will degrade the function and organization of the living system. It is impossible even to imagine how we could have anything worthy of being called life apart from the reality of this tension. "So constitutive for life is the possibility of not-being that its very being is essentially a hovering over this abyss, a skirting of its brink."[92]

The Reality of Our Hope

Fraser Watts tells us, "The more likely something is to happen, by definition, the more optimistic you are that it will happen. This is not true of hope. Indeed, hope characteristically occurs in situations of darkness or uncertainty in which optimism would be impossible or out of place. . . . If you are being held in a concentration camp, you may hope to live and eventually to be released, even in circumstances that hardly justify optimism."[93] A hope that inspires must be built on a promise, not an extrapolation.

It does not seem that an extrapolation of evolutionary processes and an

92. Jonas, *The Phenomenon of Life*, 4.
93. Watts, "Subjective and Objective Hope," 57.

understanding of organismal and ecological constraints provide warrant for futuristic optimism. They do, however, suggest grounds for eschatological hope, in two ways. First of all, recent approaches in the biosciences refuse to foreclose options, and with all the promise of brazen elusiveness they persistently challenge reified conceptualizations of the real. What bodies are, what life is, where evolutionary history is "going," all entail ambiguity underlain by mystery that resists domestication by a scheme or system — scientific or theological. Indeed, "eye has not seen, nor ear heard, nor the mind of man conceived what God has in store for those who love him" (1 Cor. 2:9). Second, in recognizing that life admits itself in degrees, we encounter warrant for eschatological hope that our own life will not just be continued but intensified in resurrection. But we also confront the *need* to have hope continued in resurrection: if we have more life, we have more peril. The above rumination by Fraser Watts may be an analogue of eschatological hope longing for release. But release does not eliminate the abyss, or our experience of its possibility; it only delivers us from it. Once released, I believe we will continue to hope for that never wholly comprehensible end for which we have been released, "the breadth and length and height and depth of the love of God, which surpasses knowing" (Eph. 3:19).

PART II

BODILY RESURRECTION AND PERSONAL IDENTITY

Scripture and Resurrection

FRANK CRÜSEMANN

Within the wide spectrum of contemporary New Testament and systematic research, within the efforts to attain a theology of the entire Bible and to delineate the relationship of the testaments as well as the relationship between Christians and Jews, that which is specifically and decisively Christian is seen in the resurrection of Jesus. That which is really new over against the Old Testament is the "'fundamental assertion' of the New Testament that God resurrected Jesus from the dead," that it is said of one human being who died that God "has already resurrected him so that this person has death once and for all behind him."[1] The meaning of this new experience and the relation to the Jewish tradition are described in very different ways. So, for example, B. S. Childs sees "something totally new" beginning "with the resurrection": "The old came to an end; the new began," and this "discontinuity" is "properly reflected in the formation of two individual and separate testaments."[2] Others such as Klaus Wengst emphasize continuity: precisely "this assertion, too, presupposes specific experiences of Israel with its God and could only be made in this way in Israel."[3] For this reason the Old Testament necessarily precedes the New Testament and remains related to it. The difference does

---

1. Klaus Wengst, "Was ist das Neue am Neuen Testament?" in *Ich glaube an den Gott Israels*, ed. F. Crüsemann and U. Theissmann, Kaiser Taschenbücher 168 (Gütersloh: Christian Kaiser, 2d ed. 2001) 26.

2. *Biblical Theology of the Old and New Testament: Theological Reflections on the Christian Bible* (London: SCM, 1992). Original translation from the German edition, vol. 1, p. 266.

3. Wengst, "Was ist das Neue am Neuen Testament?" 26.

This essay was translated into English by Dr. Clarke Seha, Bielefeld.

not actually appear to be too large.[4] In what follows I will try to show how the New Testament itself sees the interrelation between the resurrection of Jesus and the Scriptures.

This question is not at the center of the broad spectrum of new litera-ture concerning the theme of resurrection.[5] What we see rather is an attempt to define the mutual interplay between "history and promise," between "con-tingency and identity" more precisely as found above all in Traugott Holtz's treatment of Acts 2 and 13 (as well as Romans 4).[6] Accordingly, "the experi-ence of the resurrection" takes "the person who engages him or herself with it into the whole history of God who is experienced in such an event — that means into the history of God as it is witnessed in Scripture." Yet it does not result "as it were logically from an obvious forerunning history" so that it could be "made accessible deductively" from it. Even though this tension without question pertains to the New Testament texts, the theological defini-tion of the new (and therewith the definition of the relationship of the New Testament to the Old) is intertwined with two other assertions. For Holtz it is "completely clear that the experience of the resurrection of Jesus lies before the identification of a so grounded faith with the structure of the faith of Abraham." This means that the encounter with the resurrected Christ evokes a faith that can then be, and surely must be, subsequently identified with the faith of Israel as it is witnessed to in the Scriptures. Added to this is the asser-tion that the resurrection finally and ultimately defines the history of God, for it is the "goal" toward which "the forerunning history of God with His people is moving." In what follows we will pursue these questions of the evi-dence of the experience of the resurrection on the one hand, and of the rela-tionship to the history of God with Israel on the other hand, using Luke and Paul, so that we will be able to describe the relation of the testaments and the reality that is called resurrection.

---

4. So Michael Wyschogrod and Peter von der Osten-Sacken, "Auferstehung Jesu im jüdisch-christlichen Dialog: Ein Briefwechsel," *Evangelische Theologie* 57 (1997): 197.

5. Cf. *Evangelische Theologie* 57 (1997): 177-272; Stephen Davis, Daniel Kendall, S.J., and Gerald O'Collins, S.J., eds., *The Resurrection: An Interdisciplinary Symposium on the Resurrec-tion of Jesus* (Oxford: Oxford University, 1997); Friedrich Avemarie and Hermann Lichtenberger eds., *Auferstehung — Resurrection*, Wissenschaftliche Untersuchungen zum Neuen Testament 135 (Tübingen: Mohr Siebeck, 2001); Hans-Joachim Eckstein and Michael Welker, eds., *Die Wirklichkeit der Auferstehung: Biblische Zeugnisse und heutiges Erkennen* (Neukirchen-Vluyn: Neukirchener, 2001).

6. Traugott Holtz, "Geschichte und Verheißung: Auferstanden nach der Schrift," *Evangelische Theologie* 57 (1997): 179-96. The following citations are from pp. 195-96.

Presupposition and Foundation: Luke[7]

As in the other Synoptic Gospels, the Lukan Jesus committed himself against the Sadducees to the expectation of the general resurrection of the dead. Jesus connected it with the concept of God itself and with the central Jewish tradition according to which God introduced himself to Moses at his call as the God of the living, namely, as "the God of Abraham and the God of Isaac and the God of Jacob" (Luke 20:37-38). But Luke had already staked out the relationship between Scripture and resurrection in the fundamental teaching of Jesus that the resurrection of a single human being in no way touches the validity of the Torah and the prophets. Abraham himself, who is in heaven with God, answers the petition of the rich man to send certain news to his relatives from the world beyond, "If they do not listen to Moses and the prophets, neither will they be convinced even if someone rises from the dead" (Luke 16:31). That is the teaching of Jesus, whom Luke and the congregation for whom he writes know and confess as the Resurrected One. The combination of a word of Jesus with one of Abraham has an authority that is hardly surpassed. The validity of the Torah and the prophets is accordingly not touched by any resurrection. It is also bluntly clear that individual resurrection or eternal life with God does not depend on the resurrection of Jesus or faith in it. Therewith an accent is set that makes one eager to anticipate the question of what such a resurrection should and can then convince.

Experience and Scripture in the Encounter with the Resurrected

After the death and burial of Jesus Luke first of all tells a massively negative story in 24:1-11. The sight of the empty grave, the presence of the angels, and their message of the resurrection of Jesus, along with their reference to the teachings of the earthly Jesus and the personal remembrance of them — all of this is carried to the disciples by the women, but they consider it an idle tale that cannot be believed (v. 11). And it is not said that the women who communicated this message believed it or that it effected anything in them.

With this unbelievable tale is contrasted the story that, as no other, makes the resurrection believable: the Emmaus story. It is the story of a way

---

7. Cf. esp. Günter Wasserberg, *Aus Israels Mitte — Heil für die Welt: Eine narrativ-exegetische Studie zur Theologie des Lukas*, Beihefte zur Zeitschrift für die neutestamentliche Wissenschaft 92 (Berlin: de Gruyter, 1998); K. Löning, *Das Geschichtswerk des Lukas*, vol. 1, Urban Taschenbücher 455 (Stuttgart: Kohlhammer, 1997).

that leads from having closed eyes, from not perceiving and not understanding (24:16), to having open eyes and knowledge (v. 31). What effects this turnabout is presented in the clearest fashion: Scripture. Both disciples tell the whole story to the still unknown fellow traveler. In spite of the angelic message that he lives, it is a story of disappointed hopes: "But we had hoped that he was the one to redeem Israel" (v. 21). Those who have experienced, heard, and even transmitted all this must allow themselves to be depicted as foolish and slow of heart (v. 25). Why? Not because they did not believe the message of the angels and the women, but solely because they did not believe "all that the prophets have declared" (v. 25). It is faith in the witness of the prophets and in all that is to be read there that is the deficiency. If one takes the wording of the statement seriously, it is faith in the prophets that is the key that decides everything. What is to be believed here stands in the prophets.

The instruction, then, is of the same sort: "Then beginning with Moses and all the prophets, he interpreted to them the things about himself in all the scriptures" (v. 27). It is the Tanach, the three-part Hebrew canon, that comes into play here: the Torah, the prophets, and the writings. And the double *"all"* that emphasizes and radicalizes *"all the prophets"* in verse 25 shows that this does not involve individual words and proof texts, not *dicta probantia,* but the entirety of Scripture. It involves something that is found there from beginning to end and that demands faith and makes faith possible. Ultimately it must involve the living God, who is the God of the living. That is the hermeneutic — the word that stands in verse 27 — that this interpreter demonstrates. This is really amazing: the Resurrected One makes himself known in that he reads and interprets the Scripture. He can apparently be known only in this way, and he apparently wants to be known only in this way. No glory, no miracle, no overwhelming experience evokes faith and knowledge, but only the horizon that is opened by the interpretation of Scripture.[8]

The two disciples invite this still unknown and still anonymous interpreter to stay with them for the night. "When he was at the table with them, he took bread, blessed and broke it, and gave it to them" — in this they recognize him, but in the moment they identify him he disappears. Then they re-

---

8. The decisive point is therefore not that the Resurrected "opens" the Scripture or is reading it in "new" way, as Anna Maria Schwemer, like others, put it ("Der Auferstandene und die Emmausjünger," in *Auferstehung — Resurrection,* ed. Friedrich Avemarie and Hermann Lichtenberger, Wissenschaftliche Untersuchungen zum Neuen Testament 135 [Tübingen: Mohr Siebeck, 2001], 95-118), but Scripture is necessary even to recognize the Resurrected One as such. It is exactly not Jesus who is already recognized as resurrected who interprets Scripture in a new way, but only interpretation of Scripture leads to his identification.

member what happened. But what they remember is not really the presence of the Resurrected One as such. They are not thinking about the moment of identification of the Living One with the earthly Jesus, but the process of interpreting Scripture: "Were not our hearts burning within us while he was talking to us on the road, while he was opening the scriptures to us?" (v. 32). Where Scripture is so interpreted that it is talking about the God of the living, the heart burns, and the reality that is signified as resurrection is present; against that the identified disappears.

Learning depends on repetition, and this is the way Luke further depicts the same learning process. In spite of the message of these two disciples and the personal experience of Peter (vv. 33-34), the appearance of the Resurrected One in the midst of his disciples still causes them to be startled and terrified the next time around (vv. 36-37). The Dead One who returned appeared to them to be a ghost. And even the bodily identification (v. 39) or the joy in having the Resurrected One among them did not lead to faith. Instead of this there is the strange sentence: "In their joy they were disbelieving" (v. 41). The joy-inciting encounter with the Living One in no way leads to the faith involved here. Once again knowledge, understanding, and faith take place only when Scripture is interpreted. The Resurrected One reminds them first of the scriptural interpretation of the earthly Jesus (v. 44), and again the whole Scripture is named programatically: Torah, Prophets, and Psalms. Only as a whole and in all its parts together does Scripture speak of what is involved here. But, indeed, remembering the scriptural interpretation of the earthly Jesus was not sufficient: "Then he opened their minds to understand the scriptures" (v. 45). He taught them what stands written, that and how Scripture speaks of the suffering and resurrection of the Christ, and he instructed them in such a way that repentance and forgiveness of sins might be proclaimed to all nations in his name (vv. 46-47). Only here does a goal and a commission come into sight: the mission to the nations is the only named goal of the resurrection.

In Luke's Gospel, no faith is evoked by the experience of the resurrection without the medium of Scripture. Scripture as a whole is necessary even to recognize what is happening and who is there. Only Scripture and its interpretation lead people to recognize the unknown man or something like a ghost as the resurrected Christ. Theologically the Emmaus story says precisely what is involved here: the resurrected Christ is dependent on the interpretation of Scripture to make himself known to the disciples.

FRANK CRÜSEMANN

Preaching the Resurrection of Jesus

Both of the first fundamental sermons of Peter (Acts 2:22-26) and Paul (Acts 13:16-41) in which Luke develops the witness of the disciples to the Resurrected One — in both cases he puts the relationship to Scripture at the center — are characterized by Holtz in this way: "Most obviously the scriptural proof presupposes the experience of death and resurrection and interprets this path of thought proceeding from the witness of the prophet David stated in Scripture." The goal of the sermons is presumably the attestation of resurrection by "eyewitnesses"; throughout "the resurrection is [presumably] confirmed by the scriptural proof."⁹ With these formulations the differences from Luke are, in my opinion, slightly but decisively altered. As in Luke 24, so here in Acts the experience of the respective eyewitnesses is never independent of Scripture; it is never presupposed as an independent experience and can therefore not be "confirmed by scriptural proof."

In Acts 2 Peter tells the history of Jesus until his death and resurrection beginning with the gift of the Spirit according to Joel 3. From the very beginning this is described in verse 24 with words of Scripture and then established with a long quotation from Psalm 16 ("therefore" in v. 25). Only after a thorough exegesis of the quoted passage of Scripture in verses 29-31 is there a brief and thematic allusion to personal experience in verse 32: "of that all of us are witnesses," in order to go on immediately with the exposition of the meaning of words of Scripture. It is unequivocally not so that the personal encounter with the Resurrected One is to be viewed as the starting point and the goal of the argumentation; the witness of the eyewitnesses plays a very secondary role. And the resurrection is always described with scriptural quotations; it can therefore simply not be confirmed by Scripture.

Still less does Paul, whom the Resurrected One also encountered, in the presentation of Luke support his first fundamental sermon with this encounter and with his personal experience. It does not even appear. In the form of an exposition of Scripture in a worship service of the synagogue (Acts 13:14-15), he relates the history of Israel starting with Abraham and then comes to John the Baptist and Jesus and ends with his death and resurrection along with a brief mention of resurrection witnesses (Acts 13:16-31). The central point, the goal, that which follows from this story as proclamation, message, and commission, begins as follows: "And we bring you the good news that what God promised to our ancestors" (Acts 13:32) is now fulfilled. Only in this perspective of the old promise to the fathers and in connection with it does

---

9. Holtz, "Geschichte und Verheissung," 185, 189.

94

what happened become "good news." And that is then developed with quotations from Psalm 2, Isaiah 55, Psalm 16, and Habakkuk 1.

Finally, let us have a short look at the encounter of Paul with the Resurrected One. It is reported three times. If the theologically relevant succession of events is really the way Holtz claims it is, then this should come clearly to the fore here: first the experience that is at first independent of Scripture and nevertheless incites faith and then its explication on the basis of Scripture. After Luke relates it in chapter 9 he lets Paul himself report it twice in chapters 22 and 26, both times, moreover, only as an apologia for his work and not as part of his missionary preaching directed at arousing faith. In chapters 9 and 22 only a short conversation takes place in the encounter itself, which concludes with the self-introduction of the one persecuted by Saul, without an interpretation and without a commission. That must all be done by Ananias or his congregation, to whom Paul is referred. Only in the third variation in chapter 26 does a commission for proclamation follow in this encounter (vv. 16-18). But precisely in this wording Paul afterward formulates explicitly that he testifies to both small and great, "saying nothing but what the prophets and Moses said would take place" (26:22). This sounds similar to what Paul would say in 1 Corinthians 4:6, and it is a fundamental theological principle of the greatest weight: precisely the unique experience of Paul itself is nothing that would be independent of Scripture and that would in any way go beyond it. Looked at theologically, there is nothing to be said even by an eyewitness that is not already found in Moses and the prophets, nothing that leads "beyond the Scripture."

And how does the resurrection of Jesus present the goal of the history of God with his people such that it finally and ultimately defines it? If I am seeing correctly, the only reason Holtz offers for this is the closing position of this event in the sermons of Acts 2 and 13. The history of Israel is indeed told in such a way that it ends with this event. But a final event does not necessarily finalize history. The Deuteronomic history with its conclusion in 2 Kings 25 does not mean that exile is the final end, nor do other historical summaries want to say that the land conquest under Joshua is such a final end. The conclusion of many recitals of history often describes above all the hermeneutical starting point of what is said, to be sure. But this does not mean that history has come to an end. The history recorded in the book of Acts ends with the arrival in Rome. Yet history goes on. We cannot identify the goal with the sentence: "Because the resurrection of the dead is an eschatological event it defines the history of God finally."[10] As long as the dead have not been resur-

---

10. Ibid., 196.

rected, history continues. And whoever belongs to history is still decided on the basis of Moses and the prophets.

Paul

Paul is in agreement with the original Christian tradition in 1 Corinthians 15:3ff. that he has taken over, "that Christ died for our sins in accordance with the scriptures, and that he was buried, and that he was raised on the third day in accordance with the scriptures." Now this tersely phrased tradition underscores the fundamental significance of Scripture for every understanding of the cross and resurrection, but it unfortunately reveals hardly any details, neither which passages of Scripture are in view nor above all how the relationship between Scripture and the experience of resurrection is being thought about theologically.[11] For this reason, we ask how Paul defines the relationship between Scripture and the resurrection of Jesus in his own theology. Since the Resurrected One himself "last of all appeared" to him (15:8) and since this encounter turned him from being a persecutor of the church to an apostle, his definition of the relationship between contingent experience and tradition, the Christian *novum*, and the continuum of Scripture would be of special weight.

The Theological Logic of 1 Corinthians 15:13ff.

The witness to the resurrection founded on Scripture in 1 Corinthians 15:13ff. serves as an introduction to the debate with opinions in the Corinthian congregation that fundamentally deny the Jewish tradition of the general resurrection of the dead. In verses 12ff. Paul develops the inner, theological connection between the resurrection of the dead and the resurrection of Jesus in this way:

> If there is no resurrection of the dead, then Christ has not been raised; and if Christ has not been raised, then our proclamation has been in vain and your faith has been in vain. More than that, we are then found to be false witnesses about God, because we testified of God that he raised

11. For discussion see Wolfgang Schrage, *Der erste Brief an die Korinther (1Kor 15,1–16,24)*, Evangelisch-katholischer Kommentar zum Neuen Testament VII/4 (Düsseldorf: Benziger; Neukirchen-Vluyn: Neukirchener, 2001).

Christ — whom he did not raise if it is true that the dead are not raised. For if the dead are not raised, then Christ has not been raised either. And if Christ has not been raised, *your* faith is futile and you are still in your sins. . . . we are of all people most to be pitied. (15:12-19)

The usual Christian interpretation presumes the Christian faith in the resurrection of Jesus, as it is witnessed here in verses 3ff. and then again in verse 20 as in verse 12. If the Christian belief in the resurrection would be solely in the contingent event of the resurrection of Christ, then the argumentation carried out in verses 13ff. would be highly problematic, really un-understandable; it would be considered only as a sort of thought experiment. It would then be a matter "that a resurrection event should be viewed as thinkable and not as un-thinkable or impossible respectively."[12] But such a reading would not do justice to Paul's argumentation. In the parallel chain conclusions in verses 13-15 and 16-19, Paul pronouncedly does not proceed from the individual case of a resurrection of Jesus but from the promise of a general resurrection of the dead. It is indeed the framework of apocalyptic thinking that is presupposed here.[13] And for Paul this is not only presupposition and background. Instead, theologically the God who overcomes death is the weight-bearing foundation: when it falls everything falls. Historically speaking, this belief is fully developed in apocalyptic thinking. In this he includes everything that composes the Christian faith: proclamation, faith, forgiveness of sin, and hope. If Paul really means what he says here, then the whole of the Christian faith hangs on what the Scripture and Jewish tradition — Paul would say since Abraham (see below) — view as a fundamental given with the God of Israel.

Amazingly, this applies to Paul himself: the witness that he and the other witnesses have given — by the way, from God! — could be false testimony (v. 15).[14] Did Paul "see" anything? Paul's "seeing" the resurrected Jesus

---

12. So Andreas Lindemann, *Der Erste Korintherbrief,* Handbuch zum Neuen Testament 9/1 (Tübingen: Mohr Siebeck, 2000), 339.

13. See Wolfgang Schrage, *Der erste Brief an die Korinther,* 126. But even Schrage says that it is the resurrection of Christ that leads to the hope of resurrection of the dead (132) or implies this hope (129; cf. 127 and passim). The text itself says it vice versa.

14. It is especially the fact that Paul includes his own witness, his own experience in his argumentation, that is overlooked in the long and intensive work on understanding the logical structure of argumentation in vv. 12-19. From M. Bachmann ("Zur Gedankenführung in 1 Kor 15,12ff," *Theologische Zeitschrift* 34 [1978]: 265-76) to J. S. Vos ("Die Logik des Paulus in 1 Kor 15,12-20," *Zeitschrift für die neutestamentliche Wissenschaft* 90 [1999]: 78-97) one finds here the so-called *modus tollens:* (1) If there is no resurrection of the dead, Christ has not been resurrected. (2) But now Christ has been resurrected (v. 20). (3) Therefore there will be a resurrection of the dead. But Paul does not argue in this way.

is not independent of Scripture and cannot therefore be confirmed by it subsequently. Rather, Paul's "seeing" is an experience of the resurrection of Jesus because it confirms the foregoing witness of Scripture. In this chain of thought Scripture and its promises become the theological foundation not only of the resurrection of Jesus and the Christian faith but also of the witness of the eyewitnesses. On this Paul and Luke agree.

To what extent the foregoing faith of Israel is faith in the resurrection of the dead Paul declares above all in Romans 4, where he makes Abraham the father of all believers, even the father of the Gentile Christians who have just recently come to faith in the God of Israel. Abraham was the first who believed; Gentile Christians believe as he did. And the faith of Abraham is faith in the resurrection of the dead. According to Romans 4:17 Abraham became the father of many peoples — "in the presence of the God in whom he believed, who gives life to the dead and calls into existence the things that do not exist." The faith that concerns Paul and is reckoned as righteousness — the faith that Abraham as we know already had, as well as all who believe in the Messiah Christ — this faith is, so to speak, *per definitionem* always already faith in the God who overcomes death. Faith in Abraham's God who overcomes death precedes the resurrection of Jesus; it is the precondition of its perception. In it an action of God is shown that faith has always already believed him to be doing.

What of Paul's own commissioning through the encounter with the Resurrected One? In Galatians 1:11ff. he founds, as we know, the origin and authority of his gospel in this. It does not come from human beings, but from a revelation — *apokalypsis* — of Jesus Christ (v. 12). Paul persecutes the church out of zealousness for the ancestral traditions (vv. 13ff.). He describes the about-face in this manner: "But when God, who had set me apart before I was born and called me through his grace, was pleased to reveal his Son to me, so that I might proclaim him among the Gentiles, I did not confer with any human being . . ." (1:15-16). The complete independence from flesh and blood is emphasized, the one defined goal of the revelation is unequivocal, the commission to proclaim among the Gentiles, his installation as the apostle to the Gentiles. It is not unequivocal, however, whether the proclamation — "so that I might proclaim him" — has Christ or God as its immediate content, but in the light of the connection between the two nothing crucial depends on this. What is crucial is the definition of the relationship between being set apart and being called to reveal the Son and to be installed as the apostle to the Gentiles. The usual exegesis alludes to passages like Jeremiah 1, but it hardly ever deals with the theological questions inherent in it.

Two participial wordings precede the decisive sentence about the revelation of the Son. Their formulation in the aorist allows only a reference to an event that precedes the revelation, for which the mentioning of his mother's womb and of birth is a clear factual indication. Long ago, before the beginning of his existence, Paul is set apart by God just as Jeremiah was. Does the parallel formulation *"called through his grace"* mean the same act? Does this calling, too, exist since the beginning of his life, but was discovered only retrospectively through the revelation? The concept of calling makes this improbable. But then Paul knows himself to be called by God not just since the revelation of the Son. The one long since called by God rather receives a new, crucial commission through the revelation of the Son. A long-standing call is filled with a new content. Whatever this foregoing call by the grace of God exactly was, it must be connected with his previous life as a Pharisee, his education, and the like. That he mentions this calling when he talks about the decisive turnabout in his life can only mean that in spite of the contrast the common foundation remains and is merely confirmed by the new revelation, which plays a crucial role.

Theological Consequences in the Form of Two Theses

In two theses I will attempt to formulate some consequences from these findings. They are far-reaching, and for that reason they can be developed and founded here only in an initial fashion.

Thesis 1: The resurrection of the dead is a predicate of God and belongs to God the creator and his power, as it is expressed in the first article of the Christian creed. The second article of the creed on redemption is to be read in this perspective biblically.

Here lies common ground with Judaism. Resurrection faith is not developed solely on the basis of Christology. The resurrection of the dead is spoken about already six times in the second petition of the Amidah, the central Jewish prayer:

> You are powerful in eternity, Lord, enliven the dead. You are strong in helping. You nourish the living with grace, enliven the dead in great mercy, support the falling, heal the sick, liberate the bound up and maintain loyalty to those who are sleeping in dust. Who is comparable to You, Lord of all power, and who is like You, King, who kills and enlivens and lets salvation spring up? And You are loyal to enliven the dead again. Praise be to You, Eternal One, who enlivens the dead again.

"It is to be heeded," writes Michael Wyschogrod on this point, "that this praise is formulated in the present and not merely in the future. . . . It can not be reserved exclusively for the future because God's power can not be reserved exclusively for the future. God lives *now* and death stands in opposition to God; it is the principle that negates God's power. For exactly this reason there must be already a present and not just a future victory over death."[15]

Here the Old Testament precedent should be retrieved. The customary picture according to which the dead are totally cut off from God because the God of Israel has no power over death, and that this changed only in some late apocalyptic texts,[16] must be combated with the Old Testament. It is not true that the initial beginning took place in Christian faith in resurrection, accompanied by only a few unclear beginnings in Judaism. Already in the later years of the kings the might of the Israelite God over death is epigraphically indicated.[17] The famous rhetorical questions of the Psalter such as in Psalm 88:11ff. — "Will you do a miracle on the dead?" — presuppose indeed that God has not done it until now, but it also presupposes that he could do it.[18] And already Elijah and Elisha talk about the power of God to resurrect the dead (1 Kings 17:17-24; 2 Kings 4:8-37). Over and over Israel spoke in hymnic formulations (1 Sam 2:6; Ps 139:8) and in prophetic sentences (Amos 9:2) about the power of God to rule over the kingdom of death and to enliven the dead.

Certainly the promise that the dead, especially the just, will rise was explicitly formulated in the Persian era or even in Hellenistic times. But that God has the power to enliven the dead belongs to the God of Israel from the beginnings of the exclusive worship of one God *(Alleinverehrung)*.[19] Israel's God has might even over Mot, the God of death and the netherworld.

The path to monotheism also consists in the ever clearer formulation of this hope. The open questions of the Psalms remain true; they formulate

---

15. Cf. *Evangelische Theologie* 57 (1997): 207.

16. Cf. K. Müller, "Das Weltbild der jüdischen Apokalyptik und die rede von der Auferstehung Jesu," *Bibel und Kirche* 52 (1997): 8-18.

17. For the meaning of the inscriptions of Khirbet el Kom and of Ketef Hinnom see now Bernd Janowski, "Die Toten loben JHWH nicht: Psalm 88 und das alttestamentliche Todesverständnis," in *Auferstehung — Resurrection*, ed. Friedrich Avemarie and Hermann Lichtenberger, Wissenschaftliche Untersuchungen zum Neuen Testament 135 (Tübingen: Mohr Siebeck, 2001), 3-45.

18. Cf. Janowski, ibid., 23ff., who understands them as a "Grenzaussage."

19. Cf. Frank Crüsemann, *Elia — die Entdeckung der Einheit Gottes: Eine Lektüre der Erzählungen über Elia und seine Zeit*, Kaiser Taschenbücher 154 (Gütersloh: Kaiser, n.d.), 37ff., 144ff.

nothing other than the human situation in which we Christians as well as the Jews and all other human beings find ourselves without change. This condition has also not been changed by the resurrection of Jesus: that the dead remain dead and in the grave although God, as we believe, can and wants and will change this; we are, indeed, hoping and waiting for the resurrection of the dead made possible by God as evidenced in the resurrection of his Son, Jesus Christ.

The God of Israel, the God of Abraham, either is the one who enlivens the dead, or he is not. That is the perspective in which the events after the death of Jesus can effect faith. In passing, it is certainly anything other than an accident that Paul, precisely in the chapter in which he deals so basically and extensively with the resurrection, more clearly than anywhere else designates the dominion of Christ as limited. "When all things are subjected to him, then the Son himself will also be subjected to the one who put all things in subjection under him, so that God may be all in all" (1 Cor. 15:28).

Thesis 2: The enduring impulse resulting from the short period of the appearances of the resurrected Jesus is the commission to win the Gentiles for the God of Israel.

First of all, it must be emphasized that the special experiences after Easter are restricted to a very short time and to few witnesses. For Luke they cease with the ascension, and Paul himself views himself as the last in a series. "What these humans transformed was not only the moment but also the loyalty that they preserved after this moment. That is the paradox of revelation. It breaks through the order of things and is then dependent on this order."[20] And for the revelation of the Resurrected One there is added to this that it does not take place without the medium of Scripture and that it contains in concentrated form that which Scripture and tradition already knew beforehand. The tradition does not change; it does not even appear in a truly new light. It simply receives anew the illuminating power that it has already had since Abraham or that it could have been perceived to have had. Just as the faith of Abraham was always possible, so is faith in the overcoming of death.

The resurrection adds nothing to Scripture. The new revelation is a moment between Scripture and Scripture. Scripture is necessary even to be able to perceive the resurrection of Jesus appropriately. That is valid for the moment of appearance; that is most surely valid for the transmission of the experience. The one who is known with the help of Scripture disappears; what remains is memory. That was the way it was in the Emmaus story, and that

---

20. Leon Wieseltier, *Kaddish* (New York: A. A. Knopf, 3rd ed. 1998), 71. Original translation from the German, 2000.

was the way it was during the history of original Christianity. Perhaps this can be said with a picture that turns around the pictorialness of many biblical pictures. Just as a moment of darkness can nevertheless allow a previously and subsequently illuminated room that has neither been changed nor differently lighted to be perceived anew, so is the relationship of the resurrection of this one human being to the foregoing and further going, the unchanged biblical tradition.

What has changed can be described in this way: the resurrection of Jesus actualizes the promises for the Gentile peoples. In any case, for Paul in Galatians 1 and for Luke (as well as for Matthew) the foundational encounter with the Resurrected One moves toward a single impulse: the commission to bring the gospel to the Gentiles. The amazing clarity and explicitness with which that is formulated should not be prematurely covered up by pointing to other motives that are undoubtedly operating alongside this, for example, the installation of Christ as a messianic Ruler. The resurrection of the One is viewed in many texts as the beginning of the general resurrection. There is, for example, the picture of Christ as "the first fruits of those who have died" (1 Cor. 15:20). That does not involve the first one numerically, but the first fruit at the beginning of the harvest. The resurrection of Jesus is the signal that the grand promises are beginning to realize themselves. This brings a process in motion for which Israel did not and does not have a mandate — winning all people for their creator.

Paul's Concept of a Spiritual Body

PETER LAMPE

It is sown a physical body, it is raised a spiritual body. If there is a physical body, there is also a spiritual body.

1 CORINTHIANS 15:44

Systematic theology is constructed on a foundation of sound biblical exegesis. To ready theology for engagement with science, it needs to know what Scripture says. Our task here is to discern just what St. Paul says about the self who dies and rises in Christ.

Paul's Holistic View versus the Corinthians' Dichotomous Anthropology

In the collection of the Museo Nazionale in Rome, there is a touching relief on a pagan child's sarcophagus.[1] The living soul of the deceased infant is reclining on a bed, enjoying the pleasures of the Elysium in the iconographic center of the relief. The soul is depicted as an adolescent — as the person this child was supposed to become. Under the *klinē* (the bed), the corpse of the deceased infant is depicted, the small body stretched out, marked by death — a hollow shell, which the soul has left.

In Corinth, Paul faced the same dichotomous anthropological concept,[2] which was widespread in the Greco-Roman world. This typically Greek di-

1. Museo Nazionale, inventory number 535.
2. See esp. 1 Cor. 6:12-20; 1 Corinthians 15.

chotomy was different from the Jewish holistic view of the human being. Jews traditionally did not separate the physical body *(sōma)* from the immortal soul *(psychē)* or spirit *(pneuma)*. Whenever traditional Jews said "body," they did not mean just the tangible, physical parts but rather the entire person.

Paul has often been presented as a protagonist of this kind of Jewish, holistic anthropology. But things are a little more complicated. After all, he was a Hellenistic Jew, and, as such, he *could* distinguish the person's self from his or her physical body.[3] However, he saw other consequences in this dichotomy than the Corinthians did. And at the same time, he maintained a different kind of holism than traditional Jews who followed the author of the book of Daniel.

The Greek concept, which was shared by the Corinthians, could also be interpreted as a dichotomy between the inner and the outer person. The importance of the body as the exterior of the personality was then downplayed and neglected; only the inner person mattered. The Corinthian enthusiasts thought that in baptism their inner person, their soul or spirit, was endowed with the Holy Spirit, immortalized and saved. They saw this as an already present salvation that they experienced tangibly in ecstatic spiritual phenomena, especially speaking in tongues (1 Corinthians 12–14). Compared to this, the outer nature — the physical body and behavior in everyday life — was of little importance to them. One could eat whatever one wanted (cf. 1 Corinthians 8; 6:13) or have sex with whomever one desired (cf. 1 Cor. 6:12ff.; also 5:1ff.); these were external matters of the physical body, *quantitées négligables,* which did not affect the salvation of the inner soul. Thus, the Corinthians' anthropological dichotomy divided the human personality into sectors that were independent of each other — sex and food for the body, Christ for the spirit. And at the moment of death, the immortalized human spirit (or soul) is freed from the perishing physical body and ascends to the Lord. Consequently, a future eschatological "resurrection" was not necessary in the Corinthians' eyes.[4]

---

3. See esp. 2 Cor. 12:2-3; 5:6 below. Differently, see, e.g., Dan. 12:2 as the oldest certain testimony of Jewish belief in an eschatological resurrection of the dead: "Many of those who sleep in the dust of the earth will awake, some to everlasting life, and some to . . . everlasting contempt." Here the deceased person's *self* is pictured as being buried together with the *physical body.* Both are inseparable. Other variants of the expectation of a resurrection of the dead can be found in, e.g., *1 Enoch* 22–27; 51; 102–104; *Psalms of Solomon* 3:12; 13:11; 15:13; *2 Baruch* 49–51; *4 Ezra* 7.

4. "There is no resurrection of the dead" (1 Cor. 15:12), some Corinthians said, meaning that baptized Christians do not undergo a *future, postmortem* resurrection. What they called "resurrection" or "eternal life" is already encountered *now* in baptism and in spiritual,

In Paul's holistic perspective, on the other hand, the reality of salv̦
is not *another* reality apart from the outer everyday life, not just a religiou̦
ality for the *inner* life of a person. It grasps and embraces the whole of human
existence, the entire personality.[5] This principle is also applied very consistently to the eschatological concept of a postmortem life: this life will not only
involve *parts* of a human being, a soul or a spirit, but the entire personality,
including his or her bodily existence. For exactly this reason, Paul talks about
"resurrection" and not of such things as "spiritual immortality" and "ascending souls." Or, in other words, without the bodily aspect there is no legitimate
usage of the word "resurrection," according to Paul.

In summary, God's salvation, including the raising of the dead, grasps
more than just parts of a human being, than just a soul or a spirit. It grasps
the entire person and subjects this person to a transforming[6] and newly creating act called "resurrection." Consequently, the resurrected person will have a
bodily existence.

How Does Paul Envision the Bodily Side
of the Resurrection of Human Beings?

If the resurrection is such a comprehensive reality, as described above, it also
must be *future and eschatological.* This is a logical consequence of the com-
prehensiveness, because the present is imperfect, characterized by the absence
of total salvation. For Paul, resurrection of humans therefore is an "eschatological" reality, that is, something at the end and outside of our present reality,
something beyond our present life and death, something for which we only
can hope (Rom. 8:24). Contradicting the Corinthians, Paul emphasizes this
future aspect by choosing apocalyptic language when describing resurrection
(1 Cor. 15:23-28, where he lays out an apocalyptic timetable). In his Christology, he also emphasizes that in the present the *crucified* Christ is central, and,
correspondingly, Christians in the present are conformed to this crucified
Lord (e.g., Rom. 6:3-8a). Only in the *future* will they be conformed to the resurrected Lord (Phil. 3:21; Rom. 6:5b, 8b).

---

ecstatic, or charismatic experiences, such as speaking in tongues or prophesying. In baptism,
Christians meet Christ and participate in his resurrection, gaining new, eternal life already in
the present (see similar views in John 5:24-25; Eph. 2:5-6; 5:14; Col. 2:12-13; 3:1; 2 Tim. 2:18).

5. See esp. 1 Cor. 6:12ff. The entire physical existence belongs (6:19-20) to the Lord and
is grasped by him. Therefore, in Paul's view, the Lord competes directly with the courtesan
with whom a Corinthian Christian unites himself physically.

6. Cf. *metaschēmatizō* (Phil. 3:21).

Now in the old aeon, characterized by death and imperfection, Christians catch only anticipating glimpses of this future reality, for example, by experiencing love (cf. 1 Corinthians 13).[7] But it would be a poor illusion to identify anything elating in the present, such as a fantastic ecstatic-spiritual phenomenon, as a wonderful manifestation of eternal life. Speaking in tongues and prophesying belong to the old aeon and will come to an end (1 Cor. 13:8-10). Resurrection will be encountered only at the end of all times.

At first glance, the emphasis on the future eschatological aspect of the resurrection seems trivial. But it was not self-evident for the ancient Corinthians — as it might not be for modern existentialists. For Paul, however, there was no legitimate usage of the word "resurrection" *without* the future eschatological horizon. It is exactly this future eschatological perspective that might open up a common platform for discussion with natural scientists, who are familiar with linear time frames,[8] who on the basis of quantum physics are familiar with speculations about other universes beyond our universe, and who also reckon with the finality of this universe.

The next aspect directly corresponds to the previous one. In fact, it is just the flip side of it. There is a quantum leap between the present physical body of the human being and the future spiritual body of resurrected individuals. In other words, rising with a new spiritual body does not mean returning to one's old physical body and existence — like Lazarus was said to have come out of his grave, being restored to his previous natural human self (John 11:17-44), which was marked by mortality, weakness, insufficiency, and the capacity for suffering. "Flesh and blood cannot inherit the kingdom of God, nor does the perishable inherit the imperishable" (1 Cor. 15:50). Whoever dies and "is with Christ" is "not in the flesh anymore" (Phil. 1:23-24). Therefore, the spiritual body of the resurrected is something "unnatural," that is, something beyond the possibilities inherent in the present creation. It will be part of a new creation with new possibilities.

7. For another anticipating glimpse, see Romans 6, esp. v. 4: since Christ was raised, Christians in their moral behavior are capable of "walking in newness of life" already in the present, although their own resurrection remains a strictly future event (vv. 5 and 8). 2 Cor. 4:10b and 11b also seem to talk about a foreshadowing of the future resurrection. These verses probably are to be interpreted in parallel to the immediately preceding vv. 8-9 and to v. 16. Then they refer to the present favors God bestows on the apostle: God encourages him so that he does not lose heart and is being renewed every day. This loving care of God makes the "life of Jesus" manifest "in our bodies" and "in our mortal flesh" already now, although the resurrection itself remains a future event (4:14).

8. Maybe because their sciences are deeply rooted in a culture influenced by the Judeo-Christian world of thought?

Paul uses images to depict this difference in quality. Illustrating with the imagery of seeds and fully grown plants in 1 Corinthians 15:36-38, the apostle tries to answer the question about "with *what kind* of body" the deceased will be raised. He plays on a note of Greek culture when picking up the imagery of grain and sowing. The pagan Corinthian environment cultivated a strong religious interest in the world of the dead and its deities. In the Corinthian Demeter cult, for example, the dying Persephone became more and more prominent. Persephone, Demeter's daughter and the goddess of Hades, represented not only the dying vegetation but also human mortal destiny. And as dying vegetation is always revived in the circle of nature in the spring, humans also may hope for immortality. Demeter, the goddess of the grain-bearing earth, cared for more than the seeds of grain in the fields. The crowds of deceased humans also belonged to her "seeds." These human seeds of Demeter, called *demetrians* by Plutarch (*Moralia* 943b), thus may hope for revitalization.

This is a glimpse into the cultural milieu in which Paul spoke his verses about dying and reviving seeds. This imagery was neither particularly Pauline nor Christian. It evoked associations in the Corinthians' minds that differed from ours. Paul met his Hellenistic readers with cultural presuppositions familiar to them. At the same time he modified this imagery by integrating it into a particularly Christian frame. For him, resurrection had no cyclical aspects at all, as the linear eschatological timetable in 15:23-28 shows. The Jewish and Christian faiths, based on the Old Testament, stress the linear perspective of history and deemphasize the religious significance of nature's cycles — contrary to many other religions. Moreover, the only basis for all hopes for revitalization is Christ, raised by God (see, e.g., 15:23-28).

What did Paul learn from the imagery of grain and sowing? "What you sow does not come to life unless it *dies*" (15:36). This underscores the future, postmortem aspect of the resurrection and the discontinuity. You sow "a *bare* seed, perhaps of wheat or of some other grain." "You do not sow the body that is to be." "God gives a body as he has chosen" (15:37-38). Thus, we again learn that bodily resurrection does not mean a simple return to the earthly conditions of the past. It does not entail a restoration or revivification of our present flesh, blood, and bones. Our present earthly body will not see eternity (15:50).

What positively can be learned from the imagery of seeds and grain? For Paul, the postresurrection body will transcend the earthly body in the same way that a beautiful, intricate plant transcends the plain seed of grain from which it grows. There is an enormous leap in quality from the bare seed to the full-grown plant. Analogously, there will be a huge leap in quality from the earthly person to the postresurrection person, or, as verse 44 words it, from the "physical body" to the "spiritual body."

First Corinthians 15:39-49 illustrates the same idea. The examples in verses 39-41, taken from creation, try to make plausible that two qualitatively different "bodies" can exist side by side (the flesh of humans differs from that of animals and from that of birds and fish; celestial bodies and terrestrial bodies are different; so are the glory of the sun, the moon, and the stars). The underlying thought runs like this: if these quality differences are possible *within* the *present* cosmos, they are all the more likely between the present and the future eschatological realities. The distinctions listed in verses 42-44 (perishable versus imperishable, dishonor versus glory, weakness versus power) emphasize the immense difference in quality between the two "bodies," that is, between the preresurrection and postresurrection human being.

Verses 45-49 illustrate the same difference in quality by picking up the Adam-Christ typology and its category of "corporate representation." Adam represents our earthly selves; we bear "the image of the man of dust." The resurrected Christ represents our future, heavenly selves; "we will bear the image of the man of heaven." Thus the difference in quality between my preresurrection and postresurrection existence will be as huge as the difference between Adam and Christ.

Surely, there is continuity between the seed and the full-grown plant. However, two important things happen in between: the *dying* of the seed and an act of *creation* by God (15:38). Our whole perishable person will be transformed (*metaschēmatizō*, Phil. 3:21) into a new and imperishable heavenly personality that will be qualitatively different from our first. It will be — thank God — much better! This transformation, called "resurrection," will be a new and powerful act of creation by the sovereign God (compare also Rom. 4:17).

What Does Paul Mean by "Spiritual" or "Pneumatic" Body (1 Cor. 15:44)?

The word "spiritual" — and this may come as a disappointment to modern readers — does not say anything about the material or energetic structure of this new body. It does not try to describe a *Lichtleib*, some sort of concentration of light or other energy. Nor does it convey that this new body is composed of miniature particles of matter, as the Stoics would have described the *pneuma* (spirit). All this would be misunderstanding Paul, who refrains from such speculations and stays with simple metaphors.

For him, the term "spiritual" emphasizes that God's Spirit is the *only* force that creates the new body. The creation of this new body is totally *beyond* all the possibilities of the present nature and creation. That is all that Paul wants to convey with this term. Therefore, I do not see how the natural sciences could help us to understand the totally different "nature" of this future body — unless natural science were able to transcend the nature of this universe.

Paul asserts that our spiritual body will be very similar, even "conformed" *(symmorphon),* to that of the resurrected Christ (Phil. 3:21). But he refrains from giving further details, which later evangelists pretend to "know" by describing the resurrected Christ.[9] The apostle only affirms that our spiritual body "in heaven" will be a "body of glory" as opposed to the "body of lowliness" in which we now live (Phil. 3:20-21).

For Paul, Christ's resurrection included his elevation to a position of Lordship and sovereignty over "every authority and power," even death.[10] Correspondingly, Christians after their resurrection will participate in Christ's heavenly glory and reign (1 Cor. 4:8),[11] although they will not be elevated to quite the same majesty as the risen Christ (15:23-27).

This Christocentrism of the early Christians' hope for resurrection is crucial. Since God raised Christ from the dead, and since Christ is the representative of a whole new aeon, all people of this new aeon — Christians (1 Cor. 15:23b) — will also be raised by God. The hope for resurrection is anchored exclusively in the Christ event. Paul therefore talks only about the resurrection of "those who belong to Christ" (15:23). He does not speculate whether or not non-Christians will be raised. This remains an open question in Paul's writings (also in 2 Cor. 5:10; Rom. 2:16, contrary to Daniel 12, for instance).

Is this all that we can say about Paul's concept of the "spiritual body"? We can be a little more specific about one particular point. God's Spirit *(pneuma),* which is the only force that creates the new spiritual *(pneumatic)* body, *already dwells in Christians now* (Rom. 8:9–11:23). This pneumatological statement presents an interesting piece of realized eschatology — in spite of all the emphasis on the future aspect of resurrection, the external force that *will* resurrect us *is* already *in* us. However, although perceived as a force inherent in the Christian, the *pneuma* is not a human force, not an anthropological

---

9. According to Luke 24:43, e.g., the resurrected body of Christ can consume fish!

10. Cf., e.g., Rom. 15:24-27; 1 Cor. 1:4. Only later Christians began to differentiate between resurrection and ascension to heavenly power as two separate events (Luke 24; Acts 1).

11. The Corinthians mistakenly assumed that they were ruling with Christ already in the *present.* This is what Paul contests in 4:8, not the idea of ruling itself.

factor of the natural person, but given to him or her as a gift of grace. This inherent and at the same time external force will overcome death and revive the person to eternal life.

Continuity

If there is so much discontinuity, do we have to go by the *Ganz Tod* theory, according to which the entire person dies? Continuity then would be guaranteed only by God's memory: God remembers me and therefore can re-create me in new ways. According to Paul, things are more complicated than that because more factors of continuity are involved.

Paul describes the status of a deceased person *before* the eschatological resurrection of the dead as that of not being in the physical body anymore but as "being with Christ." It is a status for which Paul is longing (2 Cor. 5:8; Phil. 1:23-24; cf. 2 Cor. 5:6). He does not specify this status, which Luke will do later.[12] Nevertheless, we gain several important insights from these Pauline passages.

Even Paul espouses a certain dichotomy after all: a separation of the physical body and the self, the "me," during this temporary stage after death and before resurrection. In order to verbalize the "me," Paul simply uses personal pronouns and not terms such as "spirit" or "soul."

The most important information we get about this intermediate stage is that the "me" is "with Christ" *(syn Christō)* — not "in his memory" or anything like that. *Syn Christō* is a relational term. The existence of the "me" in this intermediate stage is stripped of any substance. It is stripped of the old physical body, which decays in the grave, *and* it has not received the new spiritual body yet. In other words, it is stripped naked (regardless of how we want to interpret 2 Cor. 5:3). Thus, the "me" of this stage *cannot* be described in substantial terms.

The existence of the "me" during this intermediate stage can only be described in *relational* terms. In fact, the "me" is reduced to *a single* relation; it is reduced to the *syn Christō,* to being "with Christ." Paul describes this reduced relational existence as "sleeping," again using a metaphor.[13] Was the idea of sleep and rest the reason why he yearned for this status? Was he longing for rest from all his apostolic troubles? Or did he expect to "see" Christ already during this stage? He did not go into these details. Maintaining his Christocentrism, he was totally content to state: I will be with Christ after my

---

12. See below, and also the essay by Prof. H.-J. Eckstein in this volume.
13. Cf. 1 Cor. 7:39; 11:30; 15:18, 51; 1 Thess. 4:14.

individual death, even much closer to Christ than was possible during my pre-mortal, physical existence (2 Cor. 5:6). This is the only thing that matters, and I do not care *how* this will take place.

The mode is irrelevant. In this intermediate stage, the lack of a body and the lack of relations except for one go hand in hand. For Paul, a multitude of relations apparently requires bodily existence. Thus Paul has not only two but rather *three* stages or qualities of life in mind: a premortal life, a postmortem but preresurrection stage, and a postresurrection eternal life. The second phase can be described only in terms of a relational ontology.[14]

If we combine our passages here with Romans 8:11, which was quoted earlier (God's Spirit already dwells in us *before* our death), then we may conclude that the dormant postmortem *syn Christō* status will also be surrounded by this divine *pneuma*, this force through which God will resurrect the deceased and create anew. Interestingly enough, in 2 Corinthians 3:16-17 the *pneuma* is even *identified* with Christ as *kyrios*. In other words, to be *syn Christō* specifically means to be with the *pneuma*, God's life-giving power.

One might be tempted to interpret the *syn Christō* of the intermediate stage also in other ways. To be "with Christ" could possibly mean to be with the future eschatological judge. The *syn Christō* relation then would imply that the "me" is still encumbered with its past and its shortcomings; the "me" remains responsible and awaits the final judgment. On the other hand, to be "with Christ" could mean to be with the redeemer. However, Paul does not spell out such specifications of the intermediate *syn Christō* relation. They might suit the systematic theologian, but not the exegete.

The reason that Paul insists that his "me" or "self" will be separated from his physical body at the moment of his death[15] seems to lie in his ecstatic experiences. In 2 Corinthians 12:2-4, a highly important text because it is our only firsthand autobiographical account of such an experience from the Second Temple period, he reports: "I know a person in Christ who fourteen years ago — whether in the body *(sōma)* I do not know, or out of the body I do not know, God knows — was snatched up[16] to the third heaven. And I know that such a person — whether in the body or apart from the body I do not know; God knows — was snatched up into Paradise." As in 2 Corinthians 5:6 and 1 Corinthians 5:3, *sōma* here denotes the present physical body

14. An analogy for the three qualities of life can be found in biotic systems, described by Prof. Schloss in this volume.

15. Differently, e.g., Daniel 12. See above, n. 3.

16. The same term is used as in 1 Thess. 4:17, where the eschaton is described! For the "third heaven" and "Paradise" cf., e.g., 2 *Enoch* 8. According to this text, God can be seen in this heavenly place when "taking a walk" there and "taking a rest" under the tree of life.

in which the self "lives" as in a dwelling (2 Cor. 5:1, 6). According to Paul, the self *can* already leave this dwelling in premortal ecstatic experiences.[17]

We would like to know more about Paul's concept of an intermediate stage, but he refrains from further speculations and specifications. He left this to later generations. Luke, for example, used the Hellenistic and dichotomous categories of the human spirit *(pneuma)* and the physical body in order to depict the intermediate stage more clearly. He thinks along these lines: the dying Jesus committed his *pneuma* into the hands of the Father, so that at the moment of his death, it left the physical body and was welcomed into paradise. Only the physical body was buried. Christ's resurrection then meant that his *pneuma* and physical body were reunited on Easter Sunday.[18] Paul was not yet so specific. According to Romans 8, the *pneuma* dwelling in Christians is *not* human but external and divine.

The Question of the Empty Tomb

Now let us ask: Was there an empty tomb at Easter, and will there be empty graves at the eschaton? For Luke and the other evangelists, the answer was Yes. During the resurrection, the physical body is "snatched up" from the grave and transformed. An empty tomb is left behind.

Paul was less clear in this respect. Already at the moment of death, his "me" will be with Christ. At the moment of his individual death, the "me" will be "stripped" of the physical body (2 Cor. 5:3-4) and will be "naked" until the moment of resurrection, when it will be "dressed" with a new body, which will be vastly different in quality from the first physical body. Then "we will not be found naked" anymore (cf. 2 Cor. 5:3). Thus, the present physical body will be "destroyed" and replaced with an eternal one of heavenly origin (2 Cor. 5:1).[19] All of these mainly metaphorical statements do not necessarily

---

17. Cf. also 1 Cor. 5:3: Paul physically *(sōmati)* is in Ephesus, while at a decisive moment he mentally *(pneumati)* is present in Corinth, excommunicating somebody in Corinth "as if" he were physically present. This is not a dramatic ecstatic split of the person into physical and mental existence; it is just an everyday experience. But it foreshadows the split that happens in the moment of death.

18. See Luke 23:42-43, 46, 55; 24:3, 23, 39-43; and cf. Ignatius, *Ad Smyrnaeos* 3; Justin, *Dialogue* 80:5. In late medieval times, William of Ockham, e.g., taught that between death and bodily resurrection souls are able to see God's glory. However, the perfect vision of God will not be possible until after the resurrection and the final judgment, when the soul is given a body again (*Dialogus* 2; Dr. Annette Weissenrieder, Heidelberg, kindly pointed me to this reference).

19. I translate 5:2-4 in this way: In the present body "we groan, longing to be further

presuppose an opening of graves and a transformation of remnants of physical bodies into these new heavenly bodies. The spiritual body of the resurrection can be created *with or without* transformed particles of the old one! For Paul, this question seems to be irrelevant. Only later theologians, such as Luke and the other evangelists, decided that they needed to know more at this particular point. Nevertheless, are there clues that Paul may have leaned in one direction or the other?

(a) 1 Thessalonians 4:17 and 1 Corinthians 15:51-54 consider those persons who will still be alive at the time of the eschatological *parousia*. In this particular case, the physical bodies — with all their energy and particles of matter — will be "snatched up . . . in the clouds to meet the Lord in the air," and in that moment they will be "swallowed up by life" (cf. 1 Cor. 15:54; 2 Cor. 5:4) and "transformed" (1 Cor. 15:52) into the new resurrection existence, so that those who are raised and those who are still living at the time of the *parousia* will not be distinguishable from one another anymore (cf. 1 Thess. 4:15). The analogy between these two groups might point us in the direction that Paul indeed had in mind, that in the resurrection process energy and particles of matter were also taken from the graves and "snatched up," "swallowed up," and "transformed" into the new heavenly body.[20] The tombs then would be empty.

(b) In 1 Corinthians 6, Paul argues that God will resurrect the Christian's physical body, and therefore, he concludes, one should not defile this body by playing around with prostitutes. This nexus between ethics and the concept of resurrection seems to hint at some kind of continuity between the present physical body and the totally transformed resurrection body — in spite of all discontinuity.

---

clothed with our dwelling from heaven in addition (to our present body); being clothed we will not be found naked" . . . "we groan, being burdened, because we do not want to be unclothed but to be further clothed, so that what is mortal will be swallowed up by life." These sentences do not attempt to present eschatological "facts." They describe human longing. Human beings long to be "further clothed" in their heavenly body. They do not want the present body to die and to be separated from them, but they want it to be "swallowed up" by the new body. However, this is an unrealistic hope for most people because most Christians die before the resurrection; they *are* unclothed and stripped naked in death. Only a few will be living in their present bodies when Christ comes again. They, indeed, will not be stripped but "further clothed" with their heavenly body, while the present physical body will be transformed (*metaschēmatizō*, Phil 3:21; *allassō*, 1 Cor. 15:51) and "swallowed up" by the new life. 1 Thess. 4:17 describes this transfiguration of the still living: "Then we who are alive and remain will be snatched up . . . in the clouds to meet the Lord in the air, and so we shall always be with the Lord" (see also 1 Cor. 15:51-52).

20. Cf. also possibly the *pantes* in 1 Cor 15:51: not all die, but "all" will be transformed, both those who will still be alive *and* those who will be raised.

(c) The oldest certain Jewish statements about an eschatological resurrection of the dead presuppose empty tombs. Daniel 12:2, for example, reads: "Many of those who sleep in the dust of the earth will awake, some to everlasting life, and some to . . . everlasting contempt." Although the apocalyptic author from the 160s before Christ does not specifically say it, he surely presupposes empty graves in this statement. Therefore, one could argue that Paul hardly deviated from this Jewish tradition. On the other hand, however, we could argue that Paul *did* deviate in a Hellenistic manner from Daniel 12:2 in that he could distinguish between a person's self and the physical body — which the author of the book of Daniel was unable to do. The apostle also differed from Daniel 12 by avoiding the notion of a resurrection "to everlasting contempt." Why couldn't Paul also deviate in an additional aspect? Again, Paul leaves us with a *non liquet* in matters unimportant to him.

Conclusion

In summary, a person's "self," his or her "me," continues to exist throughout death and resurrection.[21] God carries it through three stages of life. Temporarily, between individual death and resurrection, the self exists even without a "body," without the first physical one, which is stripped off in death, and without the future spiritual one, which will be given at the resurrection. Paul calls this status "sleep." Later Hellenistic theologians were ready to define this self as an immortal nucleus within us, whether a divine spark, as the Gnostics described, or an immortal spirit or soul.

Paul, however, avoids all these terms. He stays with simple personal pronouns. The "me," the self, continues to exist as a relational entity between death and resurrection. But Paul does not spell out in detail *how*. His renunciation of detailed speculations is impressive — especially considering all the related speculative concepts that abounded in the Hellenistic world. Maybe we should learn to appreciate this kind of "theological asceticism," which abstains from trying to take all mysteries from God. All ecumenical dialogues would benefit from such humility.

God is *faithful*, and we will be *with Christ*. These two promises are the only consolation a dying person really needs to know about his or her immediate future.

---

21. Among the texts quoted, see esp. 2 Cor. 5:1-4 with its personal pronouns and its metaphors of unclothing and clothing of the self.

Bodily Resurrection in Luke

HANS-JOACHIM ECKSTEIN

The reports of Jesus' empty grave, and his subsequent appearances as one who had been raised physically from the dead, are inclined to seem particularly offensive these days. It is nevertheless the case that it is precisely these two traditions that are presupposed in all four New Testament Gospels as fundamental to faith. Certainly, the records differ concerning the persons who, with Mary Magdalene, discovered the empty tomb on Easter morning;[1] and, as is well known, the accounts of Jesus' resurrection appearances presuppose a number of different recipients, places, and circumstances.[2] It is indisputable, however, that all four Gospels unanimously testify that Jesus of Nazareth was crucified and buried and rose on the third day from the dead, and that for this reason his mortal body was no longer to be found in his grave on Easter morning.

In the face of this consistent combination of motifs of "bodily resurrection" and "empty grave," the first question that confronts the exegete is not: How *full* can the grave be without *emptying* faith in the resurrection? Nor is it: How can the testimony of the empty grave be assessed and explained plau-

---

1. Was Mary Magdalene all by herself (John 20) or was she accompanied by other women (Mark 16; Matthew 28; Luke 24)? Did Peter also go to the empty grave after the women's testimony (Luke 24:34)? Was he alone or in the company of this unnamed disciple, who in the Gospel of John is called the disciple "whom Jesus loved" (John 20:1ff.)?

2. Places of appearance: (1) Jerusalem (Matt 28:9-10; Luke 24/Acts 1; John 20); (2) Galilee (Mark 16:7 par. Matt. 28:7, 16); (3) Damascus (Gal. 1:15-17; cf. Acts 9:22-26) — (a) at the grave (John 20:19-26); (b) on the way (Matt. 28:9-10; Luke 24:13-15); (c) at the disciples' gathering (Luke 24:36ff. [*esthē en mesō autōn*]; John 20:19-26 [*ēlthen ho Iēsous kai estē eis to meson*]); (d) on the mountain (Matt. 28:16-17); in the open air at Bethany (Luke 24:50-51; Acts 1:3ff.).

sibly according to historical criteria? His or her first task is to address, on the basis of the texts, a more basic issue: Why is it so important for all the Gospel writers to record that the grave of the Risen One was *empty*? And why did not or could not the early Christians combine their faith in the continuous living and working of their crucified Lord with the concept that his dead body had decayed in the grave?

The Physical Resurrection in the Synoptics

If, in order to answer these questions, we concentrate specifically on the Gospel of Luke among the Synoptic Gospels, then that is for two crucial reasons. First, Luke's reports of the resurrection appearances strike us as particularly heavy-handed and, for modern sensibilities, clearly very provocative. Second, Luke contains at the same time some remarkably subtle anthropological notions of the continued existence of the dead in the heavenly realm and of physical resurrection, that is, of the relationship between the body and identity.[3]

In its original version, the Gospel of Mark presumably ended with the commissioning of the women by the angels, and thus contained no extensive account of the appearances of the Risen One to his disciples in Galilee. With Jesus' earlier promise in Mark 14:28 and the angel's reminder at the empty grave in 16:7, of course, the oldest Gospel leaves its readers in no doubt that the disciples will see the bodily risen Christ there; but the portrayal of the particulars is apparently not considered part of the description of the "beginning of the gospel of Jesus Christ" (Mark 1:1).

If Matthew, on the other hand, offers us additional, detailed accounts of the appearances of the Risen One to the women on their way back from the tomb (Matt. 28:9-10) and to the eleven disciples on the mountain in Galilee (Matt. 28:16-20), his main interest is nevertheless in the theological significance of the so-called "Great Commission," in which the disciples receive their final teaching on the authority of the Risen One as well as on the goal and content of their own authoritative commissioning. The Risen One overcomes his disciples' doubts with his *word* (Matt. 28:17-18) and settles the open questions with his authoritative *instruction*. In this way, the conclusion of the Gospel becomes for Matthew the hermeneutical key to the whole account of

3. On all this see H.-J. Eckstein, "Die Wirklichkeit der Auferstehung Jesu: Lukas 24:34 als Beispiel früher formelhafter Zeugnisse," in *Die Wirklichkeit der Auferstehung: Biblische Zeugnisse und heutiges Erkennen*, ed. H.-J. Eckstein and M. Welker (Neukirchen-Vluyn: Neukirchener, 2001), 1-20.

Jesus' teaching and work that has gone before; and the words of the Risen One serve the church as a criterion for the assessment of controversial traditions.[4]

The third Synoptic Gospel also knows of the significance of the teaching of the Risen One. Nowhere else is the instruction of the resurrection witnesses by Christ himself described in as much detail as in the two Lukan writings. Whether on the way to Emmaus (Luke 24:25-27, 32), in front of the disciples gathered in Jerusalem (Luke 24:44-47), or during the forty days until his ascension (Acts 1:3ff.), the Risen One proves himself to be alive by opening the Holy Scriptures to his disciples and teaching them how his suffering and his resurrection are connected. Nevertheless, Luke distinguishes himself among the Synoptics by relating this teaching and knowledge explicitly to the truth and reality of the *bodily* resurrection of Jesus — according to the central and fundamental confession in Luke 24:34: "The Lord has risen indeed [i.e., truly, really], and he has appeared to Simon."

But why, in order to prove the physical nature of the resurrection, does Luke fall back on such concrete and drastic motifs and traditions, which in the history of research have given rise not only to objection but also to a number of misunderstandings? The Risen One encounters two men who are discussing the puzzling event of the crucifixion on the road to Emmaus, in human form, and accompanies them on their way. He stops at their place in the evening, sits down with them at table until they finally recognize him as their Lord in the giving of thanks and the breaking of the bread, and he disappears from their sight again (Luke 24:13-35). When later Jesus appears among the gathered disciples, he explicitly urges those who are afraid and full of doubt to look at his hands and feet and literally "grasp" him as bodily risen (*psēlaphēsate me*, 24:39). When because of joy they are unable to believe what they have seen and are amazed, he has his disciples give him a piece of fried

---

4. Those controversial questions, which are supposed to find "final" clarification for the Matthean church from the conclusion of the Gospel, are, e.g., the problem of the legitimacy of Christian mission among Gentiles and how Gentiles are reckoned among the "people of God," the controversial issue of the relationship between Jesus' instructions and Moses' Torah, and the clarification of the risen Christ's authority compared to that of "Moses and the prophets." What can serve the disciples as orientation in their teaching of those whom they "make disciples"? What can take the place of circumcision as initiation into the church of Jesus Christ? And what characterizes the life of a Christian in similarity to and difference from his or her previous life? On this cf. H.-J. Eckstein, "Die Weisung Jesu Christi und die Tora des Mose nach dem Matthäusevangelium," in *Jesus Christus als die Mitte der Schrift: Studien zur Hermeneutik des Evangeliums,* ed. C. Landmesser, H.-J. Eckstein, and H. Lichtenberger, Beihefte zur Zeitschrift für die neutestamentliche Wissenschaft 86 (Berlin, 1997), 379-403.

fish and eats it in front of their eyes (Luke 24:41-43: . . . *kai labōn enōpion autōn ephagen*).[5] Does not all this amount to a materialistic misinterpretation of the eschatological reality of the resurrection — as if the Risen One had been raised back into his *old* physical nature? Does not Luke presuppose by this that the one who was raised from the dead remains tied to space, time, and matter and dependent on drink and food like all mortals?

Luke and Dichotomous Anthropology

The answer is given by Luke himself in the course of his description. The Gentile Christian evangelist knows of his Hellenistic readers' dichotomous image of the human being according to which human beings consist of a mortal, transient body and an eternal spirit *(pneuma)* or immortal soul *(psychē)*.[6] Given this philosophical presupposition, the unique mystery of the eschatological resurrection of the Crucified One on the third day, for which there is simply no analogy, cannot be made sufficiently clear by the mere mention of appearances in front of the disciples alone. Could they not just as easily be interpreted as the appearances of the spirit of someone who was violently put to death and now wanders around restlessly? The disciples themselves — according to Luke's account — at first react to the appearance of Jesus with shock and fear and believe they are seeing a *spirit* (*edokoun pneuma theōrein*, Luke 24:37).

Both the invitation to "grasp" the resurrection body and especially the demonstrative eating of the fish in front of the resurrection witnesses serve to counter the misinterpretation of the appearance of the Lord as that of a "ghost." This is because, according to ancient understanding, a ghost can neither eat nor drink, and it does not have a material body that can be touched. For this reason Jesus, according to Luke 24:39, explicitly urges his disciples, "Touch me and see; for a ghost does not have flesh and bones as you see that I have."

It is evident that in a Hellenistic environment the emphasis on the *empty grave* and the demonstration of the *physical nature* of Jesus' resurrection are intended to resist the likely misunderstanding that Jesus' body (*to*

---

5. Many later manuscripts (which follow the *Koine* text) add to 24:42, "and from a honeycomb" *(kai apo melissiou Kyriou),* which may have to do with the use of honey in the celebration of the Eucharist, a tradition that finds evidence in the ancient church.

6. For description and discussion cf. P. Hoffmann, "Auferstehung I/3, II/1," *Theologische Realenzyklopädie* 4 (Berlin u.a., 1979), 450-67, 478-513, esp. 461-63, 503-5.

sōma autou, 23:55; 24:3-23) might have remained in the grave and therefore in death, while only his spirit (*pneuma*, Luke 23:46) or soul (*psychē*, Acts 2:27 par. Ps. 16[15]:10) had appeared several times and ultimately ascended to God. On the other hand, Luke in no way presupposes that Jesus had returned to his previous, earthly life and to his *old* physical nature, as he can report of the widow's son in Nain (Luke 7:11ff.) and Jairus's daughter (Luke 8:40ff.), of Tabitha (Acts 9:36ff.), and Eutychus (Acts 20:7ff.).[7] On the contrary, the Risen One in his new identity can apparently take on human form and allow himself to be recognized, without being principally or always recognizable to the human eye as such; he is able to appear perceptibly in space and time but also to withdraw in order to ascend physically to his Father into the heavenly realm in front of the witnesses' eyes, and by this be hidden from their sight for the last time (Luke 24:50-53; Acts 1:6-11; cf. v. 9: *blepontōn autōn epērthē kai nephelē hypelaben auton apo tōn ophthalmōn autōn*).

As far as this is concerned, Luke advocates a very subtle concept of "body and identity." To the disciples, the Risen One shows the scars on his hands and feet so that they recognize him as their crucified Lord: "Look at my hands and my feet; see that it is I myself" (. . . *hoti egō, eimi autos*, 24:39). And the disciples on the road to Emmaus identify Jesus at the particular moment when he, as so often before, breaks bread in front of their eyes with a blessing and hands it to them (Luke 24:30-31). The identification of the person takes place through the demonstration of *continuity!* At the same time, however, the reality of the resurrection is described by Luke in a pointed *contrast* to the old physical nature: the Risen One no longer suffers, is not mortal, and is not subject to transience; he is not restricted to space and time, and he is not rooted in this world; rather, he is depicted as living in the heavenly world. The new reality of this resurrection implies such a fundamental transformation that the disciples do not recognize their Lord after the resurrection as the one they have known; instead, they identify him first of all and for the first time as the Risen One. Therefore the identity of the risen Lord cannot be grasped without recognizing the *dis-*

---

7. Concerning Jairus's daughter, Luke expressly talks about the *return* of the deceased's *pneuma: kai epestrepsen to pneuma kai anestē parachrēma* (Luke 8:55). And, according to Acts 20:10, Paul states that the *soul* had not left dead Eutychus for good (*mē thorybeisthe hē gar psychē autou en autō estin*). Cf. the raising of Lazarus (John 11:1ff.) and already in Old Testament traditions (1 Kings 17:17ff.; 2 Kings 4:31ff.; 13:20ff.). The account in Matt. 27:52-53 that many saints were rising from their graves is more difficult to assess (*kai ta mnēmeia aneō chthēsan kai polla sōmata tōn kekoimēmenōn hagiōn ēgerthēsan*) in the context of Jesus' crucifixion and resurrection. Does Matthew think of an anticipation of the eschatological, bodily resurrection of some individuals who then "appear" in analogy to their Lord in front of many in Jerusalem (*kai enephanisthēsan pollois*)?

continuity of his physical existence. On the other hand, the reality of the Risen One cannot be understood detached from the identity of the Crucified and without the *continuity* of his life for God and his disciples.

In Jesus' invitation in Luke 24:39, "See . . . that it is I myself" *(idete . . . hoti egō, eimi autos)*, insight into this complex identity of the Risen One is in no way presupposed as natural, but is instead first disclosed to human beings and spoken to them in such a way that it leads to insight. Thus Luke also testifies that the eyes of the Emmaus disciples in Luke 24:31-32 first have to be opened by the Risen One so that they can recognize him as such *(autōn de diēnoichthēsan hoi ophthalmoi kai epegnōsan auton)*. "Were not our hearts burning within us while he was talking to us on the road, while he was opening the scriptures to us?" (24:32).

Luke on Jesus' Spirit

Now if Luke takes the dichotomous image of humans prevalent in his environment into consideration on the one hand, but deviates from all non-Jewish-Hellenistic concepts by labeling the resurrection reality of Jesus "physical" on the other, this raises the question of the detailed realization of his concept of "spirit and body" and of his idea of the "bodily" resurrection of Jesus. As it turns out, in the Gospel as well as in Acts, Luke develops his christological and anthropological convictions in a thoroughly consistent and firm manner. Taking up the anthropological dichotomy with its Hellenistic distinction of "body" *(sōma)* and "spirit" *(pneuma)*, Luke tells us that Jesus on the cross hands his *pneuma* over to his Father while his mortal body dies. In allusion to Psalm 31 (30):5, the dying Jesus cries out in a loud voice: "'Father, into your hands I commend my spirit.' Having said this, he breathed his last" (literally, "he breathed out his spirit"). *Pater, eis cheiras sou paratithemai to pneuma, mou touto de eipōn exepneusen* (Luke 23:46). Only the dead man's "body" *(sōma)* is then buried, so that the women at the funeral can see how the *sōma* of Jesus is laid in the tomb on the evening of the day of his death *(etheasanto to mnēmeion kai hōs etethē to sōma autou*, Luke 23:55).

Qua pneuma, with his "spirit," Jesus enters into the heavenly paradise immediately after his death — "today" *(sēmeron)*. As he entrusts his spirit to his heavenly Father, he does not lose his communion with God even in death, but instead, *qua pneuma*, reaches the heavenly sphere on the same day on which he died. Only so can it be explained with logical consistency how, according to Luke, Jesus can promise one of the two criminals being crucified with him: "*Today* you will be with me in Paradise" *(Amēn soi legō, sēmeron* met' emou esē *en tō paradeisō*, Luke 23:43). This man, recognizing his own guilt, had just asked him urgently: "Jesus, remember me *when you come into your kingdom*" (23:42). So all of this happens according to Luke's account on the day of death and not later at the moment of bodily resurrection. Even for Jesus this happens on Good Friday — and not later on Easter Sunday![8]

The ascension of the *pneuma* into the heavenly paradise after leaving the earthly *sōma* is also presupposed in Luke's parable of Abraham and Lazarus, since the poor man is seen after his demise in paradisiacal table communion with his progenitor Abraham (Luke 16:23). He is immediately taken by angels into "Abraham's bosom," that is, into heavenly table communion with Abraham (*egeneto de . . . kai apenechthēnai auton hypo tōn angelōn eis ton kolpon Abraam*, Luke 16:22). In Acts 7:59 Luke can also say that Stephen calls upon Jesus at his execution, just as the latter had called to his heavenly Father, and dying asks him to receive his *pneuma*: "Lord Jesus, receive my spirit" (*Kyrie Iēsou dexai to pneuma mou*).

Now for Luke, even with all this, the mystery of Jesus' resurrection on Easter morning has by no means yet been adequately portrayed. For the testimony to the resurrection concerns not only the heavenly reception of the person *qua pneuma*, but rather the transformation of his *sōma* and the reconciliation and redemption of his past "physical" existence. On the third day after his crucifixion, God already did to Jesus what the Old Testament–Jewish — and there specifically apocalyptic — tradition hopes for and expects on the day of God's coming.[9] But while "the righteous" must await the eschatological uniting of spirit and — resurrected and transformed — body, the body of Jesus — as the one truly "righteous" (Luke 23:47) — has already been raised into the eschatological reality out of the grave on the third day. This is why the angels can reproach the women who on Easter morning search in vain for "the *sōma* of the Lord Jesus" in the empty grave (*ouch heuron to sōma tou Kyriou Iēsou*, Luke 24:3; cf. 24:34): "Why do you look for the living among the dead?" (*ti zēteite ton zōnta meta tōn nekrōn*); "He is not here, but has risen" (*ouk estin hōde, alla ēgerthē*, Luke 24:5-6).

That Jesus could in no way be held by the realm of the dead, but instead was to be redeemed from the pain of death in a comprehensive sense by God

---

8. Thus Luke himself obviously would scarcely assume that Jesus had spent the three days between his cross and his bodily resurrection altogether in "Hades," in the underworld. In contrast, see the apocryphal *Gospel of Peter* 41–42 ("Did you preach to those who are fallen asleep?"); cf. 1 Peter 3:19; 4:6; less obvious Eph. 4:8-9.

9. In the history of reception, 1 Sam. 2:6; Job 19:26-27; Isa. 25:8; 26:19; Ezek. 37:1-14; Dan. 12:2-13; Hos. 6:2; 13:14 could be understood as Old Testament references for an eschatological resurrection brought about by God.

through the resurrection is something that Luke finds already predicted in a prophecy of David in Psalm 16(15):10 (Acts 2:22-32); and with this he himself gives an example for the teaching about Jesus' resurrection from Scripture, which is mentioned occasionally. In the christological part of Peter's programmatic "sermon on Pentecost," David's psalm of trust is interpreted as a prophetic announcement of the *bodily* resurrection of Jesus (*proidōn elalēsen peri tēs anastaseōs tou Christou*, Acts 2:31) — even before the decay of his body! God neither wanted to leave Jesus' *soul* to Hades (*ouk enkataleipseis tōn psychēn mou eis Ḥạdēn*, Acts 2:27/Ps. 16[15]:10), nor was even the transient *flesh* of Jesus ever to see decay (*oute enkateleiphthē eis Ḥạdēn oute hē sarx autou eiden diaphthoran*, Acts 2:31). The exuberant joy of the one praying in Psalm 16:9 is grounded in the fact that "his *flesh* will also live in hope" (*eti de kai hē sarx mou kataskēnōsei ep' elpidi*, Acts 2:26).

Now Luke is not only concerned about the formal indication that Jesus' crucifixion and his resurrection from the grave have already been foreseen by Scripture — in the sense of Luke 24:46: "Thus it is written, that the Messiah is to suffer and to rise from the dead on the third day." The reference to the event being in accordance with Scripture implies at the same time that it does not have to be interpreted as contingent or absurd. By proving itself to correspond to the providence and will of God, it can be recognized as *meaningful* and *indispensable*: "Was it not *necessary* that the Christ should suffer these things and then enter into his glory?" (*ouchi tauta edei pathein ton Christon kai eiselthein eis tēn doxan autou*, Luke 24:26; compare 9:22; Acts 17:3). Thus *in our context* the question inevitably arises again, What did Luke — following his traditions and in his own theological assessment — see to be the *meaning* and the *necessity* of the bodily resurrection of Jesus?

Glory beyond Physical Resurrection

Alongside a large number of other christological and soteriological issues, Luke focuses on one thing that he describes variously by means of his so-called "scheme of contrast":[10] humanity rejected and killed Jesus of Nazareth, "the Holy and Righteous One" (Acts 3:14), in whom God himself acted (Acts 2:22). But God confirmed and vindicated him by raising him from the dead and by proving him before the world to be "Lord and Christ" (Acts 2:36), "Leader and Savior" (Acts 5:31). By this, God not only rehabilitated him formally, but showed him effectively to be the "Author of life" (*ton de archēgon tēs zōēs*, Acts

---

10. With this scheme of contrast cf. Acts 2:23-24; 3:15; 4:10; 5:30; 10:39-40; 13:28-30.

3:15) and redeemed him completely from the pain of death (*hon ho theos anestēsen lysas tas ōdinas tou thanatou*, Acts 2:24) so that he can no longer die or decay (*mēketi mellonta hypostrephein eis diaphthoran*, Acts 13:34).[11]

But if God has "exalted" Jesus Christ into his presence and glory — far beyond mere rehabilitation and compensation (Luke 24:26; Acts 2:33; 5:31; cf. 1:6-11), then new life cannot be second to the old one in its fullness and complexity, but can only exceed it. And if the "physical" existence of the earthly Jesus is not characterized negatively, but is in the context of the Old Testament–Jewish theology of creation connoted altogether positively, then for Luke as well as for the other New Testament witnesses it goes without saying that God at Jesus' redemption does not leave the *sōma*, the mortal body, to the reign of death but transforms him physically. If this is true for the "Author of life," the *archēgos tēs zōēs* (Acts 3:15), then for those who follow him and seek their salvation in his name it cannot be described otherwise. The *reality* of the comprehensive resurrection of Jesus assures those who believe in him concerning their own hope of resurrection; and the *physical nature* of Jesus' resurrection from the grave contradicts all reductionist misunderstandings of continuation after death. For Christ was not intended to rise from the dead as the *only one*, but rather as the *first* (*ei prōtos ex anastaseōs nekrōn*, Acts 26:23).

The Greeks in Athens may ridicule the thought of bodily resurrection (Acts 17:18, 22-32), and even Jewish circles like the Sadducees may contradict the hope of resurrection (Luke 20:27ff.; Acts 4:1f.; 23:6ff.); but for Luke this conviction cannot be given up: after they die God does not restrict the paradisiacal communion of those who surrender to him to living *qua pneuma* or *qua psychē*, but they — like Christ before them — will rise finally and comprehensively, that is, "physically" or "bodily."[12] Then, as the resurrected, they will live in reconciled continuity with their complex bodily existence and in liberating discontinuity with their vulnerable and transient body, that is, they will live in fullness.

Admittedly, Luke is not so interested in the question, How *full* can Jesus' grave can be without *emptying* faith in the resurrection? But with an abundance of sophisticated and consistent arguments he answers the question of why, for him — just as for the other Gospel writers — it is so important that Jesus' grave was *empty*.

11. Accordingly, the "children of the resurrection" will be like the angels in "that they cannot die anymore" — *oude gar apothanein eti dynanti, isangeloi gar eisin kai huioi eisin theou tēs anastaseōs huioi ontes* (Luke 20:36).

12. On the resurrection of the dead according to Luke see Luke 14:14; 20:27-39; Acts 4:2; 10:42; 17:18-31; 23:6; 24:14-25; on eternal life Luke 10:25-28; 18:30; 20:38b (*theos de ouk estin nekrōn alla zōntōn· pantes gar autō zōsin*; Acts 13:46-48; cf. 5:20; 11:18.

Resurrection in Ancient Egypt

JAN ASSMANN

"Resurrection" is a Christian term and a Christian idea. To ask for "resurrection" in ancient Egypt smacks of heresy: of the heresy of reducing the Christian kerygma to just a variant of the Near Eastern myth of dying and rising gods, for example, Tammuz, Attis, Adonis, Osiris, and Persephone, behind whose dying and rising we easily discern the rhythms of nature, such as the sprouting and fading of vegetation, the coming and disappearing of the inundation, the growing and decreasing of the moon, and so on. The death and resurrection of Christ happened once and for all; it belongs to the course of history and not of nature, to linear not to cyclical time. To be sure, the Egyptian concept of immortality cannot be separated from these natural associations. We are dealing with a religion of divine immanence where natural processes were regarded as divine manifestations. Yet I hope to be able to show that the Egyptian idea of immortality has quite another origin that has more to do with political than with natural theology. In the frame of this new interpretation, the question of possible connections between Egyptian and Christian ideas of resurrection appears in a different light.

The Binary Structure of the Egyptian Hereafter

As far as human existence is concerned, virtually all the religions of the ancient world around the Mediterranean and in the Near East make the distinc-

---

This chapter is based on my book *Tod und Jenseits im Alten Ägypten* (Munich: C. H. Beck, 2001).

tion between the world of the living and the world of the dead, the upper world and the underworld. There is also the world of the gods, but this does not concern human existence. The underworld or world of the dead is the realm where human beings continue their existence after their life in the upper world. They do not "live on" in this realm, but are dead. Being dead, however, does not mean they disappear from this world altogether, but they pass from the realm of the living to the realm of the dead. "Resurrection," in this context, would mean to return to life in the upper world. This is what Orpheus aspired to achieve with Eurydice and what Jesus achieved with Lazarus, and this is what Ezekiel saw in a vision happening to thousands of dead whose bones left their tombs, were covered with flesh and skin, and returned to the world of the living (Ezekiel 37).

In the context of these religions, ancient Egypt seems to have been the sole exception. Only here, human existence encompassed three worlds, the world of the living, the world of the dead, and an Elysian world for which there are many names and descriptions in Egyptian texts such as "field of rushes," "field of offerings," "bark of millions," and "house of Osiris." Here "resurrection" does not mean to return to life on earth, but to be redeemed from the world of the dead and to be admitted into the Elysian world (I prefer the term "elysium" to the term "paradise," because the latter term has connotations of origin, primordial time, and prelapsarian state that are not present in the Egyptian context). It is this ternary distinction between (a) the world of the living, (b) the world of the dead, and (c) the Elysian world, that in my opinion marks the exceptional structure of ancient Egyptian religion and its concept of immortality. Again, the distinction between the world of the dead and the Elysian world, in order to make this absolutely clear, consists in the fact that the world of the dead is a place where the dead are dead, whereas the Elysium is the place where those who were granted resurrection from death lead a new, eternal life.

In Greece, there are already adumbrations of such an Elysian world, especially in the context of Orphism and the Dionysian mysteries. The Greeks have always related these ideas to ancient Egypt. They believed that Orpheus, Homer, and others had brought these concepts from Egypt. In Egypt, however, the idea of an Elysium has its traditional place in the official cosmology and does not belong to some special cult, but to normal funerary religion. This exceptional structure of Egyptian religion has not been recognized so far. It was generally believed that the ancient Egyptians made the same binary distinction as their neighboring cultures and knew of only two worlds, a world of the living and a world of the dead, the only difference being that they pictured their world of the dead in much more friendly and beautiful colors than did the Babylonians, the Israelites, and the Greeks. The Egyptian Duat was held to be a world of the dead just as Sheol, Hades, Orcus, and the Mesopotamian land of no return, with the only difference being that it showed Elysian traits. This, however, is not correct, as a closer look at the texts shows. Ancient Egypt confronts us with an enormously rich corpus of funerary literature that in its size and complexity is certainly unparalleled in any other ancient or modern civilization. These texts know very well of a world in which the dead are nothing but dead, and they depict this world in rather crass colors. It is a world of inversion where the dead walk upside down and are forced to live on their excrement, a world without light and water, full of demons and monsters. Every living being on earth is doomed to descend into this world, but everybody gets the chance of redemption and resurrection, not in the form of a return to the world of the living but of a passage to the Elysium.

Royal Resurrection and the Myth of Osiris

If we ask for the origins of this division of the hereafter into a realm of the dead and an Elysium, we meet with concepts and structures that belong to political theology: the institution of pharaonic kingship. During the Old Kingdom, the Elysian world was reserved for the king; he alone was able, after death, to fly up to heaven and to join his father, the sun god, and the other gods, whereas ordinary mortals, as we read in the texts, had to "hide" in the earth. Resurrection was an exclusively royal privilege and the distantiation of the royal hereafter from the destiny of nonroyal beings forms the central theme of the Pyramid Texts. The Elysium, therefore, was originally a political concept: it surpassed the world of the dead in the same way as the figure of the pharaoh surpassed the world of the living.

In order to release the deceased king from death and earth, he had to be separated from his own death. The mythical model for this operation was the myth of Osiris. Osiris, a god and a king of Egypt, had been killed by his brother and rival Seth, who, moreover, tore his body apart and scattered his limbs all over Egypt. Isis, the sister and wife of Osiris, traverses Egypt in search of the *membra disiecta* of her brother, reassembling them into the shape of a body. Together with her sister Nephthys she bewails the body in long songs of lamentation using the power of speech as a means of reanimation. Isis and Nephthys were so successful in their reanimating recitations that Isis was able to receive a child from the reanimated body of Osiris. This is the first step toward resurrection.

The appearance of Horus, the son and heir of Osiris, marks the second scene of the myth and initiates the second phase of resurrection. In the same way as Isis and Nephthys are occupied with restoring the body, Horus is occupied with restoring the social personality of Osiris. We meet here a very pronounced gender differentiation. The restoration of the body is a female preoccupation. The means that are utilized in this respect are lamentation, mourning, affective language, and expressions of desire and longing. Everything in this female part of the ritual aims at recollecting the scattered limbs and restoring the dismembered body. Female mourning is concentrated on the bodily sphere of the dead. The restoration of the social sphere of the dead, on the other hand, his status, dignity, honor, and prestige, is constructed as a male preoccupation and the task of the son. Resurrection, thus, has two aspects: a bodily one and a social one. Bodily resurrection overcomes the dismemberment of the body, while social resurrection overcomes the isolation and dishonor of the victim and turns it into a situation of highest status, general recognition, honor, prestige, respect, and majesty.

Bodily resurrection, as effectuated by Isis and Nephthys, uses lamentations and similar spells, in which the enumeration of the various bodily parts from head to foot plays an important role. To quote just one typical example:

> Your head, O my lord, is adorned
> with the tress of a woman of Asia;
> *your face* is brighter than the mansion of the moon.
> Your upper part is lapis lazuli,
> your hair is blacker than all the doors of the netherworld on the day of
>   darkness.
> (. . .) Your visage is covered with gold,
> and Horus has inlaid it with lapis lazuli.
> (. . .) Your nose is in the odor of the place of embalming,
> and your nostrils are like the winds of the sky.
> Your eyes behold the Eastern mountain;
> your eyelashes are firm every day,
> being colored with real lapis lazuli.
> Your eyelids are the bringers of peace,
> and their corners are full of black eye-paint.
> Your lips give you truth and repeat truth to Re
> and make the gods content.
> Your teeth are those of the coiled serpent
> with which the two Horuses play.
> Your tongue is wise,

and sharper is your speech than the cry of the kites in the field.
Your jaw is the jarry sky.[1]

That much for the head alone; the text continues in the same vein for pages and pages until it reaches the feet.

These texts are immediately reminiscent of love poems, to quote only a very ancient and prominent example:

> Behold, thou art fair, my love; behold, thou art fair;
> thou hast doves' eyes within thy locks:
> thy hair is as a flock of goats,
> that appear from mount Gilead.
> Thy teeth are like a flock of sheep that are even shorn,
> which came up from the washing;
> whereof every one bear twins,
> and none is barren among them.
> Thy lips are like a thread of scarlet,
> and thy speech is comely:
> thy temples are like a piece of a pomegranate within thy locks.
> Thy neck is like the tower of David builded for an armory,
> whereon there hang a thousand bucklers, all shields of mighty men.
> Thy two breasts are like two young roes that are twins,
> which feed among the lilies.[2]

The form is also very popular in ancient Egyptian love poetry. With regard to these love poems, Emma Brunner-Traut has attributed to the ancient Egyptians a "dismembering glance." The ancient Egyptians, she holds, were unable to perceive the body and other complex phenomena as a coherent whole. Instead, they arrived at a notion of the whole only by addition, by enumerating the constituent parts. They perceived of the body not as a coherent organism where the various parts are moving in interdependent interaction, but as a mechanical *Gliederpuppe*, a puppet or robot whose members lead a life of their own without interaction, interdependence, and interconnection.[3] This statement, however, seems to me to contain only one half of the truth. It is true that the ancient Egyptians were fond of differentiation and enumeration,

1. Book of the Dead, ch. 172.
2. Song of Songs 4:1-5.
3. See Emma Brunner-Traut, "Der menschliche Körper — Eine Gliederpuppe," in *Zeitschrift für ägyptische Sprache und Altertumskunde* 115 (1988): 8-14 and idem, *Frühformen des Erkennens: Am Beispiel Altägyptens* (Darmstadt, second ed. 1992; third ed., *Frühformen des Erkennens: Aspektive im Alten Ägypten* [Darmstadt, 1996]).

but their main concern was always the "connective" principles that integrate the various parts into a coherent whole. The point is not dismemberment but re-membering. Therefore, instead of calling the Egyptian attitude toward the world "dismembering" or "additive," I would prefer to call it "embalming." They were interested in the parts only in order to join them and to find out the connective principles that bring about their combination. The "embalming look" they were casting on the body led to a kind of "connective physiology." They identified the heart and the blood as such a connective principle and arrived at a theory of circulation more than three thousand years before William Harvey. It is the heart, they said, "which speaks in the vessels," meaning the beat of the pulse. The heart, by pumping the blood through the vessels, combines the limbs, ties them together, and integrates them into a coherent whole, the living body. This living connective device has to be replaced, under the conditions of death, with magic devices such as recitation that integrates the dismembered limbs by enumeration into the coherent structure of a text.

Horus, in his attempts at restoring the social self of his slain father, uses a very different kind of recitations; cf., e.g., spell 371 of the Pyramid Texts:[4]

> O Osiris the king,
> Horus has placed you in the hearts of the gods,
> he has caused you to take possession of all that it yours (or: the white
>   crown, the lady).
> Horus has found you, and it goes well with him through you. . . .
> Go up against your foe, for you are greater than he
> in your name of Pr-wr-shrine.
> Horus has caused him to lift you
> in your name of "Great lifted one."
> He has saved you from your foe, he has protected you
> as one who is protected in due season.

Horus and Osiris are united in the concept of *Ka.* PT 364, a particularly long and significant Horus Text, states: "Horus is not far from you, for you are his Ka." PT 356, another typical Horus Text, closes with an invocation summarizing the roles of deceased father and surviving son in the concept of *Ka:*

> O Osiris the king, Horus has protected you,
> he has acted on behalf of his Ka, who is you,
> so that you may be content in your name of "Contented Ka."

---

4. For an English translation of the Egyptian Pyramid Texts (abbr. "PT") see Raymond O. Faulkner, *The Ancient Egyptian Pyramid Texts* (Oxford, 1969).

The *Ka* is linked to the constellation of father and son; and it bridges the borderline between life and death. The *Ka* is written in hieroglyphs as a pair of arms that are raised as in adoration; in reality, however, they are meant as outstretched in a gesture of embracing. PT spell 1652, for example, states that the creator put his arms around his twin children Shu and Tefnut, in order that his *Ka* may be in them:

> You set your arms about them
> as the arms of the Ka,
> that your Ka might be in them.

This constellation of father and son, one in the hereafter, one in the world of the living, is one of the most fundamental elements of ancient Egyptian culture. The funerary cult is based on the idea that only the son is capable of reaching into the world of the dead and of entering a constellation with his dead father that bridges the threshold of death and that is mutually supportive and life-giving. This is what is meant by the Egyptian word *akh*. A widespread sentence says: *Akh* is a father for his son, *akh* is a son for his father.

This originally mortuary constellation provides the model not only for the mortuary cult but for cult in general. Pharaoh, the only being living on earth capable of entering into communication with the divine world, approaches the gods as their son. In cult, he plays the role of the living son vis-à-vis his dead fathers and mothers. Filial piety is the basic religious attitude toward the gods.

Horus restores the social personality of his dead father Osiris by overcoming his isolation and his dishonor. He assembles the gods around Osiris and takes care that they are not allowed to escape and to leave him alone. He makes the gods recognize Osiris as their overlord and to give him honor. He restores honor and dignity to Osiris by humiliating his enemy, who is forced to carry Osiris. All these various ritual actions concern the social self as opposed to the bodily self.

The various actions of Horus for Osiris that in the Egyptian language are subsumed under the verb *nedj* (with a broad range of applications stretching from protection to revenge) culminate in a scene where Osiris is restored to life to such a degree as to be able to confront his murderer, Seth. Seth, in this confrontation, represents death, while Osiris represents the victim of death, the dead. This form of decomposing complex experiences seems to me one of the particular achievements of the mythical modeling of reality. By personifying death in the figure of Seth, death is made "treatable." It can be brought to court, accused, and sentenced. The justice that has been violated by the murder committed by Seth can be restored. In the view of this mythology, there is no natural death. Every death is a crime that must be vindicated, and the ritual treatment of death culminates in the enactment of this vindication. There is guilt behind every death, and this guilt has to be removed in order to restore the deceased to status and position in society. Every death is murder and injustice. Therefore, it can be "healed" in a way by punishing the murderer and restoring justice. Osiris has defeated Seth, which means that he has vanquished death.

Thus death becomes in a way objectified and treatable. Osiris is given full justice against Seth, that is, death. He cannot be restored to life upon earth, but he is given life in the other world as he is reintegrated into cosmic existence. The mythical Osiris was made ruler of the netherworld and king of the dead. The dead king follows his example. He is called Osiris and takes his place on his throne in order to rule the dead and the spirits, while his son Horus takes his place on his former throne among the living. This is the meaning of resurrection in the Old Kingdom. It is the exclusive privilege of the pharaoh. *Resurrection* is a proper term for this idea because the dead king is constantly summoned to "rise." "Raise yourself" *(wtz tw)* is the typical address to the deceased, and it means not only to get up but to ascend to heaven.

The myth of Osiris is, at least as far as its "core meaning" is concerned, not about the cycles of nature, the seed that is buried in order to sprout again, the waxing and the waning moon, the rising and the falling inundation, but about kingship. Osiris is first of all a king. The lawsuit with Seth is about the throne of Egypt. The myth of Osiris is first of all about kingship, in the second place about death and resurrection, and only in a rather peripheral and associative way about nature and cyclical time. It is the Egyptian myth of the state.

The Demotion and Moralization of Resurrection

With the fall of the Old Kingdom, however, the royal hereafter and the mythical model of resurrection became extended to all human beings. Due to this process of demotion, the distinction between "realm of the dead" and "Elysium" lost its political meaning and became a matter of moralization. Not the divine quality of royal office, but the virtue and justice of a deceased person were now believed to be the conditions and prerequisites of resurrection and immortality. Therefore, the lawsuit and the idea of justification change their meaning in a very fundamental way. The dead no longer has to be justified "against" death as a murderer but "before" a divine tribunal, and the guilt that is inherent in death is no longer externalized in the form of a scapegoat, Seth, but is interpreted as the deceased's own guilt, which he has accumulated during his life on earth. The texts deal with the concept of justification in the closest possible association with ideas related to embalmment and mummification. Guilt, accusation, enmity, and the like are indeed treated as forms of impurity and pollution — as "immaterial pollutants," as it were — that must be eliminated in order to bring the deceased into a state of purity that resists putrefaction and decomposition. Justification is moral mummification. When the embalmer's work on the body is finished, the priests take over and extend the work of purification and preservation onto the whole person. The Egyptian word for mummy also means "dignity" or "nobility." At the last stage of mummification, the deceased passes through the postmortem judgment and is assigned the nobility of a follower of Osiris in the netherworld. He is justified against all accusations and purified from every guilt, every sin that might have obstructed his passage into the other world, even from the solecisms of early childhood. After the cleansing and immortalization of the body, the embalmment and mummification ritual turns in its last stage to the social self. The judgment is nothing other than a purging of the soul from guilt. The idea of a general judgment postmortem develops during the Middle Kingdom, at the beginning of the second millennium B.C. It is clearly expressed in a wisdom text dating from that time:

> The court that judge the wretch,
> You know they are not lenient
> On the day of judging the miserable,
> In the hour of doing their task.
> It is painful when the accuser has knowledge.
>
> Do not trust in length of years.
> They view a lifetime in an hour!
> When a man remains over after death,
> His deeds are set beside him as a sum.
>
> Being yonder lasts forever.
> A Fool is he who does what they reprove!
> He who reaches them without having done wrong
> Will exist there like a god,
> free-striding like the lords of eternity![5]

5. Instructions for Merikare P 53-57; cf. J. F. Quack, *Studien zur Lehre für Merikare,* Göttinger Orientforschungen 23 (Wiesbaden, 1992), 34-35.

This is what resurrection means in the context of ancient Egyptian funerary beliefs: "to exist in an Elysium hereafter like a god, free striding like the lords of eternity."

With the rise of the New Kingdom and the recension of the Book of the Dead,[6] the rules of admission into the other world became codified, and they form chapter 125 of the Book of the Dead. The mythical model of a lawsuit between Osiris and Seth had disappeared altogether. The whole procedure resembled now more an examination and an initiation.

The deceased had to present himself before Osiris, the president of the court, and before a jury of forty-two judges. He knew the accusations beforehand and had to declare his innocence. All of the possible crimes and violations that could constitute an obstacle for passing the exam had been spelled out and laid down in two lists, one of forty entries, the other of forty-two. The deceased had to recite these lists and explicitly to declare his/her innocence in each individual item. One list had to be recited before Osiris, the other one before the forty-two judges. During this recital, the heart of the candidate was weighed on a balance against a figure of Truth. Every lie would make the scale with the heart sink a little deeper. In the case of a heart found too heavy and irredeemably charged with guilt and lies, a monster that is always shown close to the balance and watching the weighing would swallow the heart of the culprit and annihilate his/her person.

By reciting these lists of negations — "I did not do this, I did not do that" — the deceased purged himself of all possible charges that could constitute "immaterial pollutants" causing his final destruction. He thus entered the other world in a state of imperishable purity. The spell in the Book of the Dead is entitled, "Purging N of all the evil which he has done, and beholding the faces of the gods." Again, there is no question of innocence. Nobody is innocent. What matters is whether a person is able or not to get purged of his/her sins. In the title of chapter 125, the ideas of moral purity and an immediate vision of the gods are brought into close relationship. According to Egyptian convictions, nobody (except perhaps the king) was able during his or her lifetime to see the gods, to have a vision and to enter the divine world. There are no traces of shamanism, prophetism, or mysticism in Egypt before the Greco-Roman period. All forms of immediate contact with the divine world are referred to the life after death and resurrection: all the gods that you have served on earth, you will confront face-to-face.[7]

---

6. For a recent English translation see R. O. Faulkner, *The Book of the Dead* (London, 1985).

7. Song III; cf. R. Hari, *La tombe thébaine du père divin Neferhotp, Teologisk tijdschrift*

From this text and countless others, we learn that the Egyptian Elysium was the same as the world of the gods. The dead who proved worthy of being justified before the divine tribunal were admitted into the divine world and were permitted to confront the gods face-to-face. The world of the gods did not form a fourth realm besides the other three, but was identical with the Elysium. Egyptian cosmology, therefore, showed the same tripartite structure as all the other cosmologies of the ancient world: heaven, earth, and underworld or world of the gods, world of the living and world of the dead, with the one exception that the dead were believed to be capable of managing the passage from the world of the dead to the world of the gods if they proved innocent or at least "justifiable" in the judgment of the dead.

This has consequences not only for anthropology but also for the Egyptian notion of divinity. If the dead are capable of passing from the world of the dead to the world of the gods, the gods are susceptible of dying and of passing through the world of the dead. The sun god Re does so every night, and the "decan stars" do so after almost two hundred days of nocturnal visibility, after which they disappear into the world of the dead for a period of seventy days. The Egyptian gods die, but there is always rebirth and new life, and this is what the Egyptian ways of treatment of the dead strive to imitate. Seventy days, which the decan stars were believed to spend in the world of the dead, was also the ideal period of performing the ritual of embalmment and mummification. It was the time span a deceased person was supposed to spend in the world of the dead before he rose like the decan stars from the dead and entered Elysium. The gods were as close to death as death was believed to be a passage to divinity. The ascension myth, which is so prominent in the Pyramid Texts, has its counterpart in the descensus myth, which is depicted on the walls of the royal tombs of the New Kingdom. There we see the sun god enter the earth in the western horizon and descend into the deepest depth of the underworld where he unites with Osiris at midnight, in order to be reborn in the East in the morning and to ascend to heaven.

In the light of these mythical images it becomes clear that funerary religion and religion in general belong together. If the Egyptian idea of resurrection is very exceptional in the context of ancient Mediterranean religions, the

---

50 (Genf, 1958), p. 4; cf. my article "Fest des Augenblicks — Verheißung der Dauer: Die Kontroverse der ägyptischen Harfnerlieder," in *Fragen an die altägyptische Literatur,* Gedenkschrift für Eberhard Otto (Wiesbaden, 1977), 69; E. Hornung, "Altägyptische Wurzeln der Isismysterien," in *Études Isaiques* (*Hommages à Jean Leclant,* vol. 3), ed. Cathérine Berger, Gisèle Clerc, and Nicolas Grimal, Bibliothèque d'étude 106/3 (Cairo: Institut Francais D'Archélogie Orientale, 1994), 289.

same applies to the Egyptian concept of a god. Gods die and mortals rise from the dead — the two ideas presuppose each other.

Conclusion

The Christian idea of resurrection presupposes the death of Christ. This, as stated in the beginning, was a fact of history, not of nature, belonging to linear time and to the category of once-for-allness. Still, through his death and resurrection, Christ has paved the way to paradise or Elysium in a way not altogether dissimilar to that of Osiris, who also, through his victory over Seth, opened a realm beyond the realm of death. The decisive common denominator of Christianity and ancient Egyptian religion is the idea of redemption from death, that beyond the realm of death there is an Elysian realm of eternal life in the presence of the divine. Christianity shares this concept not only with Egyptian religion but also with many or most of the Greek or hellenized mystery cults, with some trends in Early Judaism, and later also with Islam, but it seems that Egypt is the likely original source of these ideas.

A Hope for Worms: Early Christian Hope

BRIAN E. DALEY

One central feature of their faith on which virtually all early Christian writers agreed was that the confession of the risen Jesus as Lord implies the hope that his disciples, too, will someday share in his resurrection. The Acts of the Apostles tells us that what annoyed the temple priests and Sadducees about the early Jerusalem community was that they were "proclaiming in Jesus the resurrection of the dead" (Acts 4:2). And Paul, discussing the implications of the Easter kerygma in 1 Corinthians 15, points eloquently to the link between the news of Jesus' resurrection and hope for our own: "If for this life only we have hoped in Christ, we are of all people most to be pitied. But in fact Christ has been raised from the dead, the first fruits of all who have fallen asleep" (1 Cor. 15:19-20). The point seems immediately to have been assimilated into the developing body of distinctive Christian teaching, so that by the middle of the second century Polycarp of Smyrna and Justin Martyr could confidently assert that those who deny a bodily resurrection, or who simply hope for an immortality of the disembodied soul, are no Christians at all.[1] Tertullian, writing in the first decade of the third century, puts it even more challengingly in his anti-Gnostic treatise *On the Resurrection of the Flesh:* "The Christian's confidence is bound up with the resurrection of the dead. That makes us believers; truth compels it, and truth is revealed by God."[2] In that same tradition, Augustine would preach two centuries later, "If faith in the resurrection of the dead is taken away, all Christian doctrine perishes."[3] That

---

1. Polycarp, *Letter to the Philippians* 7; Justin, *Dialogue with Trypho* 80.

2. *On the Resurrection of the Dead* 1, trans. Alexander Souter (London/New York: SPCK, 1922), 1.

3. Sermon 361.2.

faith, which would eventually be articulated in the various churches' baptismal creeds, was understood from the very start as a central dimension of the Christian preaching of salvation in Jesus Christ.[4]

What Does "Resurrection of the Body" Mean?

The question, of course, for the earliest Christians as for ourselves, is just what one understands this hoped-for "resurrection of the body" to mean. In fact, the attempt to make sense of the resurrection hope — and often, after the mid-second century, of the millenarian expectations commonly associated with it[5] — within the larger context of biblical faith, and to defend its reasonableness against the derisive critique of traditional Jews and philosophically minded pagans, seems to have been one of the earliest stimuli to theological reflection in the long Christian tradition: Christian theological debate began, in many respects, with eschatology. Eschatology, on the other hand, then as now, never stands alone: it is rooted in an understanding of the provident and saving God and of the person of the Savior, "the firstborn from the dead" (Col. 1:18), just as it is rooted in a vision of God's relationship to the world of intelligent and material creatures and in a Christian sense of the natural identity and the transformed status of the human person before God. It belongs to a theological whole.

The intellectual interlocutors for early Christian theologians in their discussion of life after death were, in general, their philosophically and scientifically educated pagan contemporaries. Opinions varied greatly in the late Hellenistic world about the possibilities and modes of human survival after death. While Plato had argued strongly for the soul's immortality on the grounds of its identity as the principle of life and of its kinship with the eternal, immaterial forms of intelligible being,[6] the "Middle Platonists" of the

---

4. For early articulations of the "rule of faith" or "rule of truth," which included an affirmation of hope in the resurrection of believers, see Irenaeus, *Against the Heresies* 1.10.1 (referring to the "future manifestation from heaven" of the glorified Jesus, "to raise up anew all flesh of the whole human race . . ."); Tertullian *Prescription against Heretics* 13 (Christ will come again in glory as judge of saints and sinners, "after the resurrection of both these classes shall have happened, together with the restoration of their flesh"); cf. ibid. 36; *On the Veiling of Virgins* 1.

5. For a closely reasoned and convincing argument that genuine millenarian hope is in fact not clearly articulated in surviving patristic documents before Justin and Irenaeus, see Charles E. Hill, *Regnum Caelorum* (Grand Rapids: Eerdmans, 2nd ed. 2001).

6. See, e.g., *Apology* 40c-41c; *Phaedo* 72e-77d, 102d-107b; *Phaedrus* 245c-246d; *Timaeus* 41d.

second century after Christ and later were less unanimous and clear on the subject; nevertheless, most of them held for some continuation of the intellectual element of the human person, once it was freed from the limitations of a material body.[7] To thinkers in this tradition, the Christian expectation that believers will survive a final conflagration and be raised in their bodies from the dead, wrote the Middle Platonist Celsus, was simply

> the hope of worms. For what sort of human soul would have any further desire for a body that has rotted. . . . For God is not the author of sinful desire or of disorderly confusion, but of what is naturally just and right. For the soul he might be able to provide an everlasting life; but as Heraclitus says, "corpses ought to be thrown away as worse than dung."[8]

The "Neoplatonic" tradition, beginning with Plotinus in the third century, clearly emphasized that the soul, which is the core of human identity and the animating and sensible principle that informs and directs the body, is a "fallen" or individualized aspect of the eternal, divine Mind, and is therefore incapable of death.[9] Aristotle, on the other hand, thought of the soul as the "actuality" or "realization" *(entelecheia)* of the organic, material body: its characteristic functioning at the highest level rather than an entity in itself. As such, it shared the body's mortality.[10] The Epicurean school was more frankly materialistic and regarded the soul as simply a refined aspect of the body, composed, like all matter, of atoms and perishable with the rest of the body.[11] The Stoics took a more complex approach to the question; later members of the school thought it was possible that at least some souls survived for a time after death, although the school generally took the monistic view that all reality is material and that all aspects of the living individual are eventually reunited with the continuing, ordered process of the universe.[12] Galen, a con-

7. See John Dillon, *The Middle Platonists* (Ithaca: Cornell University, 2nd ed. 1996), 96-101 (on Antiochus of Ascalon [born c. 130 B.C.E.] and Cicero [106-43 B.C.E.]).

8. Quoted by Origen, *Against Celsus* 5.14, trans. Henry Chadwick (Cambridge: Cambridge University, 1965), 274. Celsus has already insisted that "the soul is God's work, but the nature of the body is different. In fact, in this respect there will be no difference between the body of a bat, or a worm, or a frog, or a man. For they are made of the same matter, and they are equally liable to corruption" (ibid. 4.56; Chadwick, 230).

9. See esp. Plotinus (205-269/270 C.E.), *Ennead* 5.7 — Plotinus's second earliest treatise.

10. See *De Anima* 2.412b.

11. See, e.g., Epicurus (341-270 B.C.E.), *Kuriai Doxai* 2; *Letter to Herodotus* 63; Lucretius, *De rerum natura* 3.830-68.

12. For the earlier Stoic position, developed by Zeno (335-263 B.C.E.) and Cleanthes (331-232 B.C.E.), which regarded the soul as simply a functional aspect of the body, see Hans

temporary of the early Christian apologists and perhaps the most influential of later Greek medical scholars, recognized the existence of the soul as the principle of voluntary movement and sensation in the body, but declared himself agnostic about whether or not it is an independent and immortal substance; even if it is, he argued, it is always heavily influenced by the body in its experience and its operation.[13] It was against the fabric of this range of views, and in the face of the contemptuous skepticism of pagan writers with regard to what Christians hoped and believed, that early Christian theologians developed their arguments for a coming resurrection of the body.

What I propose to do in this brief essay is not simply to offer another overview of early Christian views on the resurrection of the body,[14] but to examine more closely the connections between different ways of interpreting this central hope and implied or explicit understandings of what it is to be human: of human bodiliness, human intellectuality and spirituality, and the relationship of the whole human world to its creator. To do this, I propose to look briefly — in more or less chronological order — at the main theological treatments of the resurrection of the body in the first four centuries of the church

---

von Arnim, *Stoicorum veterum fragmenta*, 1 (Leipzig: Teubner, 1905), nos. 518-21; for Chrysippus's (c. 280–207 B.C.E.) more complex position, that the soul, while itself corporeal, survives separation from the visible body at least for a time, see ibid. 2 (Leipzig: Teubner, 1903), nos. 809-22. See also R. Hoven, *Stoïcisme et Stoïciens face au problème de l'au-delà* (Paris: Belles Lettres, 1971); John M. Rist, "On Greek Biology, Greek Cosmology and Some Sources of Theological Pneuma," *Prudentia* supplement 1985 (Auckland, 1985), 27-47 (repr. in *Man, Soul and Body* [Brookfield, Vt.: Variorum, 1996], V).

13. See esp. Galen's (129-199/216 C.E.) late treatise *On My Own Opinions* 3.14-15, ed. Vivian Nutton, Corpus Medicorum Graecorum 5.3.2 (Berlin: Akademie Verlag, 1999), 59-61, 111-21. See also Luis Garcia Ballester, "Soul and Body: Disease of the Soul and Disease of the Body in Galen's Medical Thought," in Paola Manuli and Mario Vegetti, eds., *Le opere psicologiche di Galeno* (Naples: Bibliopolis, 1988), 116-21.

14. A number of such surveys are already available. For a thorough summary of New Testament teaching on the resurrection hope, as well as a brief overview of second-century material, see Pheme Perkins, *Resurrection: New Testament Witness and Contemporary Reflection* (New York: Doubleday, 1984), esp. 293-391. For a survey of eschatology through the end of the patristic period, see my book *The Hope of the Early Church: A Handbook of Patristic Eschatology* (Cambridge: Cambridge University, 1991); and in a briefer, more popular mode, "The Ripening of Salvation: Hope for Resurrection in the Early Church," *Communio* (USA) 17 (1990): 27-49. See also A. Fierro, "Las controversias sobre la resurrección en los siglos II-V," *Revista española de teología* 28 (1968): 3-21; and on the particular problems of the phrase "resurrection of the flesh," G. Kretschmar, "Auferstehung des Fleisches: Zur Frühgeschichte eines theologischen Lehrformel," in *Leben angesichts des Todes*, Festschrift für Helmut Thielicke (Tübingen: Mohr/Siebeck, 1968), 101-37; Horacio B. Lona, *Über die Auferstehung des Fleisches: Studien zur fruhchristlichen Eschatologie* (Berlin: de Gruyter, 1993).

and to group them, in terms of their implied anthropology, into four main types: (1) resurrection as the completion and perfection, by the gift of God's Spirit, of what is at present an incomplete human reality; (2) resurrection as a way of reinterpreting human existence, now burdened with materiality, in an "enlightened," noncorporeal way; (3) resurrection as God's creative reassembling of the scattered particles of the decomposed human body; and (4) resurrection as the adaptation by the soul of its continuing bodily "vehicle" or instrument to suit the more transparently spiritual conditions of life with God.

Our procedure will, of course, involve some oversimplification and may obscure the overlapping that in fact exists among the authors I will mention. Nevertheless, I hope the result may promote a more highly nuanced understanding than the standard histories of dogma tend to offer of what theological stakes were involved, and what philosophical, biblical, and scientific suppositions were at play, in patristic discussions of the hoped-for human resurrection.

1. Resurrection as the Completion of the Human Potential

The first approach to articulating an understanding of Christian hope, which appears most characteristically in the works of the late-second-century Greek writers we call the "Apologists," not only understands the future resurrection of the body as the final achievement — the ultimate historical outcome, one might say — of the reconciliation between God and humanity achieved in the death and resurrection of Jesus; it also assumes that the human person himself is in some sense incomplete, his potential for life unfulfilled, until the bodies of all are raised from death at the end of history: it assumes what we might call an "anthropology of human incompleteness."

Most of the Apologists argued, in different ways, that the survival of the soul after death, in any sense worthy of the term "life," is not guaranteed by the soul's nature, and that the fulfillment of our natural desire for continued existence can come only as a gift of God, enabling the whole human person, as a composite of flesh and spirit, to participate in an incorruptible life that properly belongs to God alone.

Justin, for instance, in his one explicitly philosophical discussion of the nature of the soul in the introduction to his *Dialogue with Trypho*, argues that since souls are created and so have a beginning in time, they cannot strictly be immortal; if they survive at all — and Justin agrees that they do — it is because God wills it so.[15] In contrast to the Platonic view, Justin here observes

15. *Dialogue with Trypho* 5. In other passages, Justin does speak of the souls of the dead

that life is not something that the soul *is* — not part of its substance or definition — but something the soul *has,* by participation in what belongs only to God. As a result, death is, in natural terms, the extinction of both soul and body:

> For to live is not its attribute, as it is God's; but as a human being does not live always, and the soul is not forever joined to the body — since whenever this harmony must be broken up, the soul leaves the body and the person exists no longer — so whenever the soul must cease to exist, the spirit of life is removed from it, and there is no more soul, but it goes back to the place from which it was taken.[16]

So the incorruption and eternal fellowship with God that Christians hope for[17] is to be understood as God's gift, not as a claim of nature.

> Justin's emphasis on human dependence on God for any robust kind of immortality is expressed in more categorical terms in the works of two contemporary Syro-Greek apologists, the East Syrian Tatian and the Antiochene Theophilus. Theophilus's treatise *To Autolycus,* written around 180, is mainly an extended comparison of the story of human origins in the Octoteuch with classical myths. Here Theophilus elaborates the thesis that the human person is by nature neither simply mortal nor simply immortal, but of "a middle nature," capable of both, so that if he should incline to the things of immortality, keeping the commandment of God, he should receive as a reward from him immortality, and should become God; but if, on the other hand, he should turn to the things of death, disobeying God, he should himself be the cause of death to himself.[18]

Immortality, in Theophilus's view, will be a gift bestowed by God on both body and soul, and will be centered on our ability to see the one who is immortal by nature.[19]

---

as surviving in some form and as being capable of sensation and communication; see *Dialogue* 105; 1 *Apology* 18, 20. He seems to understand this essentially in terms of the biblical Sheol or the classical Hades.

16. Ibid. 6 (trans. *Ante-Nicene Fathers* 1.198 [modified]).

17. See, e.g., 1 *Apology* 10; *Dialogue* 45.

18. *To Autolycus* 2.27; see 2.24. It is often pointed out that in these passages Theophilus is the first Christian writer to speak of the fullness of salvation as divinization, "becoming God" — perhaps in dependence on 2 Peter 1:4. He seems to equate this divine status with immortality, since only God is naturally immortal.

19. Ibid. 1.7.

In his *Address to the Greeks,* written about 165, Tatian — a pupil of Justin — develops in clearer terms an anthropology that emphasizes human dependence on God for the fullness and permanence of life.

> Man is not, as the croaking philosophers say, merely a rational animal, capable of understanding and knowledge. . . . But man alone [among the animals] is the image and likeness of God; and I mean by "man" not one who performs actions similar to those of animals, but one who has advanced far beyond mere humanity — to God himself.[20]

So Tatian distinguishes "two varieties of spirit" in the human person: the soul *(psyche),* which is what "encloses" the flesh and holds it together, and something greater than the soul, God's spirit or "representative," which forms the soul into God's image and likeness and makes it God's temple.[21] Just what Tatian understands this "spirit" to be is not entirely clear; in some passages he refers to it by the biblical terms "Holy Spirit" and "Spirit of God"[22] and points to it as the source of prophecy and our guide to union with God;[23] in other places it seems to be a dynamic cosmic life-force, like the Stoic *pneuma,* which exists in various forms and degrees in different creatures.[24] It is itself "an image and likeness of God," and by dwelling in the soul and acting as its "constant companion," as it did in the first human beings, it allows them to rise above the limitations of their material nature.[25] Those who are "obedient to wisdom," which Tatian seems to identify with the divine Logos, receive this spirit and live by its power. And though Tatian believes that all people will eventually be raised from the dead and receive retribution for their deeds, the presence of this spirit confers a higher, more permanent quality of life on the soul, which is itself mortal:

> The soul is not in itself immortal, O Greeks, but mortal. Yet it is possible for it not to die. If, indeed, it knows not the truth, it dies, and is dissolved with the body, but rises again at last at the end of the world with the body, receiving death by punishment in immortality. But if it acquires the

---

20. *Address to the Greeks* 15.

21. Ibid. 12, 15.

22. Ibid. 15.

23. Ibid. 13.

24. Ibid. 12. For a discussion of the biblical and Stoic background of Tatian's use of the word *pneuma,* see Martin Elze, *Tatian und seine Theologie* (Gottingen: Vandenhoeck und Ruprecht, 1960), 68-69, 86-88.

25. Ibid. 13, 12.

knowledge of God, it does not die, although for a time it is separated [from the body].[26]

Life in the full and lasting sense, life worth living, comes only from participation in the spirit conferred by God on the disciples of the Logos.

The anthropology and eschatology expressed in these passages from the Apologists of the late second century seems to be driven by the concern to contrast the biblical promises of the salvation of the whole human person with the hopes of their philosophically minded pagan neighbors: the Stoics' expectation of a peaceful, natural absorption into a monistically conceived cosmic process, or the Platonists' more individualistic hope for the bodiless survival of a soul that has cultivated its own moral and intellectual integrity. Key to early Christian apologetic is the conviction that the human person is, in fact, not "whole" apart from God's active involvement within it, and that the survival of the person after death, in flesh and in spirit, is thus what later theology would call a work of grace, God's gift rather than a natural right.

This is most clearly expressed, perhaps, in the fifth book of Irenaeus's monumental treatise *Against the Heresies,* a work not usually categorized among the Apologists even though it shares many traits and themes with them. Irenaeus, of course, is mainly concerned to expose the theological weaknesses of the various Christian Gnostic sects of the late second century, who offered their initiates esoteric traditions that claimed to reveal a new, hidden narrative of human origins and a new promise of salvation for the enlightened few — salvation that essentially consisted in release from the material body and from the institutions and pressures of the external world. Throughout his work, Irenaeus constantly returns to the theme that genuine Christian preaching promises the bodily resurrection of all the dead and the salvation of all flesh,[27] not simply the rescue of the spark of light in us from the darkness of enclosing matter. The Christian practice of the Eucharist — which presumably the Gnostic communities also shared — is itself, he insists, intelligible only in terms of faith in a real incarnation of God and hope for a real resurrection of the flesh.[28]

---

26. Ibid. 13 (trans. altered).

27. See, e.g., *Against the Heresies* 1.10.1; 1.22.1; 3.16.1 (all formulaic passages); also 2.33.5; 3.12.3.

28. Ibid. 4.18.5; 4.38.1; 5.2.2-3. In the last of these passages, Irenaeus connects the Eucharist with New Testament images of grain and vine (John 12:24; 15:1-8; 1 Cor. 15:35-38): "Just as a cutting from the vine planted in the ground fructifies in its season, or as a grain of wheat, falling into the earth and becoming decomposed, rises with manifold increase by the Spirit of God, who contains all things, and then, through the wisdom of God, serves for the

In book 5 of the work, where Irenaeus develops his eschatology most fully, he also sketches out a bold conception of the human person, based on his understanding of the New Testament, that stands in strong contrast to contemporary philosophical anthropologies. Taking as his key text Paul's hope for eschatological salvation in 1 Thessalonians 5:23 ("May the God of peace sanctify you wholly, and may your spirit and soul and body be kept sound and blameless at the coming of our Lord Jesus Christ"), as many later Fathers would also do, Irenaeus insists that this human whole, which God has intended from the creation of Adam and Eve, in fact includes the presence of the Holy Spirit, one of the Creator's "two hands," along with our created soul and flesh, as an integral component of its full realization.

> For the perfect human being consists in the commingling and the union of the soul, as it receives the Spirit of the Father, and the mixture of that fleshly nature which was molded after the image of God. . . . When the Spirit, here blended with the soul, is united to [God's] handiwork,[29] the person is rendered spiritual and perfect because of the outpouring of the Spirit; this is the one who was made in the image and likeness of God. But if the Spirit is lacking in the soul, he who is such is indeed of an animal[30] nature, and being left carnal,[31] shall be an imperfect being, possessing indeed the image [of God] in his formation, but not receiving the likeness through the Spirit — and so his being is imperfect.[32]

While the Valentinians and other Gnostic groups distinguished between their own enlightened members, as "spiritual persons," and other humans — the "psychics" or "animal" kind, who had enough intelligence to be capable of receiving the sect's hidden wisdom, and the "fleshly" or "somatic" kind, who were so bound to their bodily drives and needs that they were incapable of being rescued from the darkness of the present world — Irenaeus insists that the "perfect," "spiritual" persons of the New Testament are those who have received God's Holy Spirit in their human souls and bodies and who live in the

---

use of humanity, and having received the Word of God, becomes the Eucharist, which is the body and blood of Christ, so also our bodies, being nourished by it, and deposited in the earth, and suffering decomposition there, shall rise at their appointed time, the Word of God granting them resurrection to the glory of God . . ." (5.2.3: trans. Ante-Nicene Fathers 1.528 [modified])

29. In both the Latin and the Greek text, *plasma:* Irenaeus generally uses this word to refer to the material human form shaped by God in Gen. 2:7.

30. Lat. *animalis;* Gk. *psychikos.*

31. Lat. *carnalis;* Gk. *sarkikos.*

32. *Against the Heresies* 5.6.1 (trans. ANF 1.532 [altered]).

Spirit's freedom as members of Christ's ecclesial body, looking forward to resurrection, immortal life, and an ultimate transformation of both body and soul beyond our imagining.[33] Without the Spirit of God, the human person is incomplete, God's project in creation unachieved; in the presence of the Spirit, even human flesh becomes a participant in eternal life and the radiant glory of God.[34]

2. Resurrection as Reinterpretation

A second early Christian approach to interpreting hope in the resurrection, contemporary with that of the Apologists and Irenaeus, characterized most of the Gnostic sects we have already mentioned. Although the theologies of these groups, and their distance from or nearness to mainstream Christian tradition, varied considerably — so much so that the very validity of the collective term "Gnostic" has recently been called into question[35] — they shared at least a deep suspicion of the value and goodness of the human body, human institutions, and the material world, and explained the origins and state of the present order by means of elaborate cosmogonies and myths that reinterpreted Christian categories by contextualizing them within wholly alienating narrative frameworks.[36] Some of the extant Gnostic tracts speak of the goal of human history in terms of the return of the light imprisoned within us to its primordial roots;[37] others speak of resurrection, but in a way that suggests primarily sacramental rebirth.[38]

---

33. Ibid.; see also 5.8.1-2; 5.36.3.

34. The biblical image of God's glory as a kind of visual fulfillment of human need and as the source of a life beyond inherent human capacities that is also knowledge, love, and union is a main theme of book 4 of *Against the Heresies*. See esp. 4.20.5-8, including the famous sentence in 4.20.7 (usually quoted only partly, and so misleadingly): "For the glory of God is a living human being; and the life of the human being consists in beholding God."

35. See, e.g., Michael A. Williams, *Rethinking "Gnosticism": An Argument for Dismantling a Dubious Category* (Princeton: Princeton University, 1996).

36. On the eschatology of the surviving Gnostic writings, see Daley, *Hope*, 25-28 and the bibliography cited there; also Giovanni Filoramo, *A History of Gnosticism* (Oxford: Basil Blackwell, 1990), 128-41.

37. So, e.g., *On the Origin of the World* 127 (James M. Robinson [ed.], *The Nag Hammadi Library* [San Francisco: Harper, 3rd ed. 1990], 189). This treatise, heavily concerned with eschatology, is characterized by its English translators as "essentially non-Christian," but expressing "the Gnostic world view" (ibid., 171).

38. *Gospel of Philip* 67.15-30. The main image here is that of entering into a "bridal chamber" that offers the initiate access to the Truth; the author associates this "entry" with

The one treatise in the collection of Gnostic writings found at Nag Hammadi that is mainly focused on Christian hope for resurrection is the *Epistle to Rheginos* or *Treatise on the Resurrection,* apparently a Western Valentinian work of the second century (and so probably coming from Irenaeus's cultural and theological milieu).[39] This brief work, like a number of other Valentinian works, represents a serious attempt of a Christian Gnostic author to deal with the tradition of faith, specifically with the hope for resurrection proclaimed in the Pauline letters and other apostolic writings, and lacks many of the bizarre mythical and magical trappings present in other texts from Nag Hammadi. Still, it is clear that the author interprets the resurrection not as the salvation and transformation of the present body of flesh so much as release from the flesh in which the self has been burdened by entering into the present world from its prior existence.[40] Resurrection, for this author, is simply release from the weakness and aging under which we presently suffer, a discarding of "the afterbirth of the body," and therefore a gain.[41]

In the author's interpretation, this transformation has essentially already happened for those who can live with a free and undivided mind: "Do not think in part, O Rheginos, neither live in conformity with this flesh for the sake of unanimity [with other Christians?], but flee from the divisions and the fetters, and already you have the resurrection."[42] In fact, this treatise seems to identify the Christian event of resurrection with the interior discovery, on the part of the believer, of a transformation that has already occurred within him through identification with Christ and learning the secret, "genuine" Christian story. In one passage the author compares this new vision to the apostles' glorious vision of Moses and Elijah with the transfigured Jesus (Mark 9:2-8 and par.):

> Then what is the resurrection? It is always the disclosure of those who have arisen. For if you remember reading in the Gospel that Elijah appeared and Moses with him, do not think the resurrection is an illusion.

baptism, chrismation, and the Eucharist. Cf. *Tripartite Tractate* 122.19-21; *Gospel of Thomas* 75.

39. See Malcolm Lee Peel, *The Epistle to Rheginos: A Valentinian Letter on the Resurrection* (Philadelphia: Westminster, 1969), 12-17.

40. See, e.g., *Epistle to Rheginos* 47.2-10 (Peel, 32).

41. Ibid. 47.17-22 (Peel, 33).

42. Ibid. 49.9-16 (Peel, 34-35). For the Gnostic tendency to identify division and number with the world of matter and illusion, and salvation with the return to primordial unity, see, e.g., *Gospel of Thomas* 11.106; *Apocryphon of John* 18.30; in terms of gender and sexuality, *Gospel of Philip* 68.23-26; 70.9-22.

> It is not illusion, but it is truth. It is more suitable to say, then, that the world is an illusion, rather than the resurrection which came into being through our Lord the Savior, Jesus Christ. . . . The world is an illusion . . . but the resurrection does not have this character; for it is the Truth, that which stands firm. And it is the revelation of that which exists, and the transformation of things, and a transition into newness.[43]

For the Valentinian writer of this treatise, as for many of his Gnostic confrères, the key to understanding the Christian hope for resurrection was to take it as enlightenment, a profound experience of self-discovery and of the reorientation of desire through the acceptance of a radically reordered, revisionist narrative about the origin of the world and the divine plan of salvation — a narrative accessible only to the favored members of their own marginalized religious sect. The anthropology on which this interpretation of the resurrection rests is clearly of central importance: what we might call "an anthropology of beleaguered consciousness," or "an anthropology of light in darkness," in which the *darkness* is identified with moral evil, sensuality, the body, and the regnant powers of the present world, and *light* with the innate potential in at least some of us to be "awakened" from our common sleep and to read the world in a new way.[44] In this sense, resurrection for Gnostic theology could hardly be called a bodily event at all; it is an experience of inner enlightenment, of release from the present bodily world, of radical reinterpretation of the self, its history, and its future.[45]

3. Resurrection as Reconstitution

A third approach to understanding the resurrection hope began to appear in Christian apologetic and theological writings of the late second century, and was to retain its power over Christian minds at least until the time of Augustine: the conception of resurrection as the reassembly of the scattered material fragments ("atoms" in the ancient sense) into which the body has been

---

43. *Ep. Rheg.* 48.3-38 (Peel, 33-34 [modified]).

44. For this image, see, e.g., *Apocryphon of John* 28.26–31.21.

45. For this reason, it is hard to agree with Malcolm Peel's conclusion about the eschatology, "realized" and future, of the *Epistle to Rheginos:* "that our author's view of the *resurrection body* is a reasonably faithful interpretation of the Pauline view — more faithful, in fact, than that of many of the heresiologists of early Christendom!" (*Epistle* 148-49). Peel seems to be alluding to Irenaeus's emphasis on the involvement of the flesh in future salvation, and contrasting it with the "spiritual body" spoken of in 1 Cor. 15:42-50.

reduced by death and decomposition, and the rejoining of those fragments with the surviving soul to constitute a single person — the same one who now exists. Underlying this notion is what one might call an "anthropology of composition": a conception of the human person that has its roots in both common sense and in some traditions of ancient philosophy — especially scientific atomism and Aristotle's conception of the soul as intrinsically related to the material body. In this view of the human person, each of us *is* both our inner consciousness and our material body; to survive as ourselves and share immortality, to be truly raised, there must be both material and spiritual identity between the persons we now are and the glorious figures we shall be, and that identity requires that not only our minds but also the bits of our matter must all be reclaimed as ours, even if their appearance and their properties may, to some minor degree, be changed for the better.

The classic early representative of this understanding is a treatise *On the Resurrection*, attributed to the second-century apologist Athenagoras, which, if it is not by him, seems to be roughly contemporary.[46] The author insists on his point forcefully in the paragraph that concludes the work. If all beings of the same kind find their perfection in the same final state, and if that final state must correspond to their entire nature, human fulfillment must be more than simply the immortality of the soul.

> But if this is the end of both parts together, and this can be discovered neither while they are still living in the present state of existence, through the numerous causes already mentioned, nor when the soul is in a state of separation, because the human being cannot be said to exist when the body is dissolved, and indeed entirely scattered abroad, even though the soul continues by itself — it is absolutely necessary that the end of a human person's being should appear in some reconstitution of the two together, and of the same living being. . . . But it is impossible for the same persons to be reconstituted unless the same bodies are restored to the same souls.[47]

46. Robert M. Grant, "Athenagoras or Ps.-Athenagoras," *Harvard Theological Review* 47 (1954): 121-29, and his pupil William R. Schoedel, *Athenagoras: Legatio and De Resurrectione* (Oxford: Clarendon, 1972), both hold the work to be an anti-Origenist treatise of the early third century, not by Athenagoras. Its authenticity has been strongly defended by, among others, Leslie W. Barnard, *Athenagoras: A Study in Second-Century Christian Apologetic* (Paris: Beauchesne, 1972); "Athenagoras' De Resurrectione: The Background and Theology of a Second-Century Treatise on the Resurrection," *Studia Theologica* 30 (1976): 1-42.

47. Athenagoras (?), *On the Resurrection* 25 (ANF 2.162 [altered]).

Early in the treatise, Athenagoras has begun his apologetic for this central Christian belief by insisting that raising the dead is surely possible for God if God has created human beings from nothing: surely God cannot be thought either incapable of such a second act of creation, or ignorant of the whereabouts of the particles of decomposed bodies.[48] He then deals with a hypothetical case that was to become a standard objection in pagan critiques of Christian hope: How will God deal with the particles of flesh that once formed part of one person's body, but which were eaten after their death by scavenging animals or fish? If another human should later kill and eat the animal or fish, to whom will those particles belong when both are reconstituted in the resurrection?[49] Given his understanding of human identity, the author clearly regards this as a serious question; his answer is to appeal first of all to the power and wisdom of God to sort out such issues; then — borrowing an idea from Galen's understanding of digestion, in which an animal's body makes its own only those parts of its food which pertain to its own nature — he suggests that the particles that are constitutive of a person's own physical identity will not be integrated into the bodies of others.[50]

The author goes on, in the second half of the treatise, to argue on other grounds for the plausibility and fittingness of a bodily resurrection: analogies in human experience, such as waking from sleep,[51] and the requirement in justice that the deeds we perform in our bodies must receive their reward or their punishment in a bodily way.[52] But his main argument, to which he recurs several times, is anthropological and teleological: if, as is apparent, God has created human beings as a composite of an immortal soul and a material body,

> in order that they may, when they have passed through their present existence, arrive at one common end, with the same elements of which they are composed at their birth and during life, it unavoidably follows, since one living being *(zoon)* is formed from the two, experiencing whatever

48. Ibid. 2-3.

49. Ibid. 4. For later appearances of this argument, see Tertullian, *On the Resurrection of the Flesh* 4; Augustine, *On the City of God* 22.20; and in a hostile sense, Porphyry, *Against the Christians* 4.24, trans. R. Joseph Hoffman (Amherst, N.Y.: Prometheus, 1994), 90-91. For thoughtful comments on this "chain consumption argument," see Carolyn Walker Bynum, *The Resurrection of the Body in Western Christianity, 200-1336* (New York: Columbia University, 1995), 27-43, esp. 32-33.

50. Athenagoras (?), *On the Resurrection* 5-6. For the author's use of Galen, see Schoedel (above, n. 46), 101.

51. Ibid. 16-17.

52. Ibid. 18-24.

the soul experiences and whatever the body experiences . . . that the whole series of these things must be referred to some one end.[53]

Our present composition, in other words, seems to demand resurrection.

A number of Christian authors of the second and third centuries, as I have said, reproduce essentially this same line of reasoning as apologetic arguments for a bodily resurrection, understood as the reassembly of the soul and all the material components of the present body. A treatise on the resurrection ascribed to Justin, for instance, which probably is an anti-Origenist work of the third century,[54] also emphasizes the materiality of the risen body, and argues for the possibility of a resurrection by emphasizing God's creative power.[55] Along with Tertullian, whose anti-Gnostic and anti-Marcionite tract *On the Resurrection of the Flesh* comes from the first decade of the third century, Pseudo-Justin emphasizes that the resurrection of Jesus both proves the possibility of such a restoration and provides the model for our own hope.[56] The point these authors emphasize is that it is *this present flesh,* this visible and recognizable body, that will rise again.[57]

So Augustine, in the last book of *The City of God,* after dealing briefly with the now-classical puzzle of people eating the flesh of animals who have in turn eaten human flesh, still insists that all the material components of this present body will be restored to their original owner — if also rearranged for symmetry and beauty — in the body of the resurrection:

> Whatever, therefore, has been taken from the body, either during life or after death, shall be restored to it, and, in conjunction with what has remained in the grave, shall rise again, transformed from the oldness of the animal body into the newness of the spiritual body, and clothed in incorruption and immortality. But even though the body has been com-

---

53. Ibid. 15.

54. Extant only in large fragments, mainly from the eighth-century *Sacra Parallela,* this work is now generally agreed not to be a work of the apologist and martyr; see especially F. R. Montgomery Hitchcock, "'Loofs' Asiatic Source (IQA) and the Ps.-Justin De Resurrectione," *Zeitschrift für die neutestamentliche Wissenschaft* 36 (1937-38): 35-60.

55. Ps.-Justin, *On the Resurrection,* frags. 3-5, 7.

56. Ibid., frag. 9; Tertullian, *On the Resurrection of the Flesh* 51-53.

57. See, e.g., Methodius, *Aglaophon: On the Resurrection* 3.12.17, in the Old Slavonic version, ed. G. N. Bonwetsch, Die griechischen christlichen Schriftsteller der ersten drei Jahrhunderte 27 (Leipzig: Hinrichs, 1917), 409, commenting on Jesus' appearance in the upper room: "When he himself makes [his disciples] so certain that his body is composed of flesh and bones, how could we be so bold as to dare to say that another, spiritual body will rise in place of this one. . . ?"

pletely pulverized by some severe accident or by the ruthlessness of ene-
mies, even though it has been so thoroughly scattered to the winds or into
the water that there is no trace of it left, yet it shall not lie beyond the om-
nipotence of the Creator — no, not a hair of its head shall perish. The
flesh shall then be spiritual, and subject to the spirit — but still flesh, not
spirit. . . .[58]

For all of these writers, the goodness and dignity of the flesh, the material beauty of the body created by God as integral to the human person, appeared to be at stake, as well as the crucial role played by the flesh in our way
to God. "There is no soul at all that can procure salvation," Tertullian
quipped, "unless it believes while it is in the flesh; so the flesh *(caro)* is the
very hinge *(cardo)* on which salvation turns!"[59] And flesh, in their view, was
quite obviously composed of a finite quantity of material particles, without
which the ontological continuity and identity of the organic human animal
could not honestly be affirmed. Now and in the eschaton, we are not only the
conscious mind, but also the bits and pieces in which and through which the
mind engages the material world.

4. Resurrection as Transformation

As on so many subjects, it was Origen, in the early third century, who introduced into Christian reflection a new, theologically risky, yet immensely
fruitful line of thought that was to have repercussions for several centuries.
Origen was interested throughout his life in the problems surrounding embodiment and the hope for a bodily resurrection — so much so that he apparently wrote two early treatises on the resurrection, neither of which has
survived. His approach to the subject, however, would be characteristically
different from that of the authors we have been considering — many of them
contemporaries or recent predecessors; in considering the resurrection, as indeed most subjects of Christian faith, Origen can constantly be observed trying to combine his own sophisticated philosophical instincts, even a reasonable acquaintance with the Alexandrian natural science of the day, with his
commitment to the church's rule of faith and his "profession" of thorough,
painstakingly learned scriptural exegesis, into a cohesive whole that would of-

---

58. *On the City of God* 20.21, trans. Marcus Dods (altered); see 20.19; and for an earlier
discussion, somewhat less material in emphasis, see 13.17-19, 20, 22-23.

59. *On the Resurrection of the Flesh* 8 (ANF 2.551 [altered]).

fer his readers the possibility of a faith as intellectually respectable as that of any pagan philosopher.

On the subject of the resurrection, some later critics considered Origen's approach just a step short of Gnosticism.[60] The point of the third book of Methodius's dialogue *On the Resurrection,* for instance, was to show that Origen's understanding of the resurrection was so spiritualized as to imply the risen body would be like this present body simply in external shape, a spiritual form without matter.[61] A century later, the industrious heresiologist Epiphanius of Salamis, drawing on Methodius's work, seems to have regarded Origen's position to be a denial of any genuine bodily resurrection.[62] His contemporary, Jerome, assembled and translated texts to demonstrate that Origen's conception of the resurrection in fact denied its corporeal character.[63]

To the contrary, Origen makes it clear in many passages that he wholeheartedly affirms the church's faith "that there will be a time for the resurrection of the dead, when this body, which now 'is sown in corruption, will rise in incorruption,' and 'what is sown in shame will rise in glory'" (1 Cor. 15:42-43).[64] Further, he insists — despite the embarrassment of some "heretics" (read: Gnostics) at this aspect of the church's tradition — that in the final stage of salvation we will actually "use" these same bodies that have fallen: "we will not need to be in other bodies than our own."[65] Yet Origen is contemptuous of justifying this Christian hope simply by an appeal to God's power;[66] it must be intellectually justified in some responsible way.

But Origen's understanding of this glorious future embodiment differs from the approach we have just discussed — the conception of physical re-

---

60. So Epiphanius, *Panarion* 64.71.14.

61. See Daley, *Hope,* 61-63; Lloyd G. Patterson, *Methodius of Olympus: Divine Sovereignty, Human Freedom and Life in Christ* (Washington: Catholic University of America, 1997), 141-86, esp. 171-74.

62. *Panarion* 64.63-64.

63. See esp. his treatise *To Pammachius, against John of Jerusalem* 23-36, a section that Yves-Marie Duval has shown to be heavily dependent on Tertullian's *On the Resurrection of the Flesh:* "Tertullien contre Origène sur la résurrection de la chair dans le *Contre Johannem hierosolymitanum* 23-36 de saint Jérôme," *Revue des études augustiniennes* 17 (1971): 227-78. For an argument that the "Origenist controversy" of the late fourth and early fifth centuries was centered on issues of the body and asceticism, see Elizabeth Clark, *The Origenist Controversy: The Cultural Construction of an Early Christian Debate* (Princeton: Princeton University, 1992).

64. *On First Principles,* Preface 5.

65. Ibid. 2.10.1.

66. *Against Celsus* 5.23.

constitution — precisely in that it is centered on a strong notion of change within continuity and on a much more subtle, philosophically sophisticated notion than most of his predecessors had of what constitutes matter and the body. One might characterize the Origenist understanding as that of "resurrection as transformation," relying on an anthropology that conceived the human person in terms of continual psychosomatic change.

One thing Origen's ancient (and modern) critics seem to have overlooked is his clear conviction that every created living being, even an intellectual being, needs a *body* of some kind, simply in order to be in a place and to move: bodiliness, for Origen, seems to have been an aspect of finitude, the physical expression of what Augustine would later call *distentio*.[67] The divine Trinity, whose nature Origen clearly distinguishes from the realm of creatures at the end of his great work *On First Principles*,[68] is alone "without body," *asomatos* — this term, in fact, represents the one nonbiblical, strictly philosophical concept that Origen regards as utterly necessary for a correct understanding of the Scriptures and the ecclesial tradition of faith.[69] But every other intellectual being — every finite, intelligent creature or "soul" — needs to make use of a body as an instrument of activity, in Origen's view, even though its own nature is incorporeal. According to Methodius, Origen ascribed even to the souls of the dead an ethereal "vehicle *(ochema)*, similar in form *(homoeides)* to this perceptible body," which "clothed" it and enabled it to move in space.[70] And this body, which the soul always uses as its instrument,[71] its inseparable "beast of burden,"[72] remains always subject to change, as the soul does, simply because both are finite.[73] In this way, Origen accounts

---

67. See, e.g., *Confessions* 11.23-24, where Augustine defines time, the mind's internal measurement of the body's motion in extended space, as "a certain *distentio animi*."

68. *On First Principles* 4.4.8.

69. Ibid. Preface 8-9; on the purpose of *On First Principles* as a systematic guide to the understanding of faith required for correct biblical interpretation, see my article, "Origen's *De Principiis*: A Guide to the 'Principles' of Scriptural Interpretation," in John A. Petruccione, ed., *Nova et Vetera*, Festschrift for Thomas Halton (Washington: Catholic University of America, 1999), 3-21.

70. See Methodius, *On the Resurrection* 3.18.1; the Greek text of this passage is preserved by Photius in *Bibliotheca* 234.301a. On the background for this concept of the soul's "vehicle," see Henri Crouzel, "Le thème platonicien du 'véhicule de l'âme' chez Origène," *Didaskalia* 7 (1977): 225-37.

71. See Origen, *Fragment on 1 Corinthians* 30 (ed. Claude Jenkins, *Journal of Theological Studies* 9 [1908]: 371).

72. *Homilies on Judges* 6.5.

73. In his excursus on how to understand *substance (ousia)*, in *On Prayer* 27.8-9, Origen suggests that the term is "commonly used of incorporeal things by those who main-

for the variety among creatures, which were, in their original creation, all similar and equal:

> Every created thing is distinguished in God's sight by its being confined within a certain number and measure, that is, either number in the case of rational beings or measure in the case of bodily matter. Since, then, it was necessary for intellectual nature to make use of bodies, and this nature is proved to be changeable and convertible by the very condition of its being created, . . . so of necessity God had foreknowledge of the differences that were to arise among souls or spiritual powers, in order to arrange that each in proportion to its merits might wear a different bodily covering of this or that quality; and so, too, was it necessary for God to make a bodily nature, capable of changing at the Creator's will, by an alteration of qualities, into everything that circumstances might require. This must endure so long as those endure who need it for a covering; and there will always be rational natures which need this bodily covering.[74]

Origen draws several important conclusions from this understanding of the essential changeability of creatures, and of the need of all intellectual creatures for some kind of material instrument or body. First, although he does seem to accept, in some form, the Aristotelian notion of a "prime matter" underlying all qualitative change in corporeal beings, he strenuously denies that it is eternal or that it has any independent existence as an ontological principle, apart from its role as a way of conceiving the continuing "receptacle" of change in finite beings.[75] Secondly, Origen understands the qualitative

---

tain that the reality of incorporeal things is primary, such things having stable existence, not admitting of addition nor suffering diminution." He seems here to be referring to the Platonic notion of the eternal intelligible forms rather than to created intellects.

Origen was commonly understood by his ancient critics to have believed that intellectual creatures exist eternally, simply because God cannot be imagined as ever failing to share his goodness by creating. Henri Crouzel has pointed out, however, that this, too, seems to be a misreading of Origen's statements about creation in *On First Principles* 1.4.4-5, compared with his remarks about the eternal generation of the Son in 1.2.10. Origen seems to believe that "intelligible reality" *(ta noeta)*, a realm of intelligibles or forms, exists forever in the eternal Mind, the Word or Wisdom of God; but he clearly affirms that "intelligent creatures" *(ta noera)* have a temporal beginning. See *Origène et Plotin: Comparaisons doctrinales* (Paris: Tôqui, 1991), 137-38.

74. *On First Principles* 4.4.8, trans. George W. Butterworth (repr. New York: Harper and Row, 1966), 325-26 (modified).

75. So *On First Principles* 4.4.6-7; *Against Celsus* 6.77. For an explanation of prime matter as the underlying principle of continuity in limited objects, attributed to "those who hold

changes of bodies as a necessary way of adapting to their environment, and so of mediating between the intellectual being that makes use of them and the world that surrounds them. Understandably, he draws conclusions from this for Christian hope in the resurrection:

> For souls which are in bodily places must have bodies to suit the places. And just as, if we had to become water creatures and lived in the sea, we would surely need gills and the other features of fish, so, as we are to inherit the kingdom of heaven and live in places superior to ours, we must have spiritual bodies.[76]

Third, Origen uses concepts from both Middle Platonic ontology and Stoic cosmology to articulate the substantial continuity of intellectual creatures within the changes proper to their nature. In a famous passage from his commentary on Psalm 5, quoted (and clearly misinterpreted) a century later by Methodius, Origen refers to this principle of continuity as the perceptible *form (eidos),* which endures in every organic body, through the constant ebb and flow of its material composition:

> A body is controlled by nature, which puts something such as food into it from without, and as this food is eliminated, [it adds] further things, such as vegetable and animal products, in place of the other materials it had previously put there. Thus the body has not inaptly been called a river. For strictly speaking, the first substratum *(proton hypokeimenon)* in our bodies is scarcely the same for two days, even though, despite the fluidity of the nature of a body, Paul's body, say, or Peter's, is always the same. . . . This is because the form *(eidos)* which identifies the body is the same, just as the features which characterize Peter's or Paul's bodies remain the same — characteristics like childhood scars, and such peculiarities as moles, and any others besides. This form, the bodily, which constitutes Peter and Paul, encloses the soul once more at the resurrection, changed for the better — although surely not this extension which underlay it at the first. For as the form is the same from infancy until old age, even though the features appear to undergo considerable change, so we must

---

that the reality of incorporeal things is secondary" (i.e., the Peripatetics), see *On Prayer* 27.8. Origen observes that in this perspective, if one identifies *substance (ousia)* with prime matter, such substance is always qualitatively changeable.

76. This passage is from the "epitome" of a passage in Origen's commentary on Psalm 1.5, in Methodius's *On the Resurrection,* preserved by Epiphanius, *Panarion* 64.14.7-8, trans. Frank Williams (Leiden: Brill, 1994), 143. See also *Against Celsus* 7.32.

suppose that, though its change for the better will be very great, our present form will be the same in the world to come.[77]

Later in the same passage, Origen uses different language — the Stoic terminology of "seminal reasons" or "structures" *(logoi spermatikoi)* — to designate the intellectual creature, the soul, as the principle of substantial continuity within this changing, organic body. Alluding to Paul's image of the transformation of a grain of wheat into a full ear in 1 Corinthians 15, Origen comments:

> For if we have understood the illustration properly, we must hold that when the "seminal structure" in the grain of wheat has laid hold of the matter which surrounds it, has permeated it entirely and has taken control of its form *(eidos)*, it imparts its own powers to what was formerly earth, water, air and fire, and by prevailing over their characteristics transforms them into the thing whose creator it is. And thus the ear of grain comes to maturity, vastly different from the original seed in size, shape and complexity.[78]

This final form of the body, Origen implies in some passages, will recapture the beauty and refinement of the "sparkling" *(augoeides)* or luminous body its soul possessed at the beginning of its created existence, before its "descent" into its present coarseness, its "garment of skin."[79]

Origen's understanding of the resurrection, then, clearly is centered on a material body, but one whose qualities will be transformed beyond our present imaginings, in order to serve as a suitable vehicle for the soul's life in the presence of God. Origen even hints, at the end of his treatise *On First Principles,* that though the mind is made in God's image and therefore has "a certain blood-relationship *(consanguinitatem quandam)* with God," its con-

---

77. See Epiphanius, *Panarion* 64.14.2-6 (Williams, 142-43 [modified]). For a similar argument, see *On First Principles* 2.10.2. In interpreting the first of these texts, both Methodius and Epiphanius take *eidos,* "form," simply to mean the body's external appearance, but the context clearly shows that it is more: if not the full Platonic notion of an eternal intelligible form, at least the ontological principle that makes a body recognizable within the constant process of change — not unlike the Thomistic notion of the "form of the composite body" *(forma mixti corporis).*

78. Epiphanius, *Panarion* 64.16.7 (Williams, 144-45 [modified]). In *On First Principles* 2.10.3, Origen refers to this "innate structure" *(insita ratio)* as being "always preserved in the substance of the body" to control its life and growth; cf. *Against Celsus* 5.23, also referring to the image of the grain of wheat.

79. See *On First Principles* 1.26-29; 2.6-7; 3.21; on the "sparkling" character of this original body, see Procopius of Gaza, *Commentary on Genesis* (Patrologia Graeca 87.221 A9), a passage that is usually assumed to depend heavily on Origen's lost commentary on Genesis.

tinuing embodiment may justify us in supposing that some kind of sensation will always be involved in its knowledge of God — what the book of Proverbs calls "a divine sense," which the exegete strives to cultivate even now in his reading of the biblical text.[80] As a result, our ability to know God seems to involve our body as well as our spirit.

Like Irenaeus, Origen seems to suppose in the end that the full realization of the human creature's potential as embodied intellect involves, paradoxically, God's own self-communication. Crouzel has shown, by a careful comparison of various passages in Origen's works, that in his version of the "trichotomous anthropology" common in the early Fathers — seeing the human person, with 1 Thessalonians 5:23, as "spirit, soul and body" — the Spirit must be understood not as created *pneuma,* but as God's Holy Spirit, teaching and transforming the human soul.[81] In his work against Celsus, Origen speaks of what we would call the work of grace in these terms: as a transformation of human reality not to something contrary to nature, but to something that clearly lies above it:

> . . . for God's actions are not contrary to nature, even though they may be miraculous or may seem to some people to be so. If we are forced to use this terminology, we will say that compared with what is commonly regarded as nature some things which sometimes God might do transcend nature, such as lifting man up beyond human nature and making him change to a superior and more divine nature, and keeping him in this position for so long as the man who is kept shows by his actions that he desires him to do this.[82]

It does not seem unreasonable to suppose that Origen imagined the coming transformation of the body in the resurrection in just such terms.[83]

As one of Origen's great disciples and admirers, Gregory of Nyssa (c. 335–c. 394) shared Origen's conception of the resurrection as a transformation of the body to a new, yet unimagined glory, as well as most of his underlying anthropological assumptions. Gregory is always careful to distin-

---

80. *On First Principles* 4.4.10; cf. *Dialogue with Heracleides* 156-65.

81. *Origène et Plotin* 262-65.

82. *Against Celsus* 5.24 (trans. Chadwick 282 [modified]).

83. Thomas Aquinas, at least, did; see *Summa Theologiae,* Supplement Q. 75, art. 3, where he argues that the resurrection of the body is something natural in the sense of being congruent with human nature, even demanded by it for its fulfillment, yet that it is supernatural — strictly speaking, miraculous — in that human nature is not capable of attaining it through its own operation.

guish his positions from those for which Origen, rightly or wrongly, was criticized in the fourth century; so he insists that the human soul and body, while distinct in nature and function, were created simultaneously and for each other, and always — even in death — remain related to each other.[84] Although the soul's presence in the human person can be known to us only by its effects in the perceptible "world" of our body, just as God can be known only by his operations in the world of our experience, Gregory confidently defines the soul in terms of these effects: "it is immaterial and bodiless, working and moving in accord with its own nature, and revealing its motions by means of the bodily organs."[85]

Central, too, to Gregory's understanding of the human creature, in both his fall from God's original intention and in his resurrection and restoration to glory, is the principle that all created beings are subject to change:

> Uncreated nature is incapable of the movement implied in mutability, change, and variation. But everything that depends upon creation for its existence has an innate tendency to change. For the very existence of creation had its origin in change, non-being becoming being by divine power.[86]

So some of the first created intellects, Gregory continues, freely chose to realize their innate changeability by turning from God; and the human creature — formed to realize God's image in both a spiritual and a material way, and so to rule over the material cosmos[87] — when deceived by these fallen spirits, also chose evil and experienced corruption and death as a result.[88]

But Gregory develops his understanding of human salvation, of the restoration of our present humanity to holiness and glory, also in terms of change: perfection, in his view, is a never-ending process of growth toward God, an endless growth in the human subject's reflection of, and participa-

84. See esp. *On the Soul and the Resurrection* (Patrologia Graeca 46.44A-48C; 121A-128C); see also *On the Creation of the Human Person* 14.2 on the relation of soul and body to each other.

85. *On the Soul and the Resurrection* (29 B10-14; trans. Catherine P. Roth [Crestwood, N.Y.: St. Vladimir's, 1993], 37). It is in this treatise, too, that Gregory actually refers to the whole human being as "a small cosmos" (28 B9), presumably as a way of laying a foundation for his argument to the existence of the soul in the body by analogy with the more familiar argument to the existence of God in the world.

86. *Catechetical Oration* 6, trans. Cyril C. Richardson, in *Christology of the Later Fathers*, Library of Christian Classics 3 (Philadelphia: Westminster, 1954), 280.

87. *On the Creation of the Human Person* 4-5; *Catechetical Oration* 6.

88. *Catechetical Oration* 6.

tion in, God's infinite qualities of goodness and beauty.[89] And this transformation of the human, which begins now in our imitation of Christ and in our acquisition of virtue and will come to its fullness in the resurrection of our own bodies, has already begun in the transformation worked in his own human nature, as the "first fruits" of a transformation of the whole of humanity, by the incarnate Word:

> Since humanity is changeable, but the divine unchangeable, the divinity is not moveable by alteration, either towards the better or towards the worse (since it does not receive what is worse and there is nothing which is better); but the human nature in Christ does possess the ability to change for the better, being transformed from corruption to incorruption, from what is perishable to what is imperishable, from what is short-lived to what is eternal, from what is bodily and of perceptible shape to what is bodiless and without shape.[90]

Gregory is appropriately agnostic about the actual details of the form of the risen body. At least twice in his treatise *On the Soul and the Resurrection*, he makes clear that he imagines the event of resurrection essentially in terms of the reassembly of the body's dispersed "elements" *(stoicheia)* by the soul, which — as a spiritual, nonlocalized being — has remained continually present to those elements, even in their dispersion.[91] Further, he stresses that it will be recognizably the body of the person we now are, yet in the "original," "divine" form that God eternally intended for the human creature, free from those features tied to our present state of need and passion;[92] like Paul's "spiritual body,"

89. See, e.g., *Life of Moses*, Praef. 5-8 (*Sources Chrétiennes* 1.2-4); 2.219-56 (ibid. 102-14); *On Perfection* 15 (Patrologia Graeca 46.285BC).

90. *Antirrhetikos against Apollinarius* 53 (Gregorii Nysseni Opera 3/1, 222.25–223.10). For further reflection on Gregory's "Christology of transformation," see my articles, "Divine Transcendence and Human Transformation: Gregory of Nyssa's Anti-Apollinarian Christology," *Studia Patristica* 32 (1997): 87-95; and "'Heavenly Man' and 'Eternal Christ': Apollinarius and Gregory of Nyssa on the Personal Identity of the Savior," *Journal of Early Christian Studies* (forthcoming).

91. *On the Soul and the Resurrection* (44A-48C, 72C-80A). This emphasis on the reassembly of the decomposed body's scattered parts, reminiscent of the theology of resurrection we have discussed above as Type 2, seems inconsistent with the rest of Gregory's anthropology, which emphasizes constant change and the transformation of our corporeal form. He may well have introduced it into this dialogue specifically to evade the charges leveled against Origen's understanding of the resurrection. For the influence of Methodius and his anti-Origenist critique on this work, see Patterson (above, n. 61), 192-96.

92. Ibid. 145D-149D.

it no longer will have its life ordered by its natural properties, but goes over into a spiritual and immutable state (for it is characteristic of the physical body to be continuously altered from what it is and to be always changing into something different). Of those excellent qualities which we see now shared by human beings along with plants and animals, none will be left in the life hereafter.[93]

And the anthropological reason that Gregory, like Origen, gives for this way of articulating Christian hope is the changeability of human nature:

Who does not know that human nature is like a stream, proceeding from birth to death perpetually in motion, and ceasing from motion only when it ceases from being? Our nature is like the fire on a wick, which seems to be always the same because the continuity of its motion shows that it is inseparably united with itself, but in truth it is always replacing itself and never remains the same. . . . As long as our nature is alive, it has no stillness.[94]

Because it is always in motion, human nature is capable, in Christ, of endless growth in the spiritual, and even in the bodily realization of his divine image.

---

93. Ibid. 156 A13-B7; Roth, 118. Although he emphasizes that perfection will be a constant process of change, Gregory also makes it clear that its direction will be toward ever-greater union with God, without the possibility of a future, second fall; as the only reality created by creatures, evil is by nature finite, while the natural dynamism of human nature is toward the good. See *On Virginity* 12; *On the Creation of the Human Person* 21; *On the Soul and the Resurrection* 69 C1–72 B10; 102 A2-8; 104 B13–105 A2.

94. Ibid. 141 A-C; Roth, 110-11. In his treatise *On the Creation of the Human Person* (probably an earlier work), Gregory makes the same point, specifically referring to Origen's notion of an enduring "shape" or "form" *(eidos)* as the principle of continuity within change (see 27.3); for his discussion of the resurrection here, see 21-22, 26-27.
One of the distinctive features of Gregory's ontology, which — strangely, perhaps — seems not to have prevented him from conceiving of beings in terms of identity in transformation, is that he explicitly rejects the Aristotelian notion of a "prime matter" underlying such change as its continuing subject, and describes beings simply in terms of the sum total of their qualities: see *On the Hexaemeron* (Patrologia Graeca 44.69 BC); *On the Creation of the Human Person* 24 (Patrologia Graeca 44.212-13); *On the Soul and the Resurrection* (124 B-D). For comment on Gregory's argument, and on its source in a combination of the Platonic tradition of ideas and the Stoic theory of "seminal structures," see Richard Sorabji, *Matter, Space and Motion: Theories in Antiquity and Their Sequel* (Ithaca: Cornell University, 1988), 52-55. Sorabji sees in Gregory's conception of bodies as "bundles of properties" an anticipation of the ontology of Berkeley and nineteenth-century idealism.

Summary and Questions

This brief survey of early Christian ways of articulating an intelligent, reflective faith in the resurrection is necessarily sketchy in its details and somewhat arbitrary in its groupings. The point I want to make is that different conceptions of the resurrection grow largely out of different senses of the issues challenging faith and different understandings of the human person in which hope in the resurrection finds its intellectual context. All the authors we have discussed saw themselves as faithfully defending the affirmations of the New Testament and the church's rule of faith; all of them were concerned to respond to the challenges raised to the resurrection hope by both unbelievers and questioning Christians. Some of the early Apologists, and even Irenaeus, were content to develop a biblically rooted view of the human person that regarded both soul and body as incomplete in themselves, of uncertain future without the gift of God's Spirit. Gnostic writers like the author of the *Epistle to Rheginos* tended to interpret the Christian hope in wholly internal, even metaphorical terms, as the revelation of a new self-understanding that freed the believer from serious involvement with the world of ordinary material and social relationships. Still other authors, from the time of the Apologists through Augustine, made more earnest attempts to defend the plausibility of a bodily resurrection, even understood as the reconstruction of dead and corrupted bodies in their present material form, by appeals to the creative power of God. Origen and Gregory of Nyssa, in a different way, attempted to construct an apologia for a less materialistically understood resurrection — a resurrection not "fit for worms" but "worthy of God"[95] — not simply through an appeal to God's power but through a careful interweaving of biblical imagery, philosophical speculation, and scientific observation.

For all of these early theologians, the central issues in conceiving a future resurrection were surely the same questions with which contemporary theology struggles: (1) How do we bring personal continuity and identity into such a balance with qualitative and phenomenal change that the death and resurrection of one human being can be spoken of meaningfully at all? (2) What is God's role in the process, given that He has both created us from nothing and redeemed us in our weakened, fallen state? Behind their discussion of both the role of the soul and the role of God in the raising of the dead lay also — implicitly, at least — a third, more philosophical issue, with which Greek thought had wrestled since Aristotle: (3) How can an immaterial cause be understood to have material effects? How can a transcendent source of

95. See Origen, *Against Celsus* 5.14-18, 23.

change and motion be plausibly understood to be effective within the world of our empirical experience?[96] In Christian terms, the question was: (4) How could the God who has saved us from sin and death in Christ be genuinely understood as promising to raise our own bodies from the death that sin has caused, without compromising faith, religious reverence, or the intellectual integrity of a sophisticated Hellene?

And beyond these questions lay several assumptions that continued to shape their conception of the risen person: the assumption that the intelligibility of all things is fully disclosed only in terms of the thing's *end*, its perfect state or natural goal; the conviction that the human person — for most thinkers, the human soul as the seat of reason and freedom — finds its central substantial identity and goal in being the image of God; and the consequent beliefs that the human person, as a whole, is the crowning point and ruler of creation, and that the human body shares in the soul's holiness and privilege, as it shares in its life.[97]

Epilogue

Toward the end of the fourth century, a Syrian bishop named Nemesius of Emesa composed a treatise *On the Nature of the Human Person*, which unfortunately is little known today. Nemesius seems to have been a pupil of Eusebius of Caesarea and an admirer of Origen,[98] and may have been an acquaintance and correspondent of Gregory of Nazianzus;[99] he was also well

96. See Rist, "On Greek Biology" (above, n. 12).

97. See, e.g., Origen's characteristic remarks in *Against Celsus* 6.64: ". . . That which is made in the image of God is to be understood of the inward man, as we call it, which is renewed and has the power to be formed in the image of the Creator, when a person becomes perfect as his heavenly Father is perfect, and when he hears 'Be holy because I the Lord your God am holy,' and when he learns the saying 'Become imitators of God' and assumes into his own virtuous soul the characteristics of God. Then also the body of the person who has assumed the characteristics of God, in that part which is made in the image of God, is a temple, since he possesses a soul of this character and has God in his soul because of that which is in his image."

98. See Eiliv Skard, "Nemesiosstudien I. Nemesios und die Genesisexegese des Origenes," *Symbolae Osloenses* 15-16 (1936): 23-43.

99. Letters 198-201 of Gregory of Nazianzus are addressed to a certain Nemesius, a philosophically educated pagan, who was at the time — presumably the 380s — governor of the province of Cappadocia. Since Louis Le Nain de Tillemont, in the late seventeenth century (*Mémoires* 9:540-41, 601), Patristic scholars have wondered if this might be the same Nemesius as the (later) bishop and author of this treatise.

versed in the Hellenistic philosophical and medical traditions, and may have practiced as a physician himself. His treatise is a fascinating synthesis of what late antique Greek culture had to say about the human person: largely descriptive, mainly scientific and philosophical, yet deftly framed, too, in the Christian conviction that Christ had transformed that humanity by his presence and had made it his own.

Although he generally adopts the Neoplatonist understanding of the central role of the conscious soul in the definition of the human person,[100] Nemesius echoes — early in the treatise — the conviction of some of the Apologists that "the human person was created at first neither avowedly mortal nor yet immortal, but rather in a state poised between the two," in the sense that if he were to follow passion he would die, but if he pursued "the good of his soul foremost" he would live without end.[101] This very ambiguity about the future, which is built into the biblical narrative of human origins as Nemesius reads it, he later connects — as Origen and Gregory of Nyssa would do — with the human person's fundamental ability to change and to grow, focused by Nemesius into what are for him the two propensities characteristic of human creatures alone: our ability to be converted from sin and forgiven, and our ability to be raised from the dead. He writes:

> Man has two choice prerogatives, which are as follows, and are shared by no other creature. Man only, on repenting, can gain forgiveness. And only man's body, though mortal, is immortalized. This privilege of the body is for the soul's sake. So, likewise, the soul's privilege is on account of the body.[102]

Our hearts can be converted, he seems to be saying, so that our bodies can be raised; our bodies are raised to give full realization to the transformation of our hearts.

A little later, Nemesius reflects further on this uniquely privileged position of the human person within the larger cosmos in uncharacteristically lyrical terms:

> He is the creature whom God thought worthy of such special providence that, for his sake, all creatures have their being, both those that now are,

---

100. See, e.g., chs. 7 and 66. The best general study of Nemesius's anthropology and its sources is Alberto Siclari, *L'antropologia di Nemesio di Emesa* (Padua: La Garangola, 1974).

101. *On the Nature of the Human Person* 5, trans. William Telfer, Library of Christian Classics 4 (Philadelphia: Westminster, 1955), 238 (modified).

102. Ibid. 7 (244).

and those that are yet to be. He is the creature for whose sake God became human, so that this creature might attain incorruption and escape corruption, might reign on high, being made after the image and likeness of God, dwelling with Christ as a child of God, and might be throned above all rule and all authority. Who, then, can fully express the pre-eminence of so singular a creature?[103]

In the end, Nemesius seems to be saying, all Christian anthropology and all Christian hope must grow from wonder at the mystery of the incarnation of God. Perhaps that is what makes hope in the resurrection so central a feature of the Christian profession.

---

103. Ibid. 10 (254-55). Significantly, when Nemesius — using terminology from Porphyry's *Miscellaneous Investigations* — later (ch. 22) discusses the way in which a spiritual human soul can be united with a material body without confusion or limitation, he offers as a confirming analogy the "manner of union" of God the Word with an individual human nature in the incarnation.

Schleiermacher on Eschatology and Resurrection

BERND OBERDORFER

Eschatological scepticism abounds. The German New Testament scholar Gerd Lüdemann (just to name an extreme example) found it ridiculous to assume that one day all people who have ever lived on earth will be gathered on a renewed earth; it will be a bit overcrowded and narrow then, he concluded ironically. One might find it ridiculous as well that an academic theologian dares describe the Christian hope in that simplistic way. On the contrary, a well-reflected Christian piety and theology did and does not show such a naive realism.

There has always been an awareness that in eschatology we face the hermeneutical and epistemological problems of theology in a particularly dense and intensive form. In eschatology, we not only have to deal with the regular hermeneutical problems of religious language that result from the categorical distinction between Creator and creature, but we also have to take into consideration the difference between the present state of the world and a future state of complete fulfillment. This complete fulfillment may not be conceived as an immanent, entelechical development of the world itself but rather as a work of God. Nevertheless, it has to be conceived as the realization of the essential destination of the world.

Continuity and Discontinuity

How can such a state of perfection be imagined? There must be elements of *continuity* between this and that state of the world, but an elementary *disconti-*

nuity must be maintained as well.[1] In the theological tradition, either continuity could be stressed by using a evolutionary concept of perfection, or an emphasis could be put on discontinuity by using a concept of new creation. But a state of perfection cannot be conceived without a *specific difference* from the unfinished or "preperfect" states, nor can a new creation be conceived without reference to the old one (the *new* creation is still a new *creation*). It is difficult to distinguish the elements that endure from the elements destined to vanish in eternal life (which aspects of biography, for example, belong essentially to the *personality* whose identity has to be maintained provided that the individual's hope of eternal life implies an eschatological self-consciousness?).[2] Therefore, it is difficult to give a clear picture of this kind of perfection.

Moreover, every attempt to give such a picture risks being regarded as an illusionary or even ideological idealization of reality without a basis in matter. To avoid that risk, eschatological conceptions often restrict themselves to reflecting only on the destiny of the individual self without respect to the destiny of the transitory world. This results in a kind of "slim eschatology" of the self's eternal conservation in God. This conception seems to avoid the danger of colliding with modern scientific cosmologies. But, obviously, it misses humans' elementary self-understanding as essentially "being in the world" *(In-der-Welt-Sein)*.

So eschatology has to find its way between the Scylla of a quasi-scientific, quasi-realistic description of a future world and the Charybdis of the abstract evocation of the individual's eternal existence "in God."

Interpreting Schleiermacher

Friedrich Schleiermacher is regarded as one of the greatest demythologizers of Christian eschatology. He is known for asserting that "the same value cannot be ascribed" to the eschatological doctrines of the church as to the other doctrines.[3] And he distinguished the eschatological parts of the *Glaubenslehre*

1. Cf. Ernst Conradie (this volume). For the transformed bodiliness of the risen Christ in continuity with and discontinuity from his earthly body cf. Bernd Oberdorfer, "Was sucht ihr den Lebendigen bei den Toten? Überlegungen zur Realität der Auferstehung in Auseinandersetzung mit Gerd Lüdemann," *Kerygma und Dogma* 46 (2000): 225-40.

2. Cf. Nancey Murphy (this volume).

3. Friedrich Schleiermacher, *Der christliche Glaube* (Berlin: de Gruyter, 2d ed. 1830/ 1831, 7th ed. 1960), §159 Leitsatz; cf. §159,2. In the following, I will partly refer to the English translation: *The Christian Faith*, ed. H. R. Mackintosh and J. S. Stewart (Edinburgh: T&T Clark, 1928).

from its regular parts by characterizing them as "prophetical doctrines *(prophetische Lehrstücke)*" (§159,3) which are the result of an "insufficiently supported presentiment"[4] (ibid.). But when scrutinized (particularly as Eilert Herms did in a remarkable paper in 1990[5]), Schleiermacher's reflections reveal an extraordinarily subtle hermeneutics of eschatological claims. Quite contrary to his image as an anthropocentric and individualistic theologian of intrinsic feeling, he also emphasizes the cosmological and the social dimensions of eschatology. This is particularly interesting because he develops his eschatology within a theological framework that is supposed to avoid conflict between theology and the worldview of the natural sciences.

In the following, I would therefore like to interpret Schleiermacher's eschatology as a hermeneutically considered and nonreductionist eschatology that reflects on the different approaches of theology and science. It does not evade dialogue. First I will outline Schleiermacher's hermeneutics of eschatological claims. Second, I will discuss Schleiermacher's reflections on the resurrection of Christ and the general resurrection of the dead. In my presentation of Schleiermacher's eschatology, I will refer only to the eschatological parts of the second edition of the *Glaubenslehre* (1830/31) as being the most elaborated and structured form of his theology.

Recently, the Tübingen scholar Martin Weeber, in his book *Schleiermachers Eschatologie,*[6] argued that in the *Glaubenslehre* Schleiermacher did not describe his own eschatological theory but rather critically discussed the eschatological traditions of the church. And, according to Weeber, Schleiermacher, when emphasizing the cosmological focus of traditional eschatological claims, did not aim at defending them but rather at showing their inconsistency. Weeber sees Schleiermacher's own eschatology being displayed in some of his later sermons: a radically existential eschatology of the present moment that has eliminated any cosmological implications. But although Schleiermacher did not understand his *Glaubenslehre* simply as an expression of his personal faith but as a coherent exposition of the doctrines of the Protestant church, it does not seem very plausible to assume that he wrote the eschatological parts in a kind of *reservatio mentalis*. Actually, he pointed out that we cannot produce a coherent picture of eschatological fulfillment. As I will show, however, this is caused by the categorical and epistemological difference be-

---

4. "Versuche eines nicht hinreichend unterstützten Ahnungsvermögens."

5. Eilert Herms, "Schleiermachers Eschatologie," *Theologische Zeitschrift* 46 (1990): 97-123.

6. Martin Weeber, *Schleiermachers Eschatologie: Eine Untersuchung zum theologischen Spätwerk* (Gütersloh: Christian Kaiser, 2000).

tween the present state of the world and the state of its fulfillment, which makes it difficult to imagine that fulfillment; but it does not imply that this fulfillment is not supposed to be real. Even if Schleiermacher had developed an acosmic type of eschatology beside the cosmological eschatology of the *Glaubenslehre,* we would have to ask whether this alternative is convincing.

Schleiermacher's Hermeneutics of Eschatological Propositions

To understand why Schleiermacher did not count the eschatological reflections among the regular doctrines, we have to consider first how he defines Christian doctrines. According to §15 of the *Glaubenslehre,* "Christian doctrines are accounts of the Christian religious affection set forth in speech." They are expressions of the immediate self-consciousness, the feeling of absolute dependency that in Christianity is essentially related to the redemption realized through Christ.

Schleiermacher says that "All religious emotions . . . as soon as they have reached a certain stage and a certain definiteness . . . manifest themselves outwardly," at first by mimicry and gesture, at a higher stage primarily in speech (§15,1). "The whole work of the Redeemer Himself was conditioned by the communicability of His self-consciousness by means of speech, and similarly Christianity has always and everywhere spread itself solely by preaching" (§15,2). Religion, thus, is a matter of inwardness, but it does not come from the depths of the inward life. Rather, it must be evoked and shaped by communication (it "cannot, any more than anything else which is human, be conceived entirely separated from all communication"; ibid.).

In its history, Christian preaching "very soon split up into three different types of speech, which provided as many different forms of doctrine: the poetic, the rhetorical . . . and finally the descriptively didactic" (§15,2). They differ not so much with respect "to the degree or level of piety as rather to the character of the communion or fellowship and its ripeness for reflection and contemplation" (ibid.). So, as much as this communication is "something different from the piety itself," so much "the doctrines in all their forms have their ultimate ground so exclusively in the emotions of the religious self-consciousness, that where these do not exist the doctrine cannot arise" (ibid.). "Dogmatic propositions," now, "are doctrines of the descriptively didactic type, in which the highest possible degree of definiteness is aimed at" (§16). Unlike the poetic and the rhetorical type, the descriptively didactic type cannot tolerate contradictions and inconsistencies. Dogmatic theology, therefore, has to produce a coherent and consistent theory. The object of theology is piety as it is expressed in speech. Dogmatics, then, is a second-order language system because it examines critically and systematizes first-order expressions of piety.

The criterion of this examination is first whether these expressions can be understood as being expressions of an immediate self-consciousness formed by the impression of Christ's perfect consciousness of God, and second whether they can be integrated into a consistent description of the Christian faith. Due to two arguments, Schleiermacher conceives dogmatics as a coherent description of the *present* doctrine of a certain *church:* first of all, he understands Christ as the principle and beginning of a new *"Gesamtleben,"* a new totality of life that is being realized throughout history in the community of the church, and, secondly, people participate in that *Gesamtleben* through getting involved in the community of the church that communicates the content and the meaning of the *Gesamtleben.*

The object of dogmatic propositions, according to Schleiermacher, is the genesis and the shape of subjective Christian piety as described in the doctrine of the church. Church doctrines have to be evaluated as to whether and to what extent they can be regarded as expressions of Christian faith. This determines the elementary structure of the *Glaubenslehre:* it has two parts, of which the second one has two sections. The crucial part is the second section of the second part. It unfolds the renewed existence in the new *Gesamtleben* (pneumatology and ecclesiology) and the foundation of this *Gesamtleben* by Christ (Christology). The first section of the second part reflects on humankind's existence under the conditions of sin. That means, as Eilert Herms rightly put it, that it tackles the *temporal* premises of redemption. The first part entails the doctrine of creation. That means, in Schleiermacher's system, that it entails propositions that are valid independently from the opposition of sin and grace and thus are valid in the state of sin as well as in the state of grace. According to Herms, this part reflects on the *logical* premises of redemption. In each of these parts, three aspects of meaning have to be taken into consideration: the meaning for the understanding of the self (which is basic), of the world, and of God.

Interestingly enough, eschatology does not form its own part within the *Glaubenslehre.* Instead, it concludes the second half of the second section of the second part: it deals with the "consummation of the church." While the first part describes the structures of existence, which are independent from the opposition of sin and grace, the second part describes existence under the conditions of this opposition, or, more exactly, it describes existence under the conditions of sin and its transformation into existence under the conditions of grace. The old *Gesamtleben* of sin is in the state of being transformed into the new *Gesamtleben* of grace. This new *Gesamtleben* has come within the world of sin in the person of Christ (that is the topic of the first section of the second part, which entails the doctrine of Christ's person and redeeming work).

In Christ's person, creation was in a state of perfection. He was, in other words, the perfection, the consummation of creation. But it was still a perfection in opposition.

And that is still the case, although the new *Gesamtleben* is growing throughout history (the growing of the new *Gesamtleben* is the topic of the second section of the second part, tackling ecclesiology). The church in history is an *ecclesia militans*, a *fighting* church (cf. §157,1), struggling against the decreasing but still effective power of evil. Christians in history still have to be aware of the remaining power of sin within themselves and in their environment. In the future this opposition will be overcome. There will be a state of consummation without any opposition of grace and sin (*ecclesia triumphans;* cf. §157,1). Eschatology reflects on the realization and the shape of that state of perfection.

Although the position of eschatology within ecclesiology marks an essential continuity of history with the *eschaton,* there is also a radical discontinuity that is decisive for the epistemological status of eschatological propositions. Propositions, according to Schleiermacher, are dogmatic if they refer to modes of the present religious self-consciousness that in Christianity is formed by its reference to the redemption in Christ. Every present mode of religious self-consciousness, however, is involved in an opposition of sin and grace still virulent in our contemporary world. If eschatological propositions, by definition, refer to a state of the world beyond that opposition, they cannot be dogmatic propositions in the same sense as others are. That is the reason why Schleiermacher calls them "prophetic doctrines." If Schleiermacher states that "the same value *(Wert)* cannot be ascribed" to these doctrines as to the others, then he does not intend to diminish their worth but only emphasizes the epistemological difference.

So we have to reckon with a twofold difference. It is difficult to imagine the state of consummation not only due to our restricted capability of knowledge, but also due to the different state of reality itself. However, these difficulties do not give reason to deny the reality of a final fulfillment and eliminate eschatological propositions. On the contrary, this fulfillment is necessarily implied in the person of the Redeemer, who is the perfection of creation. But only in him. He is the only warrant of eschatological reality. The expectation of the world's consummation is not to be based in a natural tendency of the world itself, but can be promised only as an implication of the appearance of Christ.

In the introductory paragraphs of his eschatology (§§157-59), Schleier-macher demonstrates the hermeneutical problems with reference to the two elementary aspects of eschatological reality: the existence of the church beyond its opposition to evil, and the persistence of human personality after death.

The Church beyond Sin and the Soul beyond Death

Why is it so difficult to imagine a state of the church without continuous opposition to the *Gesamtleben* of sin? First, this must be a state in which "Christianity has spread over the whole world, in the sense that no other religion survives as an organized fellowship" (§157,1). Yet, the main problem is that in that state a new emergence of sin must be impossible. Then, according to Schleiermacher, there can no longer be physical reproduction, because "sin develops anew in each generation" (ibid.). This implies that the consummation of the church cannot take place within history.

If this is true, however, we have to locate that consummation in a "future on which (since it lies altogether beyond human experience) our action can exert no influence whatever" and of which "in the absence of all analogy we could hardly understand the picture aright or retain it securely" (§157,2). Propositions about the consummation of the church, therefore, "must contain no reference to anything in our present state due to the influences of the world" (ibid.).[7] "That these influences may be restrained, in a higher degree than the mere co-operation of individuals could secure, is the constant object of our prayers; and the consummated Church is accordingly the sphere where such prayer is answered in full measure" (ibid.). Hence, the idea of the consummation of the church, far from being formable to a consistent picture, is rooted only "in our Christian consciousness as representing the unbroken fellowship of human nature with Christ under conditions wholly unknown and only faintly imaginable" (ibid.). So it is the *unio hypostatica,* which gives reason to expect that the new *Gesamtleben* will come to a state of perfection.

The same goes for the postmortal existence of the individual (cf. §158). "As the belief in the immutability of the union of the Divine Essence with human nature in the Person of Christ contains in itself also the belief in the persistence of human personality," Schleiermacher writes, "this produces in the Christian the impulse to form a conception of the state that succeeds death"

---

7. "World" here means (in the sense in which it is used in the Gospel of John) the *Gesamtleben* of sin.

(§158, Thesis). Schleiermacher concedes that "belief in the continued existence of personality after death" (which, to his opinion, is equivalent to the term "immortality of the soul") is not exclusively Christian and, seen in the perspective of cultural history, did not arise from the experience of the *unio hypostatica*: "traces of that belief exist everywhere, and especially in the times of Christ and the Apostles it was prevalent among the Jewish people" (§158,1). But "apart from this connexion" with the *unio hypostatica* it "could not have been given a place in our Christian Dogmatic" (ibid.).

Schleiermacher and Science

Schleiermacher's argument in this regard is very subtle and touches the relation between theology and the natural sciences, and so it is worth a closer examination. Schleiermacher insists that "faith in the Redeemer . . . may develop out of a sense of sin calling for redemption, and that from it we might infer the communication of Christ's blessedness at every moment of life, including the last moment of all, *even though we had no conception whatever of a life after death*" (§158,1; my emphasis). And Schleiermacher remarks, "the whole of the preceding argument has been set forth and proved without reference to that belief" (ibid.).[8] "Thus the question naturally arises whether, and how, this belief would have come to be bound up with our religious consciousness, had not the Redeemer accepted and sanctioned it" (ibid.). Schleiermacher names two possible ways: "Either the survival of personality would have been ascertained as a truth through the activities of knowledge, that is by way of objective consciousness; or it might have been given us originally in our immediate self-consciousness" (ibid.).

In the first case, the "doctrine of immortality" would belong "to the higher natural science" (ibid.). But evidently, in natural science immortality "has always been attacked by some people as vehemently as it has been defended by others" (ibid.). No scientific consensus is available. Hence dog-

8. This obviously implies that, according to Schleiermacher, Christ's resurrection is not an essential element of the doctrine of Christ's person as being the principle of our redemption. Schleiermacher argues that as the disciples could recognize Christ as Redeemer before his crucifixion, his resurrection cannot be a necessary premise of belief in Christ. That does not mean, however, that Schleiermacher contests the reality of the resurrection. But he gives only an indirect reason: if the testimony of the disciples about their experiences with the risen Christ proved to be wrong, not only their own credibility would be destroyed, but (because of that) Christ himself would appear as not very prudent in choosing disciples whose witness could not be trusted.

matics, if it is willing "to make further use of the idea of immortality, is not entitled to adopt these proofs" (ibid.).

As to the second case, Schleiermacher argues, "there is an impious [namely, materialistic] denial of immortality." Further, "there is also a surrender of the survival of personality . . . which, far from regarding spiritual activity as a mere phenomenon of matter, or making matter superior to spirit, strictly regards spirit as the power which produces living matter and conforms it to itself" (ibid.). Then it could be said "that while spirit is essentially immortal in such productivity, yet of such productivity the individual soul is only a transient act, and thus essentially perishable" (ibid.). "Between such a surrender of the survival of personality and the predominance of the God-consciousness . . . there would be no incongruity whatever" (ibid.). Still further, whereas "there certainly is a belief in personal survival which is in harmony with the general spirit of piety . . . there is also a belief which is impious," namely, "if it merely issued from an interest in the sense-aspect of life" (ibid.). So, as Schleiermacher concludes, there is no necessary link between belief in the survival of personality and God-consciousness.

Nonetheless, this belief is profoundly based in our "faith in the Redeemer" (§158,2). Christ ascribes a survival of personality to himself when speaking about "His return or reunion with His people" (ibid.). Schleiermacher argues that Christ could "only say these things of Himself as a human person, because only as such could He have fellowship even with His disciples," and thus the conclusion is "(s)elf-evident," "that in virtue of the identity of human nature in Him and in us, the same must hold good of ourselves" (ibid.). Schleiermacher discusses the possibility that these "sayings of Christ are all figurative, and not to be interpreted strictly, and that He nowhere claims personal survival" (ibid.). He admits that "faith in Christ . . . would still be possible" then (ibid.). But "a complete transformation of Christianity would be the result were such a mode of interpretation to prevail within the Church and be made fundamental of the Christian faith" (ibid.). Schleiermacher adds, "this of itself implies that we cannot assume that such an interpretation could be put forward in good faith" (ibid.). This sentence is very significant to his theological program as a whole. He does not exclude the possibility of such a complete transformation in principle, but indirectly he reveals that he does not understand his own theology as such a complete transformation. And he confirms his conviction that Jesus actually believed in the survival of his personality.

If Christ is immortal, then it would be docetic to deny that "all who are of the human race can look forward to survival too" (ibid.). Christ is "the mediator of immortality, only not exclusively for those who believe on Him here, but for all, without exception" (ibid.). For "if personal immortality did not belong to human nature, no union of the Divine Essence with human nature to form such a personality of the Redeemer would have been possible; and, conversely, since God had determined to perfect and redeem human nature through such union, human individuals must all along have possessed the same immortality as the Redeemer was conscious of" (ibid.). In other words, the *unio hypostatica* is the only but the real base for belief in the immortality of *human nature*.

Although "this belief naturally is accompanied by a desire to form and keep clear ideas as to the condition of personality after death" (§158,3), it is impossible to fulfill this desire. The reason for this is that Christ did not unveil the concrete cosmological "conditions of existence after death" (ibid.). As much as all propositions about "times and seasons" "lie outside the range of those communications which the Redeemer had to make to us," so much the same goes for the "purely cosmological question" of "space and spatialities" (ibid.). From Christ's "figurative" or quite "indefinite" indications we can gather only the information that is indispensable to us to know if the conception of existence after death is not supposed to be "mere perdition" — and this is only "the persistent union of believers with the Redeemer" (ibid.).

Likewise, the apostles spoke on that subject only "by way of dim presentiment, and with the confession that definite knowledge is lacking" (ibid.). Therefore, Schleiermacher concludes, "we should not seek to determine our purposes by picturing to ourselves the form of our future life"⁹ (ibid.). He states that all respective "efforts . . . spring from the interest of our sensuous self-consciousness in the survival of personality" and thus "are always sensuous in character" (ibid.). He warns us not to allow them "an influence . . . which may only too easily injure Christian faith and life, and thereby spoil for us the present" (ibid.). So he is very cautious in developing a picture of the future fulfillment, and confines himself to "scrutiniz[ing] carefully the propositions put forward by others, as well as the opinions which have become dominant" (ibid.).

Despite this cautiousness, Herms rightly emphasizes that "according to Schleiermacher the continuous existence of human personality after death does not differ from its contemporary existence insofar as time and space vanish at all, but only insofar as they [namely, time and space] are qualified in a different way."¹⁰ Our problem in imagining our after-death state is not a re-

---

9. ". . . so dürfen wir uns nicht darauf einrichten, unsere Zweckbegriffe irgend durch Vergegenwärtigung der künftigen Lebensform bestimmen zu wollen."

10. Herms, *Schleiermachers Eschatologie*, 113 (my translation).

sult of the fact that this state is beyond time and space, but only of the fact that time and space will be different then. Evidently, as Herms adds, this implies "that space and time are not thought here as characteristic only of this world, but as characteristic of any possible world."[11]

The Consummate Church and the Resurrected Self

In the following §159, Schleiermacher declares that the ecclesiastical doctrines of "the Last Things" are an attempt to solve the two problems raised earlier, namely, "to represent the Church in its consummation and the state of souls in the future life" (§159, Thesis). Every eschatological doctrine refers to both of these problems. The one cannot be solved without reference to the other. For, on the one hand, "(i)f we tried to form a Christian idea of a state subsequent to this life, and it failed to agree with our idea of the consummation of the Church, we could not believe that it really expressed the absolutely final stage" because "we should have to suppose that there still remained a further development, in which the Church would be perfected" (§159,1). In other words, an individual after-death perfection would not be a real perfection without the consummation of the church as a whole. And, on the other hand, "if we viewed the consummation of the Church as arriving within the present course of human affairs, we should have to add something in thought for the state after death" (ibid.). It seems to be evident "that both elements should be thus conjoined." Because we cannot regard the consummation of the church "as possible in this life" which is characterized by the opposition of sin and grace, we seem to have to place it "in that future life," and, conversely, we have to fill out the idea of that future life — of which as such we have no concrete imagination — on the base of "fellowship with Christ" "with content from the perfected state of the Church" (ibid.).

The idea of regarding life after death and the consummation of the church as being complementary elements of a full eschatological picture becomes particularly tempting if we consider Herms's insight that the reasons for our incapacity to imagine after-death life and the consummation of the church differ from each other: while there is a *continuity* between this life and life after death (namely, the personality) that is impossible to imagine only due to the different qualification of space and time, the consummation of the church lacks imagination because there is *no analogy* between the state of the fighting church and the state of the church when an opposition of sin against

11. Ibid. (my translation).

grace no longer exists. Thus, the life after death can be conceived as *continuation* of the "new life which has started here," whereas the consummation of the church is to be conceived only as the *end* of the era of struggle.[12] If that is true, why then should the conception of the "survival of personality" not deliver to the conception of the consummated church a "place in space and time," and, conversely, why should the conception of the consummated church not deliver to the individual's continuous existence its specific eschatological character?

Hermeneutics without Analogy

But, nevertheless, "we are not in a position to exhibit the confluence of the two factors" (§159,1). Why not? On the one hand, the perfect state of the church is without analogy to its contemporary state, and thus cannot deliver concreteness to the understanding of continuous existence after death. On the other hand, "if we seek to conceive the future life by analogy with the present, as an ascending development, we cannot but have doubts whether any such development is possible in the consummated Church" (ibid.). Schleiermacher concludes: "Thus the solution of one problem never seems exactly to fit the other" (ibid.).

So, neither the after-death life nor the consummation of the church nor the combination of the two can be unfolded to a full picture of eschatological reality. As I have shown, this does not imply the denial of that reality. The certainty of it is rather rooted and warranted in the appearance of the Redeemer. But we are unable to imagine clearly that state of fulfillment. Nor can we base our imagination on the authority of Holy Scripture and its testimonies of Christ's words. For we "nowhere find in His teaching a connected and unambiguous treatment of these subjects obviously meant to convey definite instruction about them" (§159,2).

As to the form of eschatological claims, it follows from these reflections that "there is nothing for it but that we should bring up those thought-forms which early became prevalent in the Church and passed over into our Confessions without being submitted to a fresh scrutiny, and should adduce them, under the title of *prophetic doctrines*, merely as the efforts of an insufficiently equipped faculty of premonition [attempts of an insufficiently supported presentiment], adding reasons for and against" (ibid.). Schleiermacher does not categorically reject new forms of these doctrines being developed, but

12. Cf. ibid., 113ff.

warns that by doing so "the fancy (for to it belongs everything alien to the scope of our present experience which is set forth as the object of a possible future experience), if it is to remain Christian, must place itself under the protection of exegesis, and only elaborate the material which exegesis supplies" (ibid.). In any case, these new forms would not escape the hermeneutical conditions of eschatological propositions.

Schleiermacher structures the eschatological doctrines in four prophetical doctrines and one appendix. He starts with the return of Christ (§160) as the basis of the following doctrines because to it "everything which belongs to the completion of His work must be related" (§159,3). Then he tackles the resurrection of the flesh (§161) as representing "the survival of personality, above all, as the abolition of death" (§159,3). The consummation of the church is referred to in a twofold manner. First of all, in the doctrine of the Last Judgment (§162), this consummation "as conditioned by the fact that no further influence upon the Church can now be exerted by those who form no part of the Church . . . is introduced in its character as the separation of believers from unbelievers" (§159,3). Second, in the doctrine of eternal blessedness (§163), the existence of the church is described positively "as excluding (in contrast to the Church militant) all the activities of sin and all imperfection in believers" (§159,3). The doctrine of eternal damnation of the unbelieving "cannot be given the form of a special doctrine" because "it is not an anticipation of any object of our future experience" (ibid.). This is evident with reference to the character of the *Glaubenslehre* as being an explication of the immediate self-consciousness of believers: to regard eternal damnation as an article of faith would be a contradiction in itself. Eternal damnation rather is "the shadow of blessedness or the darker side of judgment" (ibid.). It has to be reflected on only because "the survival of personality, and therefore also the resurrection of the flesh," due to its being based on the *unio hypostatica,* "had to be taken as applying to the whole human race," and so "some mode of existence had to be found for those separated from believers" (ibid.).

In the following, I will remark only on Schleiermacher's understanding of the resurrection of the flesh.

Resurrection of the Flesh

At first, we have to consider whether or how Schleiermacher links the eschatological resurrection of the flesh to the resurrection of Christ. Does he understand Christ's resurrection as a "guarantee of our own resurrection" (§99,1)? It is remarkable that in Schleiermacher's Christology, Christ's resurrection plays only "a marginal role."[13] At least, it does not belong to the "genuine elements of the doctrine of His person" (§99, Thesis). "For if Christ's redeeming efficiency is based on God's being in Him, and if the impression of that causes belief in Him" (§99,1), then it must be conceded that this impression could be evoked before and without the experience of his resurrection. "The disciples recognized Him as the son of God without foreseeing His resurrection and ascension" (ibid.), and the same goes for us. Relevant to us is only his promise of "his spiritual presence" and "his continuous influence," which is expressed in the metaphor of Christ's sitting on the righthand side of God, and what that metaphor means — namely, Christ's "genuine and incomparable dignity which is lifted up beyond any conflict" (ibid.) — is conceivable without reference to Christ's resurrection.

Schleiermacher, however, does not conceal that Paul "seems to ascribe to Christ's resurrection as well as to His death a relevance to our redemption" (ibid.). But according to Schleiermacher, the way in which Paul refers to Christ's resurrection as being the "guarantee of our own resurrection" in 1 Corinthians 15 shows "that he does not understand it in an exclusive connexion with the genuine being of God in Christ" (ibid.). This argument is not entirely clear. Its sense presumably is: since Paul uses Christ's resurrection as the "guarantee" of our own future resurrection, resurrection does not belong exclusively to the doctrine of the person of the Redeemer and is not singularly characteristic of the Redeemer as the Redeemer.

But although Schleiermacher states "that we can expect of anyone who is familiar with dogmatic propositions to realize that a true impression of Christ can appear and actually has appeared without a knowledge" of his resurrection, he nevertheless maintains an "indirect connection" (§99,2) of Christ's resurrection to the doctrine of his person. Because the belief in Christ's resurrection cannot be deduced from the basic insight in God's being in Christ, this belief can arise only from the testimony of Holy Scripture. So we are dependent on the credibility of the witnesses of the resurrection, who are the disciples. If their evidence of resurrection were illusionary and they were unable to distinguish mental phenomena from objective events, we would not only lose our trust in their testimonies of Christ in any respect, but rather Christ himself would appear as not having been very prudent when choosing his disciples. So we have to trust the disciples' evidence of having met Christ after his death. But Schleiermacher does not give any further ex-

13. Markus Schröder, *Die kritische Identität des neuzeitlichen Christentums: Schleiermachers Wesensbestimmung der christlichen Religion* (Tübingen: J. C. B. Mohr [Paul Siebeck], 1996), 199 n. 43.

planation of the character of these meetings. If we take into consideration that Schleiermacher tended to interpret Christ's death as only an apparent death, it is quite likely that he understood the "resurrection" as a kind of reanimation. But anyway, he did not give any theological relevance to that aspect of Christ's appearance.[14]

It is significant that Schleiermacher, when summarizing the "essential content" of the doctrine of the resurrection of the flesh, does not refer to Christ's resurrection but rather to the "ascension of the risen Redeemer," and that means: to his sitting on God's righthand side. The doctrine essentially entails "that the ascension of the risen Redeemer was possible only if all other human individuals too can look forward to a renovation of organic life which has links of attachment to our present state"[15] (§161,3). This renovation must be thought, on the one hand, to be "dependent on Christ's divine power" (ibid.); it is not the result of natural development.[16] On the other hand, nevertheless, it must be conceived "as a cosmic event for which arrangements have been made in the universal divine world-order" (ibid.). But whereas the dependency on Christ's divine power "is certified as implied in the faith," the idea of this "cosmic event" "hovers before the mind as indicating a problem we can never completely solve" (ibid.).

Why will we never succeed in developing a concrete picture of final resurrection? Schleiermacher discusses this question with reference to the problem of continuity and discontinuity that is linked to the problem of the compatibility of the idea of individual postmortal existence and the idea of the consummation of the church. He starts his argument by stating "that we really cannot form the idea of a finite spiritual life apart from a bodily organism" (§161,1). Therefore, "it is impossible to speak of the soul's immortality in the strict sense apart from bodily life" (ibid.). So, "(s)ince the activity of the spirit as a definite soul ceases at death simultaneously with the bodily life, it is only with bodily life that it can recommence" (ibid.).

Moreover, the idea of resurrection also implies "such an identity of life that life after resurrection and life before death constitute one and the same personality" (ibid.). The idea of the soul as persisting individual entity re-

---

14. Markus Schröder speaks of a "solution which appears ghostly *(gespenstisch)*" but defends (with reference to Emanuel Hirsch) Schleiermacher's "*intention* to put the origin of the [Christian] congregation in the days of resurrection, ascension and the pouring out of the Spirit directly down to the person of Jesus of Nazareth" (ibid.).

15. ". . . sofern auch allen menschlichen Einzelwesen eine an den gegenwärtigen Zustand anknüpfende Erneuerung organischen Lebens bevorsteht."

16. Cf. §161, Thesis: Christ "in His utterances ascribed this awakening from death to His own agency."

quires "the continuity of consciousness, which again appears to us as conditioned by memory" (ibid.). Memory,[17] now, "in its turn is as much bound up with bodily states as any other mental activity" (ibid.). From that it follows that "such a unifying memory" can hardly work "under absolutely different bodily conditions" (ibid.). Thus, if the state of the after-death existence were totally different from our present state, we would lack that memory and therefore lose the "continuity of consciousness." So it seems to be evident "that the more the soul in itself remains the same, the more must the future life be a simple, easily attachable prolongation of the present" (ibid.).

That, however, is contrary to the idea of the consummation of the church because that consummation implies a fundamental *discontinuity*, namely, the end of any efficiency of sin. Because of that, "the similarity between the future organism and the present" has to be limited, which, according to Schleiermacher, is the intention of the "description of the resurrection body as immortal and without sex" (ibid.). Both fit very well with the idea of the consummation of the church. Immortality removes the "interest in bodily self-preservation" that is "so fruitful a seed of strife between flesh and spirit" (ibid.). The end of sexual intercourse prevents "new souls from being called into being through procreation," which is always the source of new sin.

Yet, immortality and the lack of sexual intercourse mark such a huge difference from our present conditions of life that these qualities "are inimical to the identity of the soul and the continuity of consciousness" (ibid.). Schleiermacher therefore concludes that both continuity and discontinuity have to be considered "but that the two really represent different interests" (ibid.). "Hence the different items cannot be combined in an idea capable of clear representation" (ibid.).[18]

17. Cf. Dirk Evers (this volume), esp. section 5.

18. In the following, Schleiermacher demonstrates that incompatibility reflecting on the question of an "intermediate state" between death and resurrection (§161,2), and with reference to the problem that, if there are "utterly different states" of the saved and the unsaved resulting from resurrection (which is implied in the doctrine of eternal damnation), then apparently "the new bodies which they receive" must also be "utterly different" because the "organism must be adapted to the conditions which are impending" (ibid.), and the question emerges whether the individuals already rise in their respective bodily state (which would mean that resurrection and the Last Judgment coincide) or all of them rise in an identical bodily shape that is being differentiated only after the Last Judgment (§161,3).

Summarizing Remarks

Unlike Martin Weeber, I do not think that in the eschatological parts of the *Glaubenslehre* Schleiermacher describes and discusses church doctrines only to show their aporetic character in order to make them dispensable to the Christian consciousness. I rather agree with Eilert Herms's emphasis that, according to Schleiermacher, eschatology, particularly in its cosmological dimensions, is a necessary element of the Christian consciousness even though there are epistemological and hermeneutical problems limiting our knowledge of the definite future and determining the specific character of eschatological propositions. Schleiermacher's reflections on eschatology are exemplary in several respects, of which I name only three:

First, Schleiermacher continuously takes into consideration the *theological* character of eschatological propositions in contrast to *scientific* theories, without, however, neglecting the cosmological implications of eschatological reality. He consistently bases eschatology on the appearance of Christ and particularly on Christ's assumption of human nature *(unio hypostatica)*, from which all certainty of persistence and perfection of humankind derives.

Second, he draws our attention to the crucial problem of eschatological imagination: the question of continuity and discontinuity between our present state and the state of fulfillment. In a very subtle way, he links that question to the two fundamental aspects of eschatological reality, the persistence of individual existence after death and the consummation of the new social life *(neues Gesamtleben)*, and thus forms a complex pattern to examine and interpret traditional eschatological doctrines. We will hardly find a discussion of the intrinsic rationality of eschatological propositions that is as sophisticated as Schleiermacher's.

Third, Schleiermacher combines an emphasis on the body-bound character of the human soul with reflections on the conditions of existence in any given world. Although we cannot portray a concrete picture of eschatological existence, we are entitled to assume that this existence will have a worldly shape, taking place not beyond time and space but in a different form of time and space. Herms rightly states that Schleiermacher maintains the expectation of "a new heaven and a new earth." So it remains indispensable to insist on the bodily character of eschatological existence. However, we will never escape the dilemma that an emphasis on the *continuity* between the present and the future state will diminish the impression of perfection, whereas an emphasis on the *discontinuity* will damage the impression of personal identity.

Obviously, there might arise critical questions with reference to many details of Schleiermacher's expositions. In the end of my chapter, I will not deal with that but rather only mark a problem that is fundamental to Schleiermacher's program as such: according to Schleiermacher, Christ's resurrection is not essential to his redemptive work. We share subjectively in redemption by participating in his consciousness of God, which was accessible before his resurrection and is still accessible independently of it. Schleiermacher thus represents a type of soteriology that focuses on the teaching of the historical Jesus rather than on his work in resurrection. But is it really true that Christ's resurrection has no relevance to our understanding of him and his redemptive work? To ask that, however, does not necessarily imply doubting the relevance and significance of Schleiermacher's eschatological thoughts as such, but anyway demands that we reflect anew on the soteriological meaning of Christ's resurrection and its impact on our understanding of eschatological reality.

PART III

RESURRECTION AND THE
LAWS OF NATURE

God Gives the Memory: Neuroscience and Resurrection

DETLEF B. LINKE

Nonparametric Identities

Particular candidates for securing concepts of personal identity are the temporal-spatial continuity of the body and the preservation of a set of psychological characteristics. From a formal point of view, identity can also be attributed when the parameters mentioned are reduced to a minimum. This is the case when, as in fairy tales, a prince is transformed into a bear or into a frog, but can still be retransformed or retransfigured. Also, in *The Odyssey,* the companions of Odysseus were thought of as preserving their identity even when they were transformed into pigs. Such conceptions of preserving identity in extremely different bodily situations have become more difficult with a differentiated development of the brain sciences. What kind of brains did the pigs have who were the transfigured companions of Odysseus? With knowledge about brains such questions can be answered only in the sense of radical nonparametric preservation of identity and/or when sticking to a strict dualism concerning the mind-brain relation. But while in fairy tales the bear sometimes can even say that he is an enchanted prince, even dualistic philosophers and brain scientists would not accept that as being possible for bears.

The reduction of bodily continuity and psychological characteristics to such a minimum that there is rather a nonparametric identity can be thought of in the act of God, who is not in need of having quantities of parameters for his actions. Gottlieb Wilhelm Leibniz made some remarkable comments on this subject. Leibniz could not think of either joy or punishment in another life without the idea of preserved identity. For the case of joy and pleasure, he chose the example of the peasant becoming the emperor of China in his next life. In Leibniz's perspective, there would be no interest in this idea if there were no preservation of memory of the former life. I do not find this argument convincing. Could not an emperor be happy about his state of being without the memory of having been a peasant in his former life? If the memory is not just weak but rather deep-rooted, as important memories of a human life are, then it would be in relation to modified traits of the new personality outside of conscious memory. In such a case, the argument could even be put in such a way that there would be the possibility of the emperor having less pleasure, because some former, but now corrected, traits could interfere with his present condition, disturbing the coherence of his new biography. So, in fact, the emperor could be even happier without memory of his former life.

Also, Leibniz's argument that identity is necessary to receive punishment allows some modification. The punishment could simply lie in the fact that the parameters of identity have changed. Such facts are well known from biographical events in which the experience of guilt changes the experience of personal identity and the perspective of the subject in such a way that all the former characteristics of the person get lost and "self" becomes either a very abstract and general notion or the description of a very new situation.

In sum, we could in principle experience joy without remembering our former existence, and we could undergo pain even when we are not able to preserve characteristics of our former personality. We may enjoy a consciousness oriented around an "I" that is freed from concrete characteristics.

This would be a very abstract form of existence, but conscious experience of pleasure and pain would nevertheless be possible in such a notion. More and more, neurophilosophy and neuroscience see consciousness as being correlated with the complexity of brain function; and one can also think of this complexity as having self-reference without complete knowledge of the characteristics of the self. Furthermore, we can see complex cognition in which there is no additional reference to the self. In physical terms it might just be a high level of brain complexity of electromagnetic patterns, for example, or of neurochemical or chemical diffusional processes that happen to be related to consciousness but not restricting conscious experience to the act of stating that one is existing (or thinking).

It would be of great interest to look for physical correlations to the dimension of "existence" or "being." Before we dare to touch such an extremely far-reaching philosophical task we would rather like to look for some dimensions of the nervous system in which complexities and the bases for their stability can be described.

Origin of Soul

Where does the notion of separate souls, and of souls for which the bodily parameters are irrelevant, come from? I think one important aspect of this notion lies in the intuition that mental functions can happen without bodily information being processed. This means that mental, cognitive, and even emotional processes can be carried out by the nervous system without using resources and feedback from the extracerebral body. This possibility of the brain can be seen as the origin of the intuitions in cultural history for a soul being able to live without the body. (In these cases the brain that could not be observed without special measures was not taken into account.)

The ability of the nervous system to perform complex processes without using feedback can be seen as the ground for a decisive step in human evolution. This step was made possible for humanity by using an "outer" space in which, after having learned its parameters, actual feedback control was not necessary. This "outer" space is the space of the articulatory system, which, different from all other "outer" spaces to a very great degree, shows constancy for the human being. In patients having lost oral-facial and lingual sensibility it can be shown that fine articulated speech is possible even when auditory feedback is excluded by white noise.[1]

On this ground, the neurons necessary for motor speech production can be active without continuous feedback. Thus they are free to perform new group arrangements and build permutations in the time series. This is the basis for the possibility of combining phonemes and words into new constellations. It is the ground for the combinatory creativity of the mind. In being free from feedback the brain can build combinations and group selections much better than by waiting for resonances[2] or coherences and "reentry."[3]

For the body-mind relation this finding means that for speech, the bodily parameters of the articulatory system can be processed without using actual feedback. The brain is thoroughly shaped in performing motor activity by the knowledge of its extracerebral body, especially as far as the articulatory system is concerned. The neurons of an individual brain, in their outreach pattern and connections, contain important information about the body to

1. D. B. Linke, "Die Stimme im Mund," in *Quel Corps?* ed. H. Belting et al., 2002 (forthcoming); and D. B. Linke, "Ein neurokybernetisches Modell der Sprechmotorik," in *Cybernetics* (München-Wien: G. Hauske and E. Butenandt, 1978), 371-72.

2. S. Grossberg, *Studies of Mind and Brain*, Boston Studies in the Philosophy of Science (Dordrecht: D. Reidel, 1982), vol. 70.

3. G. M. Edelman and G. Tononi, *A Universe of Consciousness* (New York: Basic Books, 2000).

which it belongs. Taking it the other way around, one can say that the parameters of the body will have shaped the development of the brain in some important aspects.

The stability of the neurons relevant for the articulatory nervous system, which is attained mainly by independence from feedback (when speech has been learned), opens a wide field for the investigation of stability in the nervous system. Speech development was an important step in human development. Many cognitive functions were and are structured by it. But with their brains human beings also tried to build up stability in areas of function where speech could not immediately succeed.

The Brain and Speech

The peripheral speech motor system need not be represented as a spike code in the nervous system. It is already an inherent structure of the interconnected neurons that allows certain programs to become a routine and to calculate with information. Information is implicit in the growth of the neurons relevant for speech. It operates at a level of semiotics similar to that in Edgar Allan Poe's "The Adventures of Arthur Gordon Pym," where the figures notice that by trodding a path in a valley they follow the geometry of an alphabet.

The human body develops a structure in which the parameters of the body determine the parameters for initiating cognition through speech. In this context it is of great interest to notice that the length of the right and left laryngeal nerves sets constraints for the interaction of the two brain hemispheres. The left laryngeal nerve has to run around the aorta and is therefore ten centimeters longer than the right one. The left nerve is controlled by the right hemisphere. To get synchronous motor activity for phonation it is necessary that the right hemisphere starts about six to seven milliseconds before the left hemisphere with the impulses for vocalization. In this way the left hemisphere has time to coordinate the impulses for articulation. Elsewhere we have hypothesized that the difference of conduction times for the innervation of the voice might be the basis for asymmetric hemispheric specialization.[4]

In any case, the structure of the speech system is situated between the brain and the body in such a way that the brain structures develop in close relation to the information structures of the body. This gives the brain structures a certain stability and stresses the special importance of the word. This

4. Linke, "Die Stimme im Mund."

dominance of the word can be demonstrated in studies of hemispheric relations,[5] where in dominance shift language builds clusters of coherence.

Because of the preplanned structure of the speech system with its combinatorial possibilities, the brain is equipped with anticipatory stabilities. To a certain degree, cognitive function can refer to stabilities without having to calculate surprise all the time. On this ground, the brain can develop the ability to cope with unforeseen situations and information. We would therefore like to promote a model of brain function that is different from the models of S. Grossberg and G. M. Edelman. We think that very important information in brain function is conveyed in the growth structure of the nervous system. It is well known that memory information can induce the growth of new neurons even in adults. On this basis, the neuroarchitectural basis of cognitive function has to be stressed much more.

Cognition does not start with the binding and coherence of impulses. This is not the ground but the aim of cognition. In Grossberg's model, cognition functions through the resonance between the expected and the unexpected. In the Phillips and Singer model,[6] it is the binding and coherence that constitutes the cognitive pattern for which experimental results have been found. Mostly, questions of coherence have been discussed under the heading of the "binding problem." Edelman does see the occurrence of bindings and coherences as made possible by the reentry between two systems, especially the thalamus and the cortex. I think that it is important to understand that there are structures in the brain that can perform their activities (speech production) on the basis of preprogrammed information without the need of continuously monitoring the unexpected.

Derrida's Category Mistake

Jacques Derrida makes the attempt to think the future in a radical way without anticipation. I believe that it is necessary to make the distinction between explicit and implicit anticipation. By having developed certain geo-

5. C. Helmstaedter, M. Kurthen, D. B. Linke, and C. E. Elger, "Right Hemisphere Restitution of Language and Memory Functions in Right Hemisphere Language-Dominant Patients with Left Temporal Lobe Epilepsy," *Brain* 117 (1994): 729-37; and C. Helmstädter, M. Kurthen, D. B. Linke, and C. E. Elger, "Patterns of Language Dominance in Focal Left and Right Hemisphere Epilepsies: Relation to MRI Findings, EEG, Sex and Age at Onset of Epilepsy," *Brain and Cognition* 33 (1997): 135-50.

6. W. A. Phillips and W. Singer, "In Search of Common Foundations for Cortical Computation," *Behavioral and Brain Sciences* 20 (1997): 657-722.

metric and topological structures on the basis of experience and activity, the nervous system cannot but present structures of its history for the experience of the future. Nevertheless, the inherited structures can undergo significant change and influence what is forthcoming. Experiences that can be integrated by the soul will root themselves in the stabilities of the speech system and its derivatives.

The structure of anticipation is more complicated. The motor processes of speech are largely performed without consciousness. Consciousness is most likely wired to neuronal processes in which coherence and binding (and in a more special sense reentry) are searched for. The degree of anticipation will influence what kind of and how many coherences for the future will be found by our consciousness.

What about Derrida's election of a future without explicit anticipation? It may be that Derrida's concept of *difference* as less "present" than we usually assume is fruitful in some respects; but we believe his supporting arguments rely on a category mistake. Derrida mistakenly reduces behavioral patterns to neuronal patterns.

Derrida relies on Sigmund Freud's psychology, and on one of Freud's asides, namely, that impulses in the nervous system have to show some time difference so that they can convey meaning. For Derrida this difference is transmitted to human behavior. In his perspective, we always come too late; and the principle that was claimed for the interaction of the neurons is seen as a behavioral inescapability.

I think this is a category mistake. Now there are many arguments that support the notion that time differences between the neuronal impulses are necessary so that information can be conveyed. Complete synchrony would result in the extinction of consciousness and differentiated meaning. This can occur in epileptic seizures. If we go to the other extreme, where there is no synchrony between the impulses of the nervous system, we would not have enough coherence and integration for the information. So on the neuronal level, impulses have to coincide to a certain degree, and some have to be asynchronous. On a neuronal level, some impulses come later than others. Yet, on the level of the behavior of the whole organism, this does not mean that we always search for noon at 2:00 p.m. For Derrida, we always come too late. But this is a question of the behavior of the whole. (If there were no fear, perhaps hesitation and coming too late would not be necessary.) The behavior of the whole organism cannot be demonstrated by or deduced in an isomorphic way from the differences on the neuronal level.

Neuronal impulses *do* convey information by being synchronous, and asynchrony on the behavior level *does not* say anything about coming too late.

I believe that especially for such questions it is sometimes helpful to distinguish between phenomenology and neuronal activity. Both levels show some correlation and coherence, but not in such a way that the one can be deduced isomorphically from the other.

Much caution must be applied to prevent mistakes between the categories of behavioral phenomena and neuronal activities. In many respects it is more fruitful to start with a model of the nervous system in which a reference to stability systems is used. Certainly religious decisions of women or men are not fixed by this structural characteristic of the function of the nervous system. Neuroscientific concentration on coherence phenomena, on the one side, and phonological traditions playing with differences that constitute meaning, on the other, can be lead to a more integrated model for brain function and human behavior when the resources of structural stability are examined more closely.

The Spiritual Body

If one thinks of the transmogrification of the psychic body into the spiritual body, one is reminded of Wolfhart Pannenberg's hint that *pneuma*, in some sense, was an anticipation of the field concept of physics. Such field ideas fit appropriately with the electromagnetic activities of nervous pulse conduction. One might be tempted to use metaphors of breaking waves[7] or alpine glacial melting and freezing.[8] In any case, these ideas open the door for reflections beyond the parameter of information in the constitution of personal identity. Information about a person is firmly grounded in the relation of brain and body. In speculating about resurrection one would like to think of bodily implications. Information closely related to the structure and dynamics of the body will be changed when the body is changed. If, for example, the molecules were replaced by a different set of molecules, the temporal parameters in the nervous system and the dimensions of coherence, synchrony, and asynchrony would be changed. The new meaning of the transfigured body (with perhaps a new kind of molecules) will have to be contrived by God.[9]

---

7. "Deférlement," in J. Derrida and G. Vattimo, *Die Religion* (Frankfurt am Main: Suhrkamp, 2001).

8. As in Edelman and Tononi, *A Universe of Consciousness*.

9. Ted Peters, *GOD — The World's Future: Systematic Theology for a New Era* (Minneapolis: Fortress, 2d ed. 2000). See also Peters's chapter in this volume.

Cybernetic Immortality
versus Christian Resurrection

NOREEN HERZFELD

One of Bach's most beautiful organ preludes is based on the German chorale *"Alle Menschen müssen sterben,"* all human beings must die. As the editor of the volume of Bach's organ preludes, *The Liturgical Year,* Albert Riemenschneider notes that Bach wrote his most intimate work when contemplating death. The music is introspective but not sad; it is not written in a minor key. Its motifs express tranquility and happiness, reflecting the hope and, more, the calm certitude of the Christian in death as the passage to a resurrection into an eternal and better life.[1]

Does the concept of such a resurrection violate the laws of nature? For the Christian, resurrection and its consequent immortality are not dependent on the physical structure of this world as we know it. Though Christians speak of the resurrection of the body, it is a spiritual body that is resurrected, a body that, according to Paul, is incorruptible, spiritual, immortal, not of earth (1 Corinthians 15). This conflicts with the dictates of scientific materialism, which begin with the postulate that matter is all that exists.

For the scientific materialist, soul, consciousness, and spirit are reducible to their biological origins and material substrate. Molecular biologist Francis Crick touts the materialist creed as follows: "You, your joys and your sorrows, your memories and your ambitions, your sense of personal identity and free will, are in fact no more than the behavior of a vast assembly of nerve cells and their associated molecules. . . . You're nothing but a pack of neurons."[2] The

1. J. S. Bach, *The Liturgical Year,* ed. Albert Riemenschneider (Bryn Mawr, Pa.: Oliver Ditson, 1933), 134.

2. Francis Crick, *The Astonishing Hypothesis: The Scientific Search for the Soul* (New York: Scribner's, 1994), 3.

"you" that Crick speaks of here is located in memories, ambitions, feelings, and action, all of which arise from the workings of the material brain. Without such a material basis "you" cease to exist.

Few materialists show any interest in immortality, to be sure. But when they do, they presume that postmortem life requires physical transformation. Thus, within a strictly materialist system, resurrection or immortality must involve matter. One way for it to do so is through the transfer of that which makes up the core of the person, namely, those functions that make up what we call mind, to a new material body. While cryogenics, cloning, and genetic advances might each suggest organic ways to provide such a body, the field of computer technology offers options for an inorganic body, based on the silicon of computer chips or the emerging technologies of nanotechnology or quantum computing, which hope to develop processors at the molecular or particle scale. These options of moving the human mind to a new physical location have come to be grouped together under the rubric of cybernetic immortality. If the body must fail, why not transfer the contents of the brain to a medium that does not fail, at least not so soon?

Cybernetic immortality provides one avenue for belief in a manner of human continuance that does not violate the assumption of a material basis for all existence. It appears compatible with the most rigorous scientific theories of the natural world. The philosopher Valentine Turchin notes that traditional religious concepts of resurrection or transmigration of souls are limited to the conceptual sphere. As such, they fail to hold the allegiance of those raised in a scientific milieu, who ask to see concrete evidence of concepts in physical reality. Yet Turchin notes that some concept of immortality is necessary if life is to have meaning. He writes: "The decline of traditional religions appealing to metaphysical immortality threatens to degrade modern society. Cybernetic immortality can take the place of metaphysical immortality to provide the ultimate goals and values for the emerging global civilization."[3]

Is cybernetic immortality a belief that seeks to supplant the concept of resurrection, as Turchin suggests, or is it compatible with Christian views? MIT professor Daniel Crevier believes the latter. In his book *AI: The Tumultuous History of the Search for Artificial Intelligence*, Crevier argues that immortality in a mechanical body is quite consistent with the Jewish and Christian traditions of bodily resurrection. He suggests that "the gradual and eventual replacement of brain cells by electronic circuits with identical input-output functions" presents a way for "transferring the mind from one support to an-

---

3. Valentine Turchin, "Cybernetic Immortality" (http://pespmc1.vub.ac.be/CYBIMM .html). Accessed 15 October 2001.

other."[4] Such a transfer allows for a material transcendence of the soul that Crevier finds consistent with Christian beliefs.

While the transference of human brain patterns to a machine does allow for a material, hence "bodily," continuance of one aspect of the person, I believe other factors must also be considered, factors that make cybernetic immortality incompatible with Christianity. Computer-based immortality is grounded in a very different set of assumptions regarding both the nature of humanity and the nature of immortality than those of traditional Christianity. While cybernetic immortality might provide a theory of resurrection that is adequate in materialist scientific circles, it is not adequate as a means of instantiating the Christian understanding of resurrection. To see why not, we will compare three assumptions that underlie cybernetic immortality with Reinhold Niebuhr's explication of a Christian view of resurrection, as expressed in his anthropological study *The Nature and Destiny of Man*.

What Is Cybernetic Immortality?

Cybernetic immortality is based on the assumption that thoughts, memories, feelings, and action define the human person. These are products of consciousness, which is an emergent property of the complexity of our brains. In other words, human beings are basically biological machines whose unique identity is found in the informational patterns that arise and are stored in the neuronal structures of the brain. If these patterns could be replicated, as in sophisticated computer technology, the defining characteristics of the person would be preserved.

Hopes for cybernetic immortality are rooted in the quest for a suitable mechanical platform for the neuronal structure of the brain. Prognostications for how the mind might be transferred to such a platform vary. Advances in mechanical prostheses, such as replacement limbs or corneal implants, have led the director of MIT's robotics lab, Rodney Brooks, to predict that human beings and machines will merge in the near future, as we begin to replace more and more of our biological parts, including parts of our brains, with mechanical parts. The ultimate goal is to replace all biological parts, either by uploading a person's neural patterns onto a computer or by slowly replacing part after part, till one becomes completely machine.

Robotics engineer Hans Moravec, of Carnegie Mellon, describes a simi-

---

4. Daniel Crevier, *AI: The Tumultuous History of the Search for Artificial Intelligence* (New York: Basic Books, 1993), 278.

lar process of connecting the neurons of the brain to a computer in such a way that, "in time, as your original brain faded away with age, the computer would smoothly assume the lost functions. Ultimately your brain would die, and your mind would find itself entirely in the computer."[5] The philosophers Cliff Joslyn, Valentin Turchin, and Francis Heyleighten point out the possibilities for immortality in such a transfer:

> Through such techniques, the form or organization with which we identify our "I" could be maintained infinitely, and, which is important, evolve, become even more sophisticated, and explore new, yet unthought of, possibilities. Even if the decay of biological bodies is inevitable, we can study ways of information exchange between bodies and brains which will preserve the essence of self-consciousness, our personal histories, our creative abilities, and, at the same time, make us part of a larger unity embracing, possibly, all of humanity: the social superorganism. We call this form of immortality cybernetic because cybernetics is a generic name for the study of control, communication, and organization. It subsumes biological immortality.[6]

Ray Kurzweil, in *The Age of Spiritual Machines,* predicts that by the end of this century humans will attain such immortality. We will achieve this by uploading our brains into successive generations of computer technology. Kurzweil writes:

> Up until now, our mortality was tied to the longevity of our hardware. When the hardware crashed, that was it. For many of our forebears, the hardware gradually deteriorated before it disintegrated. . . . As we cross the divide to instantiate ourselves into our computational technology, our identity will be based on our evolving mind file. We will be software, not hardware. . . . As software, our mortality will no longer be dependent on the survival of the computing circuitry . . . [as] we periodically port ourselves to the latest, evermore capable "personal" computer. . . . Our immortality will be a matter of being sufficiently careful to make frequent backups.[7]

Kurzweil is not the sole holder of this expectation, though he may be among the more optimistic in his time line. Both Tom Stonier, in *Beyond In-*

---

5. Hans Moravec, *Mind Children: The Future of Robot and Human Intelligence* (Cambridge, Mass.: Harvard University, 1988), 4.

6. C. Joslyn, V. Turchin, F. Heyleighten, "Cybernetic Immortality" (http://pespmc1 .vub.ac.be/CYBIMM.html).

7. Ray Kurzweil, *The Age of Spiritual Machines: When Computers Exceed Human Intelligence* (New York: Penguin, 1999), ch. 6.

formation, and Hans Moravec, in *Mind Children,* suggest that the intelligent computer will be not merely a vehicle for personal immortality, but the next step in the evolutionary process, a step that, while it may or may not effect immortality for the individual human being, will result in immortality for the intelligence of the species in general. As Stonier puts it, "The cosmic function of Humanity is to act as the evolutionary interface between Life and Intelligence."[8] Moravec laments that the "uneasy truce between mind and body breaks down completely as life ends [and] too many hard-earned aspects of our mental existence simply die with us."[9] Through computers, he hopes that the mind might be "rescued from the limitations of a mortal body" and we might pass on our intelligence to our "unfettered mind children."[10]

Crevier regards the uploading of one's brain as a resurrection of the body.[11] Kurzweil likewise posits mechanical bodies, stating that an intelligence without a body is likely soon to become depressed.[12] However, not all supporters of cybernetic immortality see the necessity of a body. A somewhat different avenue of escape from the biological body is envisioned through the use of virtual reality, where one's mental self might exist only within cyberspace. Nicole Stenger, a researcher at the Human Interface Technology Lab at the University of Washington, expresses enthusiasm, "On the other side of our data gloves we become creatures of colored light in motion, pulsing with golden particles.... We will all become angels, and for eternity . . . cyberspace will feel like Paradise."[13] Software engineer Michael Benedikt envisions cyberspace as a place where "we would enjoy triumphs without risks and eat of the tree and not be punished, consort daily with angels, enter heaven now and not die.... [It is] the Heavenly City, the New Jerusalem of the Book of Revelation. Like a bejeweled, weightless palace it comes out of heaven itself . . . a place where we might re-enter God's graces . . . laid out like a beautiful equation."[14] A

8. Tom Stonier, *Beyond Information: The Natural History of Intelligence* (London: Springer, 1992), 214. See also Moravec, *Mind Children,* ch. 6. Such dreams have not originated in the twentieth century. Even Charles Babbage, the nineteenth-century designer of a mechanical precursor to the computer, imagined a "future state" for humankind, "unclogged by the dull corporeal load of matter which . . . chains the ardent spirit to its unkindred clay." Charles Babbage, *The Ninth Bridgewater Treatise* (London: Frank Cass, 1967), 173.

9. Moravec, *Mind Children,* 122.

10. Ibid., 123.

11. Crevier, *AI,* 278.

12. Kurzweil, *Spiritual Machines,* ch. 6.

13. Nicole Stenger, "Mind Is a Leaking Rainbow," in *Cyberspace: First Steps,* ed. Michael Benedikt (Cambridge, Mass.: MIT, 1991), 58, 52.

14. Michael Benedikt, "Introduction," in Benedikt, ed., *Cyberspace,* 14-15.

cyberspatial instantiation of immortality would have certain advantages. For one thing, while there might be some limits on the number of avatars who could inhabit a given computer system or network, that limit would be far larger than the number of persons, biological or robotic, who could inhabit the limited space of the earth. There is potentially infinite space in cyberspace. There is also more flexibility in a cyberspace world. When one becomes pure data, one can transform oneself at will, becoming nearly anything at any time, transcending all limitations.

How real are these dreams? Little in current computer technology substantiates the projections of Moravec, Kurzweil, Brooks, or Benedikt. While computing in general has advanced dramatically in the last fifty years, advances in AI have been limited. Neural nets remain at a level far below the complexity of the human brain. Current research in neuroscience suggests that the workings of the brain are far more complicated than was initially supposed, and may not be capturable in neural net technology as we currently conceive it.[15] Virtual reality, for all its illusion of freedom, still depends on a very material body underneath the data gloves and helmets. Hubert and Stuart Dreyfus note, "Wishful thinking has probably always complicated our relations with technology, but it is safe to assert that before the computer, and before the bomb, the complications weren't quite as dangerous as they are today. Nor was the wishful thinking as fantastic."[16] The dreams of cybernetic immortality are currently more science fiction than fact; however, they do illuminate a desire in the technological sector to view computers as a way to "break free from bodily existence, . . . from the constraints that the flesh imposes."[17] And they provide a way to maintain belief in a reductionistic materialism without giving up the hope of immortality.

A Christian Critique: Reinhold Niebuhr's *The Nature and Destiny of Man*

The assumptions regarding the natures of the human person and of eternal life that underlie the hope of an immortal presence within computers are

15. See, e.g., Detlef Linke, "The Lord of Time," in *The End of the World and the Ends of God: Science and Theology on Eschatology,* ed. John Polkinghorne and Michael Welker (Harrisburg, Pa.: Trinity Press International, 2000).

16. Herbert Dreyfus and Stuart Dreyfus, *Mind over Machine: The Power of Human Intuition and Expertise in the Era of the Computer* (New York: Free Press, 1986), ix.

17. Michael Hein, *The Metaphysics of Virtual Reality* (New York: Oxford University, 1993), 99. See also n. 8 above.

quite different from those of most Christians. Cybernetic immortality assumes a dualistic understanding of the human person, a conception of eternity as "a long time," and a hubristic faith in human power. Reinhold Niebuhr in *The Nature and Destiny of Man* speaks to each of these and cautions Christians to place their hope in God rather than in a concept of an immortality of their own making and within the bounds of history.

First, despite the materialism, the cybernetic understanding of the human person is unabashedly dualistic and dismissive of the importance of the human body. It suggests that, though emerging out of matter, what constitutes the essence of the human person is the pattern of his or her thoughts, memories, and experiences. On first glance, this understanding seems not unlike Reinhold Niebuhr's conception of the image of God in humanity. For Niebuhr, this image, which lies at the core of the human person, is reason, a reason that encompasses rationality, free will, and an ability to move beyond the self that Niebuhr defines as self-transcendence. He writes:

> The Biblical conception of "image of God" has influenced Christian thought, particularly since Augustine . . . to interpret human nature in terms which include his rational faculties but which suggest something beyond them. The ablest non-theological analysis of human nature in modern times, by Heidegger, defines this Christian emphasis succinctly as "the idea of 'transcendence,' namely that man is something which reaches beyond itself — that he is more than a rational creature."[18]

For Niebuhr, self-transcendence is a consequence of reason; it is the ability both to make oneself an object of knowledge and to model oneself after something greater than the self. Because of our capacity for self-transcendence, human beings are confronted with the paradox of having a vision of what ought to be that is limitless while at the same time being constrained by a finite creaturely nature. Niebuhr notes, as have the cyberneticians quoted above, that our finite bodily nature stands in internal tension over and against this mental transcendence.[19] However, while cybernetic immortality seeks to surmount our finite body, Niebuhr sees our inability to accept our creaturely limitations as the source of sin:

---

18. Reinhold Niebuhr, *The Nature and Destiny of Man: A Christian Interpretation*, vol. 1: *Human Nature*, with an Introduction by Robin W. Lovin, Library of Theological Ethics (Louisville: Westminster/John Knox, 1992), 161-62.

    19. Ibid., 166.

Man is ignorant and involved in the limitations of a finite mind; but he pretends that he is not limited. He assumes that he can gradually transcend finite limitations until his mind becomes identical with universal mind. All of his intellectual and cultural pursuits, therefore, become infected with the sin of pride.[20]

Our finite bodies are an integral part of who we are. The essential nature of the human being always contains two inseparable elements, self-transcending mind and finite creaturely being. The denial of the latter has led to a denigration of both women and the natural environment. Cybernetic immortality leads directly into these twin denigrations. For if we could live in bodies of silicon, or in cyberspace itself, of what use is the natural world? Nor do intelligences that can replicate themselves through backup copies need sexual differentiation. However, Christians understand the creation of the human being as set in the context of the creation of the rest of the world and the creation of sexual differentiation. Our being in relationship with that which is by nature other to us, whether it be a human of the other gender or some part of the rest of creation, is an integral part of our creation in the image of a triune God.[21] Cybernetic immortality denies the importance of the body while at the same time tying immortality to the material world.

Niebuhr does the opposite. He acknowledges our dependence on our bodily nature in this life, a dependence that is concomitant to a yearning to transcend the finitude of the world. Our capacity for self-transcendence produces the dilemma that we are creatures that find our norm in something we cannot, ultimately, be.[22] Niebuhr believes that this paradox is not resolvable within history; to try to do so leads humans into the trap of either denying God and living totally within our created nature, like animals, or denying our created nature and trying to be as God (an attempt that is acknowledged occasionally within the computer technology community). We escape this paradox only when we leave the historical time-space continuum through death and resurrection.[23]

---

20. Ibid., 178-79.

21. This understanding of the image of God is fundamental to the thought of Karl Barth and explicated in *Church Dogmatics*, vol. 3: *The Doctrine of Creation*, pt. 1, ed. G. W. Bromiley and T. F. Torrance, trans. J. W. Edwards, O. Bussey, and Harold Knight (Edinburgh: T&T Clark, 1958).

22. Niebuhr, *Nature and Destiny*, vol. 1, 270.

23. Reinhold Niebuhr, *The Nature and Destiny of Man: A Christian Interpretation*, vol. 2: *Human Destiny*, Library of Theological Ethics (Louisville: Westminster/John Knox, 1996), 75.

That Niebuhr believes one both can and must go beyond the time-space continuum points to a second difference between cybernetic immortality and the traditional Christian understanding of immortality. As Robert John Russell once put it, "immortality does not just mean more time."[24] Yet those who put their hopes in cybernetic immortality precisely have in mind more time on this earth. Niebuhr notes that the concept of the *parousia* in the New Testament is not to be taken literally in a millennialist or utopian way. History will not be fulfilled within persisting conditions of finiteness, for the fulfillment of history is also its end in the quantitative sense. Niebuhr writes, "The Christian faith insists that the final consummation of history lies beyond the conditions of the temporal process." However, lest this lead to an otherworldliness, he also asserts that "the consummation fulfills, rather than negates, the historical process."[25]

> Eternity stands at the end of time in the sense that the temporal process cannot be conceived without a *finis;* and eternity cannot be conceived as having a *finis.* Eternity outlasts time, though we know nothing about either an abrupt ending of the world or the gradual dissipation of its natural energies.[26]

Niebuhr notes that we cannot picture eternity from within the temporal process. We see it as the endpoint of time, yet all points in time could be said to be equidistant from eternity. Eternity comes, not only to end time as we know it; it takes us outside of the spatial-temporal framework, while embracing the fulfillment of our destiny within that framework. Cybernetic immortality, on the other hand, posits a future that, while it might give us more time to work toward our destiny, cannot be everlasting. No matter how durable our mechanical bodies might be, they would remain finite creations on a finite planet, within a finite universe. Even scientists agree that "heaven and earth will pass away" (Mark 13:31).

Finally, Christians, particularly those following Augustine, have generally been adamant that we cannot effect immortality through our own devices. As already noted, the human being is a finite creature of limited knowledge and understanding, failing all too often in our capacity to know or to love. History continually shows the imprint of our limitations. According to Niebuhr, the process of evolution or of history itself cannot be the God of redemption. Today we tend to mistake it for such, a mistake Niebuhr attributes

24. Robert John Russell, personal interview, May 2001.
25. Niebuhr, *The Nature and Destiny of Man,* vol. 2, 291.
26. Ibid., 299.

to the "desire to find a way of completing human destiny which would keep man's end under his control and in his power."[27]

> The Christian hope of the consummation of life and history is less absurd than alternate doctrines which seek to comprehend and to effect the completion of life by some power or capacity inherent in man and his history. . . . Both the meaning [of life] and its fulfillment are ascribed to a centre and source beyond ourselves. We can participate in the fulfillment of the meaning only if we do not seek too proudly to appropriate the meaning as our secure possession or to effect the fulfillment by our own power.[28]

The central aim of science and technology is to understand and control the objective, physical world. If only this physical world exists, such understanding and control, while never absolute, might be all to which we can aspire. Cybernetic immortality, in such a world, can only be "more time"; given the limits of the physical universe, it is not unending time, nor can I suppose we would want it to be, for our condition within the physical universe would remain limited, bounded by our creaturely finiteness, the limits of our knowing and our moral failings. Life on earth is neither heaven nor hell; it is a middle realm where great suffering exists side by side with great joy.

Alle Menschen müssen sterben. All human beings must die. Life would lose its savor were this not so. Our physical and fallible bodies, our limited minds, give us our chief joys as well as our many sorrows. The Christian concept of the resurrection of the body finds ultimate security "beyond all the securities and insecurities of history."[29] It is a concept that transcends death, not by eluding it with part of our being, as cybernetic immortality does, but by passing through it with one's whole being. Niebuhr writes that if we are truly "'persuaded that neither death, nor life, nor angels, nor principalities, nor powers, nor things present, nor things to come, nor height, nor depth, nor any other creature, shall be able to separate us from the love of God, which is in Christ Jesus our Lord,' it may dissuade men from the idolatrous pursuit of false securities and redemptions in life and history [by] its confidence in an external ground of existence."[30] It is in this ground that we Christians place our hope.

27. Ibid., 320.
28. Ibid., 298.
29. Ibid., 320.
30. Ibid., 321.

The Resurrection Body and Personal Identity: Possibilities and Limits of Eschatological Knowledge

NANCEY MURPHY

My attention to the nature of the resurrected body will address the epistemological issues surrounding this topic; I shall attempt to lay out what kinds of things we can *and cannot* know about resurrection life, and why. The first sections of my essay will survey the sources of our knowledge of the resurrection and what they can tell us. I suggest that our primary sources are Scripture, Christian faith and practice, and science, especially the neurosciences, and philosophy. I conclude that we can know a great deal about the *moral* character of resurrection life; whatever sort of embodiment resurrection life involves must be seen primarily in terms of its providing the substrate for moral and social life. At the end I argue that because we know that the very laws of nature will be transformed in the eschaton we cannot know by means of what "physical" processes this body functions.[1]

What Can We Know about the Resurrection Body from Neuroscience?

Philosophers point out that developments in neuroscience cannot disprove body-soul dualism. However, it has been widely recognized for centuries that

1. This negative argument is not meant to deny the fruitfulness of Robert John Russell's project (this volume) of seeking insights for current cosmology in expected continuities between this and the final aeon.

nothing of interest *about existence* can be proved or disproved — proof is the wrong sort of standard to apply to matters of existence. I have argued that dualism and physical monism (physicalism, for short) ought to be regarded not merely as philosophical theses but as philosophical or metaphysical "hard cores" (in Imre Lakatos's sense)[2] of scientific research programs.[3] In this light, it is clear that the physicalist program is extremely progressive: all recent advances in neurobiological understanding of cognition, emotion, and action, as well as progress in certain forms of cognitive science, are the product of a physicalist understanding of human nature. In contrast, scarcely any research follows from a dualist theory; Sir John Eccles has been the only noted scientist whose research was based on body-mind dualism, and nothing has come, finally, of his project. Thus, however inconclusive the philosophical arguments may be,[4] we can say that *science* provides as much evidence as could be desired to the effect that there is no need to postulate such things as *substantial souls or minds* and that the physicalist thesis is true.

This conclusion has important implications for theology, since most theologians throughout most of Christian history have been dualists. For present purposes, two such implications are of central interest. First, if there is life after death, it depends on bodily resurrection alone, and resurrection understood in (what I take to be) its original sense as resurrection of the whole person from death, not as the restoration of bodily existence to a surviving immortal soul, as it has been for so many years in both Christian and Jewish thought.[5]

Second, recognition of our essential physicality emphasizes our unity

2. Imre Lakatos, "Falsification and the Methodology of Scientific Research Programmes," in *The Methodology of Scientific Research Programmes: Philosophical Papers, Volume 1,* ed. John Worrall and Gregory Currie (Cambridge: Cambridge University, 1978), 8-101. Lakatos describes the hard core of a research program as a theory about the nature of the aspect of reality with which the research program is concerned. It provides guidance for the development of the empirical program and is held immune from falsification.

3. See Nancey Murphy, "Nonreductive Physicalism: Philosophical Issues," in W. S. Brown, Nancey Murphy, and H. N. Malony, eds., *Whatever Happened to the Soul?: Scientific and Theological Portraits of Human Nature* (Minneapolis: Fortress, 1998), 127-48, esp. 139-42.

4. I believe that a philosophical case for mind-body dualism (or body-soul dualism) is in fact hopeless. Its ablest current defender is Richard Swinburne, in *The Evolution of the Soul* (Oxford: Clarendon, rev. ed. 1997), but I would argue for the inadequacy of the philosophical method he employs. I would also argue that the failure of three hundred years of attempts to solve the problem of mind-body interaction gives good grounds for saying that the problem is essentially insoluble.

5. For an account of Jewish doctrines, see Neil Gillman, *The Death of Death: Resurrection and Immortality in Jewish Thought* (Woodstock, Vt.: Jewish Lights Publishing, 1997).

with the rest of nature, and suggests that we are not saved *out of* this cosmos, but as part of it. That is, it leads us to expect that the entire cosmos will be transformed or re-created in the same way as we humans are.[6]

What Can We Know from the Biblical Witness?

The expectation of bodily resurrection is based (almost entirely)[7] on the scriptural witness to the resurrection of Jesus and the claim that Jesus' resurrection signals that ours will follow. The New Testament is also our source of information regarding the characteristics of the resurrection body. However, the information we receive is varied. Paul speaks only of an appearance of light, while the Gospels depict Jesus as (sometimes) identifiable by sight and capable of eating and being touched (Matt. 28:9; Luke 24:30, 39, 41ff.; John 20:27).[8] Yet the Gospel accounts do not depict Jesus as a body just like ours, in that he could enter locked rooms and was *not* always recognizable to his followers (Luke 24:16, 31). As Michael Welker points out, despite his palpable perceivability, he is an *appearance*.[9] So it is clear from the texts that the resurrection is not simply the resuscitation of a corpse, but it is *not* clear what the resurrected body is like. The texts appear to contradict one another.

A number of scholars take the discrepancies among witnesses' testimonies as evidence against any "objectivist" account of Jesus' resurrection.[10] In contrast, Stephen Davis argues that the various accounts can in fact be harmonized.[11] I take a third position: the church, in canonizing a collection of documents with genuinely inconsistent accounts of the resurrected body, is telling us something very important about resurrection — namely, that the

6. See E. M. Conradie (this volume).

7. An exception is Wolfhart Pannenberg's argument that belief in the final resurrection can be based on the fact that the human race expects to survive death, coupled with the fact that resurrection and immortality of the soul are the only available models for life after death and, finally, that immortality of the soul has been shown to be untenable. See *Theology and the Philosophy of Science* (Philadelphia: Westminster, 1976).

8. See Hans-Joachim Eckstein's excellent exposition of the appearances in Luke (this volume).

9. Michael Welker, "Resurrection and Eternal Life: The Canonic Memory of the Resurrected Christ, His Reality, and His Glory," in *The End of the World and the Ends of God,* ed. John Polkinghorne and Michael Welker (Harrisburg, Pa.: Trinity Press International, 2000), 297-97, 282; cf. Mark 16:12. See also Welker (this volume).

10. For a survey see Stephen T. Davis, *Risen Indeed: Making Sense of the Resurrection* (Grand Rapids: Eerdmans, 1993), 51-53.

11. Ibid., 53-61.

language of the present aeon is incapable of describing a resurrected body. No ordinary description is possible. Rather, we must be content with a variety of contrasting verbal pictures of Jesus.

James McClendon points out that much New Testament teaching on the last things is expressed in "word pictures," that is, words that present visual scenes. The futuristic pictures that characterize Christian belief, such as life after death and the Last Judgment, are not based on ordinary sorts of evidence, and while these pictures need to be connected aright to the rest of the Christian faith, we need not be able to specify all of the spatial, temporal, and causal connections. That is, in order to believe in eternal life we need not be able to fit it into a chronology of historical events nor locate heaven with respect to earth, sun, or stars (as so many millennialists have attempted to do).[12] What *is* required to believe in these pictures is that we find them *life-changing.*[13]

So, following McClendon, I conclude that the accounts of Jesus' appearances to the disciples after his death are to be taken as word pictures — images in an album — none adequate in itself to say what Jesus was like after the resurrection, but each setting boundaries regarding what we must *not* say: he is not a resuscitated corpse; not merely a visionary appearance to the disciples; not a ghost.[14] Christian teaching on the resurrection should not attempt to smooth over the differences, nor replace these "glimmering, haunting eschatological pictures" with something else. And the church must faithfully present all of them, since together they express the Christian hope.[15]

What Can We Know from Christian Faith and Practice?

McClendon states that proper use of eschatological word pictures depends on properly relating the collection of pictures to Christian practice (their life-changing force) and to the rest of the Christian faith. I claim that so doing provides our best (and perhaps only reliable) knowledge of the future that awaits us in the general resurrection. That is, we need an interpretive context in which to "read" the pictures of Jesus resurrected and in which to project from Jesus' resurrection to our own. The immediate context is eschatology —

12. Cf. Günter Thomas, sect. 2 (this volume).

13. James William McClendon, Jr., *Doctrine: Systematic Theology, Volume 2* (Nashville: Abingdon, 1994), 75-77.

14. See H.-J. Eckstein (this volume).

15. McClendon, *Doctrine,* 92.

doctrines of the last things — but eschatological images and prophecies themselves are subject to the most *radical* misinterpretations if they are not read within the context of the whole gospel. To do justice, then, to the topic of resurrection, one needs to take a stand on the highly contested issue of what Christianity is basically all about, and work from there to a reading of the resurrection pictures.

Eschatology is teaching about the *last* things, in two senses: that which lasts and that which comes last.[16] Thus, knowledge of what, in Christian eyes, is ultimately important *now* provides our best insights into what lasts, and so what comes last. I can only state here, but not justify, my position on what for Christians is ultimately important. I am in good company in taking the heart of Jesus' message to be proclamation of the kingdom of God. I follow John Howard Yoder, McClendon, and others in the radical-reformation tradition[17] in understanding the kingdom of God in concrete sociopolitical terms, and as already partially realized among Jesus' followers. As Yoder says:

> Jesus was not just a moralist whose teachings had some political implications; he was not primarily a teacher of spirituality whose public ministry unfortunately was seen in a political light; he was not just a sacrificial lamb preparing for his immolation, or a God-Man whose divine status calls us to disregard his humanity. Jesus was, in his divinely mandated . . . prophethood, priesthood, and kingship, the bearer of a new possibility of human, social, and therefore political relationships.[18]

While no brief statement could be adequate, George Ellis and I attempted to sum up this understanding of Jesus and the new possibility for social life that he brings as follows: "The moral character of God is revealed in Jesus' vulnerable enemy love and renunciation of dominion. Imitation of Jesus in this regard constitutes a *social* ethic" — an ethic we designate "kenotic."[19]

Yoder claims that the New Testament sees our present age, from Pentecost to the *parousia,* as a period of the overlapping of two aeons. These are not distinct periods of time, for they now exist simultaneously. They differ in nature or direction. One points backward to human history before or outside of Christ; the other points forward to the fullness of the kingdom of God, of

---

16. Ibid., 75.

17. And many outside that tradition as well, such as liberation theologians.

18. John Howard Yoder, *The Politics of Jesus* (Grand Rapids: Eerdmans, 2d ed. 1994), 52.

19. Nancey Murphy and George F. R. Ellis, *On the Moral Nature of the Universe: Theology, Cosmology, and Ethics* (Minneapolis: Fortress, 1996), 178.

which it is a foretaste.[20] This account of partially realized eschatology contrasts both with the nineteenth-century liberal Protestant view that equated the kingdom with inevitable human progress and with views such as that of Reinhold Niebuhr, according to which the new aeon begins only after the end of the present aeon. Thus, while there will be a radical transformation, we must expect continuity as well as discontinuity.[21]

Given these presuppositions, I now return to the question of what we can know about resurrected bodies. There is a great deal we *can* know on the basis of knowledge of the continuities — what lasts. But we also know that there is a great deal that we *cannot* know. In short, we know that resurrection bodies must provide all that is necessary to carry forward the moral and social relations that constitute the kingdom of God, yet we also know that no kingdom achievements can last in the physical world as presently constituted. Thus we know that our physical composition has to be unimaginably different — here there will be radical discontinuity. I first pursue the topic of what we can know if we assume both the social character of the kingdom and physicalist anthropology.

First, an obvious point: embodiment is necessary for social life. This would be true even on a dualist account — a body is the soul's only means of relating to other souls. P. F. Strawson notes that if there are disembodied consciousnesses they are strictly solitary and it is idle speculation for them as to whether or not there are other consciousnesses.[22] McClendon states that our bodies constitute the very possibility of engagement with one another in this world *or any other*.[23] Jewish scholar Neil Gillman says: "my body is the landmark which connects me with everything else that exists physically, specifically with all of history and society."[24]

On a physicalist account, bodies are essential for participation in the kingdom of God in the trivial sense that humans *are* their bodies. More interesting claims can be made based on what we are now learning from neuroscience about how intellectual, emotional, and moral traits once attributed to the soul are subserved by neural and other biological systems.

A second obvious point is that participation in the postresurrection

20. John Howard Yoder, *The Original Revolution: Essays on Christian Pacifism* (Scottdale, Pa.: Herald, 1971), 55.

21. Cf. Welker (this volume). Note that some eschatological symbols admit of gradual realization (the kingdom of God) while others do not (resurrection).

22. P. F. Strawson, *Individuals: An Essay in Descriptive Metaphysics* (London: Methuen, 1959), 113.

23. McClendon, *Doctrine*, 249.

24. Gillman, *The Death of Death*, 262.

kingdom depends on one's being the same person before and after resurrection. There is an immense literature on personal identity both with and without consideration of the problem of resurrection. The point at which an emphasis on the sociality of the kingdom sheds light on our future expectations is in seeing what the focus on sociality *adds* to current discussions of personal identity. I argue in the next section that in addition to widely recognized criteria of memory and bodily continuity, personal identity involves "*self-recognition, continuity of moral character,* and *personal relations,* both with others and with God.

Personal Identity

The term "identity" is used in reference to persons in several ways. The sense that is not at issue in this essay is the psychological sense in which people are said to seek, or lose, or regain their identities.[25] In philosophical literature, numerical identity is distinguished from qualitative identity. It is the former that is at issue here: What are the criteria by which I am the same person now as I was forty years ago, even though qualitatively I am quite different?

There is a rich philosophical literature on personal identity, in the sense of reidentification of persons after a lapse of time. Unfortunately many theological discussions of pre- and postresurrection identity overlook some of the most important contributions. First, David Wiggins has shown that to say "x is the same as y" or "x is identical to y" requires the specification of a *covering concept;* one needs to be able to answer the question: "the same *what* as y?" This solves many traditional philosophical puzzles such as whether or not one can step into the same river twice. Criteria of identity need to be tailored to fit the relevant covering concept.[26] Consequently, in discussing personal identity it is necessary to ask specifically what are the identity criteria for the covering concept *person,* and to expect that these be different from identity criteria for a material object or even for a human body.[27]

The classic work on the concept of *person* is P. F. Strawson's *Individuals.*

---

25. I believe that this sense *is* important in Andreas Schuele's essay (this volume). By the end of my discussion it will become apparent that there are important connections between this sense and the one I pursue, in that moral commitments are critical to both.

26. Wiggins's solution is to require covering concepts to be *sortal* concepts, which serve to pick out individuals. Thus, *mass of water molecules* is not an appropriate covering concept.

27. David Wiggins, *Identity and Spatio-Temporal Continuity* (Oxford: Clarendon, 1967), 1, 35-36, 50.

Strawson argues that the concept *person* is a primitive concept applying to entities to which both states of consciousness and corporeal characteristics can be attributed.[28] The concept of mental life derives from the concept of person, not the other way around.

On the basis of evidence from both neurobiology and neurology, Leslie Brothers argues that the person concept is not merely an artifact of culture; we are biologically prepared to subscribe to the concept just as we are biologically prepared to learn language. Just as we are unable to hear a word in a familiar language without perceiving the meaning, our brains have developed in such a way that when we perceive features such as bodily appearance, bodily movement, voice, and face we are compelled to experience them as indicative of the presence of a person who has subjectivity.[29]

Evidence for the direct role of neurobiology in person recognition comes from studies involving the stimulation of the amygdala in humans and from various sorts of studies of monkeys. Brothers recorded firing patterns of individual neurons in the amygdalas of macaques while they were observing video clips of social scenes (such as the yawn that males use to signal dominance).[30] These and other results indicate that individual neurons in the amygdala and nearby cortex respond selectively to features such as significant motion, identity of individuals, and particular kinds of interactions taking place between individuals.[31]

The role of neurobiology in enabling us to recognize and participate in the world of persons is further confirmed by patients who because of brain lesions or other neurological deficits are unable to use the rules of person language appropriately. For example, patients suffering from misidentification syndrome may attribute one mind to several bodies or perceive a body as having been taken over by an alien mind.[32] Thus, in the normal case our perception of "person" is an automatic and obligatory part of our experience of others — and of ourselves.

There is a longstanding argument in philosophy between those who stake personal identity on spatio-temporal continuity of the body and those

28. Strawson, *Individuals,* 97.

29. Leslie A. Brothers, *Friday's Footprint: How Society Shapes the Human Mind* (New York: Oxford University, 1997), 4-5.

30. Male monkeys, that is.

31. Leslie A. Brothers, "A Neuroscientific Perspective on Human Sociality," in Robert J. Russell, Nancey Murphy, Theo C. Meyering, and Michael A. Arbib, eds., *Neuroscience and the Person: Scientific Perspectives on Divine Action* (Vatican City State: Vatican Observatory and Berkeley, Calif.: Center for Theology and the Natural Sciences, 1999), 67-74.

32. Ibid., 73.

who tie it to continuity of memories. There are several reasons for refusing to set these two criteria in opposition to one another. First, as we have just seen, our concept of person essentially involves both a body and a subjectivity. Second, it is an empirical fact (philosophers' bizarre thought experiments notwithstanding) that continuity of memory depends on brain continuity (the physicalist thesis), and thus on some form of bodily continuity.[33]

A Continuity-of-Consciousness Criterion

I now want to argue that the combined body-memory criterion is too narrow, in that *memory* does not capture all of what we need in order to secure personal identity.[34] I recount a thought experiment devised by Bernard Williams to show that we need *something* in addition to continuity of memory, although it is difficult to state what that something is.

The first half of Williams's essay reinforces the idea that the memory criterion is the crucial one. Two persons, A and B, enter a machine. When they emerge, the A-body person (i.e., the one who has the physical features A had before) has all of B's memories and character traits, and vice versa. The experimenter announces beforehand that after the switch one person will receive $100,000 and the other will be tortured. It is entirely reasonable to expect that, given a choice, A will want the B-body person to receive the money rather than be tortured (and vice versa). Williams concludes: "This seems to show that to care about what happens to me in the future is not necessarily to care what happens to *this* body."[35] This and further considerations introduced by Williams seem to confirm the description of the experiment as "changing bodies," and suggest that "the only rational thing to do when confronted with such an experiment would be to identify oneself with one's memories, and so forth, and not with one's body. The philosophical arguments designed to show that bodily identity was at least a necessary condition of personal identity would seem to be just mistaken."[36]

Now consider a different set of cases. You are told that you are going to be tortured tomorrow; you look forward to tomorrow with great apprehen-

33. Cf. Wiggins, *Identity and Spatio-Temporal Continuity*, 43.

34. In the end I propose an account of "same body" that differs from the standard account in that it does not require spatio-temporal continuity or the same material constituents.

35. Bernard Williams, "The Self and the Future," in *Problems of the Self: Philosophical Papers 1956-73* (Cambridge: Cambridge University, 1973), 46-63; quotation, 49.

36. Ibid., 51.

sion. The person who holds this power over you says, in addition, that between now and then something will be done to you to make you forget everything you now remember. This will not relieve your fear. Then you are told that your memories will be replaced prior to the torture by a complete set of memories from someone else's life. Does this relieve your fear? Williams says that this will not only not relieve your fear but will compound it with fear of mental derangement.

If you are told that your memories will be transferred simultaneously to the other person and that other will be paid $100,000, we have the same situation with which Williams began his essay, but now our intuitions are reversed: if given a choice, A would want the A-body person to receive the money and escape the torture.

Williams's thought experiments push us to articulate the sense in which one's consciousness is *more* than a bundle of memories. There is a parallel here with assorted objections to Hume's bundle theory of the mind. Recognition of this "more" leads readily to belief in dualism, but I believe that it can be understood not as the mind's experience of its (nonmaterial) self but rather as a product of the integration of various aspects of memory and awareness — a phenomenon that emerges sometime during early childhood. The ability to recognize my conscious self over time is so unproblematic most of the time (e.g., when we wake up in the morning) that it may go unnoticed. An obvious case of failure is the phenomenon of split personality. Its absence is also striking in certain sorts of the misidentification syndrome, in which patients believe they are being transformed into someone else's psychological identity. While we might speculate that this is the effect of reading too much philosophy of mind late at night, such patients show either localized or diffuse brain damage.[37] Schizophrenia often involves the inability to take ownership of one's own thoughts and thus a misattribution of them to God or aliens. Thus there is some reason for saying that this criterion — I'll call it the continuity-of-consciousness criterion — is, like the memory criterion, contingently connected to the body criterion.

Recognition of oneself as oneself over time and after interruptions of conscious experience may have been presumed to be part of what philosophers have been referring to all along as the memory criterion; I believe Williams has done us a favor by highlighting the distinction. It is particularly helpful in discussing pre- and postresurrection identity: if God can create a new (transformed) body and provide it with my memories, is that really I? If so, then I shall *know* that I am I, just as I did this morning when I awoke.

37. Brothers, *Friday's Footprint*, 3-10.

The Character Criterion

I now want to argue that the combined body-memory-consciousness criterion is still too narrow, in that memory and continuity of consciousness together do not capture all of what we need in order to secure personal identity. Given the moral and social character of the kingdom of God, we need to add "same moral character" to our criterion.

Modern thought, following René Descartes, has presented an overly cognitivist account of human nature in general and of morality in particular.[38] However, beginning in the 1970s and 1980s both in Christian ethics and philosophical ethics there has been a significant movement to return to an understanding of ethics in terms of character. Here the emphasis is not on the rules or principles one ought to follow, but rather on the kind of person one ought to be. These approaches emphasize the development of *virtues,* the retraining of the *emotions,* and the development of new moral *perceptions.* For example, Alasdair MacIntyre argues that without the acquired capabilities we call virtues, we are not able to achieve the goods intrinsic to social practices.[39] G. Simon Harak's book bears the title *Virtuous Passions,* an oxymoron in the eyes of a purely intellectualist account of morality. His goal is to work out a moral-theological account of the sense of the rightness or wrongness of passions and to consider ways to transform morally blameworthy passions and to foster morally praiseworthy passions.[40] Stanley Hauerwas argues that Christian ethics involves more than making decisions; it is a matter of escaping from self-protective illusions and of seeing and attending to the world as it really is, in light of its relationship to God.[41]

On the basis of the foregoing, I propose that identity of persons depends as much on *character* identity as it does on memory/consciousness and bodily continuity. That is, a replica or transformed version of my body with all my memories intact would not be I unless she possessed my virtues (or vices), affections, and moral perceptions.[42]

---

38. David Hume's emphasis on sympathy and the motivating role of the passions is one notable exception.

39. Alasdair MacIntyre, *After Virtue* (Notre Dame: University of Notre Dame, 2d ed. 1984).

40. G. Simon Harak, *Virtuous Passions: The Formation of Christian Character* (New York: Paulist, 1993).

41. "The Significance of Vision," in *Vision and Virtue: Essays in Christian Ethical Reflection* (Notre Dame: University of Notre Dame, 1974), 30-47.

42. Brian Garrett broadens the memory criterion to a "psychological" criterion that includes memory together with other features such as well-entrenched beliefs, character, and

However, it is increasingly clear that, just as the physical and memory criteria are inseparable, so are the character and physical criteria. Virtues are acquired by practice; practice makes stable changes in the strength of relevant neural pathways. Antonio Damasio argues that intelligent action of all sorts is dependent on "somatic markers" that reflect one's acquired *affective* relation to the proposed course of action.[43] Perception in general is a bodily process, and moral perception may be hypothesized to depend on the downward efficacy of higher-level evaluative processes in reshaping lower-level cognitive propensities — and these changes, too, are recorded in the tuning of neural nets. McClendon argued that Christian ethics cannot be adequately captured except by means of a three-stranded analysis: body ethics, social ethics, and resurrection ethics — his terms for ethical analyses that take account of God's action breaking into established biological and social orders. Ethical theories that attend to one or both of the latter will be incomplete and most likely misleading if not balanced by recognition of the drives, needs, and capacities of the *embodied* self.[44]

Essential Relationships

Internal relations are distinguished from external in that internal relations are (partially) constitutive of the *relata;* external relations are not. Opposing philosophical systems can be constructed by assuming either that all relations are external (logical atomism) or that all are internal (absolute idealism). The sensible position is to recognize that there are some of each. Which or what kinds of interpersonal relationships are internal relations — that is, essential to one's identity? It is clear that a great deal of what lasts in the postresurrection kingdom must be those relationships within the body of Christ that now make us the people we are. Most important, of course, is our relationship to Jesus. Thus I concur with those who emphasize that God's remembering, recognizing, and relating to me are essential to my postresurrection identity.

---

basic desires. He also argues that the bodily and psychological conditions need to be taken together. See "Personal Identity," in *The Routledge Encyclopedia of Philosophy,* ed. Edward Craig (London: Routledge, 1998), 7:305-14.

43. Antonio R. Damasio, *Descartes' Error: Emotion, Reason, and the Human Brain* (New York: G. P. Putnam's Sons, 1994).

44. James William McClendon, Jr., *Ethics: Systematic Theology, Volume 1* (Nashville: Abingdon, 1984).

Personal Development

Personal identity is necessary but not sufficient for participation in the post-resurrection kingdom. Keith Ward argues, as I have, that the memory and bodily criteria combined are not sufficient for personal identity — he mentions dispositions, habits, and practices in addition to memory.[45] Ward emphasizes, in addition, that memory needs to be *transformed* since simple vivid reliving of all past experience would undesirably re-create all the suffering and distress of earthly life.

> Memory will be so transformed that suffering is set within a wider context of learning and development, and even earthly joy is relativized by a deeper consciousness of the presence of God. Yet it is important to personal survival that the memories remain, however transformed, so that people who enter into eternal bliss will always know themselves to be the same people who suffered, enjoyed, sinned and repented, learned and developed, on the long journey towards God.[46]

Perfect memory of our evil actions, apart from such a context, might better be described as hell.

Ward also argues for the possibility of further development of capacities, talents, and dispositions, and for the reshaping of habits and skills into more creative forms.[47] An interesting question is the extent to which personal identity can be maintained through the elimination of negative characteristics. We get a sense of how this can happen from narratives of sinners transformed in this life; two classic examples are Augustine's *Confessions* and John Bunyan's *Pilgrim's Progress*.

Bodily Identity

I suggest that one's body should be thought of primarily as that which provides the substrate for all of the personal attributes discussed above: it is that which allows one to be recognized by others; that which bears one's memories; and whose capacities, emotional reactions, and perceptions have been shaped by one's moral actions and experience. It is an empirical fact, in this life, that these essential features are tied to a spatio-temporally continuous

---

45. Keith Ward, *Religion and Human Nature* (Oxford: Clarendon, 1998), 304.
46. Ward, *Religion and Human Nature*, 307; cf. McClendon, *Ethics*, ch. 8.
47. Ward, *Religion and Human Nature*, 307.

material object. Thus, while spatio-temporal continuity is a necessary part of the concept of a material object, I suggest that it is only a contingent part of commonly accepted concepts of the person. That is, all of the personal characteristics as we know them in this life are supported by bodily characteristics and capacities, and these bodily capacities happen to belong to spatio-temporally continuous material objects, but there is no reason *in principle* why a body that is numerically distinct but similar in all relevant respects could not support the same personal characteristics.

This recognition allows us to avoid tortuous attempts as in the early church to reconcile resurrection with material continuity.[48] These attempts are based on failure to distinguish the covering concepts of *person* and *material object,* and also fail to recognize that material objects can retain their identity over time despite (some) change in the material of which they are composed. So, in fact, Gregory and others were operating with the (illegitimate)[49] covering concept of *same collection of particles.*

My proposal regarding the construal of "same body" also allows for the possibility of a temporal interval between decay of the earthly body and what is then essentially the re-creation of a new body out of different *stuff.*

"Stuff" in the previous sentence is used advisedly. While we can know that after the resurrection we shall *be* embodied, and that those bodies will provide the substrate for (or, in computer-science terminology, the realization of) the ongoing and endless development of our mental life and moral character, we cannot know anything more of a positive sort about the nature of that stuff. That is, we know that it cannot be the matter with which we are acquainted in the present aeon, both because of the scriptural witness to the *transformation* involved in Jesus' resurrection and because of the fact that the travail of this life is tied so directly to the physics of this world.[50]

Although the New Testament knows nothing of the modern conception of laws of nature, there are passages that can be taken to say that the laws of nature of the present aeon are imperfect, and will be perfected in the eschaton — fully subjected to the Lordship of Christ. It is now widely accepted that the Pauline concept of the "principalities and powers" *(exousiai* and *dynameis)* refers not to the angels and demons of the medieval worldview but rather to (largely) social and political powers. (There is nonetheless an echo of the

---

48. See Carolyn Walker Bynum, *The Resurrection of the Body in Western Christianity, 200-1336* (New York: Columbia University, 1995); Ted Peters (this volume); and Brian Daley (this volume).

49. See Wiggins's distinction in n. 26 above.

50. See Robert J. Russell, "Entropy and Evil," *Zygon* 19.4 (1984): 449-68.

alien gods of Old Testament understanding.) This reinterpretation of the language of the powers serves as a counterargument to the claims that Christianity provides only an individual ethic, and neither an analysis of political power nor a social ethic.

The New Testament authors saw these powers as subordinate to God — they are God's creatures (Col. 1:15-17), yet they are fallen and rebellious (Gal. 4:1-11; Eph. 2:1-3). Jesus' mission is understood both in the Epistles and Gospels as conflict with and conquest of these powers. In the Epistles, Jesus' victory over the powers is typically represented in summary and proclamatory form, as in Colossians 2:15: "He disarmed the principalities and powers and made a public example of them, triumphing over them in him" (RSV). In the Gospels the conflicts are presented in narrative form and the opponents are no longer called "principalities and powers"; rather, they are the Herods and Caiaphases and Pilates. Wherever Christ's victory is proclaimed, the corrupted reign of the powers is challenged; yet the powers remain in being, for social life is impossible without them. There are hints in the New Testament that the final destiny of all the powers will be not their abolition but their full restoration, "a plan for the fullness of time, to gather up all things in [Christ], things in heaven and things on earth" (Eph. 1:10, NRSV).[51]

The relevance of this material is that, while most of the power terms can easily be read as referring to institutional or social realities — thrones, dominions, rulers, powers, the law — there are some oddities, in particular the *stoicheia*. This term occurs seven times in the New Testament. Translations include the four physical elements, the first principles of philosophy, basic religious rituals, the precepts of Jewish law, and the stars conceived as demonic powers.[52] The most common translation in contemporary versions is "elemental spirits." Walter Wink notes that the English term "element" is a formal category that can refer to the most basic constituents or principles of anything; if *stoicheia* is used similarly, this explains the variety of referents and means that context is crucial for an interpretation. Wink argues that *stoicheia* in Colossians 2:8 ("See to it that no one takes you captive through philosophy and empty deceit, according to human tradition, according to the elemental spirits of the universe, and not according to Christ") refers to the philosophical search for the first elements or founding principles of the physical universe.[53] In current terminology we could speak

---

51. McClendon, *Ethics*, 173-76.

52. Walter Wink, *Naming the Powers: The Language of Power in the New Testament* (Philadelphia: Fortress, 1984), 67.

53. Ibid., 74.

of subatomic particles as first elements and the laws of nature as founding principles.

Another hint that the powers include what we would now call the laws of nature comes from McClendon's recognition that in the Gospels Jesus' conflicts with the powers are spelled out in narrative form. In addition to his conflicts with the Pharisees and other human powers, there are the demonic forces that sponsor illness and madness. These demons can be cast as actors in the drama, while abstractions such as "authority" and "power" cannot.[54] We, of course, see illness and madness not as the work of demonic forces but as the outcome of the regular working of the laws of nature.

My suggestion, then, is that we can read our concept of the laws of nature *back* into the New Testament texts and so find support for the following theses: (1) The laws of nature of this aeon are God's creatures.[55] (2) Yet, in contrast to early modern understandings of them as perfect expressions of God's will, they are fallen — not in the sense that they once were perfect and then changed, but in the sense that they are meant to be our servants but are instead our masters; they do not enable humankind to live a genuinely free, loving life.[56] (3) Thus, the completion of Christ's work must include a radical transformation of the laws of nature such that they do permit the fullness of human life that God intends.

Overview

We now know a great deal about how natural processes subserve human psychic life. While we can know that, in some manner, glorified bodies support the same (or enhanced) psychic and social capacities, we know that we cannot know *how* this will be in the future. This is because our knowledge of future physical processes is based on projections using current laws of nature. We also know, as argued above, that the laws of nature in the eschaton (whatever "nature" would then designate) cannot be the same as we have now. Thus, while we might say that table fellowship is so central to the life of the kingdom that we must expect it to continue after the general resurrection, we

54. McClendon, *Ethics*, 174.

55. My use of "laws of nature" is intended to be neutral as to whether the laws in some sense exist and are prescriptive or whether they are simple reflections of regularities in nature. It is interesting that the other powers include both regularities of human social behavior and the Mosaic law, the idea from which the metaphor *laws of nature* was first derived.

56. Prior to the evolution of life, perhaps the present laws did serve God's purposes perfectly.

know in advance that we cannot answer questions about digestion, metabolism, and so forth.

Ludwig Wittgenstein spent his academic life studying the limits of meaningful language; central to his moral vision is the discipline of refraining from speech that goes beyond these limits.[57] So, he once said, while we can speak meaningfully of the hand of God, we cannot speak of God's fingernail.[58] Thus I conclude that the science-theology dialogue, however fruitful in other areas of theology, must reach a point of silence when we turn to certain matters of eschatology.

Conclusion

I have suggested that there are four sources of information about post-resurrection life: "pictures" of Jesus' resurrection, the life and teaching of the church, science (especially neuroscience), and philosophical or conceptual analysis. I have attempted to support the following conclusions:

1. Current science casts a clear vote for one of three traditional accounts of life after death. A physicalist anthropology rejects the concept of an immortal soul as well as a concept of resurrection that simply restores embodiment to an immortal soul.
2. The centrality of the kingdom in Jesus' teaching calls for an emphasis on preservation of human moral character and social relations in the eschaton. Thus, "same moral character" must be central to concepts of personal identity.
3. It follows that what we can know about the resurrection body is that it will subserve memory, emotion, virtue, and interpersonal relations.
4. Finally, our hope for radical transformation of the very laws of nature compels us to recognize severe limits to our ability to say how such a body will support these functions.

"What we cannot speak about we must consign to silence."[59]

---

57. Brad J. Kallenberg, *Ethics as Grammar: Changing the Postmodern Subject* (Notre Dame: University of Notre Dame, 2001), in press.

58. I have not been able to locate this remark.

59. Ludwig Wittgenstein, *Tractatus Logico-Philosophicus,* tr. D. F. Pears and B. F. McGuinness (London: Routledge and Kegan Paul, 1961), 151.

Transformed into the Image of Christ: Identity, Personality, and Resurrection

ANDREAS SCHUELE

In a public opinion poll in 1997 the German populace was asked, "What comes after death?" From the results it has become quite obvious that the least of what Germans are inclined to believe these days is the Christian doctrine of resurrection. Just about five percent of the people asked accepted the term "resurrection" for what they imagined to come after death. Even most of the people who associated themselves with Christian faith did not choose the term to express their thoughts on this issue.[1]

Certainly, the plain statistics do not tell what interviewers and interviewees actually understood by "resurrection." At least they seemed to agree that resurrection offers an answer to the question "What comes after death?" From general experience we have certain ideas of what life and death are, and often others share what we associate with these terms: death terminates life as we know it, that is, having a body, living in company with other human beings, having certain cognitive capacities that allow us to identify ourselves as particular individuals. On the other hand, whether or not there is something beyond death seems to be a "speculative" task on which — in modern Western societies — traditions, religions, and worldviews diverge to a considerable extent. In modern times *death* is not only what terminates physical and social existence; it also denotes the limits of cultural consensus about what will be after our body has dissolved, after all we once said and did is left to the vanishing memories of others.

---

1. Data taken from R. Sachau, *Weiterleben nach dem Tod: Warum immer mehr Menschen an Reinkarnation glauben* (Gütersloh: Gütersloher, 1998), 21.

ANDREAS SCHUELE

Modernity's Loss of Death Awareness

Modernity certainly has not restricted speculation about what will be "then." Looking at recent Hollywood productions — *City of Angels, What Dreams May Come, Artificial Intelligence,* and many others — quite the opposite holds true. Furnishing the unknown space beyond physical existence has a specific appeal to the modern mind, and it takes on manifold forms. From the viewpoint of cultural studies it is, however, worth noticing that *commonly* shared beliefs in what life after death could or could not be like do not seem all that essential. In ancient and medieval societies, conceiving of the hereafter — as the underworld in Greek antiquity, as heaven, purgatory, and hell in popular medieval Catholicism, or as *paradiso e inferno* in Dante — shaped scientific worldviews as well as aesthetic imagination, moral orientation, and religious beliefs and, therefore, provided a focus for common cultural engagement.[2] In its most elaborate forms, imagining life beyond the grave was never, as moderns sometimes tend to assume, the naive, quasi-naturalistic guesswork of the pre-enlightened and prescientific ages. As pieces of art like Michelangelo's famous *Last Judgment* on the walls of the Sistine Chapel display, imagining the hereafter was not a "speculative" task in the first place; rather, it combined scientific knowledge about the world with aesthetic and moral ideals, religious truth, and norms of social and political order to depict the ultimate foundations of the cosmos — rather than the "end of the world."

Modernity, on the other hand, has shifted its focus away from the hereafter to "this life." Bernhard Groethuysen, a student of Wilhelm Dilthey, once made an intriguing comment that pointedly sums up the modern turn: "Der eine glaubt an den Tod, wie er an Gott und an die Hölle glaubt, . . . während für den anderen der Tod aufgehört hat, Gegenstand des Glaubens zu sein. Er ist bloße Tatsache. Der Tod hat seinen religiösen Charakter verloren [Some believe in death as they believe in God or in hell, . . . to others death ceases to be a subject of their beliefs. It has become sheer fact, death has lost its religious character]."[3] This statement does not imply that life in the modern world is necessarily biased toward atheism or even nihilism. What it says, however, and where Groethuysen seems to be right on target, is that modernity makes razor sharp distinctions between its view of what precedes death

2. For a recent overview of the cultural coding of death in different religions and cultures cf. C. von Barloewen, *Der Tod in den Weltkulturen und Weltreligionen* (Frankfurt am Main: Insel, 2000), especially the contributions of Zwi Werblowsky on the Jewish understanding of death and Hortense Reintjens-Anwari on death in Islam.

3. B. Groethuysen, *Die Entstehung der bürgerlichen Welt- und Lebensanschauung in Frankreich* (Halle an der Saale: Niemeyer, 1927), 1:134.

and what might follow it. The one is informed by scientifically affirmed knowledge about the human body and intellect, the other by various types of imagination and feeling.[4] There is, however, no domain in modern intellectual life that would provide some common ground for both — what we know about life and how we conceive of existence beyond death. What we have lost — some would prefer to say "overcome" — are, traditionally speaking, *religious cosmologies* that seek to integrate life, death, and what is beyond within one coherent framework of explanation.

Considering the loss of such religious cosmologies, it seems quite consistent that in major strands of contemporary sociology religion takes on a new role. It is no longer an all-encompassing type of human insight and experience but provides perspective and meaning for precisely the assumed part of existence that lies beyond death, that is, that which cannot be sufficiently envisioned by scientific expertise alone. Religion becomes a specialist for the "last questions" at the speculative end of our experience and insight,[5] and so to be "religious" becomes crucial at the point where positive knowledge about "life" indicates its own limitations. In this view the term "resurrection" gives the specifically *Christian* answer to the question: "What comes after death?" It offers *one* possible way of furnishing the open space beyond death — one that seems, however, not all that attractive to contemporary culture.

Resurrection and the Eschatological Validity of Past, Present, and Future Life

If we turn from this outside perspective to the account that Christian faith gives of its own understanding of resurrection, things turn out differently. Looking at New Testament texts, especially at the letters of Paul, one does not get the idea that talking about resurrection is primarily concerned with what will be beyond physical existence. It is quite conspicuous how little Paul actually reasons about the possibility that somebody who has died and whose body has fallen apart may return to some state of "life" and how such life

4. For a theological reflection on this distinction cf. G. D. Kaufman, *In Face of Mystery: A Constructive Theology* (Cambridge, Mass./London: Harvard University, 1993), 7. It is consistent with his existential approach that Kaufman envisions theology to be an imaginative task in the first place (ibid., 32-44).

5. For a critique of this notion of religion as incompatible with the character of Christian faith cf. D. Bonhoeffer's letters from prison, where he sets forth the idea of a "non-religious" understanding of faith.

could be imagined. Although on various occasions Paul addresses the question "What comes after death?"[6] this does not really point to the core of his interest. Resurrection is not a *datum* at some future point of existence; rather, the term denotes a specific *quality:* to become resurrected means, according to Paul, *to partake in the life of Christ* as the risen Lord.

The rhetorics of "partaking," "being in/with Christ" *(en/syn Christō)* that goes along with Paul's usage of the term "resurrection" unfolds in an array of images and metaphors: it means to be "covered over" with the life of Christ (Rom. 13:14; 1 Cor. 15:53, 54; Gal. 3:27), to assume the "shape" of Christ (Rom. 8:29; Gal. 4:19), to be "implanted" (Rom. 6:5) into the death and resurrection of Christ, to be "conformed" to the "image of Christ" (Rom. 8:29). Especially from Romans 6:5 and 8:29 it becomes apparent that what Paul envisions is a kind of organic process in which two separate entities grow together.[7] Speaking in more abstract terms, to become resurrected means to be connected with Christ[8] in a sense that includes those who believe in him in

6. Especially so in the letters to the Thessalonians, where Paul finds himself confronted with the question of what happens to those who have died before the second coming of Christ. His answer implies that even those who are "presently" dead are related to the living Christ — *syn Christō,* with Christ — in a way that will keep them in a kind of "waiting pattern" till the day of the *parousia,* when they will again be reunited with those who are still alive (cf. 1 Thess. 4:13-18). Regarding the issue of eschatological time it is worth noticing that Paul envisions a state where people, whenever they have lived and died, will arrive at the same point of time that is marked by the second coming of Christ. In contemporary theology, especially J. Moltmann has taken up this position, combining it with Calvin's idea of a "great waking and watching of the soul after death" (cf. Moltmann, "Is There Life after Death?" in *The End of the World and the Ends of God,* ed. J. Polkinghorne and M. Welker (Harrisburg, Pa.: Trinity Press International, 2000), 252-53.

7. Cf. H.-D. Betz, "Transferring a Ritual: Paul's Interpretation of Baptism in Romans," in Betz, *Paulinische Studien* (Tübingen: Mohr [Siebeck], 1994), 264-68. For the interpretation of Romans 6 as the foundation of Paul's doctrine of baptism cf. U. Wilckens, "Der Brief an die Römer II," Evangelisch-katholischer Kommentar zum Neuen Testament IV/2 (Neukirchen-Vluyn: Neukirchener, 2d ed. 1987), 48-50. For our concern it is especially important that some of Paul's most explicit accounts of resurrection are given in the context of baptism theology. This indicates that it is not physical death that early Christianity considered to be a crucial existential datum, but the point where people come to participate in the death and resurrection of Christ that is marked by baptism. This is to say that the borderline between life and death is not accepted as fixed by the physical and mental constitution of human beings, but constituted by genuinely religious experience. This, it seems, is the rationale behind statements such as that of Romans 14:8, where living and dying are equally subordinated to "belonging to Christ."

8. On Paul's understanding of the "in-Christ relation" cf. Peter Lampe's contribution in this volume.

the eschatological state of life that he himself has assumed as the first fruits of all creation (1 Cor. 15:20, 23).

Even from these rather brief remarks on Paul it becomes clear why the Christian understanding of resurrection is not limited to the question of continuity and discontinuity between life before and life beyond physical death. It is not the fact that we have to die that brings resurrection to the theological agenda. Its significance would be reduced to a problem only of *natural-scientific credibility* if the heuristic model were primarily that of a linear time line with resurrection as what follows life and death[9] — be it that of an individual being or the rise and decline of the entire universe. Understood as participation in Christ's own life, resurrection addresses the issue of *eschatological validity* and as such relates from any point of time to all three temporal dimensions. Speaking in dogmatic language, it qualifies the past in terms of redemption, the present in terms of sanctification, and the future in terms of glorification and fulfillment.

To sum up my argument so far: in the symbolism of the Christian faith, resurrection is growing into and partaking in the life of the new creation that is connected with Christ as the risen Lord. As such, resurrection obviously addresses the issue of life beyond physical existence, but it is clearly of much further-reaching significance. Living in the presence of Christ relates not only to our future, but also to our present and even to our past. Therefore, conceiving of resurrection requires us to relate what we are destined to become, as well as what we are at any present moment and what we have been in the past, to the fullness of Christ's own life.

We can make these statements under the influence of the images and metaphors that Paul employs to depict his understanding of resurrection, but a whole series of questions arises as soon as we attempt to put them in more systematic terms. How can we conceive of resurrection as an ultimate state of existence in which we already participate when we are human beings limited by space and time, with a body that is destined to die and with fallible capacities of perception and sensibility? What sense does it make to talk about being part of a new creation if this, obviously, cannot be described in the same way in which we speak of our feeling and thinking, both of which are indispensable for orientation in the world "as it is" and to which we are bound with every fiber of our being? In short, how can we reason about the eschatological validity of our very existence if this goes beyond our daily life experiences?

---

9. With regard to the resurrection of Christ, this kind of reductionism has been rightly criticized by I. U. Dalferth, "Volles Grab, leerer Glaube: Zum Streit um die Auferweckung des Gekreuzigten," *Zeitschrift für Theologie und Kirche* 95 (1998): 379-409.

ANDREAS SCHUELE

Identity and Resurrection

It seems, therefore, right on target for Wolfhart Pannenberg to point to the problem of *identity* as the crucial issue of a theological account of resurrection. Under the heading "The Inner Problematic of the Idea of Resurrection" he writes:

> The identity of future with present bodily life is basic if the hope of resurrection is to have any meaning. This hope does also involve a transformation of our present life that will, we hope, mean triumph over its wrongs and hurts and failures. Nevertheless, this corruptible shall put on incorruptibility and this mortal immortality (1 Cor. 15:53). . . . We are not referring here to an identity of that which is no different but to an identity of that which is different and even antithetical, yet still an identity.[10]

Although Pannenberg prefers temporal categories to mark the difference between this life and its eschatological destination, it becomes clear from his statement that the issue of identity is not solved by dichotomies such as "now/then," or "already/not yet." Rather, the notion of identity introduces a problem that is related to the modern understanding of individuality and personality, discussed above. It is one of the axioms of modern thinking that being a "person" involves having a particular biography, a defined set of social relations, characteristic bodily features, and the like that come together in what we attribute to ourselves as our "identity." A good number of scholars — from the natural sciences as well as from the humanities — hold that it is the capacity to establish identity that provides the human person with a sense of continuity, coherence, and stability within ever shifting natural and cultural environments.[11] If this were not the case, being an individual could be hardly more than piecemeal, being drawn apart at every point of contact with the "outside world." More recently, under the influence of "postmodern" thinking, the adequacy of such a Cartesian or Lockean version of identity has been called into question.[12] The point has been made that identity as de-

---

10. W. Pannenberg, *Systematic Theology*, 3 vols. (Grand Rapids: Eerdmans, 1991-98), 573-74.

11. Besides the towering work of G. H. Mead and H. E. Erikson cf. more recently A. O. Cohen, *Self-Consciousness: An Alternative Anthropology of Identity* (London: Routledge, 1994); Anthony Giddens, *Modernity and Self-Identity* (Cambridge: Polity, 1991).

12. For a critique especially of Descartes's approach see A. J. Cascardi, *The Subject of Modernity* (Cambridge: Cambridge University, 1992); S. Toulmin, *Cosmopolis: The Hidden Agenda of Modernity* (Chicago: University of Chicago, 1990).

scribed by enlightened philosophy is not a capacity that characterizes a unique feature of human life but rather a *task* — something that is never given or fixed but has to be achieved over and over again. Identity, in this view, is not an a priori frame in which our perceptions of reality are embedded; it is something that is created, invented, and reinvented in fragmentary and heterogeneous rather than consistent and stable modes.[13]

Despite the differences between modern and postmodern accounts of identity, there seems to be a consensus that identity can be described as *an activity of the individual human being, directed to the integration of its natural dispositions, its cultural/moral constitution, as well as its subjective cognition and feeling into a framework of experience,* regardless of how coherent or fragmented such a framework might eventually be.[14]

For theologians taking resurrection primarily as a future event, it becomes a crucial issue if in the world to come, a world that will be other than a carbon-based universe,[15] there will be "identity" again, that is, if there will be individual entities with a specific kind of self-awareness and if this will imply the capacity to relate back to what will be then their own "past." Put in more general terms, this is a question about the continuity and discontinuity between "this life" and "resurrection life" and about how both continuities and discontinuities will be recognized from the viewpoint of resurrection. A different approach is required, however, if one attempts to include the future dimension of resurrection in the more comprehensive framework of what I have called above the *eschatological validity* of created life, and, more to our

---

13. Cf. P. Wagner, "Fest-Stellungen: Beobachtungen zur sozialwissenschaftlichen Diskussion über Identität," in *Identitäten: Erinnerung, Geschichte, Identität,* ed. A. Assmann and H. Friese (Frankfurt am Main: Suhrkamp, 1999), 3:44-72. A comprehensive outline of a postmodern notion of identity is provided by K. Tanner, *Theories of Culture: A New Agenda for Theology* (Minneapolis: Fortress, 1997), 96-119, 151-55.

14. Nancey Murphy (this volume) mentions body, memory, consciousness, and moral character as crucial elements for personal identity. Drawing on David Wiggins's idea of "covering concepts," she investigates on what grounds it could be validated that these components and their interplay are constitutive for the future kind of existence that is expressed by the symbol "new creation." Consequently, her focus is on the "possibilities and limits of eschatological knowledge" from a *philosophical* point of view. With a different emphasis my own approach (which presupposes critical accounts of what we can and cannot know about the eschaton) is aimed at how identity as a characteristic of finite human beings relates to the new kind of person that is defined by its participation in the life of Christ. Paraphrasing Murphy's subtitle, my essay is, therefore, concerned with a *theological* critique of the possibilities and limits of concepts of personal identity.

15. This issue is addressed in detail by Robert John Russell (cf. his contribution to this volume).

interests here, the eschatological dignity of the human person. The question is then how we can say both: that individual persons as finite beings are characterized by their efforts to establish identity, but are at the same time, as Paul puts it, "covered over" with the life of the risen Christ. Generally speaking, theological anthropology needs to focus on two different sources of creativity that give shape to a person and to think of the relation between these two sources. To the modern, enlightened mind such an endeavor must seem paradoxical because in its view a person cannot be more than what is contained by its own identity. A Christian account of resurrection, on the other hand, differs at this point in putting forth the somewhat countermodern claim that a person is in fact more than what is contained in his or her own identity. This claim is, more precisely, that the "data" from which identity arises — having body and intellect, being part of particular social networks, and the like — *as well as identity itself* are involved in a transformative process by which a person becomes *symmorphos tēs eikonos tou Christou,* "conformed to the image of Christ."

If theology seeks to unfold the biblical metaphor of resurrection in contemporary terms, it should be clear by now that it will have to account for the modern concept of identity and, at the same time, include it in a more comprehensive understanding of the human "person." In the next part of this chapter I shall engage in a dialogue with sociological and philosophical positions that may serve as critical and constructive resources for such an endeavor. This will lead into an examination of the idea of "objective immortality" that has been set forth by Alfred North Whitehead and that has some resemblance to the philosophy of Derek Parfit.

Personal Resurrection versus Objective Immortality

Let us return for one more time to the results of the opinion poll mentioned above. About 50 percent of the interviewees sympathized with a position that one may describe as "vague belief in immortality." Death is not considered the end of everything that characterizes human existence. Although there is no concrete idea of how existence is continued beyond death, it seems a realistic perspective that we keep participating in the spheres of life especially through the words, feelings, thoughts, and deeds of other people, of the communities to which we were closely connected in our lifetime. This is not a "strong" notion of immortality as we have it in the ancient Greek idea of an immortal soul, or in the Buddhist concept of reincarnation, for example. The vague form of immortality that seems to have a voice in contemporary culture does not claim that parts of our physical or mental constitution will go on when other functions are ultimately terminated. The idea is, rather, that there are certain patterns — like long-lasting feelings, memories, or certain chains of causes and effects — through which we continue to exist even though we do not experience this continuity of existence in any active mode.

To illustrate, let me give an example from a recent movie production. The movie *Titanic,* a most successful Hollywood blockbuster, features a popular Romeo and Juliet story. On board the *Titanic* a young, upper-class girl, Rose, meets the streetboy Jack and falls in love with him although she has already been promised to a rich but snobbish member of her own social class. In one of the key romantic scenes Jack draws a portrait of Rose shortly before the ship goes headlong into disaster. In the end Jack saves Rose's life while he himself freezes to death in the icy water of the North Atlantic. This story is told from the perspective of eighty-five years later. Rose, now a hundred-year-old lady, sees the portrait again that archeologists found in the wreck of the *Titanic,* and, on beholding the image, her memories and feelings come back. She then starts to tell the old story, which is staged in the movie as Jack's virtual resurrection. Love, memory, and even material objects like an image become the very media that have power to attribute immortality to a person — a kind of immortality that transcends the limitations of bodily existence.

Psychological Mechanisms (Peter Berger)

Taking an existentialist stand, one may judge that such vague forms of immortality represent one of the contemporary ways of coping with the disturbing fact that all of us have to die, that there is an ultimate borderline that we cannot pass but at which everything that we once were will be definitely terminated. The idea that somehow we will go on in the life of others or of the community to which we belong is triggered, in this perspective, by psychological mechanisms that work to give us a hold facing the finally all-encompassing reality of death. Psychological explanations play a significant role in many schools of contemporary sociology and philosophy of religion. The following quotation from Peter Berger's book *The Sacred Canopy* illustrates this kind of approach:

> The individual *knows* that he will die and, consequently, that some of his misfortunes can never be alleviated within his lifetime. If he loses a limb, for instance, it can never be restored to him. The collectivity, on the other hand, can usually *be conceived* of as immortal. It may suffer misfortunes,

but these *can be interpreted* as only transitory episodes in its overall history. Thus the individual dying on the battlefield at the hand of the foreign conqueror may not look forward to his own resurrection or immortality, but he can do so with regard to his group. To the extent that he subjectively identifies himself with that group, his death will have meaning for him even if it is unembellished with any "individualized" legitimations.[16]

Due to their mental and bodily limitations immortality and resurrection are unavailable to individuals. The fact, however, that the individual finds himself or herself imbedded in networks of interpersonal and social relations gives him or her a perspective that is not exposed to the same limitations. Berger and others would certainly be prepared to analyze the Christian account of resurrection very much along these lines. That Christians believe that they will be transformed into the body of Christ, which is essentially a communal structure and not just another material body, and that they will not only have mind and intellect but a share in the Spirit of God, are ways of opening a perspective beyond death that is available only in patterns of what one might call "the imagination of collective immortality."

Obviously, the plausibility of a Berger-like approach depends on whether one accepts the categorical distinction between biological facts and cultural imagination. Death and life are viewed as natural/biological givens that confront the solitary individual with the fact that sooner or later his or her mind and body will come to a definite end. Cultural imagination in general, and religious imagination in particular, cannot deny this, but they open up horizons of meaning that reach somehow beyond the plain biological facts.[17] Although Berger does not expressly put it this way, it is a clear and logical conclusion that culture and religion compensate for the lack of perspective from which individuals suffer. To uncover cultural strategies and trace existential givens seems to be one of the guiding interests of this approach. Death is taken to be a "fact," and immortality, as was seen in the movie *Titanic,* and resurrection, in the Christian sense, are both constructs designed to fit this fact into a wider spectrum of meaning. Especially in contemporary society

16. P. L. Berger, *The Sacred Canopy: Elements of a Sociological Theory of Religion* (Garden City, N.Y.: Doubleday, 1967), 61.

17. For similar approaches in contemporary philosophy and sociology of religion cf. D. Pollack, "Was ist Religion? Versuch einer Definition," in *Zeitschrift für Religionswissenschaft* 3 (1995): 163-90; U. Oevermann, "Ein Modell der Struktur von Religiosität," in M. Wohlrab-Sahr, *Biographie und Religion: Zwischen Ritual und Selbstsuche* (Frankfurt am Main: Campus, 1995), 27-102.

where traditional denominational stands have lost ground, a low-profile position such as "vague immortality" seems especially suited to the job.

There seems to me, however, to be a worthwhile question here. What if, with regard to the notion of death, the presence of a physical body and a self-aware intellect are in fact *not* the most decisive criteria for establishing the difference between life and death? Let me put the question a little more provocatively: Could it be that there is a deeper rationale at work within *Titanic* — besides the fact that the movie was designed to stir emotions? Is it just romantic exuberance when the author of the Song of Songs concludes that "love is strong as death'" (Song 8:6)? Is it only skillful rhetoric when the Roman philosopher and poet Gnaeus Naevius writes for his own epitaph, "Do not cry for me at my tomb, for I will live on through the mouth of thousands!" The bondages of interpersonal relationships, love and memory, spoken words and things done, all these instances characterize a person, but they are not subjected to the differentiation of life and death that we usually apply to the physical body or the human intellect.

Let me mention two philosophical positions that seem more helpful than the one given by Berger, positions that provide a more differentiated picture that may help us to see the specificity of the Christian understanding of resurrection. I will turn briefly to Alfred North Whitehead and then in more detail to Derek Parfit.

Objective Immortality (A. N. Whitehead and D. Parfit)

One of Whitehead's basic ideas is that every actual entity, for example, a human person, introduces, as he puts it, "genuine perspective" to the physical, mental, and social universe. What was once only *possible* becomes *real* through apprehension, feeling, thinking, through symbolizing processes of actual entities. Whatever we experience as patterns of order are objective results that arise from these processes, and we constantly participate in them while we develop our own genuine perspective that again exerts influence on the emergence of other real worlds. Every instance of what we may call life is a complex phenomenon composed of such interpenetrating processes of subjective and objectified worlds.

It is quite clear that in this setting conventional distinctions between life and death do not apply to the constitution of persons. In this regard Whitehead talks about subjective mortality and *objective immortality*.[18] Our subjec-

18. For a most recent interpretation and critique of Whitehead's notion of "objective

tive perspective will break up at a certain point, but this is only part of what we actually are. In the opening section of one of his last essays, "Immortality," he sums up his basic insight as follows:

> It will be presupposed that all entities or factors in the universe are essentially relevant to each other's existence. A complete account lies beyond our conscious experience. In what follows, this doctrine of essential relevance is applied to the interpretation of those fundamental beliefs concerned with the notion of immortality.[19]

The rather unspecified term "relevance" gives expression to the idea that there is a level of creative interdependence in the universe that connects its entities/factors in a way that is not dependent on their making conscious experiences. Self-awareness and bodily perception that come together in what modernity calls identity are, in Whitehead's thinking, necessary for the universe to become concrete or "real." But if there were only concreteness, the universe could be, in the true sense of the word, hardly more than substantial chaos. In this sense, the notion of "objectivity" serves to relativize the doctrine of Enlightenment thinking that anything that could be said about life, death, and creativity is meaningful only as long as it relates to subjective awareness.

More recently, in a book called *Reasons and Persons,* the British philosopher Derek Parfit made a number of observations that resemble Whitehead's approach (although Parfit himself is certainly not a process thinker). In a chapter that is given the provocative heading "Why Our Identity Does Not Matter," Parfit explicitly focuses on the relation between identity, personality, and death. Let me quote from a central passage of this chapter:

> There will later be some memories about my life. And there may later be thoughts that are influenced by mine, or things done as the result of my advice. My death will break the more direct relations between my present experiences and future experiences, but it will not break various other relations. This is all there is to the fact that there will be no one living who will be me. Now that I have seen this, my death seems to me less bad.[20]

immortality" cf. L. S. Ford, *Transforming Process Theism* (Albany: State University of New York, 2000), 148. On objective immortality as introducing patterns of order into the empirical world cf. M. Welker, *Universalität Gottes und Relativität der Welt: Theologische Kosmologie im Dialog mit dem amerikanischen Prozeßdenken nach Whitehead* (Neukirchen-Vluyn: Neukirchener, 2d ed. 1988), 112.

19. Alfred North Whitehead, "Immortality," *Harvard Divinity School Bulletin* 7 (1941-42): 5-21.

20. D. Parfit, *Reasons and Persons* (Oxford: Clarendon, 1984), 281.

Parfit analyzes, and subsequently criticizes, a notion of death that is defined primarily as a loss of identity. By identity he has very much in mind how Enlightenment modernity has coined the term. In this setting, identity is characterized as experience that becomes conscious. Our bodily and cognitive perceptions are not like lightning flashes that appear and quickly disappear. If that were the case, so the argument runs, we would exist only in a state of affects, of ever shifting and floating impressions, but without any idea of being a definite entity emerging from a particular set of experiences. Rather, it is the case that we have the capacity to connect the multitude of sensual and cognitive perceptions into one comprehensive framework that we attribute to ourselves as our identity. What happens when we die is essentially that we lose the capacity to establish and to keep up such identity: our brain functions stop and our body decays.

Parfit's criticism is essentially that modernity, with its emphasis on identity, has come to look at death as that which terminates everything that matters in the constitution of our personality, the unique shape of our very existence. On the other hand, whatever remains after we die — the memories about our lives, maybe the books and articles we have written — does not really matter. It may comfort those who are left behind or may ensure that our names will live on, but none of that will suffice to qualify us any longer as living beings. The difference between life and death is thus established by drawing a clear-cut distinction between states of identity and non-identity.

Most recently, Peter Singer's ethical writings and the hot-tempered debates around them have brought to light the deficiencies that come with coding life and death with states of identity. Parfit takes his own stand in this discussion. Unlike contemporary postmodern thinkers, he does not seek to abandon the notion of identity altogether. It remains true for him that a good share of what constitutes us as persons is identity in the modern sense. But, and this becomes a crucial supplement to the modern conception, not everything that constitutes a person can or must be contained by identity. Parfit gives two examples: the continuation and transformation of our words and deeds in the lives of others; and the dimension of social memory that he considers not merely some kind of swan song to something that gradually falls back into oblivion, but rather a vital form of shaping personal profiles over time and history.

These examples are illustrative in a sense, but they are problematic too in that they tend to merely transform the modern paradigm of identity and non-identity into other dichotomies such as activity and passivity, cause and effect. "Life" would then be that part of our existence in which we actively generate the events and features that characterize us, whereas death would mean the loss of all creative powers, a state in which all that we once were is left to the hands of others. It is certainly a matter of perspective if, once we have come to see this, we are ready to share Parfit's comforting conclusion that "our death seems less bad" then.

But there is a stronger point in Parfit's argument that, I believe, is also of theological significance. It concerns his basic insight that our personality is composed of a variety of elements, but not all of them presuppose that they are controlled by a reflective self, or that they are subject to bodily perception. Put in other words, personality, understood as the individual composition of physical, mental, and social characteristics, does not in all its facets depend on the presence of a self-aware "I." We might think, for example, of our genetic patterns, which, as is more and more revealed to us, condition a good portion of what we are and how we can unfold our capacities, but which are not contained by a feeling and thinking "I." We might also think of social relations like the experience of being loved, which is certainly essential to our personal structure but which we can never fully embrace with our mind or body, even though this is what we seek to achieve in various forms of *agapē* and *erōs*.

When we take this account of how a person is constituted, it becomes quite clear that the differentiation between life and death does not apply to all the components of a person in the same way. Our genetic codes do not die as the physical body does, and we still participate in the memories, feelings, and actions of others even if we no longer provide them with any fresh impulse. The fact that being a person is actually more than having an identity does not negate the borderline between life and death, but it takes away some of the absoluteness of this distinction. Once we accept that personality is more than what identity encompasses, the distinction between death and life loses the appeal of being a matter of all or nothing. And maybe this is the deeper meaning of Parfit's statement that death will break "the more direct relations between present experiences and future experiences," but "it will not break various other relations."

Personhood versus Identity

I see theological significance in this way of approaching issues of personality, identity, and death in that theological anthropology in particular draws decisively on the insight that what determines us as *persons* does not necessarily coincide with what we attribute to ourselves as *identity*. When theology turns to its crucial anthropological issues, such as justification, sanctification, or life in the presence of the Spirit of God, it points to something that qualifies us as persons but that is not contained by identity in the modern sense. Justification, sanctification, and transformation into the image of Christ are not at our disposal in the same way as are our bodily perceptions and cognitive experiences.

Nonetheless, it is a claim of Christian thinking that being conformed to the image of Christ encompasses us both physically and mentally — in short, as finite beings. The theological account of a "person," therefore, focuses on certain characteristics that we cannot acquire simply because we are alive, having a body and an intellect, and that do not "melt away" once the body and intellect are terminated. It seems, therefore, of utmost consequence that Christianity had to express its understanding of life and death in a way that would correspond to its view of a "person" as that which is destined to be transformed into the image of Christ. This, it seems to me, is the very essence of the idea of resurrection that New Testament traditions elaborate in various ways on the basis of their predecessors in the Hebrew Bible.[21]

There remain, nonetheless, at least two major differences between a Whiteheadian or Parfitian account of personality, identity, life and death, and a Christian understanding of resurrection.

The first instance of difference relates back to our initial question, "What comes after physical death?" If I have paraphrased Parfit and Whitehead correctly, they both assume in their different systems that what is ultimately lost with physical death are all forms of subjective awareness, of bodily feelings and impressions, while other characteristics of our personality, which Whitehead calls "objective," remain intact. In this regard they both offer theories of *immortality* — explicitly so Whitehead and more implicitly Parfit. The Christian notion of resurrection, however, goes one step further. It is more than simply a variation on the concept of immortality in that it claims that beyond death there are not only certain personal characteristics, but that there will even be identity once more; this means more concretely that there will be subjective thoughts and feelings, there will be a body, there will be a self-aware though transformed "I" that knows itself to participate in the new kind of reality that opens up through resurrection. Whenever biblical traditions depict the reality of future resurrection, they do so not as some ghostly existence essentially devoid of sensuality and bodily perception. Resurrection has to do with thinking, feeling, and socializing entities. This, it seems to me, is precisely the point where the concept of resurrection departs from the con-

---

21. Cf. A. Schuele, "Gottes Handeln als Gedächtnis: Auferstehung und kulturtheoretischer und biblisch-theologischer Perspektive," in *Wie wirklich ist die Auferstehung?* ed. H. J. Eckstein and M. Welker (Neukirchen-Vluyn: Neukirchener, 2002).

cept of objective immortality, where it might open a more specific, more focused, and maybe even more promising perspective, but where it certainly makes claims that will not be readily approved of by the natural sciences.

Related to the first aspect is another instance where resurrection markedly differs from the above accounts of immortality. To be, in a Whiteheadian sense, "objectively immortal" means to be part of a creative process that arranges and rearranges personal characteristics in an infinite number of new forms, and it is, according to Whitehead, this objective entry of actual entities into the "real world"[22] that provides patterns of natural and cultural order. This means, however, that no single actual entity is in itself subject to this transforming process (or it is subject to this process only insofar as it gives rise to other actual entities). Resurrection, on the other hand, presupposes a type of creativity that does not merely give rise to novelty by rearranging objectively given "data." *Resurrectio,* which in the biblical languages denotes a movement of somebody rising from the ground, standing up, and getting into an upright position, is not about losing identity but about growing into the kind of identity that already belongs to a person, though it is more ample and rich than what can be contained by any finite entity. To put it pointedly, resurrection requires us to conceive of the relation between *contained* and *uncontained identities.* As we noted above, Paul employs the metaphors of organic growth and of a new *morphē* that we assume as partakers of the body of Christ. The linear time sequence (life, death, and *then* resurrection), which is crucial to apocalyptic thinking, is pushed almost entirely into the background when he talks about the presence of the Spirit who raised Christ from the dead and who makes us partakers in the life of the risen Lord (Rom. 8:11). The language of *arrabōn,* "guarantee, earnest money" (2 Cor. 1:22; 5:5), or *aparchē,* "first fruit" of the Spirit (Rom. 8:23), points to something of which we have indeed received and that we have been promised to receive in its fullness and entire glory.

Interpreting Paul's anthropology, New Testament scholar Christoph Burchard compares the time span between the life and death of a human being to a building under construction.[23] The building already shows features of what it is destined to become, though most of it might be still hidden un-

---

22. As opposed to "possible" and "potential" worlds; cf. Whitehead, *Process and Reality: An Essay in Cosmology,* ed. D. R. Griffin and D. W. Sherburne (New York: Macmillan, 1978), 45-46, 60-61.

23. C. Burchard, "1 Korinther 15,39-41," in Burchard, *Studien zur Theologie: Sprache und Umwelt des Neuen Testaments,* Wissenschaftliche Untersuchungen zum Neuen Testament 107 (Tübingen: Mohr [Siebeck], 1998), 222: "Adam blieb durch seine Sünde eine Kreationsruine. Erst im letzten Adam brachte Gott die Erschaffung des Menschen zu Ende."

der scaffoldings that will later be removed; parts of it are already inhabitable, others remain unfinished and uninhabitable. In this view Paul, unlike Genesis 1 as seen in the Priestly code, does not maintain that God, by an initial act of power, completed the creation of humanity, giving us the full dignity of the divine image. In Paul and the post-Pauline texts of the New Testament, the rhetoric of the image is not so much about traces of our origins as about eschatological shapes into which we are growing. In this sense resurrection as becoming conformed to the image of Christ counts among the key factors of, or is in fact the key symbol to, the Christian understanding of what it means to be a person.

PART IV

RESURRECTION, NEW CREATION, AND CHRISTIAN HOPE

Memory in the Flow of Time and the Concept of Resurrection

DIRK EVERS

But only in time can the moment in the rose-garden,
The moment in the arbour where the rain beat,
The moment in the draughty church at smoke-fall
Be remembered; involved with past and future.
Only through time time is conquered.

T. S. ELIOT

Modern physics in the nineteenth century had to discover the irreversible flow of time as a basic feature of physics. For classical Newtonian mechanics the course of time had been irrelevant for the description of the physical processes. As the canonical formulation developed by William R. Hamilton (1805-65) was able to show, the dynamics of a mechanical system can be represented by a single function, the Hamilton function. The canonical equations derived from it can fully describe every mechanical system as a system of independent, point-like particles that vary their components of momentum and the coordinates of their position in space only with the course of time. These differential equations are exactly solvable, and it leads to no physical contradiction if the direction of time is reversed. Newtonian mechanics was indifferent to the flow of time.

Physics Discovering the Flow of Time

It was only with the physics of the second half of the nineteenth century describing dissipative physical processes that obviously were subject to decay and decline in due course of time — like the dispersion of heat — that the irreversible flow of time was considered a basic feature of physics itself and soon also became one of the prominent properties of our universe. Modern scientific cosmology displays the cosmos as one great process that, out of primordial homogeneity and chaos, developed order, structure, and — at least in a very narrow and specific niche of the universe — living beings through evolution. In the due course of the cosmic process primordial density differences increased, matter condensed to stars, and flows of energy arose that are also the source of evolution on our planet earth and maintain all forms of dissipative systems and living beings.

But at the same time it is a broadly accepted scientific fact that the universe in the long run is moving toward an end in the sense that every structural process that comes into existence on the way is determined to decay and decline. Due to the irresistible flow of time and the overall decay linked to it all structural processes are destined to dissipation and destruction, both individually and universally. Everything that arises in the due course of the cosmic process just because of this, its origin, faces from its beginning the inevitability of its own extinction. Thus cosmic eschatology also seems to provide one of the most hindering obstacles for the development of a realistic eschatological hope. It seems that resurrection and eternal life can be perceived only as supernatural wonders, and questions arise how our transitory material existence in space and time is linked with eternity, and whether such a connection is indeed inconceivable. Physical cosmology on the whole seems to devalue the meaning of human existence as such.[1]

Heat Death

Consequently since the development of modern thermodynamics in the nineteenth century describing dissipative physical processes and its application to the cosmos, the view of a dying universe was from the first confronted with passionate denial — and still is. Most of this debate refers to the concept of Heat Death, which was first predicted in 1852 by William Thomson (Lord

---

1. Cf., e.g., the famous passage at the end of *The First Three Minutes* by Steven Weinberg: "It is very hard to realize that this all [the beauty of the earth] is just a tiny part of an overwhelmingly hostile universe. It is even harder to realize that this present universe has evolved from an unspeakably unfamiliar early condition, and faces a future extinction of endless cold or intolerable heat. The more the universe seems comprehensible, the more it also seems pointless" (Steven Weinberg, *The First Three Minutes* [New York: Basic Books, 1977], 149).

Kelvin, 1824-1907), who generalized the idea that in every mechanical process there is an unavoidable loss of energy and stated a "Universal Tendency in Nature to the Dissipation of Mechanical Energy."[2] He developed the consequences for the fate of the universe: "Within a finite period of time past the earth must have been, and within a finite period of time to come the earth must again be, unfit for the habitation of man as at present constituted, unless operations have been, or are to be performed, which are impossible under the laws to which the known operations going on at present in the material world are subject."[3]

Not much more than a decade later the German physicist Rudolf Clausius (1822-88) developed the concept of "entropy" as a measure for energy dissipation and then formulated the two fundamental laws of thermodynamics: *"1) The energy of the universe is constant. 2) The entropy of the universe tends toward a maximum."*[4] In contrast to the view of Newtonian physics, every natural process is in the long run seen as irreversible and unidirectional, with that direction being dictated by an overall increase of entropy. The second law of thermodynamics thus implies an inevitable final state of the universe for which Claudius created the term "Heat Death" *(Wärmetod):* "The more the universe approaches this limiting condition in which the entropy is a maximum, the more do the occasions of further change diminish; and supposing this condition to be at last completely attained, no further change could evermore take place, and the universe would be in a state of unchanging death."[5] The cosmic order was envisioned as a transitory phenomenon within an overall and comprehensive decay.

Although the concept of Heat Death was highly controversial,[6] the de-

---

2. W. Thomson, "On a Universal Tendency in Nature to the Dissipation of Mechanical Energy," *Philosophical Magazine* 4.4 (1852): 304-6.

3. Ibid., 306. The apparent reservation is due to the fact that Thomson did not want to exclude the possibility of "nonphysical," energy-producing forces effective, e.g., in organisms. Two years later in a well-known public lecture Hermann von Helmholtz described the final state of the universe in detail, stating that in the end every energy will be merged into heat, that every heat difference will be finally leveled, and thus that every physical process will come to a standstill. Cf. Hermann von Helmholtz, "On the Interaction of Natural Forces," in *Popular Scientific Lectures,* ed. Martin Kline (New York: Dover, 1961).

4. R. Clausius, "Über verschiedene für die Anwendung bequeme Formen der Hauptgleichungen der mechanischen Wärmetheorie," *Poggendorffs Annalen der Physik und Chemie* 125 (1865): 353-400, esp. 400: *"1) Die Energie der Welt ist constant. 2) Die Entropie der Welt strebt einem Maximum zu."*

5. R. Clausius, "On the Second Fundamental Theorem of the Mechanical Theory of Heat," *Philosophical Magazine* 4.35 (1868): 405-19, esp. 419.

6. Friedrich Nietzsche, e.g., vehemently rejected the concept of Heat Death and identi-

velopment of the standard model of twentieth-century cosmology confirmed the inevitability of a universal decline and final ending of cosmic processes. But it disclosed two possible scenarios, a "hot" and a "cold" Heat Death, so to speak. When the Russian mathematician and physicist Aleksandr Friedmann (1888-1925) developed the still valid framework for the standard model of contemporary cosmology, he was able to show that three general types of universe can be distinguished, which differ characteristically in their future fates and imply two different final states.[7] Depending on the ratio between the mass/energy-density of the universe and the velocity of expansion, gravitation either will be able to bring expansion to a halt and reverse it into a contraction that will end in a final collapse (big crunch), or the universe will expand forever.

In each case the future development of cosmic processes will be significantly different. In the case of a final collapse, the universe would reheat and gravitation would increase beyond all limits and finally concentrate all mass and energy within a singularity with infinite density of mass and energy. This final collapse would eventually destroy every structure and order of the universe and consume it into an immense oven of heat. In the case of endless expansion, all cosmic energy and matter would be dispersed to the point that all star formation and radiation would end. Locally, the galaxies might collapse into black holes, but due to Hawking radiation even black holes would slowly lose their mass. It is presumed that even protons are not eternally stable, so

---

fied in it a will for ruin or perdition as part of the decadent tendencies of the *fin de siècle*. Against Thomson's theory of dissipation and its pessimism he formulated his doctrine of "eternal recurrence of the same." In this emotional debate on Heat Death, which seemed decisive for an optimistic or pessimistic scientific worldview, the British Association for the Advancement of Science even installed a committee that debated that issue from 1891 to 1894. It gave its final report on the general meeting in 1894, which took place in the Sheldonian Theatre at Oxford not far away from the Oxford University Museum, which thirty years before had seen the other famous debate on the implications of modern science in that century, the debate between Bishop Wilberforce and G. H. Huxley on Darwin's theory of evolution. Cf. Stephen G. Brush, *The Kind of Motion We Call Heat: A History of the Kinetic Theory of Gases in the 19th Century* (Amsterdam/New York/Oxford: North Holland Publishing Company, 1976), 2:617-19; Stephen G. Brush, *The Temperature of History: Phases of Science and Culture in the Nineteenth Century* (New York: Burt Franklin, 1978), 68-69. On page 68 Brush locates the Wilberforce-Huxley debate in the Sheldonian Theatre itself, which is incorrect. The "Report on the Present State of Our Knowledge of Thermodynamics" is found in *Report of the Sixty-Fourth Meeting of the British Association for the Advancement of Science* (London: John Murray, 1894), 64-106, including an Appendix by Boltzmann, who participated in the meeting.

7. Aleksandr Friedmann, "Über die Krümmung des Raumes," *Zeitschrift für Physik* 10 (1922): 377-86. Cf. also Robert John Russell's chapter in this volume.

that all baryonic matter would in the end decay and all order and structure of the universe would be dissolved into an ever-dispersing radiation field with decaying minimal fluctuations. This undifferentiated cosmic soup would be devoid of organized structures. In this case the world would end, so to speak, "not with a bang, but a whimper" (T. S. Eliot).

Up to now, empirical evidence does not allow us to decide which type of Friedmann Universe our universe represents. What can be said is that our universe is still in the young, expanding era when the properties of the different types are still very close. And, in the range of possible universes, the mass density of our universe is located somewhere near the threshold that separates the different types.

Another consequence of the amount of mass contained in the cosmos in relation to its rate of expansion is the curvature of its space-time. A universe above the critical density parameter has a spherically curved space-time with finite volume. It is *closed* both in space and in time. A universe with a lower than critical density, on the other hand, is *open,* its space-time curvature is negative, and it ever was and ever will be infinite in extension. A universe with exactly the critical mass density would be open as well, but it would be flat in its infinite space-time, which would show a Euclidian metric. What we can say is that our universe shows a nearly Euclidian metric.[8]

The further development of cosmology in recent decades led to a powerful new model of the early universe called the *Inflation Model.* It predicts characteristic features of the universe, especially the isotropy of its radiation background, by means of an initial inflationary phase of expansion after which the young cosmos will merge into a Friedmann Model. Inflation Models are designed such that they consequently produce a cosmos with exactly the critical density parameter and with a flat, Euclidian metric. So, for empirical and theoretical reasons, an open but flat universe that will expand forever might be seen as the most plausible model at present.[9]

---

8. However, the estimations of the cosmos's radiant masses provide only a mass-energy density, which is by far less than needed to exceed critical density. It is assumed that there must be a lot of hidden, so-called "dark matter," which supplies enough mass for a nearly Euclidian universe as we observe it. Maybe neutrinos, particles that hardly interact with other kinds of matter and are therefore difficult to detect, have a certain minimal mass, which in that case would contribute significantly to overall mass balance; cf. Walter Gibbs, "A Massive Discovery," *Scientific American* 278.8 (August 1998): 9ff.

9. Cf. Peter Coles and George F. R. Ellis, *Is the Universe Open or Closed? The Density of Matter in the Universe* (Cambridge: Cambridge University, 1997).

Physicists' Resurrection?

None of the cosmological models can avoid the inevitability of the world and its processes coming to an end. Nevertheless eschatological views have been developed that — on the lines of the Heat Death debate — try to transcend the apparent futility of a dying creation and to combine cosmological eschatology with a concept of resurrection so that, in a kind of modern *apokatastasis pantōn,* in the end everything that was meaningful in cosmic history is brought back into being through a natural process. They interpret the end of the universe as the unfolding of its inner destination. I want to deal briefly with the two most prominent proposals along these lines.

Freeman Dyson, as the title of his book *Infinite in All Directions* indicates, argues in favor of an open universe. He assumes that in due course of time life will be able to adapt to "outer space" living conditions (zero gravity, zero temperature, and zero pressure) and will soon be "capable of making itself at home in every corner of the universe."[10] In addition, he employs what he calls "the hypothesis of abstraction."[11] It says that life, as well as consciousness, must be described in terms of organization rather than substance. Life and consciousness can be "detached from flesh and blood and embodied in networks of superconducting circuitry or in interstellar dust clouds."[12]

If life can be transferred to any kind of matter and can adapt to any kind of environment, then it can be assumed as highly possible that life can escape Heat Death in an ever expanding universe because low temperature favors order and at the same time lowers the rate of metabolism of energy needed to sustain order. "The colder the environment, the quieter the background, the more thrifty life can be in its use of energy. . . . In an expanding universe, life can adapt itself as the eons go by, constantly matching its metabolism of energy to the falling temperature of its surroundings."[13] "Mind" can spread all over into cosmic space and will inform and control the whole universe. Thus it will learn and grow while the universe expands and will definitely transcend by far our scale of comprehension. "Mind" might then be identified with God, the mind, which passes all our understanding. And perhaps, Dyson speculates, our personal fate might in the end be included in the universal mind that with its intellectual power might be capable of a final recapitula-

---

10. Freeman J. Dyson, *Infinite in All Directions* (New York: Harper & Row, 1988), 107.
11. Ibid.
12. Ibid.
13. Ibid., 109, 111.

tion of all things that ever happened to be. The whimpers of the freezing universe might thus be interpreted as "whispers of immortality."[14]

Frank Tipler, on the other hand, employs the scenario of a closed universe in order to establish a natural eschatology that explicitly includes immortality and resurrection. Tipler sees his argument as an alternative that avoids the pessimistic and frustrating doctrines of both Eternal Return and Heat Death. Referring to concepts and terminology of Teilhard de Chardin's theology, Tipler has developed what he calls the "Omega Point Theory." He is very close to Dyson in that he sees life as a basically structural phenomenon that is independent of its physical constituents. "The pattern is what is important, not the substrate."[15] Tipler consequently defines life as "a form of information-processing" and the human mind as "a very complex computer program,"[16] and he explicitly confesses himself to be a reductionist, for whom the human mind and the human soul are nothing more than special types of software-controlled machinery.

As with Dyson, Tipler's vision is that mind as an information-processing structure — on our planet still linked with carbon-based forms of life — will somehow take control over all cosmic processes and thus will become independent of living bodies. But, unlike Dyson, Tipler uses the collapsing closed universe to find sources of energy that could guarantee an unlimited final recollection of everything. Tipler postulates a special type of closed universe, a universe that collapses "in one direction only while remaining essentially the same size in the other two directions."[17] In such a universe its shearing will produce a radiation temperature difference, "and this temperature difference can be shown to provide sufficient free energy for an infinite amount of information processing between now and the final singularity."[18]

Within the last compressing moments, when the dying cosmos is approaching Omega Point, an infinity of information could be processed and everything that can be known would then be known by the cosmic consciousness: "it knows whatever is possible to know about the physical universe (and

---

14. Ibid., 121.

15. Frank J. Tipler, *The Physics of Immortality: Modern Cosmology, God and the Resurrection of the Dead* (New York: Doubleday, 1994), 127.

16. Ibid., 124.

17. Ibid., 136.

18. Frank J. Tipler, "The Omega Point Theory: A Model of an Evolving God," in *Physics, Philosophy, and Theology: A Common Quest for Understanding*, ed. Robert J. Russell, William R. Stoeger, and George V. Coyne (Vatican City State: Vatican Observatory, 1988), 313-31, esp. 320.

hence about Itself)."[19] The maximum that can be known, according to Tipler, is included in the wave function of the universe, which includes everything that was actualized and could have been actualized in our lives as well as in every life in the universe. Thus our whole life, with all its possibilities, would be raised again in the consciousness of the Omega Point. And in these last fractions of a second the universe, the Omega Point, the "evolving God"[20] in it, through his infinitely accelerated mind, would gain cybernetic immortality. "Thus, although a closed universe exists for only a finite proper time, it nevertheless could exist for an infinite subjective time."[21]

The Eschatological Quest

I will not deal with physical arguments against Dyson and Tipler in detail. Others have done that, to the extent that these excessively imaginative concepts require, and have pointed at their highly problematic use of speculative physics and controversial presuppositions.[22] The main point, for our argument, is that a physical cosmic eschatology that moves along the lines of Dyson and Tipler falls short of meeting the challenge of our scientific views of the transitoriness and finitude of creation. They try to encounter the apparent futility of worldly existence simply by prolonging it through physical and technological means, thus employing what Georg F. W. Hegel called "bad infinity."[23] Thus they miss the center of eschatological hope for resurrection and eternal life, which is not a simple concept reached through an excessive enhancement of physics but a complex structure that can be envisioned as an ellipse with two focal points: the Christian concept of eschatological hope, on the one side, rejects and surpasses reductionist, inhuman, and paralyzing concepts of life and creation that reduce our reality to a mere physical fact. On the other side, this is done without despising the meaning of our historical, transitory, actual existence but instead exposing its dignity, the eternal meaningfulness of its positive and creative aspects, with which each of us enriches creation.[24]

19. Tipler, "The Physics of Immortality," 154.

20. Ibid., 323.

21. Tipler, "The Omega Point Theory," 320.

22. Cf., e.g., John Polkinghorne, *Science and Christian Belief* (London: SPCK, 2d ed. 1994), 164-65.

23. Cf. Georg F. W. Hegel, *Wissenschaft der Logik*, in *Gesammelte Werke* (Hamburg: Meiner, 1985), 21:137.

24. Cf. Michael Welker's chapter in this volume.

A cosmic eschatology that is designed and conceptualized only along the tendencies of evolutionary processes is too thin a basis to meet this challenge. Although science cannot refrain from dealing with the future and from designing conjectures about the overall development of its cosmological models, it must be aware of its limits. The primary lesson to be learned from scientific cosmology is that the physical world we live in is not designed as a project that in its end coincides with its inner meaning and destination. To seek the fulfillment of creation in the cosmological destiny of the universe is to deprive this our transitory and limited but equally concrete, definite, and unique life of its own right, its dignity. And especially when life is unfulfilled, when its possibilities are spoiled and scattered, then fulfillment and eschatological hope must not be sought in due course of time, when the lived life will, in one way or another, be recapitulated in an illustrious and joyfully musing cosmic consciousness. Such cosmic eschatologies, as is the case with Tipler, often foster a naive optimism of eternal progress and remain helpless in concrete, decision-making processes, when confronted with the risks and ambiguities of scientific progress. A refutation of Heat Death does not as such establish positive and relevant hope. Instead, it tends to denounce concrete, transitory, human existence with all its physical, emotional, and social aspects.

Tipler, for example, sees every instance of the cosmic process encoded in the wave function of the universe that will be fully conceived and understood by the overall cosmic intelligence in the Omega Point. The final resurrection is nothing else than the virtual simulation of lived lives and all their possible alternatives. In the Omega Point "the physical universe is in precise one-to-one correspondence with a simulation."[25] But then the difference between our real historic life and its resurrection in the final computer simulation of the Omega Point becomes irrelevant and meaningless.[26] Why does the universe take on the burden of existence at all when the simulation is the ultimate reality?

A powerful eschatology with a realistic and effective concept of the resurrection must employ much more than simply physics. It has to take seriously our historic, religious, and social experiences and conditions. A realistic concept of the resurrection must be designed neither as a recapitulation of what was nor as its endless continuation. Instead we have to insist on the point that the Bible puts at the center of its gospel of the resurrection of

25. Frank J. Tipler, "The Omega Point as *Eschaton:* Answers to Pannenberg's Questions for Scientists," *Zygon* 24 (1989): 217-53, esp. 242.

26. Ibid.: "How do we know we ourselves are not merely a simulation inside a gigantic computer? Obviously, we cannot know."

Christ, namely, that hope for the resurrection lies *within* this transitory cosmos, the establishment of the kingdom of God that is in our midst, among us and yet still to come. Within our concrete and finite existence in space and time, we are empowered and become oriented to and engaged by anticipating eternal life within vanishing creation. Within the passing flow of time arises what transcends time. The hope of the resurrection makes our *present* life eternally meaningful and does not refer to any kind of development that is to come in the prolongation of space and time after billions of years. Right at the core of the New Testament gospel the risen Christ is identified with the historical Jesus, so that in their resurrection experiences the apostles understood that now his earthly presence, his life and death, are eternally meaningful. Resurrection was not the reversal of his death, but its acclamation. In the crucified and risen Christ, eschatological hope is definitely constituted and has already become effective in this our life.[27] Through history, history was transformed into eternal meaningfulness; through time, time was conquered.

A Theological Alternative to Eschatology and Cosmology: Conquering Time through Time via the Concept of Memory

How is that possible? Which means and structural processes are necessary to transcend time, to ascribe to lived lives eternal meaningfulness? To answer these questions we must analyze not only the time of physics but also the structured and processed time of human experience that arises within and through physical time but at the same time transcends it by constituting identity and persistence through the complex interplay of social and individual memory. The reader will note that I will not attempt to answer the challenges set out in my previous sections by physics and eschatology, regarding not only the resurrection of Jesus but also the general resurrection and the new creation at the end of the universe. Instead I will shift the discussion and focus strictly on the theological resources we have at our disposal to address the challenge of time, specifically the concept of memory.[28]

As we have seen, it is a basic feature of modern scientific cosmology that the cosmos is asymmetric in time, that history and evolutionary developments are as such deeply rooted in cosmic processes, both in the overall history and fate of space-time and in its local thermodynamic flows. Gravity in-

---

27. Cf. Peter Lampe's and Hans-Joachim Eckstein's chapters in this volume.

28. Other essays in this volume do attempt to address this challenge. See, e.g., those of John Polkinghorne and Robert John Russell.

creases local density fluctuations of matter and concentrates matter in stars such that they start to radiate. Expansion of the universe prevents gravitational collapse and guarantees the source-drain difference. "*Any* gravitating universe that can exist and contains more than one type of interacting material *must* be asymmetric in time, both globally in its motion and locally in its thermodynamics."[29]

It is only within these entropic processes that modern thermodynamics describes, and that will inevitably lead to the heat death of the universe, that life as a phenomenon of structure and organization can come into being and dissipative systems can develop. The arrow of time of cosmic dynamics that leads to local flows of energy and maintains them, the arrow of time of irreversible thermodynamic processes within which living systems evolve, and the arrow of time of our consciousness that perceives the change of time form a hierarchy of interdependences.

And within this cosmic process our personal identity evolves. Personal identity is not founded in an immortal soul added to the structural processes of ontogenetic evolution. It arises out of the temporal structure of human existence, and it dies with its destruction. If the resurrection is not the physical continuation of a cosmic process, if, in the language of physics, there are no continuous world lines in the Minkowski world that connect our present lifetime and our life in the world to come, the coherence between our present and our resurrected identity becomes the main issue.[30] We have to reconstruct resurrection as the interface, as the joint link, between cosmic finite existence on the basis of physical processes within this cosmos and eternal life in the new heaven and the new earth.

At this point an elaborated and differentiated concept of *memory* is extremely relevant. It is through *personal memory* that we gain personal identity in the due course of our lives. It is through *cultural memory* that our individual and personal identity is shaped and formed. And it is through *God's memory* that the interplay of personal and cultural memory becomes a means of God's presence in the transient world, that the world is opened toward the kingdom of God.

As St. Augustine demonstrated in his famous analysis of time in his *Confessiones,* memory can provide the link between God's imperishable, ever

29. Paul C. W. Davies, *The Physics of Time Asymmetry* (Berkeley: University of California, 1974), 109.

30. As has often been pointed out, the idea of an immortal soul was accepted within Christianity because it could provide continuity between the dead and the resurrected person; cf. Wolfhart Pannenberg, *Systematic Theology* (Grand Rapids: Eerdmans, 1993), 3.575-80.

steadfast eternity *(semper stans aeternitas)* and the ever moving, perishing time of creation. The essence, the actual being of time in its three modes of past, present, and future, Augustine points out, is difficult to grasp. The past is gone and *is not* any more, the future is still to come and *is not* yet, and the present is only the unextended turning point at which the future becomes the past. While God "is" always the same in his eternity, time "is" not but tends toward nonbeing *(tendit non esse)*[31] and is therefore profoundly detached from eternity. But we still experience time as the basic form of our existence as created beings, and we experience time not only as just coming and going, but as staying, as long or short, as something that is extended (Augustine's Latin term is *distentio)*:[32] time is the extension of the mind *(distentio animi)*,[33] and this is where memory comes in. When I live as a human being in time, "I measure something in my memory, which stays there as a fixed impression."[34]

But memory is more than just remembering the past. It owns a great power *(magna vis est memoriae)*[35] because it retains our life and identity within the flow of time. Memory is in its wider sense the integration of the three modes of time. Here Augustine refers to the temporal acoustic phenomena of words and music and might thus refer to his experience as a teacher of rhetoric:[36] while singing a song or reciting a poem, the human mind somehow comprises the whole of what has been sung or said in memory and what will be sung or said in expectation, and is, at the same time, fully present by giving sound to one note or word after the other. And it is this directed structure of life, this interplay of memory *(memoria)*, expectation *(expectatio)*, and attention *(attentio)*, that provides the basic structure of our temporal existence.[37]

And that is not only valid for particular perceptions of time. What can be said about time in the perception of music or speech is valid, accordingly, for the individual human life as a whole as well for "the whole age of the sons

---

31. Aurelius Augustinus, *Confessiones* 11.14.17.

32. Ibid. 11.23.30: "tempus quandam esse distentionem."

33. Cf. ibid. 11.26.33: "In te, anime meus, tempora metior"; cf. *Confessiones* 11.26.33: "Inde mihi visum est nihil esse aliud tempus quam distentionem: sed cuius rei, nescio, et mirum, si non ipsius animi."

34. Ibid. 11.27.35: "aliquid in memoria mea metior quod infixum manet."

35. Ibid. 10.17.26.

36. Cf. Ulrich Duchrow, "Der sogenannte psychologische Zeitbegriff Augustins im Verhältnis zur physikalischen und geschichtlichen Zeit," *Zeitschrift für Theologie und Kirche* 63 (1966): 267-88, who suggests that Augustine's interest in memory and temporal acoustic phenomena might stem from his intense exploration of language, speech, and rhetorical tradition during his time as a teacher.

37. Augustine, *Confessiones* 11.28.37.

of men, whereof all the lives of men are parts."[38] Each human act reveals this structure from past to future, and so does human history as a whole. Thus Augustine's often so-called "psychological" concept of time is thoroughly (although not fully consistently) linked with his view of history and cosmology.

But ever-fading time is also the reason for creational transitoriness. Thus we become susceptible to fading away with time, to getting lost in it. As beings existing in and through temporal processes in which we experience the extension of time we experience also the distracting power of time. Thus Augustine exploits the fact that distraction is the second lexical meaning of the Latin word *distentio.* If we do not intentionally form and shape our temporal existence, we can get lost in the flow of events, in a life overstretched and overstrained. A concentrating *intention* must correspond to the distension of temporal existence, so that we do not exist according to the distracting flow of time but according to a concentrating intention.[39] Once again Augustine employs the concept of memory. While our memory seems to be like a vast and chaotic space filled with uncountably many things,[40] it is still the place in which God resides. And, as a faithful believer, he knows that he can find God there, and that God is the one who orders and justifies his memory and his soul: "Since when I learnt Thee, Thou resides in my memory; and there do I find Thee, when I remember Thee, and delight in Thee."[41]

Thus Augustine points to the importance of memory linking the cosmic process and our individual identity and orientation in life with God's presence. But at this point we have to go further and transcend Augustine's individualistic concept of memory by including social and cultural aspects of canonic memory and embedding memory within the comprehensive realm of God's care for creation. Memory is a constructive and living cultural achievement in which traditional and innovative components interact with present experiences. Memory must be worked out, must be structured and acquired, and that is possible only within a community, within a realm of oral, symbolic, and social communication.[42] And memory always starts with memory; it can be continued only by reshaping and refreshing it. Memory, so to speak, is embedded within memory.

The comprehensive realm of memory is God remembering his creation, being mindful of us. "What is man that you are mindful of him, the

38. Ibid. 11.28: "hoc in toto saeculo filiorum hominum, cuius partes sunt omnes vitae hominum."

39. Ibid.: "non secundum distentionem, sed secundum intentionem."

40. Ibid. 10.17.26.

41. Ibid. 10.24.35.

42. Cf. Detlef B. Linke's chapter in this volume.

son of man that you care for him?" Psalm 8 exclaims in wonder. Even when life vanishes before it really begins or finally our mind and memory disintegrate as well as our body, it is not any kind of substantial soul or the computed information of the wave function of the universe of which we are part that holds us together and keeps our integrity and dignity, but God remembering us, remembering what we strived for, where we failed, what — in good terms and in evil, in its richness and its deprivation — accounts for our personal identity.

Thus the temporal structure of life can be formed according to God's relation toward his creation and can conquer time through time. I see the Augustinian concepts of *memoria, expectatio,* and *attentio* in parallel with Paul's famous triad of faith, hope, and love in 1 Corinthians 13: *faith* as the commemorative trust and belief in what God, from whom all things come, has done to us; *hope* as the faithful expectation of what God is going to bring about, historically and eternally; *love* as the attentive and intentional care for our fellow human beings, for ourselves, and for the whole creation of which we are part. Love is the greatest among these three insofar it realizes the appropriate presence and intention of mind, which forms and concentrates the actual human temporal existence.

Through the complex interaction of faith, hope, and love, we as individuals and communities can cope with times of distraction, of doubt and perplexity, with loss of perspective and intention for life. Faith, hope, and love can bring determination to unassertive situations through memory and expectation. We can develop new perspectives of action, new confidence and trust. In its temporal intention, which can cope with the distracting distension of life, faith is the never ending, never completed form of attentive existence in which we experience the power of the Creator, from whom we come, with whom we live, and toward whom we go. We can experience that through *memory, expectation,* and *attention* God himself gets involved in human history and cooperates with us as the ongoing Creator, who opened up and ever reopens new possibilities and perspectives of life. With commemorative, attentive, and intentional love and care we cooperate with the continuously creative Creator, and in doing so we actualize our destination as images of God.

God's Final End: Judgment and Shalom

The complex interdependence between individual, social, and canonic memory, which is embedded in the overall realm of God's being mindful of us and his creation, is the foundation of eternal life. Again God's memory is not just revoking past events and re-experiencing or continuing them *ad infinitum,* but a constructive and intentional concentration and healing of our lived lives. Tradition has envisioned this as the *final judgment,* an often misused concept that must be rehabilitated and renewed with fresh meaning. After all, it is the final judgment in which God, through his memory and remembrance, transforms our lived lives into our new eternal identities. It is through God's judgment that our lived life is invested with its ultimate integrity and through which it finds its fulfillment.

God's judgment must not be employed as a means of threat in order to discipline human beings by fear. God's judgment sets right, just as God's righteousness is an effective righteousness that makes righteous. It is human selfishness and self-centeredness that provoke fear and can conceive God's judgment only as destructive. But love toward God drives out all fear and can conceive God's final judgment as "the therapeutic event."[43]

The New Testament claims that it is the coming Jesus who will judge. The Son of Man who will come with his angels to judge heaven and earth is identical with Jesus the Crucified. It is the Crucified who determines what is eternally valid, what has to be destroyed forever, and what has to be set right and compensated. It is not *Iustitia,* with her eyes bound, but the friend of the lost and the sinner, the preacher on the mount, the one who gave his life for the sake of the many. The final judgment will not be simply a happy ending. It would be unmerciful if Jesus would not bring the tears and wounds into the open, wounds that otherwise would be eternally hidden, which no time could heal. The final judgment heals, it heals by revealing the wounds of the victim as well as the shame of the perpetrator. It is therapeutic in its truth, which arises out of the divine memory.

But as eternal life, judgment is not only something yet to come. It can already be identified as effective in history. In John, Jesus said that with him, with the divine light, judgment (Gk. *krisis*) came into the world (John 3:19). In him the rectifying work of God's judgment has already begun. In Jesus' encounter with people like Zacchaeus, Mary Magdalene, and the criminal at the cross, we paradigmatically see the purifying and redeeming work of God's judgment: "Remember me when you come into your kingdom," said the crucified criminal who knew his guilt (Luke 23:42).

Jesus' resurrection is God's affirmation that community and forgiveness, such as the disciples experienced with the historical Jesus, are eternally valid, and their remembrance shall and can form the shape of our lives and

---

43. Eberhard Jüngel, "The Last Judgement as an Act of Grace," *Louvain Studies* 15.4 (1990): 389-405, esp. 402.

community. He is the one who is able to establish eternal *shalom* through his judgment. And that leads to our last point.

It is *shalom* that represents the end of creation. *Shalom* is God's intention with his creation. It is the state in which every living being is an integrated part of the whole and exists with all other beings in relations of mutual enrichment. This wholeness and fullness surely transcends space and time, requiring a new heaven and a new earth in which time and history as striving toward ends have themselves come to an end. *Shalom* might thus be something like fulfillment in each moment.[44]

The *shalom* of eternal life starts in this life as well. "Natural life is a part of eternal life and a beginning,"[45] Martin Luther wrote. There is much coherence and continuity between our life in the perishing cosmos and in the world to come, when our life and community is oriented to the kingdom of God that is near. Our worldly relationships can become analogies, parables of eternal life. In the midst of profane meals we can discover a parable of eternal life as a feast of joy, in mutual respect within a definite earthly community and in just political conditions we can discover a parable of the New Jerusalem, the heavenly citizenship (Phil. 3:20), and in the *"Augen-Blick,"* the look into the other's eyes, when we meet the eyes of a person we love, we can realize that one day we will encounter the loving God face-to-face (1 Cor. 13:12).

44. Cf. Friedrich D. E. Schleiermacher: "ewig sein in einem Augenblik" ("Über die Religion: Reden an die Gebildeten unter ihren Verächtern," in *Kritische Gesamtausgabe*, ed. G. Meckenstock [Berlin: de Gruyter, 1984], 1:247).

45. Martin Luther, "Kirchenpostille (1522)," in *D. Martin Luthers Werke: Kritische Gesamtausgabe* (Weimar: Hermann Böhlaus, 1910), 10:200.

Resurrection to New Life: Pneumatological Implications of the Eschatological Transition

GÜNTER THOMAS

This is the end, for me the beginning of life.

DIETRICH BONHOEFFER[1]

The work of the Holy Spirit is the key to any sound and realistic understanding of the Christian symbol of the final resurrection that resists the lure of groundless speculation. If we correctly comprehend the role of God's Spirit in the final eschatological transition, we discover that the final resurrection, which is grounded in Christ's resurrection, is a move to a new life with its own temporal, social, and responsive dimensions. This new life reaches far beyond ideas of a manifestation or recollection of the lived life, even though it will show complex relations with our current life. This is, in short, the general thesis behind the following considerations. Yet this thesis needs to be placed within the broader frame and the specific stages of eschatological reasoning in the twentieth century.

---

1. These were the last words Dietrich Bonhoeffer told Paine Best shortly before his execution. See Eberhard Bethge, *Dietrich Bonhoeffer: Eine Biographie* (München: Kaiser, 1967), 1037 n. 54.

GÜNTER THOMAS

Three Phases of Eschatological Discourses

The history of theology is full of surprises, even paradoxes. When Ernst Troeltsch, the theologian who stood "between" the nineteenth and twentieth centuries, made his much quoted remark: "A modern theologian says: 'The eschatological office is nowadays most of the time closed,'" he did not realize that precisely those transformations of eschatological thinking that he observed and suggested provided the key to an eschatological office across the street, where overtime would become standard.[2] In his article on eschatology written for the first edition of the dictionary *Religion in Geschichte und Gegenwart* he spelled out quite clearly that religion as such is concerned about last things, things of ultimate, infinite, and absolute *value*.[3] If the revealed, truly ultimate realities are experienced as the absolute, the reality of divine life in the midst of relativity, then we touch upon eschatological questions. For this reason Troeltsch concluded: "The last things have nothing to do with time." What followed after Troeltsch's remark is well known.[4] Within the next twenty years a very large number of publications appeared that represented a move from the eschata to the eschaton. Not the individual eschatological symbols and their temporal aspects, but the co-presence of God's eternity with any finite present moment was at the center of theological interest. After this first phase of an "axiological eschatology," to use a phrase from Paul Althaus, there appeared as a second stage a number of theological projects that could be labeled eschatological ontologies. They share the characteristic feature of conceptualizing creation as moving toward the eschaton. Even more, "eschatology becomes the constitutive meaning, not only for the question of knowledge of God but also for the question about the reality of God."[5] But again, the surprising fact is that while the peculiar eschata (e.g., resurrection, last judgment, new creation, and eternal life) were no longer fully neglected as in the first stage, they were not treated

2. Ernst Troeltsch, *Glaubenslehre: Nach Heidelberger Vorlesungen aus den Jahren 1911 und 1912* (München/Leipzig: Duncker & Humblot, 1924), 36.

3. Ernst Troeltsch, "Eschatologie: IV. Dogmatisch," in *Religion in Geschichte und Gegenwart* (Tübingen: J. C. B. Mohr, 1st ed. 1910), 2:622-32.

4. For a short overview see Christoph Schwöbel, "Last Things First? The Century of Eschatology in Retrospect," in *The Future as God's Gift: Explorations in Christian Eschatology*, ed. David Fergusson and Marcel Sarot (Edinburgh: T&T Clark, 2000), 217-41.

5. Wolfhart Pannenberg, *Grundfragen Systematischer Theologie* (Göttingen: Vandenhoeck & Ruprecht, 1967), 1:5-6. The theological work of Wolfhart Pannenberg, Paul Tillich, and certainly also of Jürgen Moltmann can be categorized in such a way. However, Moltmann's later contributions also belong to the third stage.

in a way thorough enough to truly constitute a reconstruction of the eschatological symbols.

However, during recent years theological reflection has slowly and gradually entered another (third) stage in which the distinct eschatological symbols like resurrection or the Last Judgment are once again receiving more attention. The aim of this essay is to provide a particularly pneumatological perspective on the eschatological transition in the hope that this will help to tackle three problematic issues in theological eschatology: first, it will address the paramount notion of "closure" that dominates many conceptions of resurrection and suggest "openness" as the deep structure of life in the eschaton. Second, it will shed some light on the crucial issue of the temporality of eternal life. Third, it will help to uncover the distinct, and at the same time intrinsic, relational character of these symbols. Compared to alternative approaches to the final resurrection, the following considerations will be an *internal* elaboration of the Christian symbol system, which explores the way certain distinct symbols are connected.

Recent Approaches to the Resurrection: Completion, Recollection, and Manifestation of the Lived Life

To illuminate the characteristic differences between the second and third stages, I would like to start out with a short examination of the final resurrection within the work of two contemporary theologians: Eberhard Jüngel and Wolfhart Pannenberg. During the last decades both theologians have provided insightful and remarkable contributions to an understanding of the final resurrection that at the same time have excited far-reaching questions concerning the liveliness of eternal life.

In his 1971 publication *Death,* Eberhard Jüngel dealt with the issue of resurrection against a peculiar background.[6] Following Friedrich Schleiermacher and Karl Barth, he understood death as a necessary implication of the human being as a finite creature. Therefore, death as such is not here the problem, but only its dark shadow cast on this life. Human sin gives death its painful sting (1 Cor. 15:56). Given this understanding of death, the resurrec-

6. Eberhard Jüngel, *Tod* (Gütersloh: Gütersloher Verlagshaus Mohn, 1979; orig. 1971). Important subsequent publications on eschatological topics include idem, "The Last Judgement as an Act of Grace," in *Louvain Studies* 15 (1990): 389-405; idem, "Thesen zur Ewigkeit des ewigen Lebens," in *Zeitschrift für Theologie und Kirche* 97 (2000): 80-87; idem, "Ewigkeit: III. Dogmatisch," in *Religion in Geschichte und Gegenwart* (Tübingen: Mohr Siebeck, 4th ed. 1999), 2:1774-76.

tion does not mean the abolition of life's temporal limits. Instead, the resurrection means that this finite life will be made eternal *as* finite life by participating in God's eternal life. The resurrected life is not some kind of psychosomatic unity but our lived life as fully revealed and manifested (*offenbare Geschichte*). The symbol of the resurrection is concerned with the "lived life, which will be saved and honoured." All people, as they have been, will be assembled in God, who is himself life. So what will happen with my lived life? Clearly Jüngel has two changes in mind: what our life has been will be opened publicly in its full truth. In addition, he refers to God's perspective on us: while we will fully recognize ourselves, God will recognize us as we should have been. In sum: "Resurrection from the dead means the collection, the eternity and the revelation of the lived life in which I will become identical with my life."[7] The whole event is, seen from another perspective, "the completion of the *iustificatio impii*."[8] Over against any kind of "terror of the real" Jüngel emphasizes that this remembrance of the lived life includes the revelation of the possibilities that surrounded it. That means that the eternalization includes the revelation and reestablishment of those possibilities that were part of this life but could not be realized.[9] However, there is a hidden problem of continuity within the person's identity. If Jüngel declares that "we are now as God knows us to be"[10] and at the same time conceptualizes this final act of justification as a divine act of *creatio ex nihilo*, then we do not know how we can know our self as the person we have been.[11]

How should we understand the idea that we participate in God's eternal life? Jüngel also follows Karl Barth in rejecting the timelessness of God and

---

7. Jüngel, *Tod*, 153.

8. Jüngel, "The Last Judgement as an Act of Grace," 401. Miroslav Volf criticizes Jüngel for excluding human agency in God's judgment of our lived life. Yet this accusation seems to go too far. Jüngel's proposal could be read as suggesting two distinct processes: revealing actions and experiences, and affirming God's perspective on human persons as subjects of these actions and experiences during their lived lives. When Jüngel maintains that in the event of participating in God's life the human being will be a living subject, he obviously presupposes some sort of subjectivity — even though he rules out living persons. See Miroslav Volf, "Enter into Joy! Sin, Death, and the Life of the World to Come," in *The End of the World and the Ends of God: Science and Theology on Eschatology,* ed. John Polkinghorne and Michael Welker (Harrisburg, Pa.: Trinity Press International, 2000), 256-78, esp. 263-64.

9. Eberhard Jüngel, *Gott als Geheimnis der Welt* (Tübingen: Mohr, 4th ed. 1982), 293n.58; also Volf, "Enter into Joy!" 264.

10. Jüngel, *Tod*, 153.

11. For the notion *creatio ex nihilo* in this context, see Jüngel, "Das Entstehen von Neuem," in *Wertlose Wahrheit: Zur Identität und Relevanz des christlichen Glaubens: Theologische Erörterungen* (München: Kaiser, 1990), 3:132-50, esp. 147.

interprets the notion of eternity as eternal merging or entanglement of the dimensions of time. Eternity is a concentration of past, present, and future as *simul tota possessio temporum* as opposed to the successive differentiation of the modi of past, present, and future in creation.[12] God's creative action *ad extra* separates in terms of time and space what is originally together and in one another *(beieinander und ineinander)*. Over against the Aristotelian tradition Jüngel emphasizes that eternity does not exclude possibilities. Yet this move does not imply that there is genuine novelty in God (i.e., for God himself), because Jüngel insists that these possibilities will not be destroyed by realizations.[13] As a consequence, in terms of time, the only way we can think of the eternity of the lived life is as the *eternal co-presence* of the past, the present, and the future. However, in applying the theory of the modalization of time, we have to speak more specifically of the eternal presence of *past* pasts, *past* presents, and *past* futures because the temporal life in its successive and contingent *present* nature is definitely over.

While the theologies of Eberhard Jüngel and Wolfhart Pannenberg differ in many fundamental aspects, they nevertheless show a remarkable degree of congruence in terms of their eschatology. Wolfhart Pannenberg does distinguish finitude and mortality; thus he does not follow Barth and Jüngel in their close linking of the two aspects. Instead he wants to reformulate the strong link between sin and death. Thus he conceives the entangledness of sin and temporality as part of the natural conditions of our life. In the disunity of our creaturely experience of time, time shows itself to be enmeshed with sinfulness since every temporary moment is part of the self-centeredness of sin.[14] Consequently, past, present, and future are torn apart, and the totality of life is never adequately anticipated.[15] It is at this point that the resurrection of the human person comes into the picture. Pannenberg basically shares the

---

12. Rather peculiar is Jüngel's more recent attempt to give some trinitarian rationale to this concept of eternity and attribute the Father to the past, the Son to God's present, and the Spirit to God's future. See Jüngel, "Thesen zur Ewigkeit des ewigen Lebens," thesis 4.1.1, 84. In the article on eternity ("Ewigkeit: III. Dogmatisch," 1774-76), Jüngel seeks to conceptualize God's eternity in which we will eventually participate as concentrated and intensified life. While he refutes the metaphysical postulate that we find in God continuity without innovation, he emphasizes duration and a richness of events. However, if the differentiation of the past, present, and future tenses characterizes only God's creation *ad extra*, it is not at all clear how one should think of life, of events, and of real novelty in God.

13. Jüngel, "Thesen zur Ewigkeit des ewigen Lebens," 86.

14. Wolfhart Pannenberg, *Systematic Theology*, trans. Geoffrey W. Bromiley (Grand Rapids: Eerdmans, 1998), 3:561.

15. Ibid., 3:561 n.115.

idea of resurrection as a recapitulation of a lived life. However, having faced strong criticism by John Hick, Pannenberg recently emphasized a moment of transformation, completion, and glorification.[16] Such a transformation allows comfort and consolation for the suffering, a "moment of compensation," even though Pannenberg calls into question any notion of an individual eschatological body.[17] Yet even after this final transformation in the eschatological transition we remain finite beings.[18]

Resurrection and the Last Judgment are the final results of God's intentions as creator. They are an outcome of God's final consummation of creation, yet at the same time creation's end. As an outcome of Pannenberg's metaphysical grammar of part and whole as well as of his concept of meaning and totality, the completion or consummation has to be the end. The whole or totality of temporal existence will be achieved when time is taken up into eternity — hence God is the end of time. The relation between eternity and time is a relation between a simultaneity to all times and the time of creation. Through this simultaneity, whatever has been is kept in God's eternity.[19] Based on that constellation, the resurrection of the dead can become an act in which God gives his creatures the totality, the wholeness of their being in the specific self-referential mode of *Fürsichsein*. Human creatures receive their *Dasein* as a whole, yet as a *past* one anew. In this moment the distinction between moments of time as well as modi of time will not be eliminated, but they will not be separated anymore. The resurrected will participate "in the eternal simultaneity of the divine life."[20]

These two dominant positions regarding the life of the resurrection reveal a number of shared structural elements or tendencies that deserve — at least in the light of pneumatological considerations — a rather critical view.

---

16. John H. Hick, *Death and Eternal Life* (San Franscisco: Harper & Row, 1976), 221-27. For Pannenberg's response see Pannenberg, *Systematic Theology*, 3:639ff.

17. Pannenberg, *Systematic Theology*, 3:639. Regarding the body of the resurrected Christ Pannenberg plays down the bodily nature of the resurrection appearances and points to Paul's concept of the corporate body of the resurrected Christ. See ibid., 3:626-27. In the writings of Pannenberg as well as Jüngel there is an increasing perception of the intrinsic limitations of the recapitulation model, yet there is a strong conceptual impasse since nothing new — in time — can happen.

18. Wolfhart Pannenberg, "Tod und Auferstehung in der Sicht christlicher Dogmatik," in *Grundfragen Systematischer Theologie* (Göttingen: Vandenhoeck & Ruprecht, 1980), 2:146-59, esp. 153.

19. Pannenberg, *Systematic Theology*, 3:606.

20. Ibid., 3:607.

1. Eternal life is conceived of as participation in God's life. This view, however, makes it difficult to distinguish between God's eternal life and the eternal life of created, finite creatures. There seems to be a danger of confusing our eternal life and the trinitarian life of God. Correspondingly, eternal life seems to be creationless, not a new creation with its specific differentiations such as, for example, heaven and earth.

2. Almost any concept of a bodily resurrection is removed.[21] Not only temporality with an open future but also any kind of physicality, that is to say, any natural dimension of life, is left out of this bodiless existence. A bodiless identity seems to be at the center of interest.

3. The resurrection understood as recapitulation is not a gift of a *new*, intensified life, but primarily the *end* or *totality* of one's *past* life, even though this life will somehow, in some sense, be transformed.

4. Together with this sense of an ending, any responsive aspect of the resurrection is marginalized.

5. Overall, the general understanding of the eschatological transition is more a deep sense of *ending* than of joyful life. The key metaphor is *closure*. Nothing new can happen since creation comes to its end. Transience is basically equated with perishability. Yet this notion of an ending is only one aspect of the concept of consummation. The other notion of *perfection* is not necessarily coupled with closure, and completion need not imply an ending.

In my view, almost all of these characteristics will be challenged by a thoroughly pneumatological perspective in the eschatological discourse. The key question should be: What comes to light if one looks at the theological symbol of the final resurrection in the light of the work of the Holy Spirit?

Eternal Life as the Consummation of the Work of the Spirit

Since any meaningful discourse about the final resurrection has to consider the bond between Christ's resurrection and our resurrection, the first question has to be: How is the Spirit of God involved in the resurrection of Jesus Christ? What kind of future is opened up by God's Spirit? Based on some

---

21. Basing his views on the unity of body and soul, Pannenberg contends that a future beyond death can only be thought of as bodily renewal. See Pannenberg, ibid., 3:573. But this insight does not develop fully the bodily status of the resurrected life that participates in God's eternal life.

short remarks about this connection, I would like to move on to the connection between our final resurrection and the Easter event, and eventually to our resurrection as the consummation of life in the Spirit.[22]

Christ and the Spirit in the Resurrection

Basing their thoughts on the vision outlined by the prophet Ezekiel (Ezekiel 37) in which the Spirit of God gives new life to the dead, the New Testament authors interpret the resurrection as an act of the Spirit.[23] Within Pauline theology 1 Timothy 3:16 states that Jesus "was revealed in flesh, vindicated in Spirit," alluding to the vindication by the the resurrection. A similar idea is spelled out in 1 Peter 3:18: "He was put to death in the flesh, but made alive in the Spirit." In both texts the Spirit refers to the Spirit of God as the life-giving Spirit. In Paul's writings Romans 1:3-4 is the text most frequently referred to on this topic. Paul introduces himself as an apostle of Jesus, "who was descended from David according to the flesh and was declared to be the Son of God with power according to the Spirit of holiness by resurrection from the dead. . . ." In these texts, God's Spirit is the life-giving power that overcomes death.[24] The current reign of the risen Christ is enabled by the Spirit. Thus

---

22. A remark concerning method: I will not interpret the records of Christ's resurrection in the light of "contemporary" expectations regarding the future resurrection. Instead I would like to illuminate the future resurrection through an interpretive analysis of the Easter event.

23. For the life-giving dimension of the Spirit see Michael Welker, *Gottes Geist: Theologie des Heiligen Geistes* (Neukirchen-Vluyn: Neukirchener, 1992); and Lyle D. Dabney, *Die Kenosis des Geistes: Kontinuität zwischen Schöpfung und Erlösung im Werk des Heiligen Geistes* (Neukirchen-Vluyn: Neukirchener, 1996).

24. For a similar idea see Ephesians 1:19-20 and Romans 8:11. It is worth noting that *dynamis* and *doxa* are closely related to the power of the Spirit. See Walter Grundmann, "Dynamai, Dynamis: The Concept of Power in the New Testament," in *Theological Dictionary of the New Testament*, ed. Gerhard Kittel, trans. Geoffrey W. Bromiley (Grand Rapids Eerdmans, 1964), 2:299-317; and Gerhard Friedrich, "Dynamis," in *Exegetical Dictionary of the New Testament*, ed. Horst Balz and Gerhard Schneider (Grand Rapids: Eerdmans, 1990), 1:355-58, esp. 357. According to Romans 6:4, "Christ was raised from the dead by the glory of the Father. . . ." For an interpretation of the close tie between glory and the Spirit see Ernst Käsemann, *Commentary on Romans*, ed. and trans. Geoffrey W. Bromiley (Grand Rapids: Eerdmans, 1980), 166. This link between glory and the Spirit can be found explicitly in 1 Peter 4:14. *Dynamis* and *pneuma* are brought together clearly in 1 Corinthians 2:4, where Paul contrasts plausible words of wisdom to "a demonstration of the Spirit and of power. . . ."

Paul can affirm in 2 Corinthians 13:4: "For he was crucified in weakness, but lives by the power of God. . . ."[25]

How should we conceive of this life by the power of God? According to a large number of systematic theologians, the discourse about the resurrection of Christ rests on two conceptual frames: first, the resurrection is primarily a revelation of the *meaning* of the cross — which adds nothing to the life and death of Christ. This theological opinion is expressed succinctly by Eberhard Jüngel, who declares: "God is completely defined in the crucified Jesus of Nazareth."[26] In the second frame the resurrection is *inclusion into the life of God* or a life with God. Over against these two conceptual frames I would like to suggest that the resurrection is, as a matter of fact, an event in the life of Jesus, even if this event *in* Jesus' life is at the same time an event *about* his life, that is, a metacommunicative commentary that interprets his whole life and his death at the cross.[27] Accordingly, it is an event that takes place within two reference systems: our world with its space and time as well as the new world of the new creation.[28] If we take seriously the resurrection appearances, the empty-tomb traditions, and particularly the Lukan stories about the first forty days after the resurrection, four aspects of the resurrection become visible and are relevant at this point: a *bodily*, a *temporal*, a *communal*, and a *responsive* aspect of life.

First, Jesus was resurrected to a new kind of *bodily existence*, thus affirming God's faithfulness to his creation and pointing to its deep transformation. The new creation does not abandon the old one but takes the old one with it. The "hypostatic union" that characterizes the togetherness of God and the world in the person of Christ ended neither in the event of the cross

25. The Spirit's involvement in the resurrection event was already recognized in the early church. See Tertullian, *De resurrectione carnis*, 30; Justin, *Apologia* 2, 87; Irenaeus, *Adversus haereses*, 5.1.

26. Eberhard Jüngel, "Das Sein Jesu Christi als Ereignis der Versöhnung Gottes mit einer gottlosen Welt: Die Hingabe des Gekreuzigten," in *Entsprechungen: Gott — Wahrheit — Mensch* (München: Kaiser, 1980), 276-84, esp. 277.

27. These ideas are more fully developed in Günter Thomas, "'Er ist nicht hier . . .': Die Rede vom leeren Grab als Zeichen der neuen Schöpfung," in *Die Wirklichkeit der Auferstehung*, ed. Hans-Joachim Eckstein and Michael Welker (Neukirchen-Vluyn: Neukirchener, 2002).

28. *Contra* Ingolf Dalferth, "Kreuz und Auferweckung: Das Wort vom Kreuz," in *Der auferweckte Gekreuzigte: Zur Grammatik der Christologie* (Tübingen: Mohr, 1994), 38-84, esp. 79, who states: "Alle historischen Sachverhalte haben ihren Ort in unserer Welt, sind also wesentlich weltlich, die Auferweckung ist aber wesentlich göttlich." For an elaboration of the resurrection as belonging to two realities, see Thomas F. Torrance, *Space, Time and Resurrection* (Grand Rapids: Eerdmans, 1976), ch. 4.

nor in the resurrection. The resurrection in the power of the Spirit did not annihilate the movement symbolized in the incarnation. Therefore the risen Christ is the first of God's renewed community and of the new, transformed creation. The empty tomb affirms the seriousness, the breadth and the depth, of this transforming and redeeming community with God's creation, one that became a *creatio viatorum*. The empty tomb validates God's willingness to deal with the bodily nature of human life. In addition, Christ's body becomes the visible medium for his memory. The cross remains inscribed in the body of the Resurrected One. The resurrection of Christ was not built on an episode of amnesia.

Second, the *temporal* dimension of the life of the crucified and resurrected Christ shows a high degree of complexity. In Jesus Christ, the hypostatic union between God and humanity finds its *telos*. In this union, God's eternal time and creaturely time met in such a way that they can no longer be completely separated. As a consequence, the resurrection and ascension imply the taking up of human, created time into God since the resurrected logos remains the incarnated logos *(logos ensarkos)*. Yet if Jesus Christ is the first fruits of the new creation, "in the risen Christ our human nature in its creaturely and temporal existence is redeemed and renewed and established through being taken up in its affirmed reality into the life of God."[29] The appearances make apparent, in their own peculiar and perceptible way, precisely how in the resurrection time is not annihilated but re-created.[30] Jesus was resurrected not just into the eternal life of God but into a new existence that happens to include such a rich variety of times that created time is not excluded. The forty days and the time of the church (as the time of the body of Christ) make apparent that this presence of God's time in created temporality is not left behind after the resurrection. The resurrection opens up a future that will universalize, fulfill, and perfect what began in the Christ event. As a consequence, Christ's interaction with the world does not end with the resurrection. The forty days may indicate that beyond the alternative of created temporality, on the one side, and God's eternity, on the other side, the resurrected Christ opened up a third option: the time of the new creation, which should not be confused with God's own trinitarian temporality. Corre-

---

29. Torrance, *Space, Time and Resurrection*, 98.

30. The varying witnesses to the appearances make clear that Jesus Christ was embodied, but in a rather unique form. For a succinct elaboration of the resurrection appearances see Michael Welker, "Resurrection and Eternal Life: The Canonic Memory of the Resurrected Christ, His Reality, and His Glory," in *The End of the World and the Ends of God: Science and Theology on Eschatology*, ed. John Polkinghorne and Michael Welker (Harrisburg, Pa.: Trinity Press International, 2000), 279-90.

spondingly, Jesus was resurrected to a new life with a specific future.[31] Already the limitation of the appearances to forty days is a rejection of the idea that the time of the risen Christ is the endless continuation of our created time or timeless eternity. Since the event of the consummation of the new creation is realized but not fully unfolded or actualized, we are entitled to say that the risen Christ as the first fruits of the new creation has time and a future.[32] The past of the crucified and resurrected Christ is certainly present in

31. To talk about the future of Christ implies the insight that (a) the Easter resurrection and (b) the eschatological transition including the final resurrection and the *parousia* of Christ are two events — not just for us, seen from our creaturely standpoint, but also for Christ himself. The widespread theological claim that they are one event seen from the standpoint of eternity (as by Karl Barth, Wolfhart Pannenberg, and Ted Peters) suggests that for God in his eternity what happens in the time "in between" does not make a difference. The far-reaching question is whether the incarnation and the distinctiveness of the cross and resurrection imply a temporal order in God himself. To attribute, as Pannenberg does, a historical aspect of the divine reality to the economic Trinity while rejecting it concerning the immanent Trinity does not solve the problem for at least two reasons. What seems to be a possible way to describe divine involvement in time at least opens up the door for a docetic Christology. Furthermore, any reciprocal interaction between God and the world seems to be an optical illusion — if seen from God's eternity. The "one-event model" of the resurrection and *parousia* of Christ requires us to say that in God's perspective all of redemption has taken place in the cross and resurrection and to propose a "revelation of meaning model" for the eschaton. For such a model see, e.g., Pannenberg, *Systematic Theology,* 3:645, or Carl Heinz Ratschow, "Eschatologie VIII," in *Theologische Realenzyklopädie* (Berlin: Walter de Gruyter, 1982), 10:334-63, esp. 359ff. As a consequence one has to systematically downplay the agony of postresurrection history and to overlook that Christ still suffers in and with his creation through the Spirit (Romans 8). For that reason God will, at the end, do more than reveal the (so far) hidden meaning of history and his (so far) hidden love that was supposedly at work at every point in space and time through the course of history. God's justification in the face of history will be much more than a sound explanation; rather, it will be a creative act that is part of Christ's future. For a lucid discussion of these temporal aspects see Luco J. Van den Brom, "Eschatology and Time: Reversal of the Time Direction," in *The Future as God's Gift,* ed. Fergusson and Sarot, 159-80; with relation to Pannenberg, Niels Henrik Gregersen, "Einheit und Vielheit der schöpferischen Werke Gottes," *Kerygma und Dogma* 45.2 (1999): 102-29. See also the contributions in *Dialog* 39:1 (2000).

32. The temporality of Christ requires us to draw a sharp line between the appearances of the risen yet *present* Christ on the one side and the pneumatological presence of the risen yet *absent* (ascended) Christ on the other. It is the latter one who stimulates memory and imagination that intimately connect the experiences of the pre-Easter and the post-Easter Christ — eventually leading to the written Gospels. However, the fundamental reframing happened with the help of the appearances. The primary absence expressed in spatial terms in the ascension can also be explicated in temporal terms: he is absent "until he comes" (1 Cor. 11:26). On the eschatological implications of the ascension for the life of the church see Douglas Farrow, *Ascension and Ecclesia* (Edinburgh: T&T Clark, 1999), chs. 5 and 6. The

the canonical memory of the church; that is to say, it never becomes a "past past." Yet his future present in glory is so far for us only a present future.[33] For this reason, the early Christians shouted: *Maranatha!*

Third, intimately connected with this bodily and temporal dimension is the *communal* aspect of the risen Christ. Neither the resurrected nor the ascended Christ wants to be without his disciples. According to the appearance narratives, the risen Christ immediately seeks community with the disheartened and discouraged, appearing neither where he is expected nor where he is sought. Even though the communities to which he appeared and those based on the contemporary sacramental presence of Christ need to be distinguished, both testify to the intrinsic communal and communicative nature of the life of the resurrected. The bodily, the temporal, and the communal dimensions are intertwined: community and communication need time, and any bodily configuration has temporal horizons.

Fourth, and finally, as the wounds of the cross on the body of the risen Christ indicate, the resurrection has a *responsive* aspect in that it refers back to the situation on the cross. At least the oldest account of the crucifixion portrays the dying Christ as one who laments with the words of Psalm 22 about the absence of God (Mark 15).[34] As Jesus died, not only was he abandoned by his disciples, rejected by his people, judged by Jewish law, and mocked by the military and political powers — he was also abandoned by God, the source of life. The cross itself became the instance of the lamenting question, "Why?" Given that Mark, as theologian, arranges the whole crucifixion scene according to Psalm 22, the resurrection in the power of the Spirit is preeminently a response to this lament about the Father's absence, insofar as it renews the living community. Even beyond death, God responds to the pain, suffering, and lamentation of Jesus.

---

ascension means — among other things — that the fullness of the new creation, which includes new time and the overcoming of life-destroying futility, is hidden from us. It is held back and only partially present through the Spirit. See Torrance, *Space, Time and Resurrection*, 98. Seen from another angle, the temporal difference between the ascension and Jesus' return in glory does not imply that God needs time but that God *wants to take time* to bring about the final redemption and at the same time further unfold this creation.

33. This complex tension between the presence of the past, present, and future Christ is reflected in the liturgy of the Lord's Supper.

34. For a recent discussion of the problem and for an outline of the reception of Psalm 22 in Mark, see Martin Ebner, "Klage und Auferweckungshoffnung im Neuen Testament," in *Klage (Jahrbuch für Biblische Theologie*, vol. 16), ed. Ebner et al. (Neukirchen-Vluyn: Neukirchener, 2001), 73-87.

The Spirit as Nexus between Christ's Resurrection and the Future Resurrection

The Spirit's involvement in Christ's resurrection is emphasized even more where our final resurrection comes into sight. In 1 Corinthians 6:14, Paul introduces Christ's resurrection as a promise of ours: "And God raised the Lord and will also raise us by his power." But our resurrection is not just a promise based on the resurrection of Christ, as if the two events were just causally dependent and successive events. Both events are grounded in the fact that the *same power* of the Spirit is at work. This idea is spelled out by Paul in Romans 8:11, yet in this case Paul adds even more complexity to the nexus by referring to the actual and ongoing presence of the Spirit. "If the Spirit of him who raised Jesus from the dead dwells in you, he who raised Christ from the dead will give life to your mortal bodies also through his Spirit that dwells in you." The risen Christ lives through the power of the Spirit, and it is this same Spirit that dwells in Christians. The current presence of the Spirit is seen as a beginning that will be completed in the resurrection, a process that will be perfected in the spiritual body *(sōma pneumatikon)*.[35] This connection between the risen Christ and the Spirit can become so intense that Paul sees Christ as the last Adam, "a life-giving spirit" (1 Cor. 15:45). Christ and the Spirit are not blended into one being, but the Spirit who created Christ anew became the *medium* of his presence. Since it is the same power operating in the Christian life, Paul was inclined to say that we already participate in the resurrection, yet not in ours but in Christ's.

This link between the anticipatory but real presence of the Spirit and the future resurrection can also be found in the connection between the future resurrection and the gift of the Spirit, which in Paul's account of the Spirit is referred to as *aparchē*. With this term Paul alludes to the first fruits of a harvest that were given for sacrifice (Rom. 8:23). The first fruits are not the whole harvest, something that would require the eschatological overcoming of suffering and death. Similarly, the concept of the *arrabōn* (1 Cor. 1:22; Eph. 1:13-14) as a first installment binds together the present experience of the Spirit and the consummation of her work as full payment in the future.[36] Both images share three aspects. (a) The first fruits are of the same "stuff" as

---

35. Paul's contrast of the future spiritual body *(sōma pneumatikon)* and the current physical body *(sōma psychikon)* does not downgrade the current presence of the Spirit but points to a limit or approximation. It suggests that there seems to be an intrinsic limit to the current transforming work of the Spirit (Rom. 8:11, 23; Phil. 3:21) — at least as long as Christ's transformed body is absent.

36. Hebrews 6:4-5 describes the Holy Spirit as the foretaste of the world to come.

the whole harvest, and the first installment is of the same currency as the full payment. (b) What comes is in some sense "more of the same," which at the same time — as in all processes of emergence — will nevertheless add up to a decisive and far-reaching qualitative difference: the final glorification of our whole bodily existence. (c) Both emphasize an actual given, which should not be devalued, and an outstanding future with an overwhelming consummation. Nonetheless, this "given" deepens the difference between the present and the not yet given (Rom. 8:23).

Resurrection as a Consummation of Life in the Spirit: Four Traces and Tendencies

What are the implications of the fact that the same Spirit who raised Jesus from the dead and dwells in believers will be the power of their resurrection and will shape their eternal life as spiritual body *(sōma pneumatikon)?* If we think of this *continuity* in the Spirit, it seems appropriate to see the life of the resurrected ones in continuity with the other works of the Spirit that they experience already in their lives — even though the emergent processes lead to essential differences. The Holy Spirit will not reject or abandon what he began in our lives, but will complete, refine, transform, and perfect them. This perfection characterizes the life of the resurrected. Four exemplary and characteristic features of the Spirit might shed some light on eternal life and on what many call "participation in God's eternal life." All of them accord with the four aspects that designate the risen Christ (body, time, community, and response).

1. Embodiment

The power of the Spirit operates through and within embodiment — without being contained in just one body. It is the Spirit who works and operates in temporally and spatially concrete situations, within specific cultural and linguistic contexts, and finally dwells in bodily life.[37] This indwelling of the

---

37. See Welker, *Gottes Geist.* To emphasize the embodiment in human beings and in the church does not deemphasize the link between word and Spirit that was stressed so much by Luther and Calvin. Even though the word is the medium of the ongoing coming of the Spirit, the goal of the communication process based on the word is to shape personal and social life and to overcome any aesthetic distance.

Spirit is expressed in Paul's insight that we are as *sōma* the temple of the Holy Spirit (1 Cor. 6:19). The *life*-giving Spirit dwells in finite and perishable human bodies.[38] This inhabitation is not a passing event but will find its consummation in the creation of a spiritual body *(sōma pneumatikon)* (1 Cor. 15:44).[39] This move toward embodiment neither contradicts the possible field-structure of the Spirit's effectiveness nor calls into question her character as a public person.[40] Just the opposite: if the public person of the Spirit lives in communication, the embodiment is the requirement of this process out of which this communication emerges.

However, we might ask which concept of the body can clarify the bodily aspect of the resurrection? Without any doubt the body is a sensually perceptible location of the complex unity of multiple distinctions, *distinctions* between self-referential and hetero-referential processes on many levels, and in this respect an assembling of *boundaries*.[41] These levels range from physical to emergent mental and social levels and at the same time enable each other.[42] As such a location of distinctions, the body can be seen as a limitation that gives these processes their shape. These constraints are the prerequisite for re-

---

38. The indwelling of the Spirit does not lead to a new form of mind/body or body/soul dualism. The forming power of the Spirit can be conceptualized within the theoretical framework of Niklas Luhmann's complex distinction of medium and form. See Niklas Luhmann, *Die Gesellschaft der Gesellschaft* (Frankfurt am Main: Suhrkamp, 1997), 1:190-202. Forms emerge out of a coupling of elements of a medium, whereby any kind of form can itself become a medium for further forms.

39. The opposition between *sōma psychikon* and *sōma pneumatikon* can be taken as an indication that any mind/body dualism cannot do justice to the problem of the body in the eschatological transition. However, the crucial aspect of bodily existence is endangered when *sōma* is understood primarily as person. If such an understanding dominates (as in Rudolf Bultmann, *Theologie des Neuen Testaments* [Tübingen: Mohr, 3d ed. 1958], 193-203), the material aspect of eschatological hope tends to be dismissed.

40. For conceptualizations of the Holy Spirit as field see Wolfhart Pannenberg, *Systematic Theology,* 2:76-115, esp. 105, 110; ibid., 1:382-84. For an understanding of the Spirit as public person and field of resonance see Welker, *Gottes Geist,* 224-31, 286ff.

41. This definition tries to take into account that *living* bodies inevitably relate to their natural, psychological, and social environment *and* need to exercise closure and separation — if they do not want to be dissolved.

42. In other words, in bodies the levels of reality described in conceptions of nonreductive physicalism find a fragile, perishable, and yet creative unity. The unity of these distinctions can be perceived consciously only in a very selective way and manipulated or negotiated only in a very fragmentary way, even though these distinctions are in constant flux. As a consequence, one has to distinguish (a) identity as the operational unity of these distinctions that might include memory, (b) selective, fragmentary, culture-bound, and socially negotiated self-descriptions, and eventually (c) God's perspective on us.

lations to the natural and social environment. The multi-layered character of these distinctions is required in order to experience pleasure, pain, and joy, which are, after all, bodily states that can be observed and interpreted. Since this dynamic network of distinctions and relations is neither totally self-determined nor fixed, the body can become a medium of inscriptions. In this regard the body is a medium of memory that reaches *beyond* the living organ of our mind. Even though a person can attempt to transcend her or his body through imagination, communication, and action, these techniques remain bound to bodies as their base. In all these processes the body is a configuration of distinctions and relations, that is to say, a form that relies on some basic stuff or medium: matter matters since "Adam" is made out of "the dust of the ground."[43]

How do these deliberations help to understand the embodiment of God's Spirit? When the Spirit becomes embodied, the network of relations based on these distinctions becomes itself a medium that is going to be formed by the Spirit. The Spirit of God is a power that configures the network of relations that we are. In the light of these considerations, the concept of the indwelling or embodiment of the Spirit points to a process that goes "deeper" than our conscious self-perception can capture. It implies that the Spirit is eventually transforming the *whole* complex unity of our bodily life. In this respect the Spirit lives "more deeply than we can think."[44] "Because God's Spirit is generating *life*, there emerges a spiritual *body*."[45] As a consequence, the eschatological transition will be to a life with distinctions and limitations. The embodiment of the Spirit will preserve not only identities but also *shaped and thereby limited life*. The body points — among many things — to the *social* character and, as I would like to add, *temporal* character of eternal life. Without inscriptions on and in the body, there would be no memory, no history, and probably no time consciousness. Consequently, the body remains as a structure of creatures, old ones *and* new ones.[46]

---

43. The reliance on this basic stuff should not lead to any kind of physical reductionism. But whatever will be the equivalent of matter in the new creation, it will be the basis for the new bodies.

44. See Bernard Meland, *Fallible Forms and Symbols: Discourses on Method in a Theology of Culture* (Philadelphia: Fortress, 1976), 24, although Meland is referring to our own life.

45. Joachim Ringleben, *Wahrhaft auferstanden: Zur Begründung der Theologie des lebendigen Gottes* (Tübingen: Mohr [Siebeck], 1998), 112, referring to Jesus Christ.

46. In 2 Corinthians 5:1-2 Paul undermines any attempt to conceive disembodied life, pointing out that those who have died will receive an intensified body. "For we know that if the earthly tent we live in is destroyed, we have a building from God, a house not made with hands, eternal in the heavens."

2. Community and Individuation

Closely related to this drive to embodiment is the gift-giving nature of the Spirit: the gifts of the Spirit have a double effect that only seems to be in tension. They contribute to the edification of an individual personality through their link with specific persons, that is to say, their configuration of character, habit, and personality. They differentiate, inculturate, and form a distinct person and thereby individualize. Yet at the same time the Spirit is always building up and leading to community.[47] The charisms strengthen and build up communities of mutual enrichment and inclusion *and* strengthen and build up personalities, giving each person's practice of faith, love, and hope a distinctive twist. Through this double and simultaneous movement, the Spirit is the *power of individuation* without leading to privatization, as well as the *dynamic force for community* without pulling down individuality. The Spirit nourishes social life while simultaneously preserving and transcending cultural distinctions (as shown in the preservation of native languages in the event of Pentecost, Acts 2:1-13) and cultivating diversity. If we envision a perfection of these two tendencies and keep in mind the dynamic aspect of the Spirit's function, we cannot imagine the eschatological transition as leading to a steady state, changeless duration, and eternal rest without mutual social enrichment in distinct forms of social life.[48] This twofold intensification takes its perfected shape in the spiritual body *(sōma pneumatikon)*. When faith is transformed into seeing and hope is fulfilled, love will last — not only love toward the triune God but also love that will characterize our interaction with other creatures. Yet interaction and communication imply time, contingency, embodiment, and eventually justice that include the realm of memory.

47. Ephesians 3:14-21 describes this double tendency by pointing out the strengthening of the inner being as well as the love of Christ who dwells in the heart. As embodied power the Spirit becomes a perceptible power for others. If the Spirit shapes practices and habits, triggers emotions, stimulates communication, creates patterns of perception and action, helps to uncover talents, and "colors" character traits, her work cannot be conceived of without social interaction.

48. The church as an institution of the interim between Pentecost and the eschaton will not last in the life to come. But this is true only insofar as the distinction between church and non-church will disappear. Therefore, the social life that marks the church will last. See Christoph Schwöbel, "The Church as a Cultural Space: Eschatology and Ecclesiology," in *The End of the World and the Ends of God,* ed. Polkinghorne and Welker, 107-23, 114.

3. The Presence of Faith

That the presence of the Spirit is closely connected to God's saving and rescuing action is a central feature of her effectiveness.[49] The Spirit makes present the reality of God's saving and redeeming action because she effectively replaces Christ's physical presence. Through her, we can participate in Christ's intimate relationship to the Father. Instead of referring to the strong link of the Spirit's action and faith in the dogmatic tradition, I would like to draw attention to an often misused metaphor, that is, rebirth. Paul points out an interesting constellation: "He saved us, not because of any works of righteousness that we had done, but according to his mercy, through the water of rebirth and renewal by the Holy Spirit. This Spirit he poured out on us richly through Jesus our Savior, so that, having been justified by his grace, we might become heirs according to the hope of eternal life" (Titus 3:5-7). This rebirth as a present, not future new creation happens through the Holy Spirit in baptism. Human attempts of attaining righteousness through works are not contrasted with justification by faith, but with the pouring out of the Spirit.[50] The objective helplessness of the sinner destined to death is contrasted with the coming of the Spirit.[51] Yet the metaphor of a rebirth through the Spirit carries with it a strong notion of future growth. Certainly this metaphor does not completely fit into the simple scheme of a strict discontinuity set up by human death, yet it points to a pneumatological continuity between our current "in-between life" and the life to come. Through the Spirit we are already drawn into the rich reality of the resurrected Christ. If the rebirth happens to be a gift of life through the Spirit, can the final resurrection be just the preservation of the past life without being a new *life?* While the symbol of the Last Judgment captures quite well this backward orientation, the concept of rebirth and renewal by the Holy Spirit calls for a form of completion and perfection that transfigures and deeply renews the old.

4. Lament, Intimacy, and Glorification

Over against any enthusiastic or harmless interpretation of the presence of the Spirit, the dangerous and possibly painful side of this presence has to be

49. In Welker, *Gottes Geist,* this appears to be a feature of the Spirit that spans the two testaments.

50. 1 Peter 1:3 presents the resurrection of Jesus Christ from the dead as an account of rebirth into a living hope. This can be seen as a variant on the same idea, given the involvement of the Spirit in the resurrection.

51. This text resonates with many other texts, such as Joel 3:1 and Isaiah 32:15ff.

pointed out: the already given presence of the Spirit deepens the perception of fundamental differences. Life in the Spirit makes perceptible the difference between the already given and the future redemption, and encourages "hope for what we do not see" (Rom. 8:25). The consciousness of this difference opens up an intensified sensitivity to death, suffering, and pain that results in a deep solidarity with the groaning of human and nonhuman nature (Rom. 8:19-25). At this point a paradox needs to be acknowledged: for Christians the presence of the Spirit also leads to lament about the absence of God, about the redemption whose consummation is still to come.[52] Without the real presence of the Spirit, this qualified difference could not be articulated in the Christian form of lament, nor could it be addressed to God. In this regard, lament presupposes trust and hope as well as the experience of God's healing and life-giving presence in the Spirit.[53]

The Spirit, who enables lament and provides consolation, will finally open up our lives to the full recognition and glorification of God. Participation in God's life implies an unsurpassable intimacy with and closeness to God. Yet this closeness will require a creative response to suffering that will end all conflicting dialogues *(Konfliktgespräche)* with God. God, who is already in this life revealed by the Spirit (1 Cor 2:10-11), will be praised and glorified in an undisturbed relationship full of responsive love. The Spirit, who is already the subject (Gal. 4:6) and medium (Rom. 8:15) of our communication with God, will enable trustful closeness beyond the crisis of death. By means of the Spirit we will participate in Christ's trustful yet dynamic relationship to the Father, a relationship that includes the cross as well as the resurrection. As the resurrection of Jesus encompassed God's answer to the lament at the cross, our resurrection is part of an eschatological process that will eventually encompass God's final loving response to the pain, suffering, and evil in this world.[54] The intimacy already anticipated in the Lord's Prayer will be perfected in the life to come.

---

52. For illuminating contributions on lament see Ebner et al., ed., *Klage (Jahrbuch für Biblische Theologie,* vol. 16), and esp. Ottmar Fuchs, "Unerhörte Klage über den Tod hinaus! Überlegungen zur Eschatologie der Klage," in *Klage,* 347-79.

53. There is a strong link between lament and the Lord's Prayer (Matt. 6:9-13), insofar as Jesus himself teaches us to ask for our daily bread *and* our rescue from evil. Any Christian lament takes this prayer seriously and challenges God on the basis of his gracious and merciful relationship with us. Lament insists on the eschatological horizon of the Lord's Prayer.

54. While the resurrection and God's response are intimately related, they are two events. The resurrection is the condition of the possibility that human lament is not eternally silenced by death. See Ottmar Fuchs, "Dass Gott zu Rechenschaft gezogen werde — weil er sich weder gerecht noch barmherzig zeigt?" in *Das Drama der Barmherzigkeit Gottes,* ed. Ruth Scoralick (Stuttgart: Katholisches Bibelwerk, 2000), 11-32.

The Relational Character of the Final Resurrection — Eschatological Complementarities

To sum up, the present life in the Spirit suggests that the very liveliness of the life to come is intimately connected with time, social interaction, embodiment, and creative responsiveness on God's part. The four tendencies mentioned above as well as the resurrection of Christ in the power of the Spirit indicate that God's eschatological actions transcend the unified event of a recollection of one's finite life. At the same time the pneumatological implications of the final resurrection make visible its deeply relational character and shed some light on the network of eschatological symbols.[55]

There seems to be a *complementary temporal* orientation and a similar *complementary continuity-related* orientation in, on the one hand, the resurrection, and, on the other hand, the Last Judgment. The Last Judgment presents primarily an orientation to the past and only rather indirectly an orientation to the future.[56] While the resurrection presents a strong notion of discontinuity on the human side (new body) and continuity on the Spirit's side (the same life-giving Spirit), the Last Judgment points out the continuity of our life and the discontinuity enabled by Christ the graceful judge. While the resurrection confronts us with the issue of the new life beyond death, the Last Judgment refers to the selective, lasting significance of this "first" creation and the identities built in this life-history. But far from being just the memory of the whole first creation, God will take a differentiating stand toward it in which he *actively and selectively relates* to the past.

The openness of the resurrection to a new future resonates with God's new creative acts in the creation of a new heaven and earth, a creation that obviously preserves distinctions that are characteristic of creation. If we take seriously the notion of a resurrection to new life with a personal identity, neither total amnesia nor total anamnesis regarding the past would address the

55. This relational character should not lead to the false assertion that the various eschatological symbols like the Last Judgment, kingdom of God, eternal life, second coming of Christ, resurrection, and new creation fit together like a jigsaw puzzle in order to provide one big and unified picture of God's eschatological action. A better image might be that of a mobile, in which all the parts have their own places yet are counterbalanced and interpreted by each other. The mobile also makes visible that the eschatological transition consists of a complex network of interrelated events.

56. Volf's insistence on the inclusion of a process of reconciliation has to be read as an inclusion of a future orientation. Seen in this perspective, the Last Judgment makes the future life in the Spirit possible. See Miroslav Volf, "The Final Reconciliation," *Modern Theology* 16.1 (2000): 91-113.

questions posed by injustice and suffering in the first creation. On the one hand, total amnesia would cynically forget the history of unsurpassable pain and suffering and dissolve any idea of responsibility as well as of a preservation of identity. On the other hand, total anamnesis would be hellish because it would in its own way repeat what has already happened. But in order to shape the future opened up by the resurrection, God has to address the past selectively and transformatively, and do so in at least three modes.

The Last Judgment reveals God's love for detail and his willingness to search for the victims. This will pertain to the restoration of the dignity of victims as well as the confrontation of perpetrators with their actions. However, the social dimension of the life to come requires the reconciling confrontation of the victims with their perpetrators. This creative and differentiating recollection of human life will necessarily affect, and hence transform, personal identities. The network of relations that we are will be transfigured in this graceful renegotiation of our identity.[57] While the recapitulation model of resurrection and judgment concentrates on the preservation (Jüngel) and final fulfillment (Pannenberg) of our identity, it seems more adequate to think of a deep *renegotiation of identity* in the light of past and future. The symbol of the Last Judgment states in a very convincing way that the resurrection event will be part of a *creatio nova ex vetere* (not *ex nihilo*), in which this past life matters. Eternal life will not be disentangled from this life because "the Holy Spirit is the eschatological perfecting cause of the creation."

As the Gospel of Matthew indicates, the Last Judgment will also make public where Christ was present in the distress and misery of this world (Matt. 25:31-46). As such, this revelation will be a public acknowledgment of the depravations of life in the "old world," of God's deeply affective entanglement with the world in suffering and blessing. In this regard, the Last Judgment shows God's search for the shadows and defects of the first creation. Christ will point out his suffering presence and reveal where he tried to encounter the church and his disciples. To phrase it differently, God will face the traces of the work of the Spirit, in all its depth and all its limitations. The Last Judgment makes evident — *post festum* — the need for the completion of the work of the Spirit. But knowledge about God's own suffering presence will not answer the questions arising out of suffering and pain itself. On the con-

---

57. Since personal identity emerges, among other things, out of *processual selectivity* — that is to say, out of the selective treatment of selectivity — the total recapitulation of the past would destroy any present, actual identity. Only because some aspects of the past are forgotten am I who I am right now. Only because some present moments become past and remain past do specific future possibility spaces open up. This intrinsic processual selectivity vanishes in the fullness of time.

trary, such a knowledge intensifies those questions and calls for a third mode of relating to the past.

Beyond the symbols of the Last Judgment and the resurrection God will turn to his own history with the creation and respond to it in an innovative, intensive, and expansive way. All lament over evil, suffering, and pain and all the unanswered petitions will call for a creative response that goes far beyond the revelation of some meaning to the whole of history. As part of this response, which presupposes the resurrection from the dead, God "will wipe every tear from [human] eyes" (Rev. 21:4) and will provide an emotionally and cognitively satisfying consolation that does not leave any question unanswered. This justification of God is a promise implied in the eschatological transformation of lament into praise. The need, even the urgency, on God's side to react to the immeasurable suffering in his creation (which is articulated and remembered by human beings with the help of the Spirit) is, on the one hand, aggravated by the resurrection of Christ and, on the other, addressed. This final response will be made in the power of the Spirit, even though it will not surpass the Easter resurrection but merely communicate it into the past. For this response God will take all the time necessary. And the resurrected ones, who live in the power of the Spirit and close to the trinitarian life, will also have all the time they need to have their social and individual lives judged, healed, and redeemed. The burdens, pains, and sin of the past will no longer overshadow the future and tie down the dynamic of life.[58] Intimately connected with God's creative act of a new creation and the redemption of the past is his willingness to forget. Isaiah 43:25 spells it out: "I will not remember your sins," even though the very possibility of this "forgetfulness" is itself forever "remembered" in the wounds of Christ.[59] Through resurrection in the power of the Spirit, the life of the Resurrected One did not come to an end but experienced a new beginning as perfected eternal life, a life filled by the Spirit and marked by time, relationality, sociality, activity, and dynamic and eventually unendangered openness.

---

58. For similar considerations regarding the dynamic and relationality of the life to come see Luco J. van den Brom, "Ewiges Leben: V. Religionsphilosophisch; VI. Dogmatisch," in *Religion in Geschichte und Gegenwart* (Tübingen: Mohr [Siebeck], 4th ed. 1999), 2:1765-69.

59. See also Jeremiah 31:34; Hebrews 8:12, "I will remember their sins no more."

Resurrection, Finitude, and Ecology

ERNST M. CONRADIE

Is Christian eschatology an opiate, inoculating us against responsibility for this earth? Is belief in resurrection escapist? Is otherworldly hope anti-ecological? Does hope for a new creation promote precisely the kind of other-worldliness and escapism that is not conducive to a commitment toward this earth?

Indeed, what on earth could be the ecological significance of the Christian hope for the resurrection of the dead? What could be the positive ecological significance of the hope for the resurrection of the dead?[1] Many contributions in the field of ecological theology emphasize the need to accept human finitude.[2] This need arises from the acknowledgment that there are indeed limits to growth on a finite planet. Accordingly, finitude is regarded as

---

1. See E. M. Conradie, *Hope for the Earth* (Bellville: University of the Western Cape Publications, 2000), for a more detailed exploration of the relationship between soteriology and eschatology. My argument is that Christian eschatology should maintain the soteriological focus of the gospel. However, like creation theology, eschatology cannot be reduced to soteriology. This calls for a more integrated vision of creation, salvation, and consummation.

2. I have argued in *Hope for the Earth* that Christian eschatology has traditionally responded to three dimensions of the human predicament, namely, (1) sin and the evil impact of sin in the world, (2) temporal finitude (mortality and transience), and (3) spatial finitude as this is evident in the limitations of human knowledge and power. In response to these predicaments, Christian hope has been extrapolated beyond the desire for salvation from sin, liberation from oppression, and an ultimate victory over evil to incorporate the hope for life beyond death (as expressed in the personal image of the resurrection of the body and the cosmic image of the new earth). It has been extended even further toward the hope to transcend the limitations of human knowledge and power in the presence of an omniscient and omnipotent God (epitomized by the *visio Dei*).

part of God's good creation, not a predicament from which human beings need to be "saved."[3] Salvation can be only an affirmation of the finitude of human nature, not an escape from it.[4] But what are the implications of such an assessment for the hope for the resurrection of the dead?

Ruether versus Moltmann

The issue that is at stake here may be illustrated in terms of the contrasting views of Rosemary Ruether and Jürgen Moltmann. Ruether argues that the relentless quest for immortality is related to the unwillingness of the male to acknowledge his own limitations. The female body symbolizes corruptible bodiliness that one must flee in order to purify the soul for eternal life. In numerous classical theological texts female life processes (pregnancy, birth, lactation, indeed female flesh as such) are portrayed as vile and impure. They carry with them the taint of decay and death. She says, "The problem of personal immortality is created by an effort to absolutize the personal or individual ego as itself everlasting, over against the total community of being."[5] Instead, Ruether suggests that we as human beings should accept our own finitude, our own human scale, and death as the final relinquishment of individuated ego into the cosmic matrix of matter and energy. The earth is the womb out of which we arise at birth and into whose womb we are content to return at death. All the component parts of matter and energy that coalesced to make up our individuated self are not lost, but they are taken up into the great matrix of being and thus become food for new beings to emerge.

Moltmann has criticized Ruether for these views. He argues that Christian hope is thus turned into "a pantheistic omnipresence of the everlasting matrix of life." He adds that "this eulogy on the good earth overlooks the fragility and destructibility of the earth's organism and thus the earth's own need of redemption."[6] It cannot take account of the earth's own finitude. This

3. See Michael Welker, "Resurrection and the Reign of God," *The Princeton Seminary Bulletin Supplementary Issue* 3 (1992): 3-16.

4. I have argued in *Hope for the Earth* (165-90) that the eschatological tension between continuity and discontinuity should be understood in terms of a response to the predicament of finitude. Likewise, the typical eschatological tension between the "already" and the "not yet" should be understood as a response to the predicament of sin and evil.

5. Rosemary Radford Ruether, *Sexism and God-talk: Toward a Feminist Theology* (London: SCM, 1983), 257-58.

6. Jürgen Moltmann, *The Coming of God: Christian Eschatology* (Philadelphia: Fortress, 1996), 276.

leaves the earth itself without hope. Ruether's reluctance to allow for God's transcendence leaves room for little more than a pantheist appreciation of the cosmic cycles of matter and energy.

By contrast, Moltmann has often been criticized for his notion of the eschaton as a radically new creation that will come into being beyond the finite history of the planet and of the cosmos (thus stressing the discontinuity between creation and the eschaton). For Moltmann, the eschaton has to overcome not only the suffering caused by sin but also the suffering resulting from the predicament of finitude. Creation as we know it is frail and still in bondage due to transience *(Knechtschaft unter die Vergänglichkeit).*[7] Only a radically new creation can provide an adequate solution to the predicament of transience and the immense suffering resulting from it. This emphasis on a radically new creation *(nova creatio* instead of *re-creatio)*[8] may well compromise the goodness of this creation.[9] It can also easily lead to rampant theological speculation and mysticism.

These observations raise numerous further questions. Does the Christian hope for the resurrection of the body imply a transcending of planetary and human finitude? If so, in what way is finitude transcended? Let us investigate these questions in more detail.

Assessing Finitude

It is necessary to distinguish carefully between the human predicament of sin and that of finitude. Environmental degradation is primarily the product of human sin, of the pervasiveness of evil on earth. Finitude is not the primary problem that we are faced with. Sin is. However, it is important to acknowledge that suffering, violence (natural evil), decay, death, and the extinction of species formed an integral part of nature from the early history of the planet.

---

7. Jürgen Moltmann, *God in Creation: An Ecological Doctrine of Creation* (London: SCM, 1985), 69.

8. See A. A. van Ruler, *Theologisch Werk* (Nijkerk: Callenbach, 1972), 6:222-23, for the use of the term *re-creatio* instead of *nova creatio* to formulate the relationship between creation and eschaton. The latter term cannot do justice to the concern that it is this earth, this life, this body that will be saved. The new earth is not a different earth, but this, the old earth, radically renewed, no longer broken by sin. See also the contribution by John Polkinghorne in this volume on the notion of *creatio nova ex vetere*.

9. See Steve Bouma-Prediger, *The Greening of Theology: The Ecological Models of Rosemary Radford Ruether, Joseph Sittler, and Jürgen Moltmann* (Atlanta: Scholars Press, 1995), 89, 247.

This assessment is abundantly clear from scientific reconstructions of the evolution of life on earth. Evolutionary science has rendered the assumption of an original cosmic perfection obsolete and unintelligible. Although suffering is amplified by evil, it is an inherent part of God's creation in time. Death did not enter the world merely as a result of human sin.[10] Sin is the sting of death, not its physical cause. A theological distinction between the (environmental) effects of sin and the suffering resulting from finitude (of the natural environment) is therefore important, if only for the sake of clarity and honesty.

There are several manifestations of finitude. The most obvious one is that of mortality. Finitude implies a limited life span, not only for human beings but also for every living organism. Moreover, the biological sciences have helped us to appreciate the finitude of entire species and not only of individual specimens. This also applies to the human species. We are nothing more than a brief episode in the cosmic drama. Even mountains, rivers, ecosystems, oceans, and whole continents are exposed to the arrow of time. Many of the earth's prominent topographical features have emerged relatively recently in geological time. Likewise, the astrophysical sciences have helped us to understand the finite life span of the earth, the solar system, galaxies, and possibly the universe itself. The experience of finitude is therefore not limited to human beings; it has cosmic dimensions. The world itself is destined to pass away.

Anxiety over Space, Time, and Change

As self-conscious and reflective human beings, we inevitably experience finitude (mortality) with a certain anxiety. However, this should not distract us from recognizing two other aspects of finitude that are of ecological significance:

First of all, finitude in space is a function and precondition of creation itself. The restrictedness of material bodies (including the human body) is necessary to allow for the differentiation and individuation that is so typical of creation. The history of the cosmos is certainly one of staggering differentiation and individuation, evolving into millions of species and individual

10. G. C. Berkouwer, *Man: The Image of God* (Grand Rapids: Eerdmans, 1962), 234-78, argues persuasively that the limits of Scripture have to be recognized in this regard. One cannot determine on the basis of Scripture alone whether humans have been created mortal or not. However, if Scripture cannot provide a conclusive answer to this question, the contemporary scientific reconstruction of the history of the cosmos can. To say that mortality is an integral function of creation is therefore not so much a theological truth claim as a theological acknowledgment of insights derived from science.

specimens, each with its own unique characteristics. No two specimens from the same species are, or have ever been, exactly the same. This incredibly rich diversity of life on earth is a source of awe and wonder, and is celebrated in myth and ritual. Every material object is distinct from others and can interact in a network of relations with other objects only on that basis. Such differentiation is regarded as a threat only within a preconceived Parmenidean monism, a culture of homogeneity or imposed totalitarian structures.[11] Any Christian notion of the eschaton clearly needs to allow for such differentiation and individuation.

At the same time it has to be acknowledged that the finitude of material bodies leads to a certain anxiety. "Finitude in awareness is anxiety."[12] We as human beings have to come to terms with the spatial limitations set by our bodily rootedness. All living beings strive for space, a physical location, a body, a piece of soil, a home, a city, a country, a planet. The need for space also has social dimensions, that is, a sphere of influence in a family, a community, a vocation, the institutions of civil society, and so on. The limitations of these social dimensions of space constitute the finitude of human freedom. And to be finite is to be insecure. This has important implications for human *power* and *knowledge*.

We experience restrictions to the spatial territory that we are able to exert an influence on. There are limitations to human power. We may extend our physical power and control through social institutions, political authority, organized labor, and improved technologies, but such power finally remains limited. Unlike God we are not omnipotent. Likewise, human knowledge remains limited due to the restrictions set by our bodiliness. Our physical location in space and the limited size and abilities of the human brain imply that there are limits to the knowledge that we can assimilate and accumulate. We simply cannot know everything. We may extend the frontiers of knowledge through the wisdom accumulated in human history and through cooperative research projects and ever more advanced information technologies, but such knowledge ultimately remains limited. Unlike God we are not omniscient.

Human wisdom may arise from an acceptance of these limitations of human knowledge and power. This is especially important within the context of basic scarcity. A finite planet cannot sustain continuous, expanding de-

---

11. See Colin Gunton, *The One, the Three and the Many: God, Creation and the Culture of Modernity* (Cambridge: Cambridge University, 1993), on a culture of homogeneity.

12. See Paul Tillich, *Systematic Theology* (Chicago: University of Chicago, 1951), 1:191-94.

mands on its resources. The notion of "limits to growth" is indeed a function of finitude in space. However, such an acceptance of material finitude does not eliminate a sense of insecurity and anxiety. Together with other living organisms, human beings therefore create systems of security to protect and increase their space. Subsequently, the pursuit of culture, philosophy, the arts, and the sciences has been to extend the frontiers of knowledge (and power) as far as this is possible. This quest is radicalized in numerous religious traditions to gain insight into the ultimate mysteries of the cosmos and whatever may transcend the cosmos.

Second, temporal finitude must be recognized as a function of life itself. Life implies, by definition, the possibility and inevitability of continuous change and movement. Although living organisms require some stability, the joy of life is closely related to the possibility of responding to new impulses and of adapting to changing circumstances. This also implies that any state of relative equilibrium in a living organism has limited duration. What is durable is of limited value in the life cycles of living organisms. Such a limited duration is regarded as a threat only within a Platonic assumption that what is true cannot be subject to change. That the universe itself is in a constant state of flux has been illustrated dramatically in evolutionary biology and in the discovery of an expanding universe in astrophysics. This awareness that nature (and not only humanity) is inherently historical constitutes one of the most significant discoveries of modern science.[13]

Nevertheless, such an acceptance of temporal finitude (limited duration) leads to a different form of anxiety, experienced in the form of transience. While life endures amid the always-imminent threat of death, the predicament of finitude is experienced in the form of transience, or "perpetual perishing" (Whitehead). The predicament of transience is related to the fleeting nature of the present moment and the inability of humans to return to what has once been. It therefore always implies a sense of loss — of every precious moment and each opportunity just gone by. It also applies to the cycles of weeks and seasons, the passing of each Christmas and each birthday celebration. This awareness of transience is exemplified precisely by experiences of "kairotic time" in which time "seems to stand still" — in celebrations of the liturgy, in myths and rituals, or in a walk through the forest on a day of rest.

13. See J. F. Haught, "Ecology and Eschatology," in *And God Says That It Was Good: Catholic Theology and the Environment*, ed. D. Christiansen and W. Grazen (Washington: United States Catholic Conference, 1996), 57.

Sin and the Sting of Finitude

We have to remind ourselves continuously that human beings experience these manifestations of finitude primarily as a function of the impact of sin. We find it possible to accept limitations to our knowledge and power — as long as our personal, social, economic, and political space is not threatened by the power (and the technical know-how) of others. We find it possible to accept the transience of what is beautiful and joyous in life — as long as the passing moments, days, and years are not filled with the memories of lost opportunities, spoiled plans, or, worse, a legacy of suffering, injustices, sexual harassment, oppression, starvation, and so forth. Nothing, not even a happier end or a later vindication, will then alleviate the feeling that so many years have gone by in misery. We find it possible to accept death at a ripe old age, an end to a life lived to the fullest — as long as my life (and the lives of those close to me) is not prematurely and brutally interrupted by death. The reality is that millions of people die a premature and violent death through war, murder, starvation, tragic accidents, or deadly diseases (AIDS!). A purely "natural death" is indeed rare, especially in the so-called Third World. Indeed, the sting of finitude is the impact of human sin in the many forms of evil that we experience. Nevertheless, a theological response to the predicament of finitude itself (as mortality, transience, and spatial restrictedness) is difficult to avoid, precisely as a result of the impact of sin. This accounts for the persistent inclination in Christian eschatology to move beyond the scope of soteriology in order to address the predicament of finitude.

What exactly, then, is the sting of finitude? What aspects of finitude may Christians legitimately hope to overcome in the eschaton and, more specifically, in the resurrection of the body? I would suggest that the sting of finitude is twofold.

First, an acknowledgment of (human) finitude in time implies that we cannot hope for an endless continuation of life. Nor can we expect any moment to endure forever. Unlimited duration is not necessarily a characteristic of the eschaton. However, we do sense a desire for a narrative completion of our own life stories. That is why premature death is more traumatic than death in old age. However, my own life story is not completed with my death. My story continues as long as my life is still honored in the memory of subsequent generations and as long as the material impact of my life's work is still evident. Thereafter, my life (and my bodily remains) seems to dissipate into oblivion. However, even then the story has not reached its narrative conclusion. My story forms part of the larger (hi)story of the particular genealogy, culture, species, planet, and galaxy in which I participate. My history will in this sense be completed only when the history of the cosmos comes to an end. This is why there is a longing in almost all cultures and religious traditions to transcend the boundaries of death, to maintain a certain presence, and preferably a conscious presence, in the continuation of history.

Second, at the same time the completion of one's life story is not sufficient. In fact, one may be happier not to know exactly what will happen after one's death! What is also necessary is a reintegration of the whole story to prevent the threat of disintegration (epitomized by death). We therefore sense a need for a retrieval of the past in order to reintegrate, to restore, to heal the story. Amid the constant flux of life in all its transience this is only partially possible. It may be possible to retrieve some previous experiences and to heal the negative impact of such experiences, for example, the harm that others caused me, or the harm that I may have caused others. However, it is not possible to heal all such experiences while life continues. Some experiences cannot be restored and healed in principle as a result of the impact of sin on both transience and mortality. A retrieval of the past requires a degree of simultaneity and spatial proximity in order to relate and coordinate past, present, and future in the lived moment.

Various Responses to Finitude

The following possible, if problematic, theological responses to the predicament of (human) finitude may be identified:

First, one option may be to accept human mortality as final and to rejoice in the continuation of the cycles of life and energy on earth. It provides sufficient solace to know that our existence is taken up in the ecological processes of death and new life. At best we can hope for a continued existence in the genes and perhaps in the memory of our descendants. This position begs the theological question whether God does not transcend the dimensions of space and time (including death)?

Second, one may also argue that a recognition of human and planetary finitude can only add urgency to the struggle to establish "Justice, Peace and the Integrity of Creation" within the confines of history. Any (escapist) hope for restitution in a dispensation beyond this life can only divert our responsibility toward this life and this earth. We are called to hope and work for a better future, here on earth. Although little can be done about past suffering, we have a responsibility to alleviate present and future suffering. This position offers little solace to the victims of the past. The establishment of a just society on earth could be a penultimate but never the final aim of creation.[14]

The third position regards finitude as the primary problem that has to be overcome in the eschaton. If finitude (and death) is a necessary function of time (and of life), the eschaton has to involve an abolition of time (and of change). Eternity is thus understood as timelessness. This position clearly cannot do justice to the involvement of the living God in history as portrayed in the biblical roots of the Christian tradition. Typically, such a notion of the eschaton has a narrow noetic focus. The eschaton will provide an opportunity to see God face-to-face, to know God fully. Eternal life is thus a form of knowledge, not a form of life.

Fourth, one may also ignore finitude as transience and focus only on the predicament of mortality. Eternal life is subsequently understood as an endless continuation of life. This is the way in which eternity is understood in popular piety, that is, as "a very long time." Eternal life is therefore viewed as a continuation of temporal life after death, not as life that includes but also transcends temporality as such. This position does not take the finitude of the planet itself into account. The resurrection hope cannot be reduced to hope for "life *after* death."

Fifth, any adequate theological response to finitude has to be based on a more sophisticated understanding of the relationship (the continuity and discontinuity) between cosmos and eschaton. This relationship is often understood in terms of the relationship between time and eternity. Two classic strategies to account for the difference between eternity and the finitude that characterizes our existence in time may be identified here: the simultaneity strategy and the duration strategy.

The simultaneity strategy emphasizes the presence of eternity within time. It is the "eternal now" *(nunc aeternum)* within the temporal now that stops the flux of time (Tillich). It is an attribute of eternity (Augustine), an "atom of eternity" (Kierkegaard). A sense of simultaneity is crucial and also powerful. Simultaneity allows for an interaction between past, future, and present. Without remembrance and expectation we would not be able to hear a melody or perceive any movement. More importantly, it accounts for the possibility of healing the past through the power of forgiveness and reconciliation. It also accounts for the possibility of planning for the future based on promises, covenants, and contracts. The eternal now therefore has eschato-

14. See Bram van de Beek, *Schepping: De Wereld als Voorspel voor de Eeuwigheid* (Baarn: Callenbach, 1996), 207-8.

logical significance — as Kierkegaard and Barth recognized. It also has significance for existential decisions, as Bultmann and Tillich recognized.

However, this present simultaneity remains fragmentary. It is only partially and transitorily that we can retain as a simultaneous unity that which is separated in time. The experience of any "now" has no duration. In the flux of time, each "now" is replaced by another "now."[15] This also limits our ability to heal the past and to structure the future. In a necessarily limited life span, one has to recall the past and imagine the future while living anew in the present. There is simply not enough time to heal the past and to live in the present. The past therefore becomes continuously more complex while the future becomes more limited.

The duration strategy seeks to account for the possibility of the duration that an "eternal now" lacks. Without such a sense of duration, Christian hope will be reduced to ciphers of inner self-consciousness only. Then Christian hope can offer nothing more than an enriched existential experience of the kairotic moment. The possibility of such duration is usually postulated in terms of the realm of eternity. In the famous definition of eternity by Boethius both simultaneity and duration are incorporated: eternity is the "simultaneous and complete presence of illimitable life." Duration may therefore also be regarded as a "picture" or "image" of eternity.[16]

These two aspects of simultaneity and duration correspond loosely (not exactly) to the two aspects that I identified as the sting of finitude, that is, the need for narrative completion (requiring a sense of duration), and the need for a retrieval of the past in order to heal its brokenness (requiring some form of simultaneity). However, the question remains whether the eschaton can be adequately understood in terms of the "taking up" of time into eternity. Does this not fall into the trap of a sterile totalization and a rigid unification of time that leaves little room for temporality and subsequent change?[17]

15. See Wolhart Pannenberg, *Systematic Theology* (Grand Rapids: Eerdmans, 1998), 3:598.

16. Ibid., 3:601.

17. The danger is that eternity may yet again be conceived as a mere abstract totality (duration) or as a unifying incorporation of all times, without allowing for a differentiated plurality of times. See Michael Welker, "God's Eternity, God's Temporality, and Trinitarian Theology," *Theology Today* 55 (1998): 317-28, on the notion of eternity as a "collection of times."

The Hope for the Resurrection of the Dead

The Christian hope for the resurrection of the dead is not based merely on the desire to transcend human finitude. It is also not based primarily on the hope for vindication in a life after death. It cannot be based on a speculative postulation that there is a realm of eternity beyond the boundaries of space and time either. Instead, the hope for the resurrection of the dead is essentially a hope in Godself. It arises from the complex and pluralistic witnesses in the Judeo-Christian tradition to the promises and the everlasting faithfulness of the living and eternal God. It is an extrapolation and radicalization of a trust in God the Creator who transcends human and cosmic finitude and who maintains an unconditionally creative relationship with the created order. More specifically, it is a confirmation of the Christian belief in Jesus Christ, the Risen One. It expresses the Christian hope in the power of the Spirit, who makes all things new. This comes to fruition in the hope that in death we will meet not nothingness but Someone: the God of grace who raised Jesus Christ from death.

But how should this hope be articulated anew? How can this hope address the Nietzschean suspicion that any hope for life after death constitutes a form of escapism? Can the hope for the resurrection of the dead remain true to this earth? How can we avoid the trap (that Jesus warned the Sadducees about in Matt. 22:29) of merely speculating about a virtual reality beyond the realm of this world? How can a "realistic eschatology"[18] help us to understand this earthly reality better in order to take up our responsibilities here on earth? Does this hope imply that human finitude will be transcended, or are some aspects of finitude also characteristic of the eschaton? How should the continuity between human bodiliness and a resurrected body be understood? This begs the further question of the continuity between this earth and the new earth. An adequate cosmic eschatology clearly forms a prerequisite for an adequate personal eschatology.

I would like to offer the following tentative pointers toward a constructive response to these questions:

a. The continuity and discontinuity between my body and the hope for the resurrection of the body is best understood in terms of the analogy with the bodily resurrection of Christ. There seems to be a growing consensus that the bodily resurrection of Christ cannot be understood in terms of the resuscitation of a corpse. Resurrection is not a return to this earthly form of life.

---

18. See John Polkinghorne and Michael Welker, ed., *The End of the World and the Ends of God: Science and Theology on Eschatology* (Harrisburg, Pa.: Trinity Press International, 2001), 4-5.

ERNST M. CONRADIE

The appearances of the risen Christ should be understood as an eschatological event that is of a different order than the bodily presence of Jesus Christ before his death. Likewise, the hope for the resurrection of the dead cannot be understood in terms of an endless continuation of earthly life.

The problem for theological imagination here is indeed one of understanding the difference between creation and eschaton, between time and eternity, between the finite and the infinite. What makes this particularly difficult is that this difference is something that we as finite human beings will, in principle, never be able to understand adequately. How can we begin to comprehend transcendence if it transcends the limits of our knowledge by definition? We can speak about eternity only in terms of metaphors and analogies. Moreover, we have to use these metaphors and analogies in the hope that our metaphors refer to more than mere imaginative human constructs (otherwise these metaphors will become illusionary and escapist).[19] Nevertheless, we cannot avoid this problem, if only to guard against the inadequate conceptions of eternity that are rife in Christian discourse. Perhaps a *via negativa* offers the best theological route in this regard. The refusal to address this question, for example, on the basis of an apophatic acknowledgment of this unapproachable mystery, remains short-lived. As Paul Tillich observed, religion has always trespassed, in poetry and myth, to express this mystery.[20] We therefore cannot avoid reflecting on the eschaton, but in doing so we are faced with the recognition that we will never be able to grasp it.

b. In searching for metaphors and models to describe the relationship between creation and the eschaton, it seems to me that the notion of multiple dimensions[21] offers an attractive way of comprehending transcendence, especially since it can do justice to the material (and ecological) rootedness of our human existence.

The model of multiple dimensions may be helpful to comprehend the

---

19. The dream of life beyond death and of a new earth beyond this earth can, as Marx and Nietzsche realized, easily become escapist. While a utopian vision of liberation from oppression (responding to the predicament of sin) may perhaps be inspiring and liberating, this does not apply to visions of life beyond death (responding to the predicament of finitude). Clearly, if these images are nothing more than language, mere human constructions, beautiful but seductive metaphors, they should either be avoided or be reinterpreted as a response to the predicament of sin only.

20. Tillich, *Systematic Theology* (Chicago: University of Chicago, 1963), 3:396.

21. On the model of multiple dimensions, see L. J. van den Brom, *Divine Presence in the World: A Critical Analysis of the Notion of Divine Omnipresence* (Kampen: Kok Pharos, 1993). This notion of multiple dimensions does not necessarily presuppose a view of space as the container within which matter moves.

288

relationship between space-time and eternity. Accordingly, eternity is conceived as a "depth" dimension beyond the edges of the space-time continuum. Eternity is not simply a very long time that somehow remains open to the future. That would understand the transcendence of eternity above time purely on the basis of the directionality of time. The realm of eternity includes space and time but also transcends these dimensions. More specifically, the relation between time and eternity may be understood as analogous to the relations between length and area, or area and volume, or volume and time. In each case, a qualitatively new dimension is introduced: area is not simply a very long line, volume is not simply a very large area, and time is not simply very voluminous. What is the new "depth" dimension introduced by eternity in relation to time? Here one may surmise that the dimension of eternity would at least include the possibility of simultaneity and duration that our experience of time lacks. Past and present events may be experienced together in the realm of eternity. The new creation will not necessarily begin "after" the ending of the old. This possibility may have profound implications for some classic theological problems such as the incarnation (the divine and the human nature of Christ), the coming of Christ, and the so-called intermediary state (the status of the dead between death and resurrection). The dead may be with God on one axis even while their dead bodies remain on earth on another axis.

It should be noted that each new dimension includes all the "lower" dimensions. Time implies space, volume implies area, and area implies linearity. The relation between time and eternity is therefore always a relation between time *including space* with eternity. Eternity implies neither timelessness nor spacelessness. Eternity does not imply an erasure of temporality. Nevertheless, a realm with three dimensions may be quite distinct (to use a spatial term) from a realm with only two dimensions. If these two realms intersect with one another, what is three dimensional can be perceived only in two dimensions in a two-dimensional world. Yet, in this intersection the three-dimensional realm cannot be reduced to only two dimensions.[22]

One of the advantages of such a dimensional notion of God's transcen-

---

22. This distinctness and possible intersection of two such realms may be helpful to understand the resurrection of Christ. The resurrected Christ appeared to the disciples in a bodily form that they could recognize (e.g., showing them his wounds, eating fish). However, the resurrected Christ cannot be reduced to the body of the crucified Jesus. Hence Jesus could appear and disappear from the sight of the disciples. In addition, the notion of "intersection" can do justice to those biblical traditions that refer to the eschaton as "breaking into" this world (e.g., the coming of the kingdom, the coming of Christ). Creation is not only being transformed toward the eschaton. The eschaton also breaks into this world. These insights are derived from comments by David Field.

dence is that it is indeed conceivable[23] but not reductionist. Any higher dimensions can, by definition, never be fully comprehended. Our human minds are simply too "flat" to do so.[24] Higher dimensions would, by definition, be inaccessible to scientific investigation and would therefore transcend any scientific competence — although one may fully acknowledge the limited abilities of science to comprehend the dimensions of space and time.[25] There is even a degree of commonsensical naivete about the acknowledgment of richer dimensions to reality. There is more to reality than what meets the eye. To speak of God's existence in dimensions beyond ours may therefore reaffirm the pious recognition that God is in heaven while we are mere earthly creatures. Let our words therefore be few (Eccl. 5:2)! This affirmation therefore need not lead to a form of speculative theology but is precisely an attempt to guard against it by acknowledging the limitations of human knowledge. It acknowledges God's transcendence *as this can be known, here on earth.* Since the very postulation of the existence of the realm of eternity may well become purely speculative, the model of multiple dimensions is best regarded as a reflective attempt to account for the affirmation of the Christian tradition that God is the Creator of the universe and that God therefore transcends the known dimensions of the universe.

c. Nonetheless, the eschaton cannot be adequately understood in terms of the abstract distinction between time and eternity. The Christian hope does not necessarily imply that what existed in time will become eternal or that what is finite will become infinite. It remains important to distinguish

---

23. Van den Brom, *Divine Presence in the World,* 264. Not only the *possibility* but also the *plausibility* of such a dimensional model has to be demonstrated. This plausibility criterion should not be formulated on the basis of what may be plausible to the natural sciences, though.

24. The metaphor of "flatness" is derived from Edwin Abbott's *Flatland: A Romance of Many Dimensions* (London: Seeley, 1884). See my *Hope for the Earth* (360-61) for a more detailed discussion.

25. This has important implications for long-term scenarios regarding the future of the universe. Christian theology, together with contemporary science, may accept the ultimate finitude of the universe. Christian hope is not based on an endless continuation of the universe itself. It does not expect to escape death but can accept finitude as an integral part of creation. Whichever scientific scenario may prove to be the more plausible one will therefore not falsify eschatological assertions. Christian hope remains ultimately in God, who is present in space-time but also transcends the dimensions of space and time. Christian hope trusts that the whole cosmos will be transformed in this transcendent presence of God. This hope in God cannot be falsified by new scientific theories, precisely because it pertains to "higher" dimensions that are not accessible to the physical sciences. See the contribution by Robert John Russell in this volume for a different view on this point.

carefully between creation, eschaton, and God to prevent a confusion of God with eternity or infinity (e.g., in abstract theism). Eternity is not God, and God does not exist "in" the realm of eternity. Eternity may be an attribute of the divine life (the "eternal God") but not of the eschaton.[26]

In my view, the category of heaven may be helpful at this point. The Christian hope is to be with God in heaven, or (better) to experience God's heavenly presence here on earth, not to become divine or eternal. The duality of heaven and earth may provide a clue to the relation between creation, eschaton, and God. Heaven is a dimension of creation (not of God), a dimension that is open to God, where God dwells, and where God's presence may be discerned (e.g., by the angels). Heaven can be God's dwelling place even though the highest heavens cannot contain God (1 Kings 8:27-30). Heaven is the relative transcendence of the earth, while the earth is the relative immanence of heaven.[27]

In terms of a dimensional model of transcendence one may argue that heaven is a dimension that transcends but also includes the earth (and, indeed, the cosmos). However, the heavenly cannot be equated with God or with the realm of eternity. The dimension of eternity, one may postulate, transcends that of heaven. God's dwelling in heaven is not so much a reference to God's eternity as to God's relationship with those dimensions of creation that transcend the space-time continuum. I propose that the relationship between creation and eschaton may be imagined on this basis. The eschaton involves a transformation of the cosmos in the realm of the heavenly. Or, in language reminiscent of traditional Christian piety, the earth and my body, after death and decay, will "go" to heaven; that is, it will enter into a new dimension where death and decay will no longer have an effect. What is perishable will be clothed with the imperishable (1 Cor. 15:53). It should be noted that the language of "going" to heaven unfortunately suggests spatial movement and therefore a spatial notion of higher dimensions (e.g., the "highest" heavens). This has to be avoided at all costs since such spatial move-

---

26. Pannenberg distinguishes between the finite and the infinite but not clearly enough between God and the eschaton. He often speaks of finite creation *participating* in the eternal glory of God and the *incorporation* of creation into God's eternal present (see, e.g., Pannenberg, *Systematic Theology,* 3:594, 601). But what is the eschatological difference between God and the eschaton if both exist in the realm of eternity? What characteristics of the infinite (and thus of God) are not applicable to the eschaton if creation participates in God's realm of eternity?

27. See Moltmann, *God in Creation,* 163-64, and Michael Welker, *Creation and Reality* (Minneapolis: Fortress, 1999), 33-34, who uses the contrast between what is relatively accessible and what is relatively inaccessible to us instead.

ment can easily lead to a form of escapism from the earth. Heaven has to be understood as a transformation of this earth into a "higher" dimension that includes the earth and its dimensions of space and time. The value of the notion of multiple dimensions is precisely that any one dimension includes all the "lower" dimensions.

d. In what way does the category of heaven as a "higher dimension" allow for the sense of narrative completion and a retrieval of the past that is the sting of finitude? Although the danger of speculation again looms large here, I propose that one may visualize this possibility in terms of the metaphor of "material inscription."

The history of the cosmos, this great "cosmic pilgrimage," is *inscribed* in the eschaton. Our life histories are, moment by moment, written down in the "book of life" (Hartshorne). When the story is completed (i.e., at the moment of death), the book is finished but not destroyed. Once this inscription has taken place, it can never be obliterated — not even by an omnipotent God. Eternity does not imply the annihilation of time and space. Nothing that is past can pass away (Georg Picht). Nothing is lost; everything remains inscribed forever. This inscription will be completed when the history of the cosmos finally comes to an end *(finis)*. This "objective immortality" (Whitehead) allows for the possibility of duration.

The notion of material inscription should not be misunderstood as referring merely to a form of writing. The inscription does not take place only in the mind of God either. The whole history of the cosmos is *materially* inscribed, that is, it is fixated in the three dimensions of space and the added dimension(s) of time. This would affirm forever the goodness of the material creation. One may imagine this inscription on the basis of the analogy of the front cover of a book, perhaps the "book of life." The history of the cosmos is, as it were, written down on the front cover of the book (in at least four dimensions, though, not just in the two dimensions that the metaphor of inscription seems to suggest). For Christians the work of the Father, Son, and Spirit is reflected in the very title of the book. The book of life cannot be reduced to the front cover, though. The eschaton has much richer depth dimensions than what the history of the cosmos on the cover page may suggest. This allows for an eschatological transformation of the history of the cosmos.

It is important to note that such material inscription provides (and limits!) the building blocks that would be available in the eschaton. The eschaton does not nullify human mortality and transience. In the eschatological "book of life" we remain the finite and mortal creatures that we are. Eternal life does not imply an endless extension of this life. The symphony of the history of the cosmos may well come to an end, perhaps in a long, hovering silence in which every note of the symphony reverberates. The cover page of the book of life is indeed finite. This also implies that every moment in the earth's journey is not only of ecological but also of eternal significance. That is why it remains imperative to care for the earth and all its creatures and to prevent any tragic accidents on this journey. As we care for the earth now, the contents of the cover page are finalized and the building materials for the new earth are being gathered.

e. The inscription of the history of human pain and suffering would not by itself elicit hope. It would be a source of fear, not joy. It would, in fact, constitute a harrowing, tormenting image of hell.[28] It would give eternal duration to all the evil, suffering, and pain of history. It would open the door for a continuous ritual reenactment of such evils. The models of multiple dimensions and of material inscription have no soteriological thrust; they are not liberating by themselves. This is why the possibility of a retrieval of the past is important in order to allow for a healing of history as a whole.

The models of multiple dimensions and material inscription cannot provide any guarantee that such healing will take place.[29] However, for Christians the eschatological book of life has to be read in the light of what happened in Jesus Christ. On the basis of multiple witnesses to the faithfulness of the God of Israel and to the power of God's Spirit in the church, Christians may hope that the content of the book will allow for an eschatological healing

---

28. Moltmann's warning in this regard is important for the subsequent argument:

The idea about an objective immortality in God's eternity is still not in itself a consoling idea. Would we really like to be reminded to all eternity of everything we said, did, and experienced? But according to the Psalms in the Old Testament, God's memory is not a video of our lives, recorded from heaven and played back to all eternity. It is a merciful, healing remembrance that puts things to rights. "Remember me according to thy mercy." And "remember not the sins of my youth." It is the shining countenance of God's love which looks at us, not the cold, impersonal lens of a monitor set up by a state security authority. ("Is There Life after Death?" in *The End of the World and the Ends of God*, ed. Polkinghorne and Welker, 245)

29. These models can help those who already affirm the hope for the resurrection of the body on *other* grounds to imagine the possibility for that *retrospectively*. These models may remind us that there is more to reality than what meets the eye, that scientific reductionism cannot do justice to our multi-layered experience of reality. The Christian hope is not merely for eternal duration, though. A reintegration of the predicaments of sin and of finitude is called for. The scandal of the hope for the resurrection of the dead is not the cognitive problem of imagining the possibility of such a resurrection. The soteriological thrust of Christian hope is that the powers of death and destruction will be exposed, judged, and conquered through God's love. The primary scandal is that this has taken place through the cross of Jesus Christ.

of history. The Christian hope is thus that God's loving and healing presence, epitomized in Jesus Christ, will permeate the cosmos in the eschaton ("on earth as it is in heaven"). Space and time are not abrogated in the eschaton; they are healed and restored.

If this healing took place, not "immediately" (as is often imagined in Christian piety), but through the mediation of our own embodied human consciousness, this would leave an endless(!?) amount of "unfinished business" for the eschaton. The added dimensions of the eschaton, the "many houses" of the Father's home, may allow us sufficient room (space) and opportunities for change (time) to address this unfinished business. Thus, lured by God's loving presence, we may have sufficient opportunities (requiring duration) to address the now limited building blocks of our past (requiring simultaneity) to heal the brokenness of our past and to celebrate the joy of forgiveness, with Christ and together with the community of all creatures in the presence of God. There is no resurrection of the dead without the communion of the saints.

f. How should the resurrection of the body be conceived within the context of such a notion of the eschaton? Does this allow for some form of bodily existence that would do justice to the material dimensions of eating and drinking, of swimming and dancing, of sexual pleasure, of praise and worship that characterize our earthly existence? And in what way would this existence be a "resurrection" of the body? Can such a notion help to clarify that resurrection is neither a physical resuscitation nor a mere memory of a bygone dispensation? Can the hope for the resurrection of the body do justice to the ecological integrity of the ecosystems that form the precondition for bodily existence? Or does the eschaton allow only for an ephemeral sense of embodiment (e.g., a "body" of knowledge) that has to be abstracted from ecological life cycles?

If I may be allowed some further imaginative indulgence, I propose that the metaphor of material inscription may again be suggestive in this regard. If the whole history of the cosmos is materially inscribed, then every moment, every life lived, every epoch would be together in God's presence in the eschaton. In the end, the whole story of the cosmos, the whole cosmic pilgrimage, would reach its completion. Nothing would be lost, though; everything would be retrieved. At the homecoming after the cosmic journey, the festivities can begin. One may imagine God as retrieving numerous "photos" (or "videos") of the journey during the festivities. Every video brings a particular epoch back to life, not only in memory or in "virtual reality," but as a lived and embodied experience. These experiences are not "inscribed" in only two dimensions (here the suggestion of videos is misleading). They are inscribed in space and time so that the retrieval of these events would be as real and concrete as the original lived experiences. The only difference is that the outcome of each story will be known in hindsight. Everything and everyone (not only God) would be able to relive the events in God's presence. The focus therefore remains on this life and not so much on life beyond death. Indeed, God is the God of Abraham, Isaac, and Jacob, the God of the living, not of the dead (Matt. 22:32).

All the retrieved events will have to pass through God's judgment and mercy. All will appear in the light of Christ's redemptive work. Every retrieval will take place through the power and love of the Spirit. Of course, some photos are less memorable than others. It is perhaps better to forget some events completely. Some embarrassing photos may have to remain hidden in albums forever. But some tragic and destructive moments during the journey simply have to be addressed. The reign of God cannot come without judgment, without confronting the many evils that characterized human history. This may require a final reconciliation between those present.[30] Perhaps one may imagine that the inscriptions are less similar to a video recording than to the script of a drama or a musical composition. The "gaps" (Iser) in this script allow for improvisation and for ceaseless "variations on a theme," not merely for retrieval. They therefore allow for reintegration, for healing to take place in the presence of God. Perhaps there may even be room for a new completion of the life stories of those who died violently and prematurely. In the eschatological book of life, there may be room in the contents pages for multiple layers of inscription that would not obliterate the inscription on the cover page, but that would transform its meaning. In this way the whole history of the cosmos may come alive again in God's presence. This coming alive is more than a mere memory of a distant past. It is an embodied celebration in which everyone, inscribed in the history of the cosmos, can participate in God's presence.

Does this moment of imaginative indulgence remain true to the biblical witnesses about the hope for resurrection of the dead? Is this a legitimate reflective extrapolation of the hope expressed in the Christian tradition? Does it express the continuity and discontinuity between creation and eschaton adequately? This is for biblical scholars, historians, and for you as the reader to judge.[31]

---

30. See Miroslav Volf's suggestion of the need for final reconciliation ("Enter into Joy! Sin, Death, and the Life of the World to Come," in *The End of the World and the Ends of God*, ed. Polkinghorne and Welker).

31. For me, some unresolved questions regarding the model of multiple dimensions remain. Does the notion of dimensions assume a panentheist understanding of the relationship between God and the world? Can the notion of multiple dimensions help us to understand what happened to the body of the crucified Christ after Easter?

Conclusion: The Resurrection of the Dead
in Ecological Perspective

What on earth, then, could the ecological significance of the hope for the resurrection of the dead be? A few brief concluding comments will have to suffice here.

An emphasis on the continuation of the life cycles of ecosystems (Ruether) does not necessarily provide a guarantee for their integrity. This does not take the impact of human sin into account sufficiently. At the same time the finitude of creation need not be regarded as something that should be overcome in the eschaton (Moltmann). Finitude in time is a condition of life and of change while finitude in space is a requirement for differentiation and individuation. The sting of finitude is not so much mortality as the impact of sin, that is, the disruption of a narrative completion and the inability to retrieve and to heal the past amid the transience of history.

How should the eschaton and, more specifically, the resurrection of the dead be understood in the light of human finitude? The notion of a material inscription highlights the importance of every moment in the history of the cosmos. The materiality of such an inscription is important to maintain the ecological significance of the hope for the resurrection of the body. Too often an ephemeral notion of bodiliness provides an escape route to understand the continuity between creation and eschaton. This cannot do justice to the earth or to the integrity of creation. The notion of a narrative retrieval of history in the eschaton allows for a concrete healing (not only a noetic healing of memories) of the history of the earth.

The discontinuity between creation and eschaton as expressed in the Christian hope for life beyond death has often been criticized as escapist. The danger of an exclusive emphasis on such discontinuity is that hope may function as a dangerous illusion that could only detract from our responsibility for this life and for this earth. However, a preoccupation with this life may also lead to serious distortions. A denial of life beyond death does not necessarily encourage responsibility for this earth but may degenerate into the caricatures of triumphalism, hedonism, and consumerism. Without a vision of what transcends this life, we may easily become preoccupied with this life.

The hope for the resurrection of the dead does not necessarily constitute a form of escapism. It may suggest a more profound affirmation of the significance of this earth, this life, this particular body. The hope for the resurrection of the body may help us to put this life into the wider perspective of eternal life. Paradoxically, a vision of the resurrection of the body may in this way empower and encourage a commitment toward this life and toward this earth.

Resurrection: The Conceptual Challenge

TED PETERS

Death is not extinguishing the light;
it is only putting out the lamp
because the dawn has come.

RABINDRANATH TAGORE

Why do we theologians make life so difficult for ourselves? Why do we choose to believe apparently unbelievable things and then try to justify them? With Anselm's *credo ut intelligam* we do it the hard way: we first believe and then we try to make it intelligible. Why do we not follow the easy route allegedly taken by scientists: remain skeptical until empirical proof requires belief?

Perhaps we have elected to follow the difficult path because we have been victimized by divine revelation. Heaven has visited earth. The transcendent has invaded the immanent. The infinite has challenged the finite. The mysterious and unfathomable has redefined what is natural and understandable. God, the ultimate reality through whom all penultimate realities must be interpreted, has altered the otherwise normal course of the human intellect.

Yet revelation has done us few if any favors. What we might like from revelation is a window that opens out toward a visible landscape of the transcendent; but the window remains closed and, like a mirror, turns us back to look toward our own mundane reality. What we might like from revelation is a yellow brick road leading us directly to supracosmic understanding; but we find ourselves having to draw our own maps and blaze our own trails with little more than a vague sense of direction. Revelation reminds us *that* there is a divine reality standing over against our world, but to know exhaustively *what* that divine reality is like is impossible within the scope of knowledge circumscribed by this world. This leads to epistemological frustration, to say the least.

It would appear at first glance that natural scientists escape this frustration, that they easily find fulfillment in their quest to expand human knowing. After all, if the quest is limited to an intracosmic understanding of the natural world, scientists can escape the inevitable conundrums that entangle theologians who are haunted by transcendent challenges. Scientists, of course, would not wish their Herculean efforts to be trivialized as merely cosmic because, after all, the cosmos is quite large and riddled with countless natural mysteries. So this is not a quantitative comparison regarding whose head knocks harder at the stubborn brick wall of ignorance. Rather, the point here is that the theologian's task comprises in significant portion the attempt to understand what is transcendent in terms of available knowable reality, including what is knowable scientifically.

This certainly applies to the challenge theologians face when conceptually explicating the biblical and creedal symbol, "resurrection of the body." In a recent study of the resurrection, I formulated four knotty problems: (1) the place of the body *(sōma)*, especially the flesh *(sarx)*, in the resurrection; (2) the role divine power plays in raising the dead; (3) the problem of individual identity when discerning the continuity and discontinuity between what dies and what is raised; and (4) the problem of chain consumption — that is, the problem of identifying just which physical elements, if any, belong inextricably to an individual body.[1] My task here will be to pick up where this earlier discussion left off, to tease out further implications of these problems, and to search for a direction to take to resolve them.

Theological explication and conceptual construction begin with two sets of New Testament texts, the Gospel accounts of Jesus' original Easter resurrection and St. Paul's description of our resurrection in the fifteenth chapter of 1 Corinthians. The two are in concert, to be sure, because Christ is the "first fruits of those who have died" (1 Cor. 15:20).[2] We will begin here by

---

1. Ted Peters, "Resurrection of the Very Embodied Soul?" in *Neuroscience and the Person,* ed. Robert John Russell, Nancey Murphy, Theo C. Meyering, and Michael A. Arbib (Vatican City State: Vatican Observatory; and Berkeley, Calif.: Center for Theology and the Natural Sciences, 1999), 305-26.

2. Although Paul in 1 Corinthians 15:20 stresses the continuity between Jesus' Easter resurrection and our eschatological resurrection, some interpreters fall short of granting exhaustive identity. The apostle "does not present Christ's resurrection as being a precise prototype for ours," writes Gerald O'Collins, because the soteriological event of Christ is more important than what happens to us human beings who benefit from it. *Jesus Risen: An Historical, Fundamental and Systematic Examination of Christ's Resurrection* (New York: Paulist, 1987), 180.

looking carefully at what Paul says about the *spiritual body* in 1 Corinthians 15, the focal biblical symbol for the Christian conception of resurrection. We will then ask to what extent the concept of a resurrected body can be coherent, especially in light of the biological interdependence our bodies share with the surrounding physical world illustrated by the problem of chain consumption.

The discussion that follows might belong to what some are calling a "theology of nature." Ian Barbour employs *theology of nature* to refer to a "critical reflection, within a tradition based on historical revelation and religious experience, in which theological beliefs concerning nature are reformulated in the light of contemporary science."[3] Whether traditional beliefs will be reformulated remains to be seen; but certainly they will be examined and analyzed in light of nature apprehended by contemporary science.

To pursue this examination and analysis, we will look at conceptual expositions of the symbol of resurrection in patristic theologian Gregory of Nyssa and contemporary physicist Frank Tipler. For both the human being is made up of body and soul, the soul being the form or pattern of intellection or information processing. We will ask about the coherence of maintaining individual identity between life in our present physical bodies and life as we will enjoy it in resurrected spiritual bodies. We will face the question of continuity and discontinuity as we move from the present creation to the new creation, from death to resurrection.

John Polkinghorne provides a compass, a way of showing the direction a theology of nature might take us beyond Gregory of Nyssa and Frank Tipler. We will have to take the road that leads to a dialectic between continuity and discontinuity. Because of the discontinuity, we will have to rely upon a "theological understanding of reality. . . . If the universe is to make complete sense, it will be through something like the continuity/discontinuity of the Christian resurrection hope. The theological motivation for entertaining that hope lies in the resurrection of Jesus and the faithfulness *(ḥesed)* of God."[4]

---

3. Ian Barbour, *Religion and Science: Historical and Contemporary Issues* (San Francisco: HarperSanFrancisco, 1997), 360.

4. John Polkinghorne, "Eschatology: Some Questions and Some Insights from Science," in *The End of the World and the Ends of God,* ed. John Polkinghorne and Michael Welker (Harrisburg, Pa.: Trinity Press International, 2000), 18.

The Spiritual Body

With the topic of resurrection we find ourselves inescapably entangled in two vines, immanent continuity and transcendent newness. At root here is the concept of total death and total new life. This is forcefully expressed in Paul's appeal to the image of the seed sown in the ground. The flower or tree that grows up looks quite different from what had been planted. Whereas the seed looks as if it is dead, the new plant lives; and through its future seeds it will be capable of regeneration. Paul exploits the moribund appearance of the typical seed to say, "What you sow does not come to life unless it dies" (1 Cor. 15:36). This analogy is delicate. Paul wishes to affirm continuity and discontinuity between present and future realities. Resurrection is not exactly creation out of nothing, but rather creation of something out of something else. A dead seed is sown, but what is harvested is new life.[5]

Once he has cultivated the image of a seed sown in the soil like a body buried in the grave, Paul then describes an eschatological harvest in terms of four complementary contrasts.

> So it is with the resurrection of the dead. What is sown perishable (corrupt, *phthora*) is raised imperishable (incorrupt, *aphtharsia*). It is sown in dishonor *(atimia)*; it is raised in glory *(doxa)*. It is sown in weakness *(astheneia)*; it is raised in power *(dynamei)*. It is sown a physical body *(sōma psychikon)*; it is raised a spiritual body *(sōma pneumatikon)*. (1 Cor. 15:42-44)

For Jesus or for us to be raised "imperishable" is to be raised to everlasting life. One's body is not resuscitated for the purpose of simply returning to one's daily toil. *Doxa,* which in reference to the heavenly bodies usually means luster, here means we are raised in honor. The power into which we will be raised, *dynamis,* is the same power by which miracles of healing are performed (1 Cor. 12:28).

That we find ourselves on the doorstep of transcendence is clear from

---

5. Roy Harrisville notes that Paul's seed analogy emphasizes the discontinuity between death and resurrection. "But in neither instance is the move from agronomy to Christian existence, but exactly the reverse. The analogy is warped to what it serves, and here it is made to fit the assertion of discontinuity, the contention that there is no resurrection unless 'from the dead'. What that warping and twisting of the figure to serve its topic means is that there is, after all, no analogy in nature to the activity of God envisioned here, but only a refraction; no possibility of inferring the 'wisdom of God' from what can be observed in the world." *1 Corinthians* (Minneapolis: Augsburg, 1987), 274-75.

St. Paul, who speaks of heavenly bodies *(sōmata epourania)* with their *doxa* — connoting glory or radiance or luster — and identifies them with the resurrection of the dead. To be raised in glory is to be raised into the new creation, not to return to the present creation. In order to pass into the new, we must die to the old. Glory here does not emphasize a body with radiance or any other such quality. "Rather, this reflects Jewish eschatological language for the future state of the righteous."[6] This denies any abiding life force that perdures through death. "Between 'is sown' and 'is raised' lies an infinite gulf which the body cannot span."[7] If there is resurrection, it is new creation.

Paul describes the earthly body as a "psychic" body *(sōma psychikon)*. Here the *psychē* or soul is the source of life, earthly life. What dies and is buried is a breathing body. Paul says that it is not the *psychē* that we find in the resurrection; it is the *sōma*. What we know as the psychosomatic unified person gets buried. If we take note of the terminology in the transition from *sōma psychikon* to *sōma pneumatikon*, it is the *sōma* or body, not the *psychē* or soul, that reappears in the spiritual body. Joel Green summarizes the implications in terms of Hellenistic body-soul dualism.

> There is a profound continuity between present life in this world and life everlasting with God. For human beings, this continuity has to do with bodily existence. . . . Paul does not here think of "immortality of the soul." Neither does he proclaim a resuscitation of dead bodies that might serve as receptacles for souls that had escaped the body in death. Instead, he sets before his audience the promise of the transformation of their bodies into glorified bodies (cf. Phil. 3:21).[8]

The term "spiritual body" is the best description we have of the transformed state. Elsewhere in the Pauline corpus we see Paul contrasting this spiritual body with the fleshly body as well as the ensouled body. In depicting the tension that characterizes Christian existence, Paul frequently portrays it in terms of a war between the flesh *(sarx)* and the spirit (Gal. 5:13-26). Flesh is the power of sin that leads to death. Spirit is its great antagonist. Spirit is the power of creation and new creation. Both powers attempt to invade and control us.

6. Gordon D. Fee, *The First Epistle to the Corinthians*, The New International Commentary on the New Testament, ed. F. F. Bruce (Grand Rapids: William B. Eerdmans, 1987), 785.

7. Harrisville, *1 Corinthians*, 276.

8. Joel Green, "Bodies — That Is, Human Lives: A Re-Examination of Human Nature in the Bible," in *Whatever Happened to the Soul?* ed. Warren S. Brown, Nancey Murphy, and H. Newton Malony (Minneapolis: Fortress, 1998), 170.

It is important to see here that when Paul uses these terms he does not intend to make metaphysical statements regarding human nature — that is, flesh and spirit are not distinct ontological components of each human being. This is not another version of body-soul substance dualism. Rather, flesh and spirit are proclivities or forces that contend for domination of the whole person, body and soul included. Oscar Cullmann goes a bit too far when he hypostatizes them, describing flesh and spirit as "two transcendent Powers" that can enter us from without. Yet he is correct in saying that "neither is given with human existence as such."[9] With this background, we can see why Paul might say, "flesh and blood cannot inherit the kingdom of God" (1 Cor. 15:50).

Be that as it may, the concept of flesh as that which corrupts cannot be separated from its metaphysical designation as the physical body that simply decays, and both meanings seem to be present in 1 Corinthians 15. Hence there is overlap between flesh *(sarx)* and body *(sōma)*, despite how some scholars such as Oscar Cullmann have tried to drive a wedge between them. That there is room for some interchangeability is evidenced by the writings of the Greek Fathers such as Justin Martyr, who could use the phrase "resurrection of the flesh" and declare that because flesh was created by God it must be deemed valuable by God.[10] Early versions of the Apostles' Creed rendered part of the third article as "I believe in the resurrection of the flesh." This upset Cullmann, who complained that this is "not biblical." Instead of "flesh" it should read "body," he wrote. In my judgment, against Cullmann, it appears quite biblical. The challenge to Doubting Thomas to place his hands in the wounds of the resurrected Jesus in Luke 24:39 makes it clear, especially as interpreted by Augustine, who affirms that even in our resurrected spiritual bodies the term "flesh" may apply just as it did to the post-Easter Jesus.[11] Maybe Cullmann's problem is that he wants to deal with the issue strictly as a matter of word choice without looking at the conceptuality being conveyed. Maybe his assumption is that the term "flesh" *(sarx)* refers to flesh contaminated by sin *(hamartia)* rather than flesh as merely the breathing body *(sōma psychikon)*.

Still, in the train of Cullmann, we might be able to get at Paul's underlying conceptuality here by thinking of *sōma* as the form that can exist with one

9. Oscar Cullmann, "Immortality of the Soul or Resurrection of the Dead?" in *Immortality and Resurrection*, ed. Krister Stendahl (New York: Macmillan, 1965), 25.

10. Justin, *On the Resurrection*, sections 2 and 7, in *The Ante-Nicene Fathers* (9 vols.; Grand Rapids: William B. Eerdmans, 1982), 1:194 and 297; abbreviation: ANF.

11. Augustine, *Enchiridion*, ch. 91, in *Nicene and Post-Nicene Fathers* (14 vols.; Grand Rapids: William B. Eerdmans, 1994), first series, 3:266; abbreviation NPNF.

or another force, either flesh *(sarx)* or spirit *(pneuma* or *doxa).* Hans Conzelmann proffers such a form-substance theory and contends that there is no such thing as a *sōma* all by itself. *Sōma* always exists in a specific mode of being, either as *sarx* or as *doxa.* The form is always related to its concrete mode of being. It is always either heavenly or earthly. It does not constitute the individual human being as such. It exists on its own only as an abstract concept.[12] Although Conzelmann helps us here, his theory is not careful to show just how this idea takes account of the fact that Paul's contrast is actually between a psychic body and a spiritual body, not between a fleshly and a glorified body.

Theologically, it seems to me, the spirit is not simply one substance interchangeable with others. The spirit is the power of God whereby reality itself is determined. The *sōma pneumatikon* is the resurrected body that is determined by the Holy Spirit. It is the reality that we will be because God will have created us — re-created us — in this form. Because it is an eschatological reality belonging to the new creation, and because we still live amid the old creation, we cannot expect to apprehend clearly just what this means. Now we can only look through a mirror dimly, and Christ is that mirror reflecting the light of future glory amid our present darkness. What we can say with confidence is that there will be a resurrection of the human self. What we cannot say at this point is precisely what that resurrected mode of existence will look like.

It appears to my reading that Paul is thinking this out for the first time in his dialogue with the Corinthians.[13] He is not simply restating an already existing set of ideas that previously belonged to any established worldview. He is not proposing one theory of immortality among others. Paul here is struggling to explicate the gospel, to apply what he knows about the resurrection of Jesus to our promised resurrection. Paul has already confronted the gospel and is now trying to re-present it to an audience that probably believes the material body is inimical to the spirit. The readers of his letter in Corinth, probably heavily influenced by the Hellenistic intellectual tradition, have misunderstood what the significance of the gospel is for human mortality and eternal life. Today's readers do not know exactly how Paul thought of the gospel before explicating it to the Corinthians, so for us this letter serves as a primary stage of thinking through the implications of a gospel that begins with the Easter announcement that "He is risen!"

---

12. Hans Conzelmann, *1 Corinthians* (Philadelphia: Fortress, 1978), 282.

13. See additional elaboration in Ted Peters, *Science, Theology, and Ethics* (London: Ashgate, 2002), ch. 19.

Identity This Side and the Other Side of Death

The above theological discussion loosens, even if it does not entirely untie, three of the problematic knots: (1) resurrected existence will be embodied existence even if the negative moral force of the flesh will be extinguished; (2) passage through death to new life is not a capacity lying within us by nature; rather, it requires a special act of divine power; and (3) who is raised will in at least some sense be recognizably in continuity with who dies — that is, identity will be maintained.

This third item, the problem of identity, involves two continuities. First, we recognize the continuity between the Easter Christ and your and my future resurrection, which I here refer to as *prolepsis*. Second, we recognize the continuity each of us as individuals will have between life now in our earthly bodies and our future life as a spiritual body.

Although the term "prolepsis" has been used theologically to denote anticipation in the sense of a present incarnation of a future reality, it also denotes incorporation or inclusivity. "Prolepsis" describes Jesus' Easter resurrection in both senses. When St. Paul refers to the risen Christ as "the first fruits of those who have died" (1 Cor. 15:20), we understand Christ as the anticipation of our own future resurrection.[14] When St. Paul adds that "as all die in Adam, so all will be made alive in Christ" (1 Cor. 15:22), we see that our resurrection is incorporated into Christ's resurrection. They belong together. They come in a single ontological package, even if separated in time.[15] Hans

---

14. We can liken the Pauline notion of Christ as the first fruits of those having fallen asleep to childbirth. Gerhard Sauter, when expositing Martin Luther on this point, notes how in childbirth the head emerges first; and then it pulls all the other members out with it. So also, the body of Christ is at one with its head, and all the members follow. "Luther on the Resurrection," *Lutheran Quarterly* 15.2 (Summer 2001): 195-216, esp. 206. Translated by Austra Reinis from "Die Verkundigung des Auferstandenen als Zusage des Lebens bei Gott," in *Relationen-Studien zum Übergang vom Spatmittelalter zur Reformation: Festschrift zu Ehren von Prof. Dr. Karl-Heinz zur Muhlen*, ed. Athina Lexutt and Wolfgang Matz (Munster: Lit, 2000), 383-98.

15. "For us, therefore, the [Easter] resurrection and the *parousia* are two separate events. But for Him they are a single event. The resurrection is the anticipation of His *parousia* as His *parousia* is the completion and fulfilment of the resurrection." Karl Barth, *Church Dogmatics* (4 vols.; Edinburgh: T&T Clark, 1936-62), III/2:490; see IV/1:756. "The coming again of Christ will be the completion of the work of the Spirit that began in the incarnation and with the resurrection of Jesus. From the standpoint of eternity we have here one and the same event because the incarnation is already the inbreaking of the future of God, the entry of eternity into time. For us, however, confession of the incarnation has its basis in Jesus' resurrection, and only at his return will debate concerning the reality of the

Frei puts it this way: Christ's "identity as this singular, continuing individual, Jesus of Nazareth, includes humankind in its singularity. He is the representative and inclusive person."[16]

Frei reminds us of the continuity question, both with respect to Jesus and to us. On the one hand, the Bible attests to personal continuity between who we are this side of death and in the resurrection. On the other hand, we lack a physical or even metaphysical understanding of the eschatological reality. "Mystery" becomes the word we must fall back on when trying to explain it.

> The mystery to which the New Testament accounts testify — or which they render for us as texts inadequate yet adequate — is the continuity of the identity of Jesus through the real, complete disruption of death. He is the same before and after death. We know nothing of a reversal of the physical conditions of full death once it has set in; moreover, we also know nothing of a human identity that is not physical. . . . It is Jesus Christ who remains capable of saving us in our mortal condition, who continues to be efficacious on our behalf. . . . This message is far more important than any theories we may form about the nature of the resurrection. . . .[17]

For Frei this is "at once the *truth* claim and the *mystery* of this message."[18] Michael Welker formulates the continuity problem by analogy to the Copenhagen principle of complementarity in the field of quantum physics. "One could talk of an 'eschatological complementarity,' which on the one hand makes it necessary for us to grasp and to think the transformation of earthly life into eternal life, and on the other the difference between earthly and eternal life."[19]

From where does this continuity derive if it is not inherent in our present nature? It is a continuity God provides in a divine creative — re-creative

---

Easter event be at an end and will that reality definitively and publicly come into force, for the resurrection of Jesus is the proleptic manifestation of the reality of the new, eschatological life of salvation in Jesus himself. . . ." Wolfhart Pannenberg, *Systematic Theology* (3 vols.; Grand Rapids: William B. Eerdmans, 1991-98), 3:627.

16. Hans W. Frei, *Theology and Narrative: Selected Essays*, ed. George Hunsinger and William C. Placher (New York and Oxford: Oxford University, 1993), 204-5.

17. Ibid., 204.

18. Ibid.

19. Michael Welker, "Resurrection and Eternal Life: The Canonic Memory of the Resurrected Christ, His Reality, and His Glory," in *The End of the World and the Ends of God*, ed. John Polkinghorne and Michael Welker (Harrisburg, Pa.: Trinity Press International, 2000), 289-90.

— act. Christoph Schwöbel identifies discontinuity with death and continuity with God. It is the faithfulness of God in both creation and new creation upon which we must rely.[20]

Apocalyptic Justice and the Resurrected Body

Reliance on the faithfulness of God, even in the face of injustice, has been a historical factor in the rise of belief in resurrection. The experience of unjust suffering, especially victimage from persecution, has given rise to anticipations of divine righteousness exacted in the next life. This is the point of the judgment. "Many of those who sleep in the dust of the earth shall awake, some to everlasting life, and some to shame and everlasting contempt" (Dan. 12:2). What has been experienced as unfair in this life will be righted and made fair in the next, where the righteous will be rewarded and the unrighteous punished.

The apocalyptic horizon within which intertestamental and New Testament texts became written and interpreted prompts an acute sense of divine justice. Whether chafing under the tyranny of the Seleucids during the reign of Antiochus IV Epiphanes in the second century before Christ or under the Caesars of Rome during Jesus' time, the Jews were an oppressed people. Those most loyal to the Mosaic covenant suffered social discrimination if not persecution, whereas those who capitulated to the dominant foreign cultural and political pressures gained social rewards. This was unjust. Justice denied on earth must be affirmed in heaven! This is apocalyptic logic. In the resurrection those who suffered for their righteousness would be granted an eternal reward. Apocalyptic judgment would right what in history is wrong.

Claudia Setzer argues that Jewish communities led first by the Pharisees and later by the rabbis employed the concept of resurrection symbolically to identify and maintain Jewish social organization. *"Resurrection was fabricated out of the tool kit of Jewish culture,"* writes Setzer. "Resurrection of the dead functions as a rhetorically powerful symbol that says its adherents have a right to frame solutions to questions of justice, reward and punishment, and God's activity in the world."[21] In particular, resurrection with its accompany-

---

20. *"Die Diskontinuität des Todes und die Kontinuität der Treue Gottes werden verbunden in der schöpferischen und neuschöpferischen Beziehung Gottes in seinem Geist zu seinen Geschöpfen. . . ."* Christoph Schwöbel, "Auferstehung: 5. Dogmatisch," in *Religion in Geschichte und Gegenwart* (Tübingen: Mohr Siebeck, 4th ed. 1998), 1:919.

21. Claudia Setzer, "Resurrection of the Dead as Symbol and Strategy," *Journal of the American Academy of Religion* 69.1 (March 2001): 65-101, esp. 90, italics in original.

ing day of judgment stands as a protest against the structures of injustice prevalent under Roman subjugation.

> Resurrection of the dead serves as an implicit protest, against the world as it is, against Roman hegemony, and against the powerlessness of Israel. These, it says, will not prevail. It answers those who accept injustice, who say that there is no real justice, judge, reward, or punishment. In its insistence on resurrection instead of the more commonly held idea of spiritual immortality, this community carved out a place within but separate from the larger society.[22]

While making this argument, Setzer adds a reference to body thinking. She alludes to the anthropological work of Mary Douglas, according to which body attitudes are condensed views about the relation of society to the individual. Then she draws out some expansive implications for the notion of bodily resurrection. Ordinarily the body connotes finitude, limitation. Yet, when resurrected, the body begins to take on the meaning of infinity, of transcending limits. On the one side, the body "is subject to death, the ultimate limit, the body shorn of all possibility. Yet resurrection and restoration of the body reveal the body's other side, a complete lack of limits, a sense that it is all possibility."[23]

We have just moved from the original contextual meaning of resurrection with a concern for justice toward considerations of bodily existence in the resurrection. The body here described takes on possibilities forbidden by the physical limits we now know. It may be difficult to imagine a body in postmortem existence; but it may be even more difficult to imagine whether the resurrected body is more spiritual than our present one.

The Body, Really?

This theological commitment to a resurrected body appears to be dissonant with scientific understandings of present embodiment. This is especially the case for contemporary scientists who reduce all that we as persons are to our biological substrate. Molecular biologist Francis Crick, famed for his role in the discovery of the double helix structure of DNA, flies the flag of reductionism: "You, your joys and your sorrows, your memories and your ambitions, your sense of personal identity and free will, are in fact no more

22. Ibid., 96.
23. Ibid., 88.

than the behavior of a vast assembly of nerve cells and their associated molecules."[24]

Let us note two things about Crick's challenge. First, the immaterial sense of personhood or soul is reduced to what is material, to what is physical. Second, instead of a whole we are reduced to a plurality. We are nothing more than an assembly of "nerve cells and their associated molecules." There is no whole person or unifying soul here, only an assembly or aggregate of physical components. Thus, for Crick, no coherent person could be raised into a resurrected body because apparently no whole person exists now in the present body. Our present existence is nothing but an assembly of biological processes.

What makes this so conceptually challenging is the presumed antipathy between matters bodily and matters having to do with the soul. Yet Christian anthropology has always been holistic, thinking of the spiritual as that which holds body and soul together in complementary unity. This applies to the resurrection, as Athenegoras declared it. "It is absolutely necessary that the end of a man's being should appear in some reconstitution of the two [body and soul] together, and of the same living being. And as this follows of necessity, there must by all means be a resurrection of the bodies which are dead, or even entirely dissolved, and the same men must be formed anew."[25] Augustine similarly insisted that we humans are "whole and complete only when a body is united with a soul."[26]

Physical Retrieval: Resurrecting Our Substance according to Gregory of Nyssa

To track the constructive reasoning that begins with an explication of biblical symbols of the faith, I find it instructive to track our issues as they appear in the mind of Gregory of Nyssa. Gregory illustrates well the theology of nature alluded to above, wherein we try to think through the implications of our faith commitments in light of nature, especially a scientific approach to understanding nature.

Gregory's first observation is that for the human imagination, nature is not enough. If death is natural, then this is not enough. Something within the human soul yearns for more. "There is such an instinctive and deep-seated

24. Francis Crick, *The Astonishing Hypothesis: The Scientific Search for the Soul* (New York: Scribner's, 1994), 3.

25. Athenagoras, "The Resurrection of the Dead," ANF 2:162.

26. Augustine, *City of God*, 10:29, NPNF, first series, 2:199.

abhorrence of death in all. Those who look on a death-bed can hardly bear the sight; and those whom death approaches recoil. . . . In fact all thought about how we are to go on living is occasioned by the fear of dying."[27] This is the existential dimension of human consciousness that raises the question of immortality in many cultures. The Christian doctrine of resurrection is one answer to this universal human quest.

For Gregory, we persons are more than merely our bodies. We have a soul. What is the soul? Roughly, the soul is the mind, the intellectual dimension of what makes us our self. "The soul is an essence created, and living, and intellectual, transmitting from itself to an organized and sentient body the power of living and of grasping objects of sense, as long as natural constitution capable of this holds together."[28] Like so many in the ancient world influenced by Greek philosophy, Gregory believed the rational capacity of the mind places us in tune with divine reason: ". . . amongst all the powers endued with reason some have been fixed like a Holy Altar in the inmost shrine of the Deity. . . ."[29] "The speculative and critical faculty is the property of the soul's godlike part; for it is by these that we grasp the Deity also."[30] Yet Gregory rejected garden-variety substance dualism of the Platonic type. "We must therefore neglect the Platonic chariot and the pair of horses of dissimilar forces yoked to it, and their driver, whereby the philosopher allegorizes these facts about the soul."[31]

In contrast to a Platonic scheme wherein the soul permanently escapes the body, Gregory propounded the return of the soul and the resurrection of the body. Yet, just as we today, Gregory found it a challenge to make this understandable. "We must believe, not only that there is a Resurrection, but also that it will not be an absurdity."[32] To avoid absurdity, he sought methodologically to construct a view of resurrection that engaged in dialogue with critical appropriation of common or scientific knowledge. We "build up our doc-

---

27. Gregory of Nyssa, "On the Soul and the Resurrection," *Nicene and Post-Nicene Fathers of the Christian Church,* second series, ed. Philip Schaff and Henry Wace (14 vols.; Grand Rapids: William B. Eerdmans, 1954), 5:430.

28. Ibid., 433.

29. Ibid., 461.

30. Ibid., 449.

31. Ibid., 439. Substance dualism may actually remain in Gregory's legacy in Orthodoxy; but the difference from inherited Greek thought is that the essence of the person resides in the body as well as in the soul. Vladimir Lossky signals this double identity when he writes, ". . . the separation of body and soul [is] the fundamental aspect of death. . . . the human person remains equally present in His body recaptured by the elements, as in His soul." *Orthodox Theology: An Introduction* (Crestwood N.Y.: St. Vladimir's Seminary, 1989), 117.

32. Gregory of Nyssa, "On the Soul and the Resurrection," 464.

trine by rule of dialectic and the *science* which draws and destroys conclusions."[33]

What Gregory could observe is that dead bodies decay, their elements dissipating into the surrounding environment. Over time, decaying bodies lose their identity, merging once again with nature, becoming something else. How might such a body be reconstituted? Gregory ponders this question and then suggests that the soul, our intellectual self, watches over the atomic units that make up our bodies. The soul keeps track of where in nature our bodily atoms migrate. On the day of resurrection, then, the soul is ready to call in the inventory so that the original body can be reassembled: ". . . the soul be near each by its power of recognition, and will persistently cling to the familiar atoms, until their concourse after this division again takes place in the same way, for that fresh formation of the dissolved body which will properly be, and be called, resurrection."[34]

> Might the soul make mistakes, mixing together parts of different bodies? No. When that form has gone to pieces the soul that has been mistress of this particular vessel will have an exact knowledge of it, derived even from its fragments; nor will she leave this property, either, in the common blending with all the other fragments, or if it be plunged into the still formless part of the matter from which the atoms have come; she always remembers her own as it was when compact in bodily form, and after dissolution she never makes any mistake about it, led by marks still clinging to the remains.[35]

If Francis Crick thinks that the human body is only an assembly of chemical processes, Gregory goes on to view this assemblage as constitutive of a whole person.

> If, then, the soul is present with the atoms of the body when they are again mingled with the universe, it will not only be cognizant of the entire mass which once came together to form the whole body, and will be present with it, but, besides that, will not fail to know the particular materials of each one of the members, so as to remember by what divisions amongst the atoms our limbs were completely formed. There is, then, nothing improbable in supposing that what is present in the complete mass is present also in each division of the mass.[36]

33. Ibid., 439; emphasis added.
34. Ibid., 445.
35. Ibid., 446.
36. Ibid., 448.

Note how for Gregory this is an act of divine power, not a capacity inherent in the soul or body by nature. "Should the signal be given by the All-disposing Power for these atoms to combine again, then . . . all these, once so familiar with each other, rush simultaneously together . . . each single one of them being wedded to its former neighbour and embracing the old acquaintance."[37]

Gregory is concerned about the identity question. Continuity must be maintained, he argues. If we were to be totally annihilated in death, then what would be raised would be a new person — that is, someone different from who we are. Yet, it is we ourselves who receive the gift of resurrection.

> For if the identical individual particle does not return and only something that is homogeneous but not identical is fetched, you will have something else in the place of that first thing, and such a process will cease to be a resurrection and will be merely the creation of a new man. But if the same man is to return into himself, he must be the same entirely, and regain his original formation in every single atom of his elements.[38]

One of the ancient questions that is indirectly relevant to the contemporary discussion is this: How old will we be in the resurrection? Noting that our body is constantly changing — growing, strengthening, weakening, deteriorating, healing, and such — at which stage in our earthly life will our body be resurrected? Augustine had suggested age thirty, because this seems to be the age at which we are in our prime. Gregory, curiously, combines all ages in the life cycle. When by the resurrection our body will be restored to life again, each "single man will become a crowd of human beings, so that with his rising again there will be found the babe, the child, the boy, the youth, the man, the father, the old man, and all the intermediate persons that he once was."[39] Or, "The Resurrection is *the reconstitution of our nature in its original form.* But in that form of life, of which God Himself was the Creator, it is reasonable to believe that there was neither age not infancy nor any of the sufferings arising from our present various infirmities, nor any kind of bodily affliction whatever." It will be a life "free from evil."[40] "The Resurrection is only a return to our pristine state of grace."[41]

37. Ibid., 446.
38. Ibid., 446.
39. Ibid., 463.
40. Ibid., 465.
41. Ibid., 467.

Chain Consumption

Gregory's atomic reassemblage theory must confront two difficulties, one scientific and one theological. The scientific difficulty is the curious problem of chain consumption. If one's vision of resurrection consists in reassembling the physical atoms that once constituted the fleshly body of an individual person, then we need to ask: Which atoms belong to whom? The problem is this: given that life eats life in continuous cycles, which elements belong to which person? In the ancient Roman world the question arose with regard to cannibalism. If one person eats another, does the flesh of the eaten one then belong to the eater or to the eaten? How will God discriminate on judgment day? Although cannibalism itself was rare, that human beings should be eaten by wild beasts — such as Christian martyrs in the Roman arenas — was common, feared, and puzzling.

Ancients could pose the following problem: suppose a sailor falls overboard and is eaten by a shark. Later the shark is caught by a fisherman, prepared for a fish fry, and eaten by the community. Now, do the fish diners absorb into their own bodies the atoms of the previous human being? In the resurrection, whose atoms are these?

In our own era the matter becomes still more complicated as we incorporate into the chain consumption problem a longer sense of evolutionary time, the cycling and recycling of nature's elements through death, fertilization and growth of plants, digesting the plants as food, death, and so on. We should also take account of metabolism, the death of old cells and birth of new ones on seven-year or similar cycles. If resurrection means reassembling previous physical elements belonging to an individual, then it is not clear which elements belong to which individual, or when. In his *City of God,* Augustine addresses the issue.

> For all the flesh which hunger has consumed finds its way into the air by evaporation, whence . . . God Almighty can recall it. That flesh, therefore, shall be restored to the [person] in whom it first became human flesh. For it must be looked upon as borrowed by the other person, and, like a pecuniary loan, must be returned to the lender.[42]

Augustine thought he could solve the chain consumption problem by giving priority to the first human being to possess bodily elements. Perhaps like Gregory, he assumed that each person begins life with a fresh set of hith-

---

42. Augustine, *City of God,* 22:20.

erto unused physical elements. Given our modern understanding of the interrelatedness of elements in the ongoing life cycle, it would be difficult to arrive at such a proprietary understanding of physical elements. We all share, to greater or lesser degrees, the same physical elements.

Arthur Peacocke offers a scientifically informed solution, one that differs from Augustine's. Peacocke distinguishes slightly between transformation and re-creation. "It is only too clear," he writes, "that the constituents of human bodies are at death irreversibly dispersed about the globe, eventually contributing to the bodies of other, later persons (as well as other living organisms). Hence the actual transformation of individual human bodies could not itself secure the continuity of personal identity through death." Transformation understood as merely immortalizing our mortal bodies is conceptually inadequate because over time we share the elements of our bodies with other creatures. Thus, an adequate conceptual account must include a component of new creation, a "*re-creation* into a new mode of existence."[43] Peacocke emphasizes that the resurrected body of Jesus as well as our resurrected bodies are not miracles within the existing natural order; rather, they are eschatological realities belonging to God's re-creation. This implies that the continuity of our identity through the resurrection will be something achieved by the creative act of God.

Physical Disposal: Resurrecting Our Form according to Frank Tipler

A second difficulty in Gregory's construction is theological. It is the risk that his emphasis on retrieval of physical atoms will require a substantialist continuity that would violate Paul's principle, "flesh and blood cannot inherit the kingdom of God" (1 Cor. 15:50). Rather than everlasting flesh and blood, we look forward to a transformed or re-created body, a spiritual body; but will this transformation or re-creation require the gathering and reassembling of earlier physical atoms? If not, could we maintain identity by just replicating the form of the body without its physical substance?

Such a constructive alternative has been offered recently by physicist Frank Tipler, who projects a future virtual body — a replica of our original physical body — that continues to accompany the information processing of human consciousness. Tipler belongs to a new breed of scientific eschatolo-

---

43. Arthur Peacocke, *Theology for a Scientific Age* (London: SCM Press, enlarged ed., 1993), 285.

gists postulating *cybernetic immortality*. According to this school of thought, the soul is equivalent to consciousness; and consciousness is understood to be an emergent property of brain complexity. We human beings are basically biological machines whose unique identity is found in the patterns stored in the brain. If these patterns could be replicated by computer technology, we could duplicate and preserve the human soul. What Tipler adds is a virtual body created by the soul for its own enjoyment.

Tipler's eschatology skips over the proleptic anticipation of Jesus' Easter resurrection. Tipler overtly rejects the claim that Jesus Christ rose from the dead. Then, on the basis of this rejected claim, he declares himself to be a non-Christian and an atheist.[44] Tipler's view of resurrection is strictly eschatological, with no christological prolepsis.

Without God and without Easter, upon what does Tipler rest his scientific case for future resurrection? Evolution. Resurrection here will be the result of a future evolutionary event in which life understood as information processing will take hold of its own destiny and create a supraphysical environment for its existence just prior to the moment when the physical world self-destructs.[45]

The essence of human consciousness is information processing, says Tipler, so this is all that needs to be preserved in our future postphysical body. This future body will be an emulation of our present body, but it will not have the drawbacks of a biological body. Our future consciousness will retain the embodied form it now has; yet it will transcend its historical embodiment. This becomes the hermeneutic construct through which Tipler interprets what St. Paul means by spiritual body.

> Borrowing the terminology of St. Paul, we can call the simulated, improved, and undying body a "spiritual body," for it will be of the same "stuff" as the human mind now is: a "thought inside a mind. . . ." The spiritual body is thus the present body (with improvements) at a higher level of implementation . . . an emulated person would observe herself to be as real, and as having a body as solid as, the body we currently observe ourselves to have. There would be nothing "ghostly" about the simulated body, and nothing insubstantial about the simulated world in which the simulated body found itself.[46]

44. Frank J. Tipler, *The Physics of Immortality* (New York: Doubleday, 1994), 305, 309-13.

45. Ibid., 225.

46. Ibid., 242.

Tipler is alert to a number of theological concerns here. First, he is sensitive to the human yearning for perfection. Our present state of existence is not satisfactory. We do not hunger simply for life beyond death. We hunger for salvation. So, without using the term "salvation," Tipler announces that the simulated body will transcend the previous model by eliminating bodily defects such as missing limbs; youth will be substituted for old age; sight for blindness; etc.

Second, Tipler says that continuity of identity will be maintained. Anticipating objections that total death followed by total re-creation denies continuity, Tipler responsively argues that continuity in conscious self-identity is both necessary and possible. Replication is not annihilation. To be resurrected as a replica of one's former self does not deny that it is the same self. The identity of the information patterns within which we are aware of our experience of the world and ourselves seems to be sufficient for Tipler. In sum, what is resurrected is the immaterial form but not the material substance of who we presently are.

> An exact replica of ourselves is being simulated in the computer minds of the far future. This simulation of people who are long dead is "resurrection" only if we adopt what philosophers call the "pattern identity theory"; that is, the essence of identity of two entities which exist at different times lies in the (sufficiently close) identity of their patterns. Physical continuity is irrelevant.[47]

This is not merely another example of Platonic body-soul dualism in which a nonmaterial soul is extracted permanently from a material base. Tipler's simulation so emulates the physical body that, for all practical purposes, what resurrected souls experience is physically real. Tipler's own version of "spiritual body" is apt.

> The simulations which are sufficiently complex to contain observers — thinking, feeling beings — as subsimulations exist physically. And further, they exist physically by definition; for this is exactly what we mean by existence, namely, that thinking and feeling beings think and feel themselves to exist. Remember, the simulated thinking and feeling of simulated beings are real.[48]

According to this view, resurrected souls experience themselves in their environment; and this environment is experienced as if it were physical. In a sur-

47. Ibid., 227.
48. Ibid., 210.

prising move, Tipler reiterates Bishop William Berkeley's subjective idealism: to be is to be perceived.[49] If as a computer simulation we perceive physicality, the physicality exists thereby.

Is Tipler's replica theory in which the form but not the substance of our present physical body enters the resurrection faithful to the Pauline description? One could say that it adequately expresses in an alternative metaphor Paul's assertion that we undergo total death and total re-creation. This most likely implies that neither our physical atoms nor our soul's intellectual content perdures beyond death on its own. Despite the apparent coldness of the image of computer processing, Tipler's image roughly correlates with Paul's image of the seed dying and then sprouting.

Just how plausible is Tipler's theory, scientifically speaking? Not very, either physically or biologically. John Polkinghorne dubs these ideas as

> excessively speculative in the assumptions that they make about physical processes in unexplored circumstances, particularly in Tipler's case. The closing instants of a collapsing universe involve physical processes at energies vastly in excess of those of any regime of which we could claim to have an understanding. . . . The speculations of the physical eschatologists are also chillingly reductionist in tone. Life is equated to the mere processing of information. Only if one believes that humans are no more than computers made of meat could one regard their replacement by computers made of bizarre states of matter as affording a picture of continuing fulfillment.[50]

Even though Tipler sees this as a future extension of evolutionary history, it seems to violate the assumption in evolutionary biology that life feeds off life without direction or purpose. Molecular biologist and devout Jew Robert Pollack raises the problem of life's meaning in the face of two components of Darwinian theory: common descent and natural selection. He does not perceive an inherent thrust toward salvation within nature. The human species is merely one species among others, without design or purpose or perfectibility, and, worst of all, temporary. Neither nature nor that which transcends nature seems to care about the human race. Within this context of natural meaninglessness death plays its cold and unfeeling role. "Without the fact of mortality and the certainty that every individual of every species must die, there cannot have been the replacement of one set of forms and functions

---

49. Ibid., 211.
50. Polkinghorne, *The End of the World and the Ends of God,* 33.

by another, the slow weeding and seeding of natural selection from which both we and frogs are current outcomes."[51]

What can we learn theologically from Tipler the physicist? Rather than requiring God to locate and piece together all the molecules of our previous body, might we say rather that who we are is found in the patterning of the molecules? Rather than the molecules as matter, might we say that the form is what counts? Does God remember and reincarnate our form or pattern? Tipler is reminiscent of Origen: "The previous form does not disappear, even if its transition to the more glorious occurs . . . although the form is saved, we are going to put away nearly [every] earthly quality in the resurrection . . . [for] 'flesh and blood cannot inherit the kingdom' (1 Cor. 15:50)."[52] For Origen and Tipler the form is saved, but not the substance. Is this sufficient to guarantee continuity of personal identity, especially when we think of our identity as something gained over time and like scars embedded in our limbs as well as our remembered thoughts? Is there not more to our individual consciousness than information processing, namely, our own information processing informed and influenced by our bodily functions?

One more thought. If the key to cybernetic immortality is replication of the soul's pattern, what would happen in the event of multiple replications? We already know what computer clones are. In principle, the soul's pattern could be replicated many times, not just once. Which would maintain the individual's identity? Does continuity of unique personal identity require some degree of substance continuity?

Form with Transformed Substance:
Resurrection according to John Polkinghorne

Do we have an instance of Scylla and Charybdis here? The Scylla of Gregory is that identity is maintained by physical retrieval but at the cost of coherence. Gregory's theory is incoherent because the immaterial soul is assigned the task of remembering the material structure plus the location of the physical atoms and then, in the resurrection, reassembling the material parts. Further, by affirming physical continuity through reassemblage of original atoms, Gregory fails to make resurrection consonant with what we know about the

---

51. Robert Pollack, *The Faith of Biology and the Biology of Faith* (New York: Columbia University, 2000), 53.

52. Origen, "Fragment on Psalm 1:5," cited by Carolyn Walker Bynum, *The Resurrection of the Body in Western Christianity, 200-1336* (New York: Columbia University, 1995), 64.

relationship of our biology to the external world; and he fails to take sufficiently seriously Paul's contention that flesh and blood cannot inherit the kingdom of God.

The Charybdis of Tipler's physical disposal is that identity is maintained in the pattern of information processing, but by failing to maintain physical continuity, he loses divine reverence for the created physical world. By divesting the pattern or form of our selves from our previous physical history and then trying to substitute a virtual nonphysical information processor, Tipler ends up with a new entity that breaks sharply with the old. This is incoherent because it depends on an evolutionary or developmental scheme according to which the seeds for a future disembodied state must be sown now by the present embodied reality. Tipler builds his radical newness of spirit on an evolutionary scheme that demands physical continuity.

Critical of Tipler, John Polkinghorne argues that no pure naturalistic explanation can provide a satisfactory eschatology. He explains why an evolutionary eschatology necessarily fails.

> The bleak prognosis for the universe puts in question any notion of evolutionary optimism, of a satisfactory fulfillment solely within the confines of the unfolding of present physical process. . . . Christian theology has never staked its claims on the basis of an evolutionary optimism, of the coming of the kingdom of God simply through the flux of history. . . . An ultimate hope will have to rest in an ultimate reality, that is to say, in the eternal God himself, and not in his creation.[53]

Polkinghorne, as we saw earlier, is critical of Tipler on many fronts. Yet, Polkinghorne cannot simply follow in the wake of Gregory. Polkinghorne, in principle, adheres to Paul's signal that flesh and blood cannot inherit the kingdom of God. This acknowledges ontological discontinuity between the present creation and the new creation; and our individual resurrection depends for its place on the new creation. What is at stake here is not merely survival beyond death, survival with an opportunity to live again in the present creation. Rather, what is necessary here is a divine action of transformation that is tantamount to the creation of the world in the first place. Whereas the present creation arrived *ex nihilo*, out of nothing, the new creation will be *ex vetere*, a transformation of the existing creation. Key here is that resurrection of the individual is inextricably tied to the renewal of all things.

---

53. John Polkinghorne, 1993-94 Gifford Lectures in *The Faith of a Physicist* (Princeton: Princeton University, 1994) or *Science and Christian Belief* (London: SPCK, 1994), 162-63.

> The new creation represents the transformation of that universe when it enters freely into a new and closer relationship with its Creator, so that it becomes a totally sacramental world, suffused with the divine presence. Its process can be free from suffering, for it is conceivable that the divinely ordained laws of nature appropriate to a world making itself through its own evolving history should give way to a differently constituted form of "matter," appropriate to a universe "freely returned" from independence to an existence of integration with its Creator.[54]

Note that the present universe will have its material with its natural laws transformed. We will have new laws conducive to the avoidance of suffering and death. These new natural processes will be healing and life-giving because they will be suffused with the divine presence, the source of healing and life.

Polkinghorne emphasizes that the new creation will not evolve on the basis of existing resources within the present creation. Only an act of God can make this transformation happen. The corollary to this is that our immortality is not inherent in the human soul. Death is total annihilation of the psychosomatic person, at least from our point of view. No quality within us as mortal beings has any purchase on immortality. If we are to rise from the dead, it will be due solely to the exertion of divine power. "The Christian hope is, therefore, for me not the hope of *survival* of death, the persistence *post mortem* of a spiritual component which possesses, or has been granted, an intrinsic immortality. Rather, the Christian hope is of death and *resurrection*."[55]

Polkinghorne still relies upon the soul for continuity, however. He defines the soul as an information-bearing pattern; as in Aristotle and Thomas the soul is the form of the body. When Polkinghorne tries to describe the transition from death to new life, from the old creation to the new, he sounds somewhat like Tipler and even like Gregory. "I believe it is a perfectly coherent hope that the pattern that is me will be remembered by God and its instantiation will be recreated by him when he reconstitutes me in a new environment of his choosing. That will be his eschatological act of resurrection."[56] Where Polkinghorne differs from both Tipler and Gregory is that this pattern or soul that bears our individual identity is not maintained by who we are in this mortal life; rather, it is maintained in the memory of God. Death is complete, total. The dissipation of our biological atoms into the sur-

---

54. Ibid., 167.
55. Ibid., 163.
56. Ibid.

rounding physical environment is complete, total. Who we were physically in the past is not retrieved in its original substance. We need not concern ourselves with problems surrounding chain consumption. Resurrection consists of transformation into a spiritual body, the form of which is recalled by God into a new individual existence.

Despite Polkinghorne's clarity here, one might still ask why he places continuity in the divinely remembered soul or pattern. Recall that in Paul's vocabulary it is the body or *sōma* that is repeated; no soul or *psychē* survives in the spiritual body, *sōma pneumatikon*.

What will be changed is the material of the new creation making up the future resurrected body, Polkinghorne rightly says. The new material will obey new laws of nature, laws of life rather than laws of death. Such an idea of resurrection "is both immensely thrilling and deeply mysterious."[57]

> Thus the Christian hope centres on a real death followed by a real resurrection, brought about through the power and merciful faithfulness of God. . . . It is not necessary, however, that the "matter" of these bodies should be the same matter as makes up the flesh of this present world. In fact, it is essential that it should not be. That is because the material bodies of this world are intrinsically subject to mortality and decay. If the resurrected life is to be a true fulfillment, and not just a repeat of an ultimately futile history, the bodies of that world-to-come must be different, for they will be everlastingly redeemed from mortality. Science knows only the matter of this world but it cannot forbid theology to believe that God is capable of bringing about something totally new.[58]

In sum, with Polkinghorne we can think of the resurrected spiritual body as material, but not the same material we enjoy presently in our biological makeup. We have a soul, defined as the form of the body — that is, the complex information-processing pattern of the body. This soul or pattern, however, is not in itself immortal. Rather, it supplies the form by which the divine mind remembers us and on the basis of which God in the new creation re-creates us. Who we are in the new creation is who we are; but this continuity of identity is a gift from God.

57. Ibid., 164.

58. John Polkinghorne, *Science and Theology: An Introduction* (London: SPCK; Minneapolis: Fortress, 1998), 115-16.

Conclusion

Gregory of Nyssa and Frank Tipler leave us with a dilemma of sorts. On the one horn, Gregory's idea of atomic reassemblage has two difficulties: it fails to solve the problem of chain consumption, and it fails to take sufficiently seriously the end that death puts to the physical body. Yet, moving to the other horn of the dilemma — Tipler's idea of a replicated form of the body without its physical substance — risks losing continuity of identity. How should we proceed?

Perhaps the difficulty with both the substance and form theories is that they seek continuity through persistence, through perdurance of something we had or were in this physical existence. As long as flesh and blood cannot inherit God's kingdom — which is another way of saying that death is decisive — perhaps these problems should be shifted onto the shoulders of re-creation. This is where Peacocke puts it. Whereas for Origen the "form is saved," for Peacocke the resurrected body is tantamount to a new creation. Polkinghorne, as we saw, would vote for re-creation according to the pattern remembered by God.

The relevant locus here is not theological anthropology; rather, it is the doctrine of God. The question is: Will God act? Resurrection, if it is to take place at all, must be a divine act. As a part of that act of raising us, just as God raised Jesus on Easter, God will provide what is necessary to maintain continuity of our identity while transforming us into the new creation. Rather than locating memory of our physical atoms in the individual soul as Gregory did, it is better to locate our continuing identity in the memory of God. It is God who granted us our being in creation; and it will be God who grants us being in the new creation. Although we can attest that God is the one responsible for maintaining our identity in the resurrected spiritual body, we still fall short of an explanation. This is a transcendent reality, one difficult to explain this side of transcendence. But no demur is warranted here. Carl Braaten reminds us: "it would be foolishness to hold that an explanation is needed to gain access to the life it [resurrection] promises. That would be like refusing to watch television until one could explain electricity, or refusing to admit one had fallen in love before explaining how it happened."[59]

---

59. Carl E. Braaten, *The Future of God* (New York: Harper, 1969), 75.

Contributors

Jan Assmann is Professor of Egyptology at Heidelberg University. His main fields of research are ancient Egyptian literature and religion in the context of comparative literature and religious studies, Egyptian funerary beliefs and practices, Theban tombs of the Ramesside period, cultural theory (particularly "cultural memory"), history of religion (particularly the rise of monotheism in the ancient world), and early modern concepts of Egyptian culture ("Egyptomania"). His books in English are *Solar Religion in the New Kingdom, In Search of God: Theology and Piety in Ancient Egypt,* and *Moses the Egyptian: The Memory of Egypt in Western Monotheism. The Mind of Egypt: History and Meaning in the Time of the Pharaohs* is forthcoming in 2002.

Ernst M. Conradie is Associate Professor of Religion and Theology at the University of the Western Cape. He is author of *Rus vir die hele aarde* (Lux Verbi, 1996), *Hope for the Earth — Vistas on a New Century* (UWC, 2000), *Ecological Theology: A Guide for Further Research and Ecological Theology: An Indexed Bibliography* (both UWC, 2001), and co-author of *Fishing for Jonah* (UWC, 1995), *Die Bybel in Fokus* (Lux Verbi, 1997), *A Rainbow over the Land: A South African Guide on the Church and Environmental Justice* (Western Cape Provincial Council of Churches, 2000), and *Angling for Interpretation: A Guide to Understand the Bible Better* (UWC, 2001).

Frank Crüsemann studied theology in the years 1958 to 1964 at universities in Hamburg, Heidelberg, Mainz, and Erlangen. He received his Ph.D. in 1968 at Mainz, and completed his *Habilitation* in Old Testament at Heidelberg in 1975. Since 1985 he has been Professor of Old Testament at the Lutheran Seminary in Bethel. His publications include *Tora: Theologie und Sozialgeschichte* *des alttestamentlichen Gesetzes* (München, 1992), *Elia — Die Entdeckung der Einheit Gottes: Eine Lektüre der Erzählungen über Elia und seine Zeit* (1997), and *Ich glaube an den Gott Israels: Fragen und Antworten zu einem Thema, das im christlichen Glaubensbekenntnis fehlt,* ed. with U. Theissmann (1998).

Brian E. Daley, S.J., taught historical theology, especially the theology of the Church Fathers, at Weston Jesuit School of Theology in Cambridge, Massachusetts, from 1978 until 1996; since then he has been the Catherine F. Huisking Professor of Theology at the University of Notre Dame. He has been a fellow of Dumbarton Oaks (1981-82), a member of the Center of Theological Inquiry in Princeton, New Jersey (1999-2000), the Tuohy Lecturer at John Carroll University (1991), and the D'Arcy Lecturer at Oxford University (2002). He has also been a member of the editorial board of *Traditio* since 1978, as well as of the *Journal of Early Christian Studies.* His books include *The Hope of the Early Church: A Handbook of Patristic Eschatology* and *The Dormition of Mary: Early Greek Patristic Homilies.*

Hans-Joachim Eckstein is currently Professor of New Testament at the University of Tübingen, Germany. His publications include "Der Begriff Syneidēsis bei Paulus: Eine neutestamentlich-exegetische Untersuchung zum 'Gewissensbegriff,'" Wissenschaftliche Untersuchungen zum Alten und Neuen Testament 2/10 (Tübingen, 1983); "Verheißung und Gesetz: Eine exegetische Untersuchung zu Gal 2,15–4,7," Wissenschaftliche Untersuchungen zum Alten und Neuen Testament 2/10 (Tübingen, 1996); and *Wie wirklich ist die Auferstehung? Biblische Zeugnisse und heutiges Erkennen,* ed. H.-J. Eckstein and Michael Welker (2002).

Dirk Evers, Dr. Theol. (Tübingen), teaches systematic theology as an assistant at the Institute for Hermeneutics at the University of Tübingen (Germany). He is also an ordained minister of the Evangelical Lutheran Church in Württemberg. He received his Ph.D. in 1999. For his book *Raum — Materie — Zeit: Christliche Schöpfungstheologie im Dialog mit naturwissenschaftlicher Kosmologie* (2000) he was granted the ESSSAT prize 2002 of the European Society for the Study of Science and Theology.

Noreen Herzfeld is Associate Professor of Computer Science at St. John's University in Collegeville, Minnesota. Her academic interests include the ethical implications of computing, artificial intelligence, and spirituality and technology. Her next book is forthcoming from Fortress Press, titled *In Our Image: Artificial Intelligence and the Human Spirit.*

CONTRIBUTORS

Peter Lampe is a Professor of New Testament Theology at the University of Heidelberg, Germany. His teaching and research areas are biblical studies, early Christian archeology and epigraphics, social history of the early church, the Hellenistic background of early Christianity, and questions of methodology. He is an ordained Lutheran pastor.

Detlef B. Linke is currently Professor of Clinical Neurophysiology and Neurosurgical Rehabilitation at the University of Bonn. His research projects are in the areas of neurodynamics and selective anesthesia of human brain areas. He has received an award in epilepsy research and has more than two hundred publications, including ten books, including *Das Gehirn, Einsteins Doppelgänger — Das Gehirn und sein Ich,* and *Kunst und Gehirn.*

Nancey Murphy is Professor of Christian Philosophy at Fuller Theological Seminary in Pasadena, California. She holds doctorates in both philosophy and theology, and is the author of six books and co-editor of six. Her first book, *Theology in the Age of Scientific Reasoning,* won the American Academy of Religion's Award for Excellence and a prize for books in theology from the Templeton Foundation. Her research interests focus on the role of modern and postmodern philosophy in shaping Christian theology and on relations between theology and science. She is a member of the Board of Directors of the Center for Theology and the Natural Sciences and an ordained minister in the Church of the Brethren.

Bernd Oberdorfer received his Ph.D. in theology from the University of Munich in 1993. His thesis was on the works of young Friedrich Schleiermacher. In 1999 he completed his *Habilitation* for systematic theology at Munich in 1999. His thesis was on the *filioque* problem. In 2000 he was ordained as a Lutheran pastor. In 2000-2001 he received the Heisenberg Scholarship of the *Deutsche Forschungsgemeinschaft* for research at the University of Stellenbosch, South Africa. Since 2001 he has held the Chair for Systematic Theology at the University of Augsburg, Germany. His fields of research include dogmatics, especially the doctrine of the Trinity; ecumenical theology; Schleiermacher; and religion in the modern world, particularly with reference to Niklas Luhmann's theory of society.

Ted Peters is Professor of Systematic Theology at the Pacific Lutheran Theological Seminary and the Graduate Theological Union. A former parish pastor, Peters is ordained in the Evangelical Lutheran Church in America. He di-

324

rects the Center for Theology and the Natural Sciences Science and Religion Course Program and has authored numerous books and articles.

Sir John Polkinghorne worked for many years as a theoretical elementary particle physicist. From 1968 to 1979 he was Professor of Mathematical Physics at the University of Cambridge; then he resigned to train for the ministry of the Church of England. After working as a parish priest he returned to Cambridge, and in 1996 he retired from being President of Queens' College. He is an Anglican priest and a Fellow of the Royal Society and was knighted by the Queen in 1997. He has written many books about science and religion, including *The Faith of a Physicist* (1994). In 2002 he won the Templeton Prize for Progress toward Research or Discoveries about Spiritual Realities.

Robert John Russell is the Founder and Director of the Center for Theology and the Natural Sciences, Berkeley, California, and is Professor of Theology and Science in Residence at the Graduate Theological Union. He is ordained in the United Church of Christ to ministry in higher education. Dr. Russell serves as primary editor of the Center for Theology and the Natural Sciences–Vatican Observatory volumes on science and divine action and has authored numerous articles.

Jeffrey P. Schloss studied biology and philosophy as an undergraduate at Wheaton College, pursued postbaccalaureate study in field biology at the University of Virginia and the University of Michigan, and received his Ph.D. in ecology and evolutionary biology from Washington University. He has taught at the University of Michigan, Wheaton College, and Jaguar Creek Tropical Research Center, and is currently Professor of Biology at Westmont College in Santa Barbara, California, and Director of Biological Programs for the Christian Environmental Association. His twofold research interests include ecophysiological strategies of poikilohydric organisms and evolutionary theories of altruistic morality. His most recent project, a collaborative volume forthcoming from Oxford University Press, is *Altruistic Love: Scientific and Theological Perspectives*.

Andreas Schuele is Assistant Professor for Biblical Theology at the University of Heidelberg. His major book publications (*Die Syntax der Althebräischen Inschriften*, 2000; *Israels Sohn — Jahwes Prophet: Ein Versuch zum Verhältnis von kanonischer Theologie und Religionsgeschichte anhand der Bileam-Perikope*, 2001) focus on the language and literary history of the Hebrew Bible. In a number of essays on central theological issues like creation, resurrection and the notion of love he investigates the intersections of biblical studies and systematic theology. Presently he is working on a book called *Canon and Culture: A Theology of Scripture.*

Günter Thomas teaches systematic theology at Heidelberg University. His research includes the fields of systematic theology of the twentieth century, theology and culture, theology and science, and theory of religion. He is the author of *Medien-Ritual-Religion* (1998) and *Implizite Religion* (2001), as well as editor of *Religiöse Funktionen des Fernsehens?* (Wiesbaden, 2000). He is currently working on a project on the theme of the New Creation.

Michael Welker is a philosopher and a theologian who works through the biblical traditions to address questions of contemporary culture. Professor and Chair of Systematic Theology at the Theological Faculty of the University of Heidelberg, he has been director of the university's *Internationales Wissenschaftsforum* since 1996. Dr. Welker is a graduate of the University of Tübingen, where he studied with Jürgen Moltmann and earned a doctorate in theology in 1973. Ordained in the *Evangelische Kirche der Pfalz,* he received a Ph.D. from Heidelberg in 1978. He was Professor of Systematic Theology at the Theological Faculty of the University of Tübingen from 1983 to 1987; and, for the next four years, Professor and Chair of Reformed Theology at the Theological Faculty of the University of Münster. A member of the Consultation on Science and Religion of Princeton's Center of Theological Inquiry since 1993, he has published more than one hundred papers and has been the author or editor of nineteen books, including *God the Spirit* (1995) and *Creation and Reality* (1998). His most recent study is *What Happens in Holy Communion?* (Eerdmans, 1999).